Labor Economics: Problems in Analyzing Labor Markets

Recent Economic Thought Series

Editor:

Warren G. Samuels
Michigan State University
East Lansing, Michigan, U.S.A.

Other books in the series:

Feiwel, G., *Samuelson and Neoclassical Economics*
Wade, L., *Political Economy: Modern Views*
Zimbalist, A., *Comparative Economic Systems: Recent Views*
Darity, W., *Labor Economics: Modern Views*
Jarsulic, M., *Money and Macro Policy*
Samuelson, L., *Microeconomic Theory*
Bromley, D., *Natural Resource Economics: Policy Problems and Contemporary Analysis*
Mirowski, P., *The Reconstruction of Economic Theory*
Field, A., *The Future of Economic History*
Lowry, S., *Pre-Classical Economic Thought*
Officer, L., *International Economics*
Asimakopulos, A., *Theories of Income Distribution*
Earl, P., *Psychological Economics; Development, Tensions, Prospects*
Thweatt, W., *Classical Political Economy*
Peterson, W., *Market Power and the Economy*
DeGregori, T., *Development Economics*
Nowotny, K., *Public Utility Regulation*
Horowitz, I., *Decision Theory*
Mercuro, N., *Law and Economics*
Hennings, K. and Samuels, W., *Neoclassical Economic Theory, 1870 to 1930*
Samuels, W., *Economics as Discourse*
Lutz, M., *Social Economics*
Weimer, D., *Policy Analysis and Economics*
Bromley, D. and Segerson, K., *The Social Response to Environmental Risk*
Roberts, B. and Feiner, S., *Radical Economics*
Mercuro, N., *Taking Property and Just Compensation*
de Marchi, N., *Post-Popperian Methodology of Economics*
Gapinski, J., *The Economics of Saving*

Labor Economics: Problems in Analyzing Labor Markets

edited by

William Darity, Jr.
Cary C. Boshamer Professor of Economics
University of North Carolina at Chapel Hill

Kluwer Academic Publishers
Boston / Dordrecht / London

Distributors for North America:
Kluwer Academic Publishers
101 Philip Drive
Assinippi Park
Norwell, Massachusetts 02061 USA

Distributors for all other countries:
Kluwer Academic Publishers Group
Distribution Centre
Post Office Box 322
3300 AH Dordrecht, THE NETHERLANDS

Library of Congress Cataloging-in-Publication Data

Labor economics: problems in analyzing labor markets / edited by
William Darity, Jr.
p. cm. — (Recent economic thought series)
Includes bibliographical references and index.
ISBN 0-7923-9260-4 (alk. paper)
1. Labor economics. 2. Labor market. I. Darity, William A.,
1953- . II. Series.
HD4901.L133 1992
331.12—dc20 92-18985
CIP

Contents

Labor Economics: Problems in Analyzing Labor Markets

INTRODUCTION

William Darity, Jr.

In 1984 the Kluwer series in Modern Economic Thought, under the editorial direction of Warren Samuels, brought out a book under my editorship entitled *Labor Economics: Modern Views*. It consisted of a series of essays and commentaries that sought, in a critical fashion, to assess the state of the art in the field of labor economics with respect to several themes. These included methodology versus practice, the analysis of discrimination by gender and race, the phenomenon of persistent racial differences in unemployment exposure, occupational safety and health regulation, dual versus segmented labor markets, and the remnants of the Phillips curve trade-off between unemployment and inflation.

Nearly a decade later I was approached by Warren Samuels and Kluwer about editing a new book that would again address where things stand in labor economics. In proceeding with the development of this current book I was a struck by the extent to which the research thrust that was apparent in the early 1980s remains intact as we move toward the 21st century. The vast majority of scholarship in the labor subfield is dominated by the methodological orientation of applied neoclassical microeconomics, supplemented by incursions from the themes that occupy the so-called "pure theorists," particularly of the game theoretic variety. But there also is a lively body of work lying outside the mainstream that contests orthodoxy at the most fundamental levels—on grounds of logical consistency and empirical accuracy. I view the current book as a potpourri of perspectives on the status of labor economics both from those who work in the subfield within the terms of applied neoclassical microeconomics and those who work within the terms of alternative modes of thought.

Despite common attachment to a singular conception of how one does economic analysis—the starting point always is with the individual and individual-optimizing behavior—there is substantial dissent among labor economists. Indeed, mainstream labor economists remain in perpetual conflict over the issue of how real-world markets, especially those for employment, actually work. Does the labor market in the aggregate or do sectoral markets behave as contract markets, with comparatively inflexible wages, or as auction markets, with a high degree of wage flexibility? From the mainstream perspective, if the former is the case, there is a basis for explaining the occurence and persistence of unemployment; if the latter is the case, then either unemployment does not really occur or it is at worst a temporary and ephemeral phenomenon.

The fact that economists would even engage in debate over the theoretical existence of unemployment is bewildering to the historian Alexander Keyssar. Keyssar (1986), author of an important study of the origins of unemployment as a socially recognized phenomenon of concern to policymakers in the state of Massachusetts, sees the incidence of joblessness as so palpable, real, and devastating that he views the debate among economists as a descent into the theatre of the absurd. He says as much in his contribution in the first section of the current book.

Also in the first section Michael Syron Lawlor provides a remarkable study of the emergence of the theory of aggregate unemployment in Cambridge, England, in the 1930s. Lawlor argues that the fixprice versus flexprice view of labor markets had been a long discussed issue in Cambridge, dating at least from Alfred Marshall's lectures to the generation of dons that were to rise to prominence during the interwar years. Moreover, by making careful use of the Keynes Papers at Kings College at Cambridge University, Lawlor demonstrates that the fixprice view of labor markets and the panoply of arguments for wage rigidity utilized by the contemporary "New Keynesian" economists were well developed by Keynes's favorite whipping boy, A.C. Pigou, well before the publication of *The General Theory*. Thus, Lawlor doubts that the attribution of rigid wage economics to Keynes is an accurate account of his theory of unemployment and suggests that the contract versus auction market debate has no relevance to the legitimacy of Keynes's theory of less than full employment equilibrium. But since the New Keynesians have a broadly dismissive attitude toward doctrinal history—their major organ, *The Quarterly Journal of Economics*, has an active policy of refusing to consider papers in the history of economic thought—I suspect that Lawlor's chapter will not be addressed by any of the principals. Hopefully, others will read his chapter and be inspired to think more deeply about the limitations of how economists have come to conceive of unemployment.

The exploration of the question of how labor markets really work is pursued in a trio of essays that occupy the second section of this book. The timbre of the discussions here indicate ways in which the conventional procedures of mainstream economics can be modified or amended to accommodate potential trouble spots, rather than proposing overturning orthodoxy altogether.

The first of the three, by Alfred Field and Arthur Goldsmith, asks a seemingly narrow question that has wide ramifications for the usual empirical work performed by labor economists. Field and Goldsmith are concerned with an omitted variable from traditional studies of earnings and occupational status, formal on-the-job training. But the scope of their investigation suggests how far wrong previous empirical research could have gone by leaving out this variable. Utilizing the Bureau of Labor Statistics' January 1984 Job Training Survey as a supplement to the January 1984 Bureau of the Census Current Population Survey, they are able to demonstrate how dramatically employment and lay-off probability regression equations will be altered when formal on-the-job training is taken into account. The Field-Goldsmith investigation also suggests how poorly on-the-job training, whether formal or informal, has been incorporated into empirical labor economics, despite the importance ascribed to such training in theoretical work on human capital accumulation.

In the second essay in this group, James Heckman and Thomas MaCurdy undertake an examination of the evidence on whether labor markets are best characterized by equilibrium (in the sense of market clearing) or disequilibrium (in the sense of nonmarket clearing) modes of thought. This is the same issue that Goldsmith with an earlier coauthor, Thomas Kniesner, sought to evaluate in a major survey article that appeared in the *Journal of Economic Literature* in 1987. Both articles conclude that the issue cannot be resolved unequivocally on the basis of data available on labor market dynamics or on the basis of existing tests of whether labor markets tend to clear or not to clear.

In a related vein, William Dickens and Kevin Lang reexamine the evidence on whether labor markets should be characterized as segmented or singular. In the mid-1980s they first introduced a procedure for testing for the existence of dualism in the U.S. labor market (Dickens and Lang 1985). Their procedure, which they argued established that the structure of markets for employment in the United States is, indeed, segmented, spawned a body of research both supportive and critical of their findings. Probably the most negative assessment came from Heckman in collaboration with Joseph Hotz in an article focusing on dualism in the labor market in Panama, where Heckman and Hotz (1986) challenged the Dickens and Lang procedure (rather than necessarily disputing the Dickens and Lang conclusion). Dickens and Lang use the current essay as an opportunity to reply to Heckman and Hotz as well as other critics.

While Dickens and Lang see inadequacies in the conventional treatment of labor markets as a continuum of opportunities potentially open to all comers with the requisite skills regardless of ascriptive characteristics, they want to explain the workings of segmented markets in a manner consistent with individual optimizing behavior. Labor markets are segmented, hence imperfect, and there is nothing anyone can do about that; for Dickens and Lang it is a virtual state of nature. But given that fact, individuals then behave in an optimal fashion. Therefore, they see a convergence between the empirical observation that labor markets are segmented and the body of theory that invokes informational asymmetries, efficiency wage doctrine, adverse selection and the like—arguments that have individuals behaving optimally in the face of an immutable imperfection (although precisely why the grand imperfection is immutable is rarely, if ever, explained).[1]

Dickens and Lang view segmented labor market theory as an alternative to human capital-based explanations for wage differentials. But if segmentation exists—and their evidence seems to be reasonably persuasive that it does—the key question is why some persons or groups have a greater likelihood of being present in one segment rather than another. Is it because they are steered there, independent of their capacity to perform, or is it because their individual abilities best suit them for a particular sector? To be more direct: are black workers disproportionately found in the low-wage segment of the labor market because of discrimination or because of lower levels of human capital accumulation? Obviously, the resolution of this question lies at the heart of how mainstream economists think about the determination of income distribution and the "fairness" with which the market system treats participants.

The fairness of a putatively capitalistic marketplace is the issue that provokes Jeremiah Cotton's inquiry in the section of the book entitled "Race, Discrimination, and Inequality." Cotton contributes an essay that reasserts the real world significance of labor market discrimination while simultaneously establishing the deep range of anomalies the persistence of labor market discrimination poses for mainstream economic theory. Given a segmented structure of the labor market, Cotton would say unequivocally that the mechanisms that allocate blacks to the low-wage, low-job stability tiers are not attributable to the productivity characteristics of black laborers but due to the operation of out-and-out discrimination. Human capital theory does not explain racial wage differentials in Cotton's estimation, nor does orthodox theory *writ large*.

In the same section Rhonda Williams, while equally unimpressed with mainstream theory's approach to discrimination, also finds fault with the status quo in radical economists' approach to racial economic inequality. She calls for a nonromantic look at American labor history and a corresponding radical theory of divisions among the working class that recognizes, as she puts it, the "racialized self-understanding" of working class communities. Williams and Cotton represent a newly emerging group of labor economists whose work is richly informed by classical political economy and Marxist theory rather than by the neoclassicists. This new group is engaged in an innovative reconstruction of the theory of discrimination and the theory of intra- and interindustry competition. I also would include in this group such economists as Patrick Mason, Howard Botwinick, and Steven Shulman.[2]

The chapters in sections II and III of this book, then, represent two poles of attack on the problems that bedevil labor economists—either repair the craters from within the hole or seek a different surface altogether.

Section IV contains two chapters that are pertinent to controversies over the sources of poverty and inequality in the U.S. economy. The first chapter by Stephen Woodbury was prompted by the debate that has developed concerning the residuals in earnings equations estimated for racial or ethnic groups. One interpretation ascribed to the residuals is that they capture the unmeasured effects of discrimination. The second interpretation which gained intellectual popularity in the 1980s is that the residuals capture the unmeasured effects of culture. The debate has been characterized by Jeremiah Cotton (1992) as the "color versus culture" controversy.

Woodbury seeks to compare labor market outcomes for a racially homogeneous but culturally heterogeneous population, native U.S. blacks and blacks of West Indian ancestry in the United States. He then compares both populations with whites, and in particular he compares the West Indian blacks' experience with other nonblack immigrant populations. Certainly his findings are none too salutary for the anecdotal claims neoconservative economists like Thomas Sowell have made about culture as the decisive explanatory variable for racial and ethnic differences in patterns of economic performance. In addition, Woodbury's findings also undercut several propositions advanced by two specialists on immigrant research, Barry Chiswick and George Borjas.

The final chapter in the book, by Michael Foster, examines the growing involvement of economists in public policy analysis with respect to alteration of the American system of social welfare provision. Foster is primarily concerned with how economists think about poverty populations and the notion that poverty is a culturally generated condition. This leads to the fundamental question of the endogeneity of tastes and preferences, a matter that economists usually skirt altogether. Foster's discussion is disarming in tone, but again the depth of the problems that he raises with the research content of mainstream economics is compelling.

At base, orthodox economics does not have a theory of social stratification, hierarchy, and the evolution and transformation of social classes aside from an implicit notion that class status emerges from *individual* decisions about self-investment in human capital. Everything else is a permutation on that central idea. Rather than starting with the class or the group as the organizing *analytical* construct and working back to the individual when necessary, orthodox economics starts with the individual as the supreme actor and then tries, vainly, when forced to do so, to work its way up to the class or the group. This is supreme heresy, but perhaps economists do have something to learn from sociology after all.

William Darity, Jr.
Durham, North Carolina

Notes

1. For a critical discussion of this body of theory and its application to the problems of unemployment and discrimination, see my essay (Darity 1991, 39–54).
2. See Mason (1991), Botwinick (1988), and Shulman (1990).

References

Botwinick, H. 1988. *Wage Differentials and the Competition of Capitals: A New Explanation for Inter- and Intra-Industry Wage Differentials Among Workers of Similar Skill.* Doctoral dissertation, New School for Social Research, forthcoming as a book to be published by Princeton University Press.

Cotton, J. 1992. "Color or Culture?: Wage Differences Among Non-Hispanic Black Males, Black Hispanic Males and White Hispanic Males." Unpublished manuscript, University of Massachusetts at Boston.

Darity, W., Jr. 1991. "Efficiency Wage Theory: Critical Reflections on the Neo-Keynesian Theory of Unemployment and Discrimination." In *New Approaches to Economic and Social Analyses of Discrimination*, ed. R.R. Cornwall and P.V. Wunnava, eds., 39–54. New York: Praegar.

Dickens, W.T., and Lang, K. 1985. "A Test of Dual Labor Market Theory." *American Economic Review* 75 (September): 792–805.

Heckman, J.J., and Hotz, J.V. 1986. "An Investigation of the Labor Market Earnings of Panamanian Males: Evaluating the Sources of Inequality." *Journal of Human Resources* (Fall): 507–542.

Keyssar, A. 1986. *Out of Work: The First Century of Unemployment in Massachusetts*. New York: Cambridge University Press.

Kniesner, T.J., and Goldsmith, A. 1987. "A Survey of Alternative Models of the U.S. Labor Market." *Journal of Economic Literature* 25(3): 1241–1280.

Mason, P. 1991. "Inter-industry Wage Differentials and African-American Employment: An Alternative Theory of Discrimination." Unpublished manuscript, University of California at Riverside.

Shulman, S. 1990. "Racial Inequality and White Employment: An Interpretation and Test of the Bargaining Power Hypothesis." *The Review of Black Political Economy* 18(3): 5–20.

I UNEMPLOYMENT

1 KEYNES, CAMBRIDGE, AND THE NEW KEYNESIAN ECONOMICS

Michael Syron Lawlor

Marshall, who was more alive than many economists to the complexity of the economic world, where all things are subject to "mutual interaction," attempted to provide a synthetic view, in which the forces which affected the supply of labour and the forces which affected the demand for labour were combined. On the whole, the theory which he reached was less rigidly deterministic than the traditional doctrines: for example, it allowed scope to the influence of collective bargaining by trade unions on wages, through its effect not only on the efficiency, but also on the "supply price" of labour.

—Dobb (1938, 119)

Thanks are due to Sandy Darity, Geoff Harcourt, Don Frey, and Allin Cottrell for helpful comments. Financial support from the Wake Forest Reynolds Leave program is gratefully acknowledged. Permission to quote the John Maynard Keynes papers has been provided by the Provost and Fellows of Kings College, Cambridge.

Involuntary Unemployment Once Again

There is something very basic and relevant about the phenomenon Keynes labeled "involuntary unemployment." Modern industrial economies exhibit recurrent episodes of insufficient employment opportunities for all of the available workforce. These workers lose (as opposed to giving up) employment for general systemic reasons that generate less than sufficient demand in the aggregate to keep the workforce employed. This phenomenon is irrespective of (and not in contradiction with) the existence of unemployment due to other causes, such as search activity and shifting sectoral allocations. To the man on the street these are "hard times," where more people are "out of work," and they are clearly visible episodes.

What may seem quite incredible to the lay observer is that the very existence of involuntary unemployment is called into question by economic theory. Put simply, the question recent debates have posed is: Should economic theory, the set of generalizations and methods with which we view the economy, be able to: (1) at least admit the possibility of the existence of such states; and/or (2) allow us to analyze, however imperfectly, their causes? Keynes said yes. Increasingly over the postwar era, economists working in the vineyards of macroeconomics, the heirs to Keynes' attempts to answer 1 and 2, have come to the opposite conclusion.

The logical conclusion of this progressive retreat from involuntary unemployment was reached in the work of the new classical economists, who in the last decade have declared the concept both indefinable and useless. Robert Lucas provides the best example with his contention that "one cannot, even conceptually, arrive at a usable definition of full employment as a state in which no involuntary unemployment exists" (1987, 1).

Yet the phenomenon exists. It is not necessary to get teary and weepy, or to invoke the Great Depression, to observe that involuntary unemployment, defined quite literally as swings in total unemployment due to changes in aggregate demand, continues to be with us. In a recent survey, two labor economists summarized the empirical regularities of the postwar U.S. record as follows:

> During the typical postwar U.S. recession, which lasts about 10 to 12 months, real GNP falls 2 to 3 percent, nonfarm employment falls 2 to 4 percent, and the unemployment rate rises 2 to 4 percent. . . . The increased flows into unemployment during a recession stem mainly from new layoffs and firings. Quits, which are terminations of the employment relationship initiated by employees, fall dramatically . . . both the aggregate real wage and the aggregate nominal wage are statistically independent of real output [and] . . . cyclic movements in labor utilization appear to be dominated by changes in the number of workers with jobs rather than characterized by short hours or worksharing arrangements [Kniesner and Goldsmith 1987].

In short, the evidence attests to a degree of unemployment attached to swings in activity. This unemployment is not the result of voluntary actions of the employees, and it is not correlated with labor's price nor is it the result of reduced hours of work. This is involuntary unemployment as the statisticians see it. What of the theorists?

In 1936 Keynes attempted to launch a revolution in the theoretical treatment of unemployment. In the process he defined a new category of unemployment which he dubbed "involuntary unemployment." Now 50 years on, the concept continues to cause vexation and consternation among economists. The most recent body of literature to test its mettle against the evidently enduring enigma of involuntary unemployment has been dubbed the New Keynesian economics. This literature is both a reaction to the marginalization of the topic at the hands of the new classical economists and an attempt to refound Keynes's vision with modern techniques. One recent chronicler of the tradition makes this motivation clear:

> Yet it is now apparent that the rumors of the death of Keynesian economics were greatly exaggerated. Building on foundations laid in the late 1970's . . . , a large number of authors, young and old alike, in the past decade have produced an outpouring of research within the Keynesian tradition that attempts to build the microeconomic foundations of price stickiness. The adjective *new-Keynesian* nicely juxtaposes this body of research with its arch-opposite, the new-classical approach [Gordon 1990, 1115].

To answer just why involuntary unemployment remains such a mystery for economic theorists requires an analysis of the history and methods of economic theory, where language and definitions take on an importance and meaning that often appears fantastic to the outsider. This is particularly so in the case of unemployment theory, which in the postwar era has become progressively more difficult to evaluate as the technicalities of modern theoretical methods have accumulated. In the process, what at first (recalling the social reality of the 1930s) must have seemed a relatively innocuous term, involuntary unemployment, has become a lightning rod of debate.

This chapter is an attempt to provide an historical perspective on this most recent attempt to account for involunary unemployment by economic theorists. It consists of a look back to the intellectual setting of Keynes's own views in prewar Cambridge economics. Marshallianism was the major influence, of course, but we shall see that its legacy is ambiguous. Marshall not only spawned Pigou's (1933) amazingly out-of-touch treatment, *The Theory of Unemployment*, but also Dobb's subtle and historically informed view of labor markets in his Cambridge Handbook *Wages*.

Our examination of this context will support the view that there was more than one way to be a Marshallian (although to be fair to the master, one might say Cambridge economists at this period tended to be either

Marshallians or "Pigovians"). Thus Keynes's reaction against his upbringing in 1936, coupled with his obvious retention of Marshallian habits of thought, becomes more understandable. But of greater relevance to understanding the current work of the New Keynesians, our reading of the work of Marshall, Dobb, the early Keynes, and even the *early* Pigou, reveals a subtle and sophisticated microeconomic labor market analysis.

Significantly, most of the issues now being raised by the New Keynesians were treated by these authors going back as far as the period *before World War I*. Interestingly, though, Marshall, Keynes, and Dobb did not see such institutional realism as necessarily relevant to unemployment. Thus when Keynes came to part with this tradition of labor market theory as it relates to unemployment, he was simultaneously departing from a view in many important aspects like that of the New Keynesian analysts. For this reason, our final argument will be that Keynes's view of involuntary unemployment, while it does not deny the welcome realism of sophisticated labor market analysis such as Dobb's or the New Keynesian economics, is in fact a metaphysical category distinct from the usual categories then and now current in the literature.

New Keynesian Economics

The awful confusion of events and ideas that is modern economics cries out for order and system. Sheer volume combined with sometimes numbing complexity threatens to make sub-sub-specialists of us all. History is the proper antidote, as we are attempting to show here. But even history needs an "object" to juxtapose the old against. Inevitably these objects are open to the charge of creating "straw men," an opponent crafted to fit the argument. Keynes's "classicals," Marx's "vulgar economists," and innumerable would-be critics' "neoclassicals" all exhibit this tendency in some degree.

Thus intellectual honesty requires explicit identification of sources. Also the historian of ideas should exhibit a degree of sympathy with one's subject. Fortuitiously this job has been done for us in the case of identifying under one grand heading the disparate new work on the microfoundations of macroeconomic unemployment theory by the recent appearance of several excellent surveys by insiders to the literature (Ball 1990; Gordon 1990; Lindbeck and Snower 1989). Of these we will rely especially on Lindbeck and Snower in what follows. From their crystallization of this literature we will identify its major themes and outlook. This will then stand as our touchpoint in comparing the economics of the New Keynesians with the economics of Old Cambridge.

According to Lindbeck and Snower, and in keeping with our historical viewpoint, the most recent work in trying to account for involuntary unemployment by economic theorists arises from the unsatisfactory terms upon which the Keynesian/New Classical debate of the 1970s and 1980s ended. They describe this state of affairs as a "standoff" in which each side clung to its own beliefs and its critique of the opposing viewpoint.

The Keynesian economists objected to the new classical approach on three major grounds:

> First, they regarded the Neoclassical assumption of clearing markets as blatantly counterfactual. They found it impossible to believe that the unemployment of, say, the 1930's depression or of the 1978–1982 recession was largely voluntary.
>
> Second, they had overwhelming doubts that errors in wage-price expectations could be large enough to account for the magnitude and length of witnessed fluctuations in unemployment. ... Yet if this objection is granted and thus (in accordance with the natural-rate hypothesis) unemployment fluctuations are attributed mainly to swings in the natural rate of unemployment, there is another difficulty. The natural rate of unemployment depends soley on the tastes, technologies, and endowments of an economy and these are unlikely sources of cyclical macroeconomic activity.
>
> Third, the New Classical economists provided no microeconomic reason for why the public does not acquire those pieces of information that it needs to avoid its expectational errors [Lindbeck and Snower, 1988, 29].

Of course, the critique by the new classical economists also had an impact on the recent work, which was not prepared to accept the old Keynesian orthodoxy. It is telling that this orthodoxy, dubbed "The Reappraisal of Kenyes," is, in the telescoped historical scale of a modern theorist, here equated with the post-1975 work of Barro and Grossman (1976), Muellbauer and Portes (1978), and the French "non-Walrasian" school of Benassy (1975), Dreze (1976), and Malinvaud (1977). Its major failings for what seems to have come to be called the New Keynesian economics[1] (not to be confused with the post-Keynesians) are as follows:

> ... the quantities demanded and supplied in each market are formulated in accordance with agents' objectives and constraints, but prices are not explained in this way. ... A macroeconomic theory that covers quantity determination but not price determination—even though quantities demanded and supplied do, in general, depend on prices—must be incomplete.
>
> ... when markets fail to clear, agents face unexploited gains from trade. By changing the prices and quantities at which they trade, some agents could be made better off without any others being made worse off. ... Yet in the Reappraisal of Keynes world, these gains are exploited only through quantity adjustments, not through price adjustments. ...

> Finally, although the Reappraisal of Keynes theory implies that the way in which government policies affect unemployment depends (in part) on wage and price levels, the theory does not tell us how these wage and price levels respond to government policies. In fact, wages and prices are assumed impervious to policy influence. Now if this assumption turns out in fact to be false, then the theory provides no way of assessing what the effectiveness of government policies is [Lindbeck and Snower 1988, 29–30].

Lindbeck and Snower find commonalities in these objections concerning the failure of both theories to deal with important informational and expectational errors and to adjust behavior to exploit potential gains from trade. This commonality suggests to them that the unifying theme of the current and future work on unemployment is its setting *outside* of the standard price-taking competitive state.

> In this light it would appear eminently sensible to investigate explanations of involuntary unemployment that recognize the existence of both imperfect information and price-setting behavior. Indeed, this has been the thrust of many recent contributions to the unemployment literature. But the joint assumptions of imperfect information and price setting do not go well [with] the market-clearing foundations on which the New Classical Macroeconomics is built.... When price setters are imperfectly informed about their economic environment, there is no guarantee the set prices will eliminate all surpluses and shortages.... *Consequently, it is not surprising that many recent contributions to the unemployment literature hae moved away from the presumption that all markets clear or have rested on new concepts of what "market clearing" means* [Lindbeck and Snower 1988, 32].

Thus the thrust of New Keynesian economics becomes the assertion that labor markets may not clear [2] and that this nonclearing may be explained by the rational behavior of firms and workers operating in an environment of price-setting and imperfect information.

Note that this "metaphysic" of unemployment would not have suprised Pigou. He, as we will see, would have ascribed these conditions to a lack of "plasticity" of prices and wages. What is new in New Keynesian explanations is the extent to which the behavior of individuals is given rationalistic foundations, which were assumed in Pigou's system (but perhaps not in Marshall's, considering his social and moral outlook on labor questions), to extend only to the perfectly competitive case.[3]

Just what are these newly founded rationalizations for behavior that lead to involuntary unemployment? Gordon (1990, 1135–1160) provides the most extensive treatment to date. Lindbeck and Snower also catalogue many different approaches 1988, 32–47) but settle on four as the most viable and important. They are: (1) implicit contracts, (2) increasing returns to scale, (3) efficiency wages, and (4) insider–outsider theories. Lindbeck and Snower are proponents of one of these in particular (#4) and so are not entirely impartial in their analysis of the relative merits of these approaches, but the preliminary overview they give of each is excellent and can be consulted for full references. Here we need only give a general outline of their chosen four to get the flavor of the issues currently being raised in unemployment theory.

Implicit contracts, strictly speaking, lies outside the other three explanations both because of its comparative antiquity [stretching all the way back to Gordon (1974) and Azariadis (1975)!] and because it is classified as a "market clearing" theory. This classification devolves into a matter of semantics, though. Insurance is the underlying analogy bolstering the implicit contracts view. Workers and employers enter into an implicit agreement to smooth out employment fluctuations and guarantee stable labor costs. Since workers are more risk averse and have less access to capital markets, they receive, de facto, insurance in exchange for stable wage demands. Unemployment arises when the contingent conditions for employment are not met, as in the case of a business downturn, and the implicit contract calls for unemployment. Although the worker might like to renegotiate the terms at this point ex post, the ex ante agreements are still in force and determine what the actual trades will be be in the labor market. Thus past supply and demands are ('involuntarily'?) equal, markets "clear", even if agents might wish for a current alternation.

Increasing returns to scale, although of long and proud lineage from Smith [1937 (1776)] through Young (1928) and down to Kaldor (1985), enters the field of New Keynesiansism in the work of Weitzman (1982). In his argument it is linked with the assumption of pervasive imperfect competition and assumed to characterize the long-run equilibrium of the system so that firms' pricing decisions determine wages and the markup based on the current state of aggregate demand. Unemployment is explained as compatible with this long-run result since the usual competitive incentives to expand output are absent and individual workers cannot set up on their own due to scale disadvantages. The only cure is increased aggregate demand (combined with a "share economy").

Efficiency wages [see Weiss (1990) for an extended survey] take their cue from the problem of monitoring and selection under imperfect information that is usually associated with Akerlof's (1970) "Lemons" and the moral hazards of the agency literature.[4] In the case of the lemons analogy the firms, for various reasons such as attracting higher productivity workers and inducing existing workers to stay rather than quit, find it optimal to offer "high" wages. Similarly, in the case of difficulty in monitoring performance, the firm offers high wages and summary dismissal to "shirkers." The assumption is that "moral" and or "productive" workers can be bought. The existence of involuntary unemployment in this theory is explained by the argument that these high wages for existing employees will not be undercut in times of high unemployment because they are optimal for the firm. Thus there will be no mechanism for the unemployed to undercut the now nonmarket clearing wage. "The unemployed may be willing to work for less pay than the incumbents, but firms who hired them on these terms would find that their marginal revenue would decline more than their marginal cost" (Lindbeck and Snower 1989, 43).

Insider–outsider theories expand on the efficiency wage scheme by giving expression to the part played by "inside" labor itself against the unemployed (or newly employed) "outsiders." This theory is based on the observation that firms would find it very difficult to completely replace the existing workforce with outsiders due to various transactions costs and the insiders' firm specific human capital. The implication is that firms may find that existing workers hold some of the cards in the employment and wage setting decisions, and may be expected to exploit some of their "insider" rents. This in itself may set up the context for involuntary unemployment if it means that the insider wage is above the reservation wage of the outsiders (so the outsider would take the job for less than the going wage) but not so far above it that it would pay the firm to fire the insiders and incur the transactions costs of training the new hires. An added wrinkle is the possibility of insider harassment both of laid-off fellow insiders and of outsiders as a means by which the insiders enforce their relative position.

One cannot read Lindbeck and Snower's book and other recent "classics" of this literature without admiring the ingenuity and skill of these theorists in marrying what had been previously—say, in Pigou's (or Lucas's) hands—considered incompatible states of market metaphysics: imperfect, non-clearing-market outcomes and rational optimizing agents. Nor can one doubt that the issues raised have some relevance to the operation of real labor markets. Shorn of the imposing theoretical garb, implicit contracts recalls the fact that labor is not a standard commodity and the workplace is a social setting consisting of human institutions. After all, the efficiency wage theory harkens back to Marshall's view that firm-specific human capital makes for more productive workers and that better, higher paid workers are worth more. The insider–outsider model formalizes the view that workers themselves may gain power in a social environment like the modern workplace, and it will pay employers to heed this power in negotiating wages and employment decisions. And the increasing returns literature, on the face of it, seems to rest on the claim that modern large-scale capitalism is not that of the handicraft era; thus the roles of worker and employer involve power and position and these places are not interchanged easily.[5]

Yet when stated in this simplistic way and compared to the sometimes extreme technical lengths needed to express these notions in optimization terms, one cannot help but pause and ask what the real point is of this immense effort. Recalling Marshall's dictum, later echoed by Keynes, that formal analysis be used only insofar as it illuminates the phenomena in question, and even then better rewritten in words or relegated to an appendix, one wonders if these sorts of issues are not best treated in another way entirely. That is to say, is it not the case that the complexities of "the labor market" should be banned from ever being forced into a simplistic supply-and-demand framework and that the issues of employee relations and bargaining be treated in a comparative historical context?

Such methodological issues aside, it is clear that in the sweep of the history of unemployment theory, the work of the New Keynesians recalls a pre-Keynesian emphasis upon imperfections in the labor market for its basic outlook on what "explains" the concept of involuntary unemployment. It is this contention and the attendant differences with Keynes's own approach to these matters that are pursued in what follows.

To summarize this section, the rise of New Keynesian economics is best characterized as a *reaction* to the events leading up to what Lindbeck and Snower call the Standoff. If one looks carefully at the combined rejections by the New Keynesians of both New classical and reappraisal of Keynes notions, noted above, there is an unusual quality possessed by the New Keynesian work that should be noticed. Though the New Classical view is severely rebuked for its social unreality ("blatantly counter factual"), its underlying microfoundational method is considered valid by the New Keynesians. Contrariwise the method of the reappraisal Keynesians is found wanting ("incomplete in its scope, defective in its logic,[6] and misleading in its policy implications"), yet its object, definitions of states of involuntary unemployment, is deemed worthy of pursuit.

Thus Lindbeck and Snower (1988, 30) note "the Keynesians and New classical macroeconomists had reached a standoff. The most convincing arguments of the contestants seemed to be their criticisms of each other." The solution for the New Keynesians was to accept the criticisms of both. They were then driven to imperfectionist microfoundations (rigorously specified) to explain the imperfect operation of labor markets. But note that this left the benchmark of the New Classicals intact. Unemployment would not occur if only markets were perfect, as Beveridge and Pigou said 60 years ago. Perhaps the definition of the perfect benchmark is what needs work.

Unemployment to the Victorians: The Background to Marshallianism

One of the most striking things about the history of economists' treatment of unemployment is the comparatively late stage at which it was even considered a problem worthy of attention (see Garraty 1978). In the texts of the period of classical political economy the issue was not widely discussed, generally being considered part and parcel of the "conditions of the working class."

Thus in Smith, while wage theory and the issue of labor mobility are clearly discussed, what we might today recognize as unemployment rarely shows its head. After the incorporation of the Malthusian population doctrine by Ricardo, the general tone of the discussion of labor by economists became the "dismal" outlook of legend. In the context of the English classical system, what discussion of unemployment there was would generally have been understood as part of the Poor Law Debates. Here the issue was not so much why people did not have jobs as the proper public management of the poor, the vagrant, and the beggar. And under the influence of the Malthusian theory and the wages fund doctrine, economists—whose views were instrumental in the drafting of the New Poor Law in 1834—displayed much more of a moral than an analytical tone. As an example the poor law reform seems largely to have been an attempt to avoid encouraging slothful beggars from easily becoming wards of the state. The exception in this, of course, is the work of Marx, where a reserve army of the unemployed becomes a natural feature of a capitalist system. Be that as it may, it is noteworthy in analytical terms that the classical school of political economy did not conceptualize the analysis of labor issues primarily in terms of the market supply-and-demand approach that would later dominate discussion.

With the advent of neoclassical marginalism the attention of economics shifted from the broad classical themes of growth and distribution to the narrow ones of individual motivation in economic decisions and the operation of markets. It took the second generation of marginalists to extend this method to the issues of labor and wages with the rise to dominance of marginal productivity analysis in the 1890s. Henceforward and to the present, the marginalist supply and demand approach would dominate mainstream discussion of labor issues. The labor market was to be taken as a special instance of the general laws of markets. This set the theoretical stage for the treatment of unemployment that Keynes would later characterize as "classical."

But the use of this theoretical framework, it must be said, was not immediately taken up by economists in the pursuit of the question of unemployment. Just how this happened is a complicated issue involving the concrete historical events of the late 19th and early 20th century, the simultaneous drive to professionalize economics, and the enterprising work of various outsiders to the emerging "professional" clique.

It is instructive to concentrate on the British case because it is clearly the setting for Keynes's work, and also because, to a large extent, the intellectual tradition it spawned still dominates the economics of unemployment. With industrialization the "problem of the unemployed" became a progressively larger issue in British society. Over time its treatment came to be tied in with the issue of the trade cycle. Actual documentation and analysis of unemployment were originally spurred by social inquiries conducted by non-economists, particularly those associated with the Fabians and the Edwardian "problem-centered social investigators."[7] Most notable in this regard was the work of Charles Booth (1902) who conducted an influential statistical account of the extent of poverty and unemployment in London in the 1880s, B. Seebohm Rowntree (1902) who conducted a similar study in York, and William Beveridge (1909), whose book marked unemployment as a "problem of industry" and became a rallying point for Fabian reformers at the turn of the century. Beveridge's contribution to the economic theory of unemployment was negligible, but he was important in the wider sense of bringing the issue into such prominence that the economics profession felt required to comment.[8] Also, Beveridge explicitly tried to bring the latest economic theory to bear on the problem, to the extent that he proposed solving unemployment by reforming labor markets to resemble more closely the model provided by economic theory.

Finally, the most important direct challenge to the dominant economic *theory* of unemployment at the time was presented in the voluminous output of the self-confessed "economic heretic," J.A. Hobson. It was Hobson's role to challenge Victorian complacency regarding unemployment and to pin much of the blame on the irrelevance of the orthodox economics of his day, with its presumption of automatic adjustments via Say's Law, and what Hobson saw as its apologetic outlook. Combined with his underconsumptionist attack on the great Victorian belief in the virtue of thrift, Hobson was a marked man, and he never gained status within economics. It also is true that his formulations often lacked clarity. That his popular appeal was great, though, is attested by the frequency with which orthodox economists went out of their way to refute him.

Although mostly known for the many versions of his business cycle work, *The Problem of the Unemployed* (Hobson 1896) is Hobson's most interesting direct commentary on the issues of concern here.[9] In reading the book today, one is struck by the extent to which Hobson uses such "Keynesian" terminology as "aggregate supply" and "aggregated demand" (p. 117), and his clear identification of unemployment with "all forms of involuntary leisure" (p. 9). But in retrospect, considering Keynes's claims four decades later, what is most modern about Hobson's treatment is his strong disassociation of unemployment from the *individual* "morality" of the unemployed as opposed to the *social* causes at work:

> A depression of the staple trade in a town throws out of employment 10 per cent. of those who are normally employed. The charity organiser with his individual scrutiny sets to work, and a close investigation of each "case" discloses in most of this 10 per cent. some moral or economic defect: there is drink, laziness, inefficency, or some other personal fault discernible in, or imputed to, most of these "unemployed." Our "thorough" investigator, having, as he thinks, found a sufficient reason why each man should be unemployed, reaches the conclusion, that "unemployment" is due to individual causes. Such conclusion is, of course, wholly fallacious. Pesonal causes, no doubt, explain in a large measure who are the individuals that shall represent the 10 per cent. "unemployed," but they are in no true sense even contributory causes of the "unemployment." When economic causes lower the demand for labour, competition will tend to squeeze out of employment those individuals who, for reasons, sometimes moral, sometimes industrial, are less valuable workers than their fellows. If these individuals had not been morally or industrially defective they would have kept their work, but necessarily by pushing out another 10 per cent [Hobson 1896, 47].

Marshall

The explanation for the fact that the English economists had so little to say about unemployment in the Victorian era when it gained such prominence outside the profession probably rests, as with most of that group's strengths and weaknesses, with the work and attitudes of Alfred Marshall. Yet Marshall was a complicated personality, and his economics was dense and sometimes beclouding (as some of his Cambridge successors, such as Joan Robinson, were later inclined to say). Consequently, it is perhaps no surprise that we can trace to Marshall's influence *both* the extreme neglect and misrepresentation Keynes would ascribe to economic theoreticians concerning the nature of unemployment, *and* also the roots of Keynes's own later revolutionary outlook. But first, Marshall.

In evaluating Marshall and his influence it is crucial to recognize his methodological attitude and his vision for economics. Two strands of his general perspective seem most relevant: his attitudes toward controversy and truth (Collard 1990). It is commonplace to regard Marshall as wary of controversy, almost to the point of extreme timidity.[10] Yet this was not just a personal trait but also a strategy for gaining professional status for economists. For Marshall, professional economists were to avoid the unseemly appearance of controversy, both theoretical and practical, and were to assume a scientific objectivity on social issues. Part of this self-conscious sense of objectivity lay in the security of the method and theory of the *Principles of Economics*. "The Organon was to be a machine for the discovery of concrete truth" (Collard 1990, 167).

In line with this vision for economics was Marshall's extensive efforts to found the Tripos (Coats 1967), which supposedly would institutionalize the production of such noncontroversial "professional" economists. Furthermore, another critical aspect of Marshall's attitude toward controversy was his attempt to reconcile the old classical theory with the newer neoclassical approach. This is clearly evident in his labor market analysis, where long-run supply and demand become "indeterminate" as the old classical themes concerning labor—population, human nature, and social institutions—come to the foreground.

In retrospect, it is easy to see now that things were not quite so cut and dried. First with respect to the issue of method, one man's objectivity is often just prejudice to another. And it is only fair to note that Marshall injected into his analysis much Victorian moralizing of the type Hobson railed against—particularly with regard to labor markets because of their close connection in Marshall's though to changeable human nature. But the genius of Marshall was to weave this moral polemic so intricately into his positive analysis that is *seemed* splendidly dispassionate.[11] And, as R.C.O. Matthews (1990, 20–23) has recently stressed in his superb documentation of Marshall's views on labor markets, his fusion of morals and theory was for him a *scientific* necessity when dealing with long-run social forces in which effects today would yield changed preferences and human natures over a long future time.

Picking up on this theme, it is perhaps not unreasonable to skip Marshall's development of the apparatus of supply and demand in the labor market. This was actually treated more concisely by Dobb as we will see below. Instead, we will concentrate on some of the usually forgotten qualifications with which Marshall endlessly complicated his argument. Thus, after setting out the mechanical aspects of supply and demand for labor, Marshall (1961, ch. IV, Bk. III) stresses the long-term cumulative effects of wages:

> But some peculiarities in this action [of supply and demand on labor] remain to be studied, which are of a more vital character. For they effect not merely the form, but also the substance of the action of the forces of demand and supply; and to some extent they limit and hamper the free action of those forces. We shall find that the influence of many of them is not at all to be measured by their first and most obvious effects: and that those effects which are cumulative are generally far more important in the long run than those which are not, however prominent the latter may appear [Marshall 1961, 559].

Chief among the evil effects of adverse labor market outcomes—in Marshall's view, low wages, not unemployment—is the transmission of poverty, lack of opportunity, and poor education for children. For Marshall, the main point to stress was that the cumulative nature of social evolution meant that these effects, which "exert a deep and controlling influence over the history of the world," cannot be treated directly by the static method. It is at this juncture, clearly of high importance in Marshall's thinking, that he advocates a regime of high wages. For if low wages, though perhaps a natural short-run outcome, can have such long-term cumulative disastrous effects, the opposite is also true:

> On the other hand, high earnings, and a strong character, lead to greater strength and higher earnings, which again lead to still higher earnings, and so on cumulatively. [p. 560].

As we will see below, Dobb emphasizes this aspect of Marshallianism more than the master himself ever did and draws from it support for positive action such as minimum wage laws and union bargaining. In Marshall's hands these clear-cut policy conclusions would probably have been too "controversial" to consider. Instead we get reserved endorsement of the *goal* of agitation for higher working class incomes,[12] which is then drained away in the sand of another array of Marshall's endless qualifications (see, for example, Bk. VI, ch. XIII, esp. pp. 702–722).

Also it should be added in fairness to Marshall that he considered state action as only a last resort, while "policy" had much broader implications. Matthews (1990, 30) observes that "policy" to Marshall was preeminently a matter of educating leaders of business and labor in the macroeconomic implications of their actions, that is, they must be enlightened properly, presumably by reading the *Principles*. Finally, the Victorian faith in progress and rationality in advancing civilization is expressed in Marshall's belief that the social effects of high wages coincided with the private interests of employers and so could be expected to dominate in the long run. This is the context where we first come up against a New Keynesian notion, in Marshall's explicit and extensive references to "efficiency wages" (see Bk. VI., ch. III),

> . . . that is, earnings measured, not as time-earnings are with reference to the time spent in earning them; and not as piece-work earnings are with reference to the amount of output resulting from the work by which they are earned; but with reference to the exertion of ability and *efficiency* required of the worker [Marshall 1961, 549].

The complication for supply-and-demand analysis which this implies is a degree of interdependence between the two. High wages call forth better labor and so, in turn, affect the demand price:

> We conclude then that an increase of wages, unless earned under unwholesome conditions, almost always increases the strength, physical, mental and even moral of the coming generation; and that, other things being equal, an increase in the earnings that are to be got by labour increases its rate of growth; or, in other words, a rise in its demand-price increases the supply of it [Marshall 1961, 532].

It is in this complex setting that we are to understand Marshall's emphasis on the point that distribution theory does *not* present an exact analogue to value theory:

> The keynote of this book [Bk. VI, "The Distribution of National Income"] is in the fact that free human beings are not brought up to their work on the same principles as a machine, a horse, or a slave. If they were, there would be very little difference between the distribution and the exchange side of value [Marshall 1961, 504].

Thus, recent evidence concerning the issue of efficiency and high wages is:

> . . . forcing constantly more and more attention to the fact that highly paid labour is generally efficient and therefore not dear labour; a fact which, though it is more full of hope for the future of human race than any other that is known to us, will be found to exercise a very complicating influence on the theory of distribution [Marshall 1961, 510].

But what of unemployment in all of this? It must be said that in the treatment of this issue, which so engaged other reformers of his time, Marshall had something of a blind spot. His scant comments on it in the *Principles* (Bk. VI, ch. XII, pp. 687–688) bring it up only to dismiss it as overblown and surely improving over time (a rather large historical gaffe, considering where unemployment rates were heading as the last edition of the book came out in 1920). To account for this it is perhaps sufficient to note that Marshall's discursive-moral-evolutionary dynamics were highly dependent on the author's own peculiar prejudices. This ingredient is suggested, again, by David Collard's recent assessment of Marshall's influence on Cambridge economics when he argues that Marshall emphasized the need to arrive at "Truth" through the use of his analytic machine—a machine which for all Marshall's qualifications about the long run turned out to be remarkably unsuited to the analysis of unemployment:

> The Organon was to be a machine for the discovery of concrete truth. Keynes remarks (1926, p. 36) that Marshall was not good at the discovery of concrete truth. Beatrice Webb noticed (Koot 1987, p. 180), after staying with Marshall, that he had an extraordinary penchant for making "an astounding observation with no basis in fact" [Collard 1990, 167].

Webb's comment is telling in the context of Marshall's treatment of unemployment since it would seem that he both denied the view of the Victorian social reformers (like Webb) concerning the growing problem of unemployment and that he based his own views on what could easily be characterized as an "astounding observation with no basis in fact." In the case of unemployment R.C.O. Matthews (1991, 33–38) has noted that Marshall, somewhat astonishingly, based his analysis of unemployment on his observations of what he considered the "pre-industrial" city of Palermo during his vacation visits to Italy. Matthews summarizes his view as follows:

> It [Marshall's observations in Palermo] suggested to him that the history of hiring practices had gone in a circle, with three phases: 1. The worker permanently attached to a feudal patron, but chronically underemployed and also lacking in personal freedom; 2. labour hired and fired on a casual basis; 3. a reversion to a more or less permanent attachment of the worker to one employer, but now because of asset specificity rather than patronage, and with a full whole-time wage being paid, and without loss of personal freedom. The transition from phase 2 to phase 3 had served to reduce the inconstancy of employment [Matthews 1990, 34]

This observation sheds considerable light on the difficulties Marshallianism would present to a scholar seeking a fuller understanding of short-run changes in unemployment, just when such an understanding was urgently needed in the 1920s and 1930s. However, Marshall's own (scant) treatment of unemployment is less important than the ambiguous, but vastly influential legacy his method left to that profession. In Marshall's hands the Organon suggested that supply and demand organize the discussion, but with due regard to the evolution of social customs and the influence of the economic environment upon character. As we have seen, his analysis was wonderfully complex and subtle in the case of the labor market. Starting from the supply and demand framework, he argues that the short-period effects were dominated by long-period concerns that were not amenable to static theorizing. Of these the most important were the issues of human capital specific to individual firms and industries, the consequent peculiarities of labor as a commodity, and the influence of steady labor attachments on improving the character of the working class. Thus his complex theoretical view of supply and demand analysis, in the case of labor markets at least, became merely a skeleton upon which he hung his more evolutionary social and moral outlook (see Matthews 1990, 14–30).

Although one comes away admitting his own use of the Organon, it seems clear, against Matthews, that Marshall's emphasis on long-period normal supply and demand easily led to later confusions and dead-ends concerning employment theory. Perhaps, though, more of the blame for the confusions should be placed on Pigou than Marshall.

With regard to the labor market, the ultimate irony is that Keynes's own influential views, though clearly opposed to Marshall's conclusions on unemployment, may be more faithful to the master's careful method concerning problems of labor than the chosen successor Pigou. This is because Pigou grew ever more impatient with Marshall's qualifying and fudging, but always heeded his advice to remain noncontroversial. Thus in Pigou's hands the *mechanical* aspect of the Organon takes over, and unemployment becomes a *simple* matter of a nonclearing labor market.

Keynes, always more attuned to current social facts than either Marshall or Pigou, and ever the controversialist, perhaps took more from Marshall's moral philosophy outlook. As Marshall left the characterization of labor supply and demand and its social effects (properly) shrouded in a mysterious brew of institutional and moral analysis, there seems to hbave been plenty of room for Keynes to elaborate on this part of the Organon. In any event, as we shall see, Keynes never let the Organon blind him to current realities as it eventually blinded Pigou. And when Keynes felt the need for a new Organon to explain mass unemployment of a kind Marshall never expected, he was able to rise to the occasion as Marshall's more devout successor could not.

Dobb: Labor Market Orthodoxy in Interwar Cambridge

To set up our discussion of the immediate pre-*General Theory* context of unemployment theory at Cambridge, it is convenient and appropriate to start with that school's official orthodox view as set out in the Cambridge Economic Handbook series edited by Keynes from 1914 to 1936.[13] Maurice Dobb's *Wages* came out in that series in 1928 and eventually went through three revisions and over 20 reprintings. Indeed, it survived in print into the 1950s. We will quote below mostly from the original 1928 edition, with some minor references to the second edition written in 1938 as it elaborates upon the arguments of the first. In any case, it is clear that this treatment would have been considered fairly standard in Cambridge between the wars.[14]

Coming to Dobb's book today, the modern economist is struck by the author's thoroughness and fairness in his discussion of the "theory of wages" (ch. IV), and by the wealth of institutional detail relating to historical wage rates, the myriad variety of complex wage payment systems, and the social history of bargaining and compact. One senses the influence of Marshall strongly, but here we find that influence in an interesting and ironic blend with Dobb's Marxist historical materialism (which, incidentally, is *very* much in the background).

For our purposes here, the most important discussion in Dobb's book relates to the analysis of wage institutions in "The Payment of Wages" (ch. III), and the chapter on the "Theory of Wages" (ch. IV). In chapter III Dobb presents a detailed description of several types of wage payment systems, historical and contemporary.[15] Under the heading "The Economy of High Wages," Dobb offers a distinctly New Keynesian line of argument.[16]

> Recently a great deal has been talked and written concerning "The Economy of High Wages": if the employer pays well, it is said, he will get better work done and so gain more profit. This may come about in two ways. First if the worker and his family live at a higher standard of life, their physical and mental conditions will tend to improve and their working efficiency will tend to increase. Part of this result will tend to be mainly of a psychological character and to be more uncertain and indefinite. Second, the prospect of more wages may act as an inducement to the worker to increase the amount of work that he does, either by working longer hours or by working more intensively [Dobb 1928, 4445].[17]

Dobb then discusses in detail various alternative methods of contract between workers and employers such as piece rates, premium bonus systems, task bonus systems, and Taylorite systems. Having shown how these systems often prove superior to time rates from the standpoint of the employer's desire to maximize labor's effort, he asks why is it that we do not see them more universally adopted. His answer (pp. 51–52), citing Ford as an example of a company with a policy of exclusive time wages, is that the nature of certain processes—where the speed of the work is not up to the worker but is a characteristic of the process—many not lend themselves to piece rates. Anticipating the "shirker" version of modern efficiency wage theories, Dobb notes that the issue for the employer in these situations is the degree to which supervision is practical. And as in the "insider-outsider" view, this will be at least partly a function of workers' cooperation or resistance.[18] Furthermore, Dobb makes it clear that in the case of skilled work (firm-specific human capital?) the question often revolves as much around quality as quantity. For all of these reasons, "It is far from true that every case of low output and high costs is curable by an extension of payment by results" (Dobb 1928, 51).

Turning to Dobb's discussion of wage "theory," we get a nice historical account, stressing, in good Marshallian fashion, continuity with the classical schoolmasters and an emphasis on flexible, socially relevant theory. The classical theory is seen as "rigid and definitive" in the extreme. Against this:

> ... only in recent times [read Marshall] have serious doubts developed as to whether the conditions on which wages depend may not be more complicated, and less easily explicable by an easy mechanical formula—whether changes in wages may not react on these so-called "determining" factors as much as these latter influence wages [pp. 70–71].

The downfall of the classical theory is traced by Dobb to the chink in the Iron Law of Wages introduced by Ricardo's admission that the subsistence wage was not an absolute physical standard, but a matter of social and historic "custom and habit." This influence was eventually used by Marx to dissassociate wages from population growth altogether, except insofar as subsistence created a crude lower limit to wages. They became indeterminate in some degree and subject to struggle between workers and employers (Dobb 1928, 74–75).

But the classical introduction of a demand side argument in the form of a "wages fund" was not enough to save classical doctrine either. Although it was taken up by Victorian moralists (he quotes Mrs. Marcet) to show trade unions and working class leaders "the untutored folly of their methods," it eventually backfired when, under the influence of marginalist thinking, it was shown that the wage "fund" was in fact a "flow." It is at this stage also, according to Dobb sometime in the late 19th century, that it was realized that higher wages lead to lower birthrates. This boosts the standing of trade unions and underpins the "high wage economy" arguments.

Yet Dobb sees the marginalist revolution (at least in its sophisticated Marshallian variant) as an advance over the wage fund arguments, not because it was radically different in kind (he follows Cannan in classifying them both as "supply and demand theories"), but because it was less *deterministic* in its conclusions. Thus, quoting Marshall against Clark's crude marginal productivity ethics, Dobb (p. 83) comments that "those who were wiser and understood the situation more clearly realised that the new doctrine did not constitute a complete theory of wage" (p. 83).[19] The complete theory, of course, turns out to be a marginalist supply-and-demand schedule, handled with all the qualifications and reservations Marshall would have added. A long quotation strung together from his discussion (Dobb 1928, 87–90) is appropriate to convey the accepted version of supply and demand for labor in Cambridge in 1928:

> The supply of labour can be used in several different senses. It may be applied to the *number of workers* seeking wage-employment. It may include the *number of hours* which each worker is willing to work. . . . It may be further stretched to include the *intensity of work* that is done each hour . . . or even to include the *quality* of work done, depending on the intelligent skill with which it is applied. All of these things are likely to bear some kind of relation of to the price of labour. . . .
>
> Changes in the wage level will probably react on the quality of the labour supply; and the possibility of this reaction will have to be taken into account as a modifying factor in the theory. But more important than this will probably be the reaction of the wage level on the supply.
>
> With regard to the connection between the level of wages and the total population we cannot be more than very uncertain. . . . With regard to the supply of labour in other senses, however—the intensity of work, the willingness to work longer hours, the proportion of the population that offers itself for wage-employment—one probably can postulate some connection; and to this extent it will be possible to represent the supply prices of different quantities of labor as a "supply curve," on the assumption of a given aggregate population and a given quality of labour.
>
> The wage level is then seen to be dependent on two variable quantities—the amount of capital advanced to hire labor (or the "Wage Fund") and the supply of labour forthcoming. The former at any one time will depend on the past accumulations of capital, but modified in the course of time by the investor's willingness to add to existing capital by new investments, or on the other hand, by his unwillingness to leave existing accumulations of capital intact ["waiting"]. . . .
>
> It will, therefore, be possible to conceive of a "demand curve" for labor as well as a "supply curve," although the shape of this demand curve will differ according to the period of time that one has in mind. Putting the two curves together, we can then have the accompanying picture, with the point of intersection of the two curves as the equilibrium-point where the level of wage will tend to settle down.

Already it should be clear that, at least on Dobb's interpretation, the Cambridge tradition of labor market analysis to which Keynes reacted in the 1920s and 1930s, while clearly a supply-and-demand theory, was a rather sophisticated one. Following Marshall it made allowances for much institutional detail and was cast in a less rigid fashion than is common even today, wages often exhibiting a degree of indeterminacy. In Dobb's analysis indeterminacy constituted the justification for devoting the second half of his book almost entirely to bargaining and unions. Also, it is clear that the version presented by Dobb shows full cognizance of the issues of incentives and monitoring of labor that are the hallmarks of the microeconomics of the New Keynesian economics. Yet it is worth noting that he has next to nothing to say about the issue of "unemployment." As we will see in the section on Keynes's own writings, it was this strand of Marshallian economics which he internalized, worked within, and later rejected.

Pigou: Mechanical Marshallianism

But there is another avenue out of Marshall that Keynes implicitly identified when, in the preface to the Handbook series, he identified the founding fathers as "Dr. Marshall and Professor Pigou." It is to this strand of thought, a somewhat more precise and technical Marshallianism, as we shall see, to which we turn for the explicit reaction of Cambridge economics to the concerns of the late Edwardian social reformers about unemployment.

Marshall himself, as we have seen, actually dealt very little with the problem. Instead, the primary response from Cambridge to the growing popular literature in the early part of the century is by Marshall's chosen successor to the chair at Cambridge and later Keynes' straw (classical) man in the *General Theory*, Arthur Cecil Pigou. In 1913 Pigou's *Unemployment* was published in the "Home University Library of Modern Knowledge." Its expressed goal was to encapsulate the latest thinking of the Marshallian neoclassical school as updated in Pigou's own treatise *Wealth and Welfare*, where, according to Pigou and in keeping with Marshall's suggestion that the Organon be the guide to 'Truth,' "the special problem of unemployment is treated as a subordinate part of a larger and more general problem" (p. 253). So framed, it was natural that the question devolved into one of market-clearing equilibrium. Following the the long-run prejudices of his mentor Marshall, Pigou introduces the positive aspects of his theory as "Unemployment in the Stationary State" (ch. 5). An extensive quote reveals the core of the approach:

> Though, as just stated, the preceding chapter [devoted to criticizing "popular explanations"] has realised no positive results, it has revealed a *method*. For it has made plain the theoretical possibility that wage-rates at any moment and in every part of the industrial field can be so adjusted to the demand for labour of various grades that *no unemployment whatever can exist*. In other words, it has

shown that unemployment is *wholly* caused by maladjustment between wage-rates and demand. The road which our investigation must follow is thus indicated. It must assume the form of an inquiry into the influences by which various kinds of maladjustment may be and are brought about [Pigou 1913, 51].

Setting a standard that is very similar to the modern labor economics of rigid wages that is once again popular in economic theory, Pigou's investigation led to the imperfections of the labor market that marked it off from the textbook model. These "frictions" from which unemployment would arise even in the fictitious stationary state ranged from unions to the inability, due to custom, to grade each laborer's reward according to individual productivity, to minimum wage laws.

Outside the stationary state, dynamic conditions meant that unemployment was the result of the general phenomenon that wage rates are never "perfectly plastic" (p. 76). Thus although Pigou recognized that the change in demand for labor over the trade cycle was a proximate cause of unemployment, the root cause was the inability of wage rates to adjust. "We are then entitled to the general conclusion that unemployment is likely to be greater, the more rigidly wage-rates are maintained in the face of variations in the demand for labour."[20] Finally the lack of "the mobility of labour" (ch. 10) completes Pigou's catalogue of the causes of unemployment. It is at this point that Pigou's major policy recomendations are directed, and his argument is almost identical to Beveridge's then popular proposals for labour exchanges to increase the efficiency of the market to match employers with employees.

Actually, reading Pigou's tract of 1913 is a useful antidote to the simplistic view of him and pre-Keynesian economists that has been standard in the profession ever since Keynes singled "the Prof" out for crucifixion in his appendix to chapter 19 of the *General Theory*. In fact, the text offers support for the contention that Keynes's *General Theory*, though constituting a crucial turning point in unemployment theory, is squarely within the Cambridge tradition of his day. First, as Richard Kahn (1976, 19) remarked, it is surprising to see Pigou devoting his treatise at the very start to the issue of "involuntary unemployment," a distinction usually presumed to have begun with Keynes.[21] Moreover, it is clear that Pigou had some sort of inkling of the issue of demand-deficient unemployment, if not a coherent theory of it. Besides his remarks on the trade cycle, this is evident in his policy prescription. In addition to the endorsement of Beveridge's labor exchanges, he give a partial nod to the notion of government contercyclical spending policy:

. . . public authorities are in a position somewhat to lessen the fluctuations that occur in the demand for labour, and hence to diminish unemployment, both by fitting that part of their own demand for goods and services, which is necessarily occasional, into the interstices of the general demand, and also by avoiding unnecessary ups and downs in that part of their demand which is, or can be made, continuous. These practices constitute remedies for unemployment in all circumstances. [p. 247].

Still, although Pigou in some respects presents a fairly sophisticated analysis of unemployment, it is clear that his theoretical outlook confines the issue to the operation of the labor market and in particular to the lack of "plasticity" of wages in the face of changes in demand. In some ways this is even more evident in his later *Theory of Unemployment* (1933) which so irked Keynes that he felt compelled to devote a whole appendix to its excoriation in the *General Theory*. In fact, a comparison of the two books is rather startling in that Pigou's earlier book appears more sophisticated and alive to the issues than the later one.

Although written at the depth of the slump, the later book expresses an almost sclerotic retreat into labor market metaphysics. But since it was written exclusively for a professional audience, as compared to the popular audience for the first book on unemployment, its theoretical underpinning is more transparent.[22] As argued above, the theoretical foundation attributes all unemployment to some form of labor market disequilibrium, typically associated with rigid wages. In 1933, Pigou again timidly endorses the temporary injection of public spending in the slump, but makes clear that "wage-policy" is the ultimate "cause" of unemployment.

First he argues that any chronic insufficiency of demand cannot occur:

. . . the state of demand for labour, as distinguished from changes in that state, is irrelevant to unemployment, because wage-rates adjust themselves in such a manner that different states of demand, when once established, tend to be associated with similar average rates of unemployment [p. 252].

And, thus, by construction the unemployment that does occur is due to "frictions."

There will always be at work a strong tendency for wage-rates to be so related to demand that everybody is employed. Hence, in stable conditions every one will actually be employed. The implication is that such unemployment as exists at any time is due wholly to the fact that changes in demand conditions are continually taking place and that frictional resistances prevent the appropriate wage adjustments from being made instantaneously. [p. 252].

One wonders what Marshall (and Dobb) would have made of this. Lost is all sense of Marshall's complexity and his insight into the role of social institutions and human nature. Also absent is the Marshallian emphasis on Smithian realism in the sense of touching base with real (or even imagined) social facts now and then. It is no suprise that Keynes found this theory repellent and fascinating at the same time. Remarking to D.H. Robertson, Keynes wrote:

> Have you read the Prof's book carefully: I find it most disturbing. For if I haven't completely misunderstood, it's simply nonsense from beginning to end. . . . For heaven's sake have a good look at the work and tell me if the gist of this is right. Or am *I* talking nonsense? A.C.P. produces as great a sense of Bedlam in my mind as Hayek does. Are the undergraduates to be expected to take it seriously? What a subject! [Keynes 1973, 310–313].

So we have before us the explicit textual treatents of labor markets and unemployment by Cambridge economist other than Keynes, before the *General Theory*. It must be said that it is a mixed bag. Marshall and Dobb emphasized the nondeterministic influence of social institutions at work in labor markets. As a result they were able to account for much of the actual institutional detail of wage practices.

The issues raised by modern efficiency wage theories and insider-outsider models would have been no suprise to them. They also saw a role for unions and expressed favor, to a greater or lesser extent, for the "social" goal of a "high wage economy," as both practical and desirable.

This issue clearly sets them (particularly Dobb) off from the more mechanistic Pigovian analysis. For though Pigou might find the idea of raising wages desirable, his analysis could only see this as leading to unemployment and loss of output. Interestingly, the modern incorporation of bits of labor market reality into an even more technically oriented discussion by the New Keynesian economics seems to take Marshall's and Dobb's insights, which they did not themselves see as explanations of unemployment, and make them the explanation of what Pigou would call "lack of plasticity" in the labor market. Perhaps the crucial difference is expressed in Marshall's famous dictum, "*natura non facit saltum*." He saw the effects of steady employment and higher incomes as effecting a slow evolutionary change on society. Society would change slowly over time as a result—he thought naturally.

Dobb (1938, 56–58) in his later editions also emphasizes this evolutionary argument, but saw the need for state intervention to secure the needed reforms since the short-term interest of employers were not coincident with the desirable social effects of higher wages and stable employment. Yet New Keynesian economics professes to be a short-run equilibrium account of involuntary unemployment. In this sense the New Keynesians follow Pigou. Our task now is to look at some of Keynes's own thoughts on labor markets and unemployment, and to trace their evolution up the *General Theory*. It will be our contention that he was always much closer to Marshall (and Dobb) than to Pigou.

Keynes as a Marshallian

Given that Keynes was one of those "orthodox members of the Cambridge School" to which he referred in his introduction to the Handbook series, it should come as no suprise that he held views on labor markets and unemployment during his career that reflect the Marshallian tradition laid out above. Keynes's lecture notes prior to World War I, as we will see below, make it clear that early on he indeed did hold what is best described as a sophisticated and realistic Marshallian view on value and distribution theory.

But Keynes's attitude toward the orthodox treatment of unemployment changed significantly as the 1920s progessed. It will be our task here to show that Keynes's pre-*General Theory* writings provide evidence that the types of explanations of involuntary unemployment now being proffered as New Keynesian economics would not have been novel to Keynes even before World War I, much less in the 1930s. Moreover, his departure from the traditional view of the labor market as self-adjusting begins in the 1920s. Further it will be argued that, though of interest in themselves, these departures remained no more than elaborate qualifications of the classical theory he would eventually reject in the *General Theory*. Thus the source for his own break with classicism must be sought elswhere.

To place Keynes within the Marshallian tradition at Cambridge is to recognize both Marshall's enormous but sometimes invisible influence on his pupils and to highlight Keynes's peculiar gifts. It would appear that the characteristics that would mark his career in general, a continuing interest in current social issues, a distaste for 'pure theory' as such, and a strong attraction to controversy and political involvement, showed very early in Keynes's career as an economist.

We have much evidence to substantiate this point. Indirectly, the recent work on Keynes's philosophical apprenticeship with G.E. Moore and his professional work in the philosophy of probability (see O'Donnell 1988; Davis 1992) make it clear that he always conceived of his role as that of a moral scientist in the mold of Smith, Sidgwick, and Marshall himself. By this is meant to imply his interest in developing habits of thought that would provide practical guides to clear thinking and action about social problems. Thus his *Treatise on Probability* can be read as an attempt at formulating a justification for pursuing the Moorean "good" in the context of human affairs where the outcomes of conduct could not be rigidly specified. This, of course, required a theory that was attuned to particular situations, not a mechanical apparatus.[23]

In addition, it is evident that Keynes chose topics that were matters of current social import and controversy. At the turn of the century Indian currency reform was one such topic. Later, the problems associated with war finance and the restoration of monetary relations between the trading partners of the Western world were the dominant economic topics of the day. Of course, this also is obviously the case with employment theory as we pass into the '20s and '30s. Keynes's attempts at influencing policy and engaging in sharp polemical controversy are also well documented. And, in contrast with the retiring Pigou, this distinguished Keynes from most of his Cambridge contemporaries whose public personae tended toward the Marshallian model.

Yet for all of this Kenyes was brought up on Marshall and forever retained traces of the master's influence. These influences included the ever present attempt to blend historical and institutional analysis with the bare bones of the analytical machine, and a dislike for the purely mechanical aspects of theoretical work.[24] It is perhaps fair to say that besides his taste for controversy (or perhaps due to it), his main difference with Marshall was a more constant attention to, and a more daring theoretical use of, *current* social facts.

Keynes exhibited a lifelong interest in the gathering and utilization of economic data. Examples are his participating in the creation of the Cambridge Economics Research Service and later the Department of Applied Economics at Cambridge, and his work on index numbers (see Stone 1976). Yet as Marshall also displayed a deep interest in the social relevance of his economics, one must be careful in differentiating the two men on this head.

Interestingly, we now have evidence that this difference with regard to bending both his theory and interests to ever-changing current conditions is what Keynes saw as setting himself off from Marshall, and what Marshall very early saw as Keynes's major trait as an economist. In Keynes's memorial biography of Marshall (Keynes 1924) he laments the fact that peculiarities of Marshall's personal habits and career led him away from completing the projects he laid out for his life work in his early years. In particular, he notes how Marshall was distracted from producing the further planned volume of the *Principles* which was originally to have included treatments of money and realistic problems of industrial organization, trade, and business cycles (see Whitaker 1990), and that Marshall delayed the eventual monograph treatments of these topics until his grasp of the facts was seriously out of date. He ascribes this to a combination of Marshall's overweening caution in publication and his timidity with regard to criticism. The first trait led him to great lengths to ensure that his historical and institutional analysis was "complete" enough to withstand scrutiny. The second led him into the endless revisions and alterations of the already published volume of the *Principles*. Keynes's biography brilliantly shows both the strengths and weaknesses, the good and the bad of Marshall's work and method, and in the process highlights the differences in Keynes's approach to doing economics.

It is for our purposes useful to recall the weakness Keynes saw in Marshall for the contrast it provides with his own work. A series of observations from Keynes's (1924) essay convey the main points:

> Marshall . . . arrived very early at the point of view that the bare bones of economic theory are not worth much in themselves and do not carry one far in the direction of useful, practical conclusions. The whole point lies in applying them to the interpretation of current economic life. This requires a profound knowledge of the actual facts of industry and trade. But these, and the relation of individual men to them, are constantly and rapidly changing [p. 196].

> In publishing his intellectual exercises without facing the grind of discovering their point of contact with the real world he would be following and giving bad example. On the other hand, the relevant facts were extremely hard to come by—much harder than now. The progress of events in the 'seventies and 'eighties, particularly in America, was extraordinarily rapid, and organised sources of information, of which there are now so many, scarcely existed [p. 197].

> [Besides his bad health], he was too meticulous in his search for accuracy, and also for conciseness of expression, to be a ready writer. He was particularly unready in the business of fitting pieces into a big whole and of continually rewriting them in the light of their reaction on and from the other pieces [p. 197].

> Given his views as to the impossibility of any sort of finality in economics and as to the rapidity with which events change, given the limitations of his own literary aptitudes and of his leisure for book-making, was it not a fatal decision to abandon his first intention of separate independent monographs in favour of a great treatise? I think that it was . . . [pp. 197–198].

> Economists must leave to Adam Smith alone the glory of the quarto, must pluck the day, fling pamphlets into the wind, write always *sub specie temporis*, and achieve immortality by accident, if at all [p. 199].

> Moreover, did not Marshall, by keeping his wisdom at home until he could produce it fully clothed, mistake, perhaps, the true nature of his own special gift? . . . The building of his engine was the essential achievement of Marshall's peculiar genius. Yet he hankered greatly after the 'concrete truth' which he had disclaimed and for the discovery of which he not specially qualified [p. 199].

> Economics all over the world might have progressed much faster, and Marshall's authority and influence would have been far greater, if his temperament had been a little different [p. 199].

Thus, we may say that Keynes disputed the means by which Marshall achieved his ideal goal of a logical and realistic economics, but not the goal itself. His own method, in opposition to Marshall's meticulousness with the facts, was to take the salient features of reality that struck his intuition as relevant and important and to weave the theory around these, with the eventual goal of ordering reality and identifying causes. It is well described in an early philosophical paper in which he compares the work of the scientist with that of the artist:

> [He] is presented with a mass of facts, possessing similarities and differences, arranged in no kind of scheme or order. His first need is to perceive very clearly the precise nature of the different details. After concering himself with this precise and alternative perception, he holds the details clearly before his mind and it will probably be necessary that he should keep them more or less before his mind for a considerable time. Finally he will with a kind of sudden insight see through the obscurity of the argument or of the apparently unrelated data, and the details will quickly fall into a scheme or arrangement, between each part of which there is a real connection.[25]

Moreover, there is reason to believe that Marshall himself saw Keynes's penchant for realism as his major attraction in consideration of his future as an economist. In Keynes's papers exists a set of questions he wrote for Marshall in 1905. Copious remarks are scribbled over them by Marshall, mostly in an attempt to tone down Keynes's strong conclusions. One ends with the following, one must say in light of history, acutely drawn message from the master to the prospective follower:

> This is an admirable paper. It is one of the most interesting I have ever seen. It still has traces of the tendency to talk of things in the real world as they may be in a conceivable world. Your propositions are often too unconditional: and if you were to apply them in practice, you would come to grief.
>
> But you are working yourself to take account of realities; and comparatively seldom lash out into "the world behind the looking glass." I repeat what I said before, that I should immensely like to see you become a member of some economics staff, and especially of this. But I know the world is wide.[26]

Marshall evidently later came to believe Keynes had achieved the proper balance of theory and reality, remarking to him in a letter in 1917 that

> ... you have a better chance than any economist has ever had in their country of rendering high service to the State on critical occasions: for you will know more of economics than any professional statesmen has ever done; and you will know more of Whiteshall's difficulties—whether founded in the nature of things or in bureaucracy—than any professional economist has ever done.[27]

To follow out this theme of Keynes as a "realistic" Marshallian (as opposed to the scholastic Marshallian that Pigou, for example, was to become), and to see more deeply into the Cambridge setting of the development of Keynes's views on labor markets and unemployment, it is useful to divide his career into three phases. The first covers his period as a young Don, from 1908 when he began lecturing in Cambridge until 1915 when he went into full-time war service with the Treasury. From this period we get a glimpse of Keynes as a Marshallian on labor markets. But, as the foregoing discussion makes clear, this is a view already evidently quite sophisticated in outlook by modern standards. Second, we look at his writings after the war an running up to 1930. During this period Keynes comes to doubt the efficacy, at least in times of the rapid monetary upheaval that he was witnessing, of the automatic adjustment mechanisms that lay behind the Marshallian analysis of the labor market. Third, of course, is Keynes of the *General Theory of Employment, Interest and Money*. This will not be directly our concern here, though in the last section we will put forward various views of its break from the Marshallian positions on unemployment.

Keynes as a Young Don

Keynes's lecture notes from his early years at Cambridge survive among his papers and offer a very interesting view of the state of Cambridge orthodoxy at that period. They also reveal Keynes to have been quite hardworking (with numerous courses and students) and lively as a lecturer (bringing both his wit and many current events and statistics into the argument). It is to his course of lectures on "Principles of Economics" given over the years 1909–1914 that we turn for his views on the labor market at that time. Indicative of the state of the profession during that period, and perhaps indicative of Keynes's then current preoccupations, unemployment is not treated anywhere in his lectures as a separate topic. Instead one must glean the source of unemployment from the discussion of the labor market. In keeping with the Marshallian emphasis on normal value and distribution theory, this stands as a special case of the theory of long-run value:

> As in the case of the theory of normal value, so also in the case of the theory of normal distribution, the more abstract method of treatment must be mastered not because it describes the facts, but because it supplies an analysis and a classification by reference to which the meaning of the essential facts can be elucidated.[28]

Thus as Marshall had done in the case of the theory of normal values, Keynes treats the textbook view as merely a skeleton on which to elaborate analysis of the facts. In particular he proceeds by way of listing the conditions necessary for the textbook view to hold (essentially what we would recognize as the first order marginal conditions of a primitive general equilibrium system) and then the possible departures from these conditions met in the real world which might violate the textbook view. Referencing Taussig's *Principles* (1911), Keynes lists the conditions required for the theory of normal distribution to hold:

1) Accurate knowledge on the part of the entrepreneurs of what the marginal efficiency of each factor really is.
2) Accurate knowledge on the part of each factor as to the employments in which its marginal efficiency is greatest.
3) Freedom on the part of entrepreneurs and of the owners of the factors to adjust themselves rapidly to changing conditions.
4) Free competition and complete absence of monopoly amongst the various owners of any factor—i.e. no combination amongst them for the purpose of bargaining with the owners of other factors.
5) A tendency for the supply of each factor to rise and fall directly with its reward.
6) A tendency for the demand for each factor to rise and fall inversely with its cost.

Amongst these Keynes considers the most important divergences between actual and normal distribution to be due to the first three—what he calls "the element of ignorance and the difficulty of rapid adjustment to change." But the rise of unions and large-scale business enterprise calls for recognition of a (then) current tendency toward the violation of (4). As to the last two, he claims there are important cases—"to the possibility of which we must always be alive"—where demand and/or supply of a factor is insensitive with respect to changes in its reward. This last violation will come to play an increasing role in his view of labor markets well into the 1920s.

Keynes then proceeds to a detailed discussion of particular conditions affecting the return to each individual factor. These end up falling into one or another of the general categories.

In the case of wages he follows Marshall and gives the "normal doctrine" as follows:

> The net advantage obtained by the exercise of a given degree of efficiency tend to equality in different places and occupations: or more briefly, *efficiency earnings* tend to equality.

As of this period, Marshall's term "efficiency wages" was apparently quite orthodox, especially recalling that this was a lecture to an economics principles course. What was accepted as its meaning is indicated in Keynes's discussion, where he uses it to clarify the misleading use of "time wages" and "piece wages" in defining the equilibrium condition referred to above. In particular it was meant to provide a framework in which the divergences between wages in different firms in the same industry were to be accounted for by reference to the fact that geographical advantages (Keynes mentions "agricultural labor in the north and south" and "coal mines in different districts") and firm-specific capital advantages ("the case of mills with old fashioned machinery") altered labor's productivity. In a passage that sounds very modern, but in fact is a reference to Marshall, Keynes points out that the efficiency wage doctrine has to be qualified by "the fact that low-waged labor is generally dear if working with expensive machinery."[29] The meaning here is that the value of skilled work is jointly determined by the capital and the laborer's ability to use it.

> Thus it may be to the advantage of the employer to raise the time earnings of the more efficient workers more than in proportion to their efficiency.

As in the case of Dobb's book, this complex view of workplace realities allows the theory to accommodate the immense complexity of actual wage practices as attempts to capture the "efficiencies" of labor peculiar to individual firms. Thus, as Keynes's contrast (above) of efficiency wages with the simplistic cases of wages per hour ("time wages") and per unit of output ("piece wages") implies, there may be many variations in wage practices in reality:

> In this case [of raising the time earnings of more efficient labor] efficiency partly consists of *speed*. Some elaborate combinations of price and piece rates sometimes in force (sometimes with the object of encouraging speed, sometimes with the object of discouraging it).

Continuing with the elaboration of the orthodox maxim, Keynes next proceeds to a discussion of the term "net advantages." Here, as he admits, he follows Marshall in following Smith. Thus he lists Marshall's accounting of Smith's factors that might provide offsetting advantages and disadvantages to different employments. But again it is Keynes's *qualifications* of the doctrine that are most interesting. Here he covers the ground of information and mobility in a manner that sounds very like modern search theory:

> The normal doctrine assumes mobility between places and between occupation of the same kind. It is obvious that this condition is only partially fulfilled. Principally dependent upon degree of knowledge. Influence of labor exchanges.

Then Keynes goes on to J.S. Mill's theme of noncompeting groups, also elaborated upon by Marshall and Dobb:

> But there is a somewhat different connection in which the question of mobility is important. How far do those who supply labour of specialized kinds and of

> different grades or degrees of difficulty form distinct groups? How far is there mobility between different *groups* of labourers?

Again picking up on the basic premise of the modern efficency wage theories and insider-outsider models, Keynes notes that the answer to this question is "of great importance to the doctrine of wages." If employees have the power to alter their wage without attracting competition, then the normal doctrine is inapplicable. Bringing it down to his (and our) social reality, Keynes notes that this theoretical question depends on the actual labor institutions for compact and bargaining.

> Will a change in the wage of one group relatively to the others cause a movement of labourers into or out of it? Upon the answer to this question largely depends the answer to that other question how far one group of labourers may by compact bargaining prey upon the rest of the community and how far the rest of the community can prey upon a particular group of labourers.

His example, a prescient one concerning developments to come in the 1920s, is the "coal miners."

It is also worth noting that at this stage and perhaps later, Keynes's attitude toward unions displays a distinctly Marshallian ambivalence.[30] He notes, with Marshall, that the implicit combination of capital in large-scale enterprise puts the individual laborer at a bargaining disadvantage so that "[t]rade unions are necessary in order to counteract in some degree the initial inferiority of the labourer." Yet he often depicts the victories of unions as "preying" upon the rest of the community and inimical to the maximum national dividend. Later in the 1920s, as we shall see, this attitude would be tilted against the unions by political events and his changing approach to the theory of normal distribution.

Squarely within the Marshallian tradition, Keynes ends his discussion of mobility and its effect upon the equalization of net advantages between employments by noting the influence of heredity and parenting. Since the training and education of children so influence eventual labor supply opportunities, there may be long-term hindrances to mobility that inhibit equalization of net advantages. Nevertheless, as of 1914, Keynes considered this only a friction in the efficient operation of labor markets. "Although the original action of the parents counts for much, it is *not* final in its effects."

Thus in summary by 1914 Keynes had in hand a very sophisticated Marshallian view of labor markets that recognized the serious complications in the application of the doctrine of normal distribution. Notions very much like current theories of firm-specific human capital, information deficiencies and search behavior, efficiency wages, and insider-outsider effects were well within his theoretical purview. Yet as the following summation from his lecture makes clear, *these complications were not concerned directly with the notion of unemployment.*

> We have, therefore, a series of groups of labourers supplying different kinds of services, efficiency earnings in each group tending to equality and partial mobility between these groups. The wage of any group will depend partly upon the supply (adjusted for efficiency earnings) of their labour in relation to the demand, and partly upon their bargaining power.
>
> In these conditions of normal distribution we have the wage so fixed as to employ all, the wages of each being equal to the marginal net product of the last. Actually this state of affairs will be upset, partly by ignorance, partly by some degree of monopoly power on one side or another.

Keynes in the '20s: An Emerging Social Theory of Wages

With this background in a sophisticated and subtle Marshallianism, Keynes, fulfilling Marshall's prediction, went out into the wide world attempting to clear up current social issues with the aid of Marshall's clear thinking method. Yet, unemployment was not an issue that immediately drew his attention. His first economic works, summarized in *Indian Currency and Finance*, had little to say about unemployment. It was not until after his war experience—and the disastrous aftermath which he found so distasteful—had enlarged his worldview with a baptism by fire in social and political realities, that Keynes begins to write of the role and behavior of "the labouring classes." This was no coincidence. For the same Victorian vision of society which he viewed as destroyed by the war and as responsible for the many social evils that would follow in its wake was the background to the Marshallianism he had internalized earlier.

Keynes's break with traditional views on labor markets, an integral part of his "long struggle of escape from habitual modes of thought and expression," really began in the 1920s.[31] This struggle involved a move away from the individualistic analysis implicit in Marshall's supply-and-demand framework, but Keynes maintained the distinctive Marshallian method of integrating positive and normative analysis with reference to current social reality. The amalgam is a "social" analysis of labor markets as a setting for struggle over distributive shares, increasingly carried out in political terms. The "social justice" argument Keynes uses, with its explicitly social/institutional setting, thus marks it off from the current preoccupations of the New Keynesians. The latter are explicitly attempts to ground labor market behavior in an individualistic labor market analysis. Finally, although this vision undergirds his move toward the *General Theory*, it is still not the central theoretical basis of involuntary unemployment. It may, though, provide hints about useful macrofoundations of labor markets.

Antecedents, and perhaps the whole underlying social vision, to what became a growing preoccupation with the plight of labor show up as early as his *The Economic Consequences of the Peace* (Keynes 1919, 1–16). In its general overview of the pivotal historical epoch in which the Western nations then found themselves—between the extraordinary growth and stability from 1870 which the war had brought to an end in 1914, and an uncertain but definitely changed future—Keynes saw foreboding glimpses of conflict. Much of this he ascribed to the breakdown of the delicate conventions and psychology of the prewar era. Among these was the implicit acceptance of "*inequality* of the distribution of wealth which made possible those vast accumulations of fixed wealth and of capital improvements which distinguished that age from all others" (p. 11).

> . . . this remarkable system depended for its growth on a double bluff or deception. On the one hand the labouring classes accepted from ignorance or powerlessness, or were compelled, persuaded, or cajoled by custom, convention, authority, and the well-established order of society into accepting, a situation in which they could call their own very little of the cake that they and nature and the capitalist classes were co-operating to produce. And on the other hand the capitalist classes were allowed to call the best part of the cake theirs and were theoretically free to consume it, on the tacit underlying condition that they consumed very little of it in practice [Keynes 1919, 12].

Yet the war had disclosed the instability of this bluff and it could no longer be relied on to give order and continuity to distribution in a manner consistent with the population's notion of justice. "The war has disclosed the possibility of consumption to all and the vanity of abstinence to many. Thus the bluff is discovered; the labouring classes may be no longer willing to forgo so largely, and the capitalist classes, no longer confident of the future, may seek to enjoy more fully their liberties of consumption so long as they last, and thus precipitate the hour of their confiscation" (Keynes 1919, 13).

This view of the conflict that would rock a society in transition, free of one set of conventions of distribution but not yet in possession of a replacement, was to be borne out forcefully by the dislocations and crises that swept over the British economy for the rest of Keynes's life. At each stage Keynes's commentary, policy advice, and analysis reveal his concern with distributive *justice* as a major element in his outlook. But, ever the Marshallian, this was not just a utopian commentary from an ideal ethical standpoint, but an observation of society that became an integral part of his analysis.[32]

Analytically this concern coalesced in the 1920s around an argument that, however orthodox economic theory suggested labor markets *should* behave, in fact postwar conditions meant they no longer *could* adjust to wide swings in monetary values (as, for instance, in the case of the return to gold). Thus throughout the 1920s one could say that Keynes, though still basically orthodox in theoretical outlook, was a solid "sticky wage" man, as are so many "Keynesians" today. In his case the analysis was framed in terms of a cost-price argument in which swings in the price level called for rapid changes in cost which fell heavily on labor. The injustice deflationary price instability inflicted on the laboring classes was that it resulted in intensified unemployment. But this positive analysis of deflation was due to the conflict between the sense of fairness of the working class, no longer content to be sacrificed to rentier interests in a historic prewar exchange rate, and the politicians' and economists' belief that nominal values would automatically self-adjust. Thus the *Tract on Monetary Reform* attacked the assumptions built in to the quantity theory concerning the speed, painlessness, and neutrality of the necessary nominal price movements. This, of course, is the textual origin of Keynes's famous quip about death in the long run.

As the 1920s wore on and the crises continued, Keynes's views crystalized on unemployment as the major social ill. A common theme in his writings in this period is what he characterized as the responsibility of stupid and slavish devotion to worn-out principles as the source of the persistance of high unemployment. *Essays in Persuasion*, "the croakings of a Cassandra who could never influence events in time" (Keynes 1932, v.), is a catalogue of accusations of such stupidity by British leaders.

Of particular interest is the line of argument Keynes pursues in his polemic, *The Economic Consequences of Mr. Churchill*. Leaving aside the monetary details, Keynes's main claim against the return to gold at the pre-war parity of $4.86 per pound sterling concerned the implicit acceptance it represented of a "deliberate intensification of unemployment" (1925a, 257). Here his strong doubts about the orthodox self-adjusting school are clearly in evidence concerning the labor market. He divides the economy into two sectors. The "external" trading sector would bear the immediate brunt of the new exchange rate on its output and prices. Yet its costs, principally wage costs, would remain tied to the condition of the "sheltered" industries which had no direct connection to foreign competition. The ensuing dislocation concerned the need for the external sector's wages to fall in line with external prices while the price of laborer's wage goods were fixed in the internal market. To Keynes there was only one possible outcome; unemployment and industrial strife until the "fundamental adjustments" assumed by orthodox theory were forced to come about. Once again the issue concerns the struggle for relative shares necessitated by the lack of a social mechanism to change all money wages:

> The working classes cannot be expected to understand, better than Cabinet Ministers, what is happening. Those who are attacked first are faced with a depression of their standard of life, because the cost of living will not fall until all the others have been successfully attacked too; and, therefore, they are justified in defending themselves. Nor can the classes which are first subjected to a reduction of money wages be guaranteed that this will be compensated later by a corresponding fall in the cost of living, and will not accrue to the benefit of some other class. Therefore they are bound to resist so long as they can; and it must be war, until those who are economically weakest are beaten to the ground [Keynes 1925a, 247–248].

This is clearly a long way from the qualified acceptance of the normal theory of distribution in Keynes' early lectures. That it was the force of events coupled with a concern for social justice that led him to this position is also made clear in this essay. He mentions the colliers as the victims of this misguided policy and notes that if there were a free mobility of labor, their sacrifice would not be so great:

> If miners were free to transfer themselves to other industries, if a collier out of work or underpaid could offer himself as a baker, a bricklayer, or a railway porter at a lower wage than is now current in these industries, it would be another matter. But notoriously they are not so free. Like other victims of economic transition in past times, the miners are to be offered the choice between starvation and submission, the fruits of their submission to accrue to the benefit of other classes. But in view of the disappearance of an effective mobility of labour and of a competitive wage level between different industries, I am not sure that they are not worse placed in some ways than their grandfathers [p. 260–261].

Keynes then throws this situation into relief by examining its underlying ethical basis. Not only is it a fact to Keynes that the kind of "automatic" mobility that would ensure fundamental adjustments is gone but "on grounds of social justice, no case can be made for reducing the wage of miners" (p. 261). They are the victims of an ideological struggle that is clouded by the faults of the underlying positive economic doctrine of laissez faire.

> The truth is that we stand mid-way between two theories of economic society. The one theory maintains that wages should be fixed by reference to what is "fair" and "reasonable" as between classes. The other theory—the theory of the economic Juggernaut—is that wages should be settled by economic pressure,

> otherwise called "hard facts." . . . The gold standard, with its dependence on pure chance, its faith in "automatic adjustments," and its general regardlessness of social detail, is an essential emblem and idol of those who sit in the top tier of the machine. I think that they are immensely rash in their regardlessness, in their vague optimism and comfortable belief that nothing really serious every happens. Nine times out of ten, nothing really serious does happen—merely a little distress to individuals or to groups. But we run a risk of the tenth time (and are stupid into the bargain) if we continue to apply the principles of an Economics which was worked out on the hypotheses of *laissez-faire* and free competition to a society which is rapidly abandoning these hypotheses [p. 262].

Elaborating on Marshall's point that the labor market is much more of a social institution than an automatic mechanism for bringing supply into equality with demand, Keynes notes that "the problem of how to bring about this reduction is as much a political as an economic problem." He therefore proposes a political solution of a treaty agreement between business, labor, and the government to effect a uniform reduction of money wages and prices consistent with the new exchange, coupled with a surcharge on rentier income, to equalize the burden across all classes.

Although in one sense this is just another passing trick of Keynes's immense talent for instant policy proposals, it further illustrates the theme with which we want to end this section: at least from the mid-1920s through to the *General Theory*, Keynes saw the fixing of money wages and their stability as crucial elements of an overall macroeconomic view, and one closely linked, as chapter 19 of the *General Theory* attests, to price stability. Thus the way was cleared by this stage at least to extricate himself from the traditional emphasis on labor market analysis and concentrate on an integrated view of money and interest as the casual links to employment.

One searches *The Economic Consequences of Mr. Churchill* and Keynes's other writings of the '20s in vain, however, for any hint of an alternative macroeconomic theory. Yet he increasingly emphasized a view of the efficacy of public works policies to combat unemployment, and his attacks on the orthodox view grew ever more more shrill. Keynes was clearly shedding his old "classical skin" in this period, but the pattern of his new skin was not yet in sight. In terms of labor market analysis this involved more confident uses of his social-political view of money wage-setting. Appropriately this shows up most clearly in his political writings of the period.

In "The End of Laissez-Faire" (1926a, p. 312), Keynes declares it time to "clear the ground from the metaphysical or general principles upon which, from time to time, *laissez-faire* has been founded." There are no "natural" liberties, self-interest does not always lead to greater social interest, and groups of individuals are often superior in achieving social ends than individuals acting alone. As an alternative, state action should be directed to an agenda the aim of which is to create ways of doing well "those functions which fall outside the sphere of the individual, . . . those decisions which are made by no one if the State does not make them" (1926a, p. 317).

In "Am I a Liberal?" (1925b, pp. 335–336) we see this general position extended to a call for a new liberalism that would seek a "transition from economic anarchy to a regime which deliberately aims at controlling and directing economic forces in the interest of social justice and social stability." Acceptance of this responsibility is a matter of the facts and of public opinion. "The Trade Unions are strong enough to interfere with the free play of the forces of supply and demand, and Public Opinion, albeit with a grumble and with more than a suspicion that the Trade Unions are growing dangerous, support the Trade Unions in their main contention that Coalminers ought not to be the victims of cruel economic forces which *they* never set in motion" (p. 336).

Yet in "Liberalism and Labor" (1926b, 341) Keynes's early ambivalence against trade unions turns to antagonism. Trade unionists are "once the oppressed, now the tyrants, whose selfish and sectional pretensions need to be bravely opposed." Writing to a socialist author of this period, he is even more explicit: "My opinions on a good many matters are shifting, but I do not yet see clearly where I am being led to. But when it comes to politics I hate Trade Unions."[33] Thus it is not surprising that in "Liberalism and Industry" a proposal for state intervention in the setting of money wage bargains is offered for "the betterment of the economic welfare of the worker."

In 1930 Keynes finally brings forth his *Treatise on Money* after a ten-year gestation. As would be expected, it bears at least some evidence of the continual transition in his thought over the 1920s. Although without an adequate treatment of changes in output, the *Treatise* analysis of price fluctuations does ascribe practical significance to the social and political setting for money wage bargaining. Thus "cost inflation" (Keynes 1930, 166–170) could occur under certain organizations of the wage system. And in a passage that presages the cost-price view of wages that emerges in the *General Theory*, Keynes notes,

> If there are strong social or political forces causing spontaneous changes in the money rates of efficency wages, the control of the price level may pass beyond the power of the banking system [Keynes 1930, 351].

This theoretical viewpoint informed Keynes's re-immersion in direct policy issues arising from the worsening slump in the early 1930s, as a member of the Macmillan Committee and the Economic Advisory Council in 1930–31. Peter Clarke (1989) has recently provided a splendid account of the high policy drama of this period and its intimate relation to Keynes's evolving theoretical views. On theory he wavered, backtracked, and revised as conditions required, with a strong sense only of the need to do *something* expansionist, rather than nothing. As he remarked to the Prime Minister Ramsey McDonald:

> When we come to questions of remedies for the local situation distinct from the international, the peculiarity of my position lies, perhaps, in the fact that I am in favour of practically all the remedies which have been suggested in any quarter. Some of them are better than others. But nearly all of them seem to me to lead in the right direction. The unforgivable attitude is, therefore, the negative one—the repelling of each of these remedies in turn [Keynes 1981, 375].

The central unifying theme of his polemics at this point was the need to provide increased aggregate demand (although he did not as yet use that term) through any channel possible. And thus in various places he abandoned old positions to propose protectionist measures, restrictions on overseas lending, and reductions in bank rate. Yet he held to the rejection of the usefulness of a "wage policy" of driving down money wages throughout. Thus the addendum to the the Macmillan report, "Proposals Relating to Domestic Policy to Meet the Present Emergency," written by Keynes and signed by him and five other committee members, advocated a combination of monetary policy and expansionist spending. Labor itself was absolved of responsibility for the slump and then high real wages were absolved in another addendum written under Keynes's influence, "A Reduction of Wages and Salaries." This last document also included Keynes's old idea of a National Treaty to set money incomes equitably in times of rapid monetary change.

In debate with Lionel Robbins and Hubert Henderson in the deliberations of the Economic Advisory Council his main opposition was to their practical and theoretical reliance on wage measures. It is in Keynes's personal memorandum circulated to this committee of economists (Keynes 1973a, 180) that we get a clear picture of his final break with the classical notion of the labor market:

> Real wages seem to me to come in as a by-product of the remedies which we adopt to restore equilibrium. They come in at the end of the argument rather than at the beginning. That is to say, we arrive finally at a consideration—as having an important bearing on our choice between the different alternatives—as to how much each of the several expedients, both those which involve a reduction in money wages and those which do not, are calculated to reduce real wages. But the answer to this will not have much direct bearing on the question how much

> employment we can expect from each of the several expedients. *Employment is not a function of real wages in the sense that a given degree of employment requires a determinate level of real wages, irrespective of how the employment is brought about.*[34]

Our main conclusion from this evidence is a negative one. By 1930 at least, but actually growing out of a long gestation during the policy debates of the 1920s, Keynes rejected the notion that orthodox labor market analysis, even the sophisticated variety that he himself had learned and taught at Cambridge, was of any use in understanding the swings in employment over the short period that beset England and the world in the Great Slump. He developed in the course of this rejection a loose "social" theory of *wages* in which bargaining over relative money claims by force, fraud, or possibly by compromise might be worked out. Yet this only replaced the distributional and price level arguments of the classical doctrine. By 1930, he flatly rejected the causal influence of real wages on *employment*. Yet the world would have to wait for the *General Theory* for an alternative analysis of employment, integrated with Keynes's theory of interest and money.

Conclusion

Our negative conclusion from the evidence of pre-*General Theory* Cambridge labor market analysis is that its content makes it very doubtful that Keynes could have been attempting to found his self-described "theoretical revolution" on labor market arguments, like those of the New Keynesians. Moreover, Keynes's own writings show much evidence of a rejection of what for him would have been orthodox wage theory long before the *General Theory*. Thus arises the old bugaboo, the talmudic touchstone of Keynes scholarship, that never-ending question all these past decades of macroeconomic debate: just what did Keynes really mean by involuntary unemployment?

Of course, an answer cannot be expected here. But luckily there is much in the literature on interpreting the *General Theory* that points toward the negative conclusion our evidence has supported and analyzes the alternative offered by Keynes. It is worthwhile ending with some references to these alternatives.

First of all, the action in the *General Theory* is *not* in the labor market (Darity and Horn 1983; Lawlor 1991, Lawlor, Darity, and Horn 1987). Second, while it could be the case that Marshall's and Dobb's stress on the indeterminacy of the labor market in some sense opened the way for Keynes to derive different levels of equilibrium output and employment from the same set of Marshallian short-period data, there was still only one (full employment) long-period equilibrium to the Marshallian system.[35] For all of his qualifications about evolutionary arguments, Marshall remained wedded to a full-employment real economy model. It may have been Kahn's investigation of the short period (Kahn 1990) that finally moved Keynes away from this long-period Marshallianism (Harcourt 1991).

Yet, apparently the issue goes even deeper than this. Keynes stressed that he was rejecting the outlook of the Classicals on what constituted the basis of a modern monetary economy. Early on he worked with distinct "types" of economies (the "cooperative" and the "monetary production" being the most important) to express his fundamental departure from Marshall (see Keynes 1933, for example). Christopher Torr (1988) has shown that the use of this standpoint clears up much confusion between neoclassical non-labor-market-clearing sorts of explanations of unemployment, and Keynes's emphasis on the "Principle of Effective Demand." An alternative "model" that expresses this viewpoint clearly and concisely is available in the post-Keynesian literature (see, for example, Wientraub 1957; or Darity 1988).

In any case, the point of departure from which the *General Theory* addresses the issue of involuntary unemployment is at the *aggregate* level (recall Hobson's viewpoint, cited above), and is meant to express the influence of interest and money as fundamental building blocks of a theory of employment. But by Keynes's reasoning, the activity of asset markets and the phenomena of interest tied up with this activity can not be expressed at a micro-based, individualist level of analysis (see Keynes 1937b; and Townshend 1937).[36] This is the main point to which attention needs to be drawn in evaluating recent attempts to interpret Keynes's involuntary unemployment as just another, albeit ingeniously sophisticated, example of Pigou's lack of plasticity in the wage rate. It would thus be more historically accurate to change the label for this literature from New Keynesian to New Pigovian.

Notes

1. The term *New Keynesians*, according to Robert J. Gordon (1990, 1115) in the recent *JEL* survey "What is New Keynesian Economics?," originated with Michael Parkin. Gordon identifies the etymology of the term as follow: "The word new rather than *neo* to describe the recent work in the classical tradition distinguishes it from what Paul Samuelson in the early postwar period called the *neoclassical synthesis* of old-Keynesian macroeconomics and classical microeconomics. In turn, the word *new* rather than *neo* is used for the recent work in the

Keynesian tradition, so that it can be properly juxtaposed to the new-classical approach."

2. This same theme is echoed by R.J. Gordon in his recent survey of New Keynesian economics (1990, 1135): ". . . the essential feature of Keynesian macroeconomics is the absence of continuous market clearing. Thus a Keynesian model is by definition a non-market-clearing model, one in which prices fail to adjust rapidly enough to clear markets within some relatively short period of time."

3. To be discussed extensively below.

4. Although recent authors, Gordon (1990, 1157) excepted, do not reference it, Alfred Marshall was quite fond of the term *efficiency wages*, and in fact as we will see below offered an extensive discussion of a "high wage" economy. It is perhaps even less well known that Veblen used the term in the *Theory of Business Enterprise* (1904).

5. See Leijonhufvud (1986) for an interesting account along theses lines.

6. Incidentally, this seems like a bold claim to make against the group of French mathematical economists concerned!

7. "The economic depression of the mid-1880's led to the so called 'discovery of unemployment'. The political events of that time—especially the 1886 clashes in Hyde Park and Trafalgar Square and the 1889 dock strike—provoked a reconceptualization of the problem. . . . Within this framework, social investigators like Booth and Rowntree organized new kinds of investigation into casual labour and urban poverty which provided evidence of problems of irregular work and low wages. By the 1900s, the economists were being outflanked by a new breed of freelance social investigators who defined unemployment as a social problem in a policy-oriented discourse." (Williams and Williams 1987, 102).

8. Beveridge does, however, have the distinction of explicitly stating what many later economists have been accused of implicitly believing in their work. That is to say, Beveridge made it explicit that he saw the problem of unemployment to be that labor markets did not work like the economics textbooks said they should. Thus the cure was to make actual markets more like the textbooks!

9. Of the many statements of Hobson's underconsumptionist position, his early collaboration with Mummery, *The Physiology of Industry* (Hobson and Mummery 1889), is usually considered the best.

10. It is no surprise that Keynes's biography of Marshall first established this point (Keynes 1926 [1972], 199–200). It was to mark perhaps the biggest departure Keynes's own life as an economist was to make from Marshall's. This is particularly true with regard to their respective views on unemployment.

11. Other examples of Marshall's moralizing, to name only a few, include his treatment of: women and work (*Principles*, 9th ed., p. 695), racial superiority (*Principles*, chs. IV and V, Bk. IV; and appendix A) and Trade Unions (*Principles*, pp. 702–722). For extensive accounts of this characteristic of Marshall as regards Trade Unions, see Petridis (1973; 1990).

12. The one issue on which he rose above his timidity was education (see Matthews 1990, 29), where Marshall saw a strong role for the state.

13. As Keynes's original preface to the series states:

> Generally speaking, the writers of these volumes believe themselves to be orthodox members of the Cambridge School of Economics. At any rate, most of their ideas about the subject, and even their prejudices, are traceable to the contact they have enjoyed with the writings and lectures of the two economists who chiefly influenced Cambridge thought for the past fifty, years, Dr. Marshall and Professor Pigou [Dobb 1948, vi].

14. Since our argument here is that Keynes's views in the '20s were firmly within the Cambridge tradition of his day, it is worth noting that the correspondence over the planning

of the Handbook series shows him fully involved at every level. Thus he argues with the publisher in February of 1927 that there is "no need to go outside the Cambridge circle" for authors. On June 9, 1927, he writes to Dobb concerning his manuscript, "I think it is an excellent synopsis and I really have no criticism to make." And on January 2, 1929, he complains to the publisher, Nisbet, that he has yet to receive a copy of Dobb's book: "Since I am not only the General Editor of the series, but spent considerable time over the proofs of these volumes, this seems to me something of a discourtesy" (Keynes Papers, file CEB.1).

15. Perusal of later editions reveals that he continually updated this section as institutions changed.

16. A movement that Dobb elsewhere traces to the 1860s and the schemes of a certain Lord Brassey.

17. In the second edition (Dobb 1938, 54–60) Dobb shows an even more elaborate Marshallian approach to this issue, with a discussion of the general social externalities of a high wage economy and the generational time span involved. He also notes this as an argument for a minimum wage law.

18. For an even more elaborate discussion of the role of unions and compact bargaining in this context, see the discussion in the third edition (Dobb 1948, 72–95).

19. If there is any doubt that this refers to Marshall in the first edition, it is cleared up in the second. The discussion examined here appears in two sections of chapter 3 of the first edition (Dobb 1928) titled "The Theory of Marginal Productivity" and "Demand for Labor." These are replaced in the second edition (Dobb, 1938) with much the same argument in sections titled "The Theory of Marginal Productivity" and "Marshall and Supply and Demand." Also, in this latter section of the second edition is the glowing tribute to Marshall which appears in the epigram that opens this chapter.

20. As for causes of the trade cycle itself, though subject to much debate, Pigou neatly categorizes them into "variations in the seasons, the climate and the mood of business men" (p. 146). He thus glaringly leaves aside any mention of the underconsumptionst arguments of his underworld contemporary Hobson, who Beveridge at least had felt it necessary to attack. As will be argued below, this determination by the profession to ignore nonlabor market explanations of unemployment is significant.

21. His definition and discussion in chapter 1 is of interest in itself in that it clearly marks out unemployment as a phenomenon of "wage-earners," Pigou thus rules out of hand the currently popular interest in defining unemployment as preference for leisure or nonmarket employment: "If a wage-earner happens to possess an allotment on which he can work when discharged from his ordinary trade, or if he is able, on these occasions, to run his hand to wood-carving or some other domestic industry, we shall not, for that reason, decline to class him among the unemployed" (Pigou 1913, 14). It is to then further clarify his subject that he introduces the involuntary aspect of unemployment: "Even, however, when this is understood, it does not become possible to pass directly to a definition of unemployment. For unemployment clearly does not include all the idleness of wage-earners, but only *that part of it which is, from their point of view and in their existing condition at the time, involuntary*" (Pigou 1913, 14; emphasis in original).

22. In the preface Pigou makes clear that *The Theory of Unemployment* is designed to correct what he saw as the excesses of the profession in "advocating policy" and devoting too exclusive an attention to the "monetary side" of the problem and so neglecting what he wanted to account for on the "real side." To compare this preface with that of Keynes's *General Theory* provides a clear look at the divergence of their views. Although both were written as economic tracts *of* the time, *for* fellow economists, Pigou's comes off as sterile and defensive in the extreme, whereas Keynes's is full of the excitement of socially relevant theoretical progress and

clearly aggressive. One cannot but help thinking that Pigou had regressed from the theoretically pedestrian, but practically sensible views of his 1913 book.

23. "The object of our analysis is, not to provide a machine, or a method of blind manipulation, which will furnish an infallible answer, but to provide ourselves with an organised and orderly method of thinking out particular problems . . . ." (Keynes 1936, 297).

24. This is exemplified in the lifelong contempt he expressed for the use of mathematics in economics. As Twelfth Wrangler in mathematics and a student of Whitehead and Russell's work, it is clear that he was no fool when it came to mathematics. Yet from the beginning to the end of his career he held to Marshall's dictum that such mathematics as was useful in working out a problem was to be thrown out and disguised in expressing the idea. He explicitly "agrees with Marshall" on this topic in his early lecture notes (file MM26 of the Keynes Papers at King's College). See also his comments in the *General Theory* (pp. 275 and 297–298).

25. This quote is from a paper presented to the "Apostles" on February 20, 1909. It lies in the Keynes papers at Kings College in file no. UA10.

26. This note in Marshall's hand is appended to set questions done by Keynes in 1905 and deposited in the Keynes papers in file MM26.2 at the Kings College Modern Archive.

27. This letter is from the Keynes papers at Kings College, file EJ1.3. It is hard to resist quoting its ending, which is high Victorian Marshalliana at its best: "So when you are K.C.B. and yet thinking out your best thoughts to their foundations, and from your foundations, you are to suppose that my shade is hovering over you, and wrapping an ethereal wreath from Elysian fields on your head. Yours, till then and after, AM."

28. This and all of the quotations to follow from Keynes's lecture notes on "Principles of Economics" are part of an unpaginated file in the Keynes collection at Kings College, #MM26.4.

29. The extent to which Keynes was a slavish Marshallian at this early age is represented by the fact that most of these "examples" can be found in the *Principles* (see Bk. VI, chs. III).

30. On Marshall's attitude toward unions see Petridis (1990).

31. For a detailed study of Keynes's changing thoughts on wages, see Millmow (1985).

32. In fact this concern with social justice is probably a holdover from his basic Moorite outlook on ethics, with its call to achieve the greatest good for the greatest number. It is interesting that he refers to the issue as early as his prewar lecture notes cited above. For a thorough discussion, including the argument that Pigou's own position in his *Wealth and Welfare* bears the stamp of Moore's *Principia Ethica*, see O'Donnell (1989, 164–173).

33. This comes from a letter to H. N. Bailsford, author of *Socialism for Today*, dated December 3, 1925, Keynes papers file MM18.

34. It is worth noting that this position is even more free of the the classical postulates than Keynes's position in the *General Theory*. There real wages also were not a causal factor in the level of employment, coming in at the end once aggregate demand had determined output and employment. But there was postulated a *unique* correspondence between the level of real wages and employment.

35. Excluding Keynes's crucial addition to this data of the "state of long term expectation."

36. It is appropriate to stress how fundamentally this outlook differs from the usual analytic approach to building up theory from arguments about the atomistic behavior of individual agents. Townshend was the first to realize this about the *General Theory* and thus his 1937 paper casts that work as a fundamental *extension* of the marginalist theory of value. For an interesting "modern" statement of this point in another context, see Kirman (1989, esp. 126).

References

Akerlof, G., and Yellen, J. 1985. "A Near-Rational Model of the Business Cycle, with Wage and Price Inertia." *Quarterly Journal of Economics* 100: 823–838.

Azariadis, C. 1975. "Implicit Contracts and Underemployment Equilibria." *Journal of Political Economy* 83: 1183–1202.

Ball, L. 1990. "Insiders and Outsiders: A Review Essay." *Journal of Monetary Economics* 26: 459–470.

Barro, R., and Grossman, H., 1976. *Money, Employment and Inflation.* Cambridge: Cambridge University Press.

Benassy, J.P. 1975. "Neo-Keynesian Disequilibrium in a Monetary Economy." *Review of Economic Studies* 42: 502–523.

Beveridge, W. 1909. *Unemployment: A Problem of Industry.* London: Longmans.

Booth, C. 1902. *Life and Labour of the People in London* (17 vols.). London: Macmillan.

Chick, V. 1983. *Macroeconomics After Keynes.* Oxford: Philip Allan.

Clarke, P. 1989. *The Keynesian Revolution In The Making: 1924–1936.* Oxford: Oxford University Press.

Coats, A.W. 1967, "Sociological Aspects of British Economic Thought." *Journal of Political Economy* 75: 706–729.

Collard, D. 1990. "Cambridge After Marshall." In *Centenary Essays on Alfred Marshall*, J. Whitaker, ed., 164–192. Cambridge: Cambridge University Press.

Darity, W. 1988. "The Simple Analytics of Keynes's Aggregate Supply and Demand." In *Essays in Honor of Sidney Wientraub*, J. Kregel and P. Davidson, eds. London. Kluwer.

Darity, W., and Horn, B. 1983. "Involuntary Unemployment Reconsidered." *Southern Economic Journal* 49: 717–733.

Davis, J. 1992. *The Development of Kenyes' Philosophical Views.* Cambridge: Cambridge University Press.

Dobb M. 1928. *Wages.* London: Nisbet and Company.

————. 1938. *Wages*, 2nd rev. ed. London: Nisbet and Company.

————. 1948. *Wages*, 3rd rev. ed. London: Nisbet and Company.

Dreze, J. 1976. "Existence of an Equilibrium under Price Rigidity and Employment." *Economic Journal* 90: 309–330.

Garraty, J. 1978. *Unemployment in History: Economic Thought and Public Policy.* New York: Harper Colophon Books.

Gordon, R.J. 1990. "What is New Keynesian Economics." *Journal of Economic Literature* 29(3): 1115–1172.

Gordon, D. 1974. "A Neoclassical theory of Keynesian Unemployment." *Economic Inquiry* 12: 431–459.

Harcourt, G. 1991. "On Richard Kahn's Contribution to the *General Theory.*" *Cambridge Journal of Economics.*

Hobson, J. 1896. *The Problem of The Unemployed: An Enquiry and An Economic Policy.* London: Methuen and Co.

Hobson, J., and Mummery, A.F. 1889. *The Physiology of Industry*. London: Murray.

Kahn, R. 1976. "Unemployment as Seen by the Keynesians." In *The Concept and Measurement of Involuntary Unemployment*, G.D.N. Worswick. London: George Allen and Unwin.

————. 1990. *The Economics of the Short Period*. London: St. Martin's Press.

Kaldor, N. 1970. "The Case for Regional Policies." *Scottish Journal of Political Economy*, 17: 337–348.

Keynes, J.M. 1919. *The Economic Consequences of the Peace*. London: Macmillan.

————. 1923. *A Tract on Monetary Reform*. London: Macmillan.

————. 1924. "Alfred Marshall 1842–1924." *Economic Journal* 34: 311–372. Reprinted in Keynes (1933a).

————. 1925a [1932]. "The Economic Consequences of Mr. Churchill." Reprinted in *Essays in Persuasion*, pp. 244–270.

————. 1925b [1932]. "Am I a Liberal?" Reprinted in *Essays in Persuasion*, pp. 323–338.

————. 1926a [1932]. "The End of Laissez-Faire." Reprinted in *Essays in Persuasion*, pp. 312–322.

————. 1926b, [1932]. "Liberalism and Labour." Reprinted in *Essays in Persuasion*, pp. 339–349.

————. 1930. *A Treatise on Money* (2 vols.). London: Macmillan.

————. 1932. *Essays in Persuasion*. New York: Harcourt Brace.

————. 1933a. Essays in Biography, vol. 10 of *The Collected Writings of John Maynard Keynes*.

————. 1933b. "The Monetary Theory of Production." Reprinted in *Collected Writings*, vol. XXIX (1979), pp. 408–411.

————. 1936. *The General Theory of Employment, Interest and Money*. London: Macmillan.

————. 1937. "The General Theory of Employment." *Quarterly Journal of Economics*. 51: 209–223. Reprinted in Keynes 1973b, pp. 104–123.

————. 1973a. "The General Theory and After: Preparation." In *The Collected Writings of John Maynard Keynes*, vol. 13, ed. Donald Moggridge. London: Macmillan.

————. 1973b. "The General Theory and After: Defence and Development." In *The Collected Writings of John Maynard Keynes*. vol. 14, ed. Donald Moggridge. London: Macmillan.

————. 1981. "Activities 1929–1931: Rethinking Employment and Unemployment Policies." In *The Collected Writings of John Maynard Keynes*, vol. 20. London: Macmillan.

Kirman, A. 1989. "The Intrinsic Limits of Modern Economic Theory: The Emperer Has No Clothes." *Economic Journal* 99 (Conference).

Kniesner, T., and Goldsmith, A. 1987. "A Survey of Alternative Models of the Aggregate U.S. Labor Market," *Journal of Economic Literature* 25(3): 1241–1280.

Lawlor, M. 1991."Keynes, Meltzer and Involuntary Unemployment: On the Intensional and Extensional Logic of Definitions." *Review of Social Economy*, xvlix (3).
Lawlor, M., Darity, W., and Horn. 1987. "Was Keynes a Chapter Two Keynesian?" *Journal of Post Keynesian Economics* (Summer): 516–528.
Leijonhufvud, A. 1986. "Capitalism and the Factory System." In *Economics as a Process: Essays in the New Institutional Economics,* ed. R. Langlois. Cambridge: Cambridge University Press.
Lindbeck, A., and Snower, D. 1988. *The Insider-Outsider Theory of Employment and Unemployment*. Cambridge: MIT Press.
Malinvaud, E. 1977. *The Theory of Unemployment Reconsidered.* Oxford: Basil Blackwell.
Marshall, A. 1905. "Correspondence with J.M. Keynes." *The Keynes Papers*, copyright Provost and Fellow of Kings College, Cambridge.
———. 1961 [1920]. *Principles of Economics: Ninth (Variorum) Edition*. London: Macmillan.
———. 1919. *Industry and Trade*. London: Macmillan.
Matthews, R. 1990. "Marshall and the Labour Market." In *Centenary Essays on Alfred Marshall*, ed. John Whitaker. Cambridge: Cambridge University Press.
Millmow, A. 1985. "The Evolution of J.M. Keynes's Wage and Employment Theory 1920–1946." Unpublished graduate diploma thesis, Department of Economic History, Australian National University.
Muellbauer, J., and Portes, R. 1978. "Macroeconomic Models with Quantity Rationing." *Economic Journal* 88: 788–821.
Mummery, A.F., and Hobson, J., 1889. *The Physiology of Industry*. London: John Murray.
O'Donnell, R. 1989. *Keynes: Philosophy, Economics and Politics*. New York: St. Martin's Press.
Petridis, A. 1973. "Alfred Marshall's Attitude to the Economic Analysis of Trade Unions." *History of Political Economy* 5: 165–98.
Petridis, A. 1990. "The Trade Unions In the Principles: The Ethical Versus the Practical In Marshall's Economics." *Economie Appliquee* 42: 161–86.
Pigou, A.C. 1912. *Wealth and Welfare*. London: Macmillan.
———. 1913. *Unemployment,* London: Williams and Norgate.
———. 1933. *The Theory of Unemployment* London: Frank Cass and Co.
Rogers, C. 1989. *Money, Interest and Capital: A Study in the Foundations of Monetary Theory*. Cambridge: Cambridge University Press.
Rowntree, B.S., 1902. *Poverty: A Study of Town Life*. London: Longmans.
Smith A. 1776 [1904]. *The Wealth of Nations*, ed. E. Cannan. London: Methuen.
Tassig, F.W. 1911. *Principles of Economics*. New York: The Macmillan Company.
Torr, C., 1988. *Equilibrium, Expectations and Information*. Cambridge: Polity Press.
Townshend, H., 1937. "Liquidity Premium and the Theory of Value." *Economic Journal* 47: 197–205.

Veblen, T. 1904. *The Theory of Business Enterprise.* New York: Augustus Kelly.
Weiss, A. 1990. *Efficiency Wages: Models of Unemployment, Layoffs, and Wage Dispersion.* Princeton, NJ: Princeton University Press.
Weintraub, S. 1957. "The Micro-Foundations of Aggregate Demand and Supply." *Economic Journal* (September):
Weitzman, M. 1982. "Increasing Returns and the Foundations of Unemployment Theory." *Economic Journal* 92: 787–804.
————. 1984. *The Share Economy*. Cambridge: Harvard University Press.
Williams, K., and Williams, J. 1987. *A Beveridge Reader.* London: Unwin Hyman.
Young, A. 1928. "Increasing Returns and Economic Progress." *Economic Journal* 38: 527–542.
Young, A. 1928. "Increasing Returns and Economics Progress." *Economic Journal* 38: 533–555.

2 LABOR ECONOMICS AND UNEMPLOYMENT: AN HISTORIAN'S PERSPECTIVE

Alexander Keyssar

For an historian who spent years researching and writing about the history of unemployment, reading about joblessness in the contemporary labor economics literature can be an unsettling experience. Analytically rigorous and technically sophisticated as that literature may be, it nonetheless reveals that the scholarly world has no more of a shared understanding now than it had in 1910 about the sources or causes of unemployment. For more than a decade, moreover, one of the central debates among mainstream economists has centered around a question that also dominated late 19th century thought: does "involuntary" joblessness actually exist or not? And the current literature—far more starkly and universally than was true 50 or 70 years ago—is deeply ahistorical and static.

It is, of course, always hazardous for a practitioner of one academic trade to comment, in public and critically, about work carried on in another discipline. All the more so when that discipline, as is the case with economics, has relatively high technical barriers to entry: most historians, including this

The author would like to thank Michael Bernstein, William Darity, Lou Ferleger, and Sanford Jacoby for helpful criticism of an earlier draft of this essay.

one, do not possess the mastery of statistical and mathematical techniques required of economists. But the excursion across disciplinary boundaries may be warranted here, since there is more at stake than academic turf. Unemployment is not simply a statistical construct or an ingredient in a theory: it is (or so I read the evidence) a major social problem in the United States and elsewhere. Millions of people suffer because they do not have remunerative employment.

If this is so, or to the degree that it is so, our understanding of the phenomenon of unemployment matters, very concretely, outside the halls of academe. Public policy and consequently the welfare of the unemployed are shaped by the ideas and analyses put forward by soical scientists; and since World War II the ideas that have dominated the dialogue have been those generated by economists. Yet—from an outsider's perspective at least—that dialogue, particularly in the last decade or so, seems to have some curious, and even unproductive, features.

The most striking, perhaps, is the prominence of the debate about whether there really is much "involuntary unemployment," whether the phenomenon really does exist or can exist (except, briefly, during depressions when its existence seems to be granted). That debate seems to have surfaced (or resurfaced) in the 1970s, and it came to dominate several strands of the literature in the 1980s.

The debate was apparently launched by a branch of the profession that claimed that many people who were being counted as unemployed by the Current Population Survey were, in fact—and for various reasons—not involuntarily jobless. They were, rather, engaged in search activity, a productive use of their time aimed at locating good or better jobs. Or they were enjoying a form of contractually agreed-upon leisure, subsidized by higher-then-necessary weekly wages earned during spells of employment. Or they were, in a significant sense, *voluntarily* jobless: for example, they were exercising a preference for having leisure now and working later, or they were choosing to remain out of work rather than accept available jobs on terms regarded as disadvantageous. The unemployment of such individuals, of course, did not constitute a serious social problem and thus did not demand any public policy initiatives or programs.[1]

The counterattack from other wings of the profession consisted of new theoretical constructs and even some empirical evidence (more on that later) to support the view that the vast majority of men and women who were being counted as unemployed were, in fact, involuntarily jobless. The unemployed, they argued, were men and women who were unable to find jobs and who would prefer to be working. As Robert Solow put it in 1980, "I believe that what looks like involuntary unemployment is involuntary unemployment"

(1980, 3). A decade later, Lawrence Summers published a collection of papers rooted in and designed to buttress "the increasingly controversial premise that unemployment is an analytically meaningful and useful concept and that the extent of unemployment represents a serious and potentially remediable social problem" (Summers 1990, xv). "Involuntary unemployment," according to Summers and his co-authors, does exist and is an appropriate and feasible target of public policy.

What is striking to an historian is not the relative merits of particular arguments (although my own sympathies have already been made clear) so much as the fact that the debate has been taking place—and is being taken seriously—at all. Why is this happening? Why are sophisticated experts spending a great deal of time and energy arguing about the existence of a phenomenon whose existence seems obvious to anyone who has walked around a blue-collar, or low-income, neighborhood?

Why is the mainstream of the profession pondering the reality of a chronic social problem that was formally and officially recognized as such more than 50 years ago, with the passage of the Social Security Act (or 11 years later in the Employment Act of 1946)? Why are scholars butchering the language with redundant phrases like "involuntary unemployment" and oxymorons such as "voluntary unemployment"? (The word *unemployment* entered the English language, roughly a century ago, to refer specifically to the condition or social problem of "involuntary" joblessness. According to all dictionaries that I have consulted, that is still its primary meaning.)[2] Did someone in the 1970s find millions of the unemployed lolling around Palm Beach, cavalierly spilling red wine on the want ads in the paper?

A semi-systematic reading of the literature suggests that no such lurid event prompted the debate. It seems, rather, to have been set off by two other developments. The first was what appears to have been a long-run upwards drift in the unemployment rate, in the United States and in western Europe, in the 1970s and 1980s. This shift was difficult to explain; it also seemed to shatter the post-World-War-II hope that unemployment rates could be durably held to levels that had been defined as representing full employment (e.g., 2–4 percent). As Richard Duboff pointed out more than a decade ago, "full employment" has been a "receding target" since 1946, but it began to recede with particular rapidity in the 1970s (1977, 219–237).

The second development was that recorded unemployment rates were not behaving in conformity with prevailing mainstream economic theories, particularly—but not exclusively—neoclassical theories. The relationship between unemployment rates and wage rates confounded expectations; the Phillips curve was bent out of shape by (among other developments) the stagflation of the 1970s; the "natural rate" of unemployment appeared to be rising (which was unnatural); and in Europe unemployment rates soared to almost unprecedented levels and then, contrary to what prevailing models would have predicted, remained very high.[3]

Indeed, the debate, which still goes on, appears to be more theory-driven (or ideology-driven) than rooted in empirical observations. Those who have argued that a great deal of recorded unemployment is actually "voluntary" are not basing that argument on personal encounters with the unemployed or on studies of the behavior of jobless workers. They are, rather, reacting to the fact that the movements of the unemployment rate do not conform with their theories or models of the relationship between unemployment and other dimensions of economic life. Their explanation of this lack of conformity is that the official unemployment rate must be recording something other than levels of "involuntary unemployment." This is certainly a logical possibility. Another possible explanation, that the theories or models are misspecified, misdirected, or just plain wrong, appears to be beyond the pale of consideration—which seems strange to someone who resides in a different wing of the academy.

It would, moreover, be difficult for an historian to read this debate without hearing very strong echoes of similar arguments that raged—in less technical and more overtly moralistic language—during the late 19th and early 20th centuries. Conservative intellectuals and politicians of that era were quite convinced that most joblessness was voluntary rather than involuntary. They argued that jobs were almost always available, particularly if workers obeyed the dictates of the market by either relocating or accepting reduced wages; and they maintained that most of the so-called unemployed were unworthy "idlers" or even "tramps." They also argued against public intervention to aid the unemployed or reduce unemployment levels; such actions were deemed unnecessary or even counterproductive (e.g., they could interfere with the proper workings of the market or subsidize unworthy slackers) (Keyssar 1986, 130–42, 250–262).

The history of unemployment policy in the United States from the 1870s to the 1940s (stretching perhaps to the 1960s) is, in fact, a history of the gradual defeat of such views at the hands of liberal reformers, trade union leaders, and workers who maintained both that a great deal of "involuntary idleness" did exist and that the government could and should do something about it (Keyssar 1986, 250–298; 1987, 213–217). Against this backdrop, it appears more than coincidental that the debate among economists about the existence of "involuntary unemployment" should have flared up again during the years of conservative political ascendancy in the 1970s and 1980s. The dispute about theory—and about the "involuntariness" of unemployment—is, of course, also an argument about policy. Indeed, in the long run it seems likely that this debate will be regarded as an episode in the history of ideology and public policy rather than as a step in the evolution of economic science.

A second and related feature of the labor economics literature that seems surprising to an historian is its emphasis on theory and on model-building rather than on empirical investigation. To be sure, historians do tend to be unusually (and unduly) nervous about models and theory, and our characteristic sin is that of aimless fact-gathering, but some of the economists interested in unemployment seem to be erring in the other direction. The extensive literature about unemployment durations is, I think, a case in point.

There appears to be widespread agreement among economists (Martin Feldstein, Lawrence Summers, and George Akerloff, to cite a few of many possible names) that the length of spells of unemployment (or the amount of time that individuals spend out of work in the course of a year or two) is very important to understanding the phenomenon (Akerlof and Main 1980, 885–893; Feldstein 1973, 5–23; Summers 1990, 3–85). If, for example (and as Feldstein has claimed), the vast majority of spells of unemployment are very short (and if most people are protected by unemployment insurance during those spells), then the social welfare problem engendered by a particular unemployment rate might not be very severe. On the other hand—as Kim Clark and Summers, among others, have argued—if spells of unemployment are characteristically lengthy, that would have very different implications for our understanding of the problem and for policy. People who are unemployed for four, six, or ten months can be presumed to be feeling the pinch, a presumption borne out by sociological and psychological studies (Liem 1987, 319–353).

Unfortunately, the major source of data on unemployment, the Current Population Survey (CPS), does not yield very satisfactory figures regarding unemployment durations. The CPS determines only the length of spells of joblessness prior to the date of the CPS interview itself; therefore, a person whose unemployment spell is recorded as lasting two months was jobless for two months at the time that the survey was conducted. And then what happened? When did they get a job? The CPS does not tell. If the economy were in equilibrium and everything else were equal, it would be reasonable to assume that one could double the recorded unemployment durations, for different groups, to find out actual unemployment durations. But those are not necessarily tenable assumptions.

The primary response of economists to this dilemma has been to devise elaborate mathematical and statistical strategies and models to try to derive meaningful and useful figures from the published CPS data. They have also refined their estimates by analyzing unpublished CPS data and (less often) several other data sets that have information that is germane. But these techniques have not put the issue to rest. The utility, or validity, of different mathematical models has itself become a source of disagreement, and some analysts have argued that the CPS data are filled with errors that lead to a major understatement of average unemployment durations. There remains, in fact, no real agreement among scholars about the length of periods of unemployment in the United States.[4]

What does not seem to be transpiring is a broad-gauged effort, or assembly of efforts, to collect new data that might produce such an agreement—about what is, after all, an empirical issue. It would not be easy or inexpensive, but it would certainly be feasible to design empirical studies that would yield rich new data regarding the duration of spells of unemployment. (The government's Survey of Income and Program Participation, begun in 1983, does help, as does the older Panel Study of Income Dynamics conducted by the Institute for Social Research, but a great many questions remain unanswered.) As any 19th century historian would enviously note, the subjects of such research are still alive and can still respond to a scholar's inquiries. That so little research of this type is being carried out is truly puzzling to an outsider. It also suggests that the field of labor economics has come a very long and unfortunate distance from the thorough and extremely insightful empiricism of the pioneering scholars of unemployment, such as William Beveridge in England, and his American counterparts, such as William Leiserson and Don Lescohier.[5]

Beyond this issue is a third, of equal or greater importance. The current literature dealing with the economics of unemployment is profoundly ahistorical. References to years before 1970 are infrequent; allusions to events that occurred prior to the Great Depression are exceedingly rare. Analyses of contemporary developments, moreover, are not even informed with a long-run perspective. There is little awareness that unemployment had a history before the 1930s, or 1950s, for that matter.

Yet that history, in its basic outlines at least, has been uncovered by historians, and it is sufficiently germane to some current debates to warrant a brief re-telling here.[6] In the United States at least (the contours of the history would look different elsewhere), the problem of unemployment appears to have gradually emerged in the course of the 19th century. There were, to be sure, jobless men and women in 17th and 18th century America, but they were few in number, and the problem of "involuntary idleness" remained relatively invisible through the first half of the 19th century. Only with the triumph of industrialization and the emergence of a large, propertyless working class did the problem of unemployment (and the words to describe it) come into prominence.

By the 1870s the modern phenomenon of unemployment had become clearly visible in the United States, and within a short time both state and federal governments were trying to measure the extent of involuntary joblessness. What those statistics, and their successors, indicate is that the unemployment rate has not changed much—or, to be more precise, has not moved in any particular direction—in the course of the last 120 years. Unemployment levels are always fluid, bobbing up and down from year to year and from month to month, but there has been no long-term trend, and the range within which the fluctuations have occurred has held reasonably steady, with the exception of the 1930s. Decadal unemployment rates also display no long-run shifts. The one aggregate change that does seem to be visible in the data is that unemployment durations have increased over the long run, while the proportion of labor force members who experience some unemployment in the course of a year has declined. The social distribution of unemployment also appears to have changed: young people and black people are unemployed relatively more often than they were, while mature white males—and particularly white males over the age of 50—are jobless correspondingly less.[7]

The chronic presence of unemployment, coupled with the fact that the problem became severe during the "panics" or depressions that occurred at least once per decade, gave rise to political and social movements aimed at reducing unemployment levels and alleviating the hardships of the unemployed. These movements were extremely diverse in their precise goals and, for decades, consistently unsuccessful at achieving concrete reforms. Only during the 1930s, under the enormous pressures created by the Great Depression, did durable institutional changes take place. It was during that decade that an unemployment insurance program was adopted (years after such programs were created in some European nations); that federal and state governments became active counter-cyclical employers; and that the use of seniority systems to allocate layoffs became widespread among unionized workers. These institutional developments were extended during the 1940s, a decade when the federal government also assumed formal responsibility for minimizing unemployment levels.

This history raises serious questions about some of the arguments that appear in contemporary debates. It seems, for example, to be a widely accepted view among economists that a fundamental source of unemployment is the downward stickiness of wages; linked to this view is the claim, heard quite frequently in the 1980s, that the minimum wage contributes to unemployment by enhancing the stickiness of wages (and that an increase in the minimum wage would produce more unemployment). Similarly, unemployment has been attributed to (and sometimes blamed on) trade unions because they keep wages up for their members and, in so doing, prevent market-recovery mechanisms from operating. The unemployment insurance system has also received its share of analytic fire: according to this view, the insurance system actually creates unemployment (or raises the official, recorded unemployment rate) by making it possible for workers to remain jobless for longer periods without feeling compelled to accept whatever jobs might be available.[8]

All of these arguments are, to some degree, undercut by the long-run historical record. The unemployment insurance system was not created until 1935; there was no minimum wage until 1938; unions were barely present in the mass production industries until the late 1930s, and even in the crafts they had relatively little market strength until after 1900. Yet unemployment rates were just as high before the 1930s (or 1900) as they have been since the Great Depression. The pre-1930s world was one in which unions had comparatively little economic or political power and in which there was relatively little government intervention in the economy. But nonetheless unemployment existed, in roughly the same proportions as exist today. Given that fact, it seems unlikely that the source or cause of unemployment really resides in institutions that were created (or widely implanted) in the 1930s. To be sure, it is possible that unemployment had one set of causes before 1935 and has had another set of causes thereafter, or even since 1970. But that would be a different argument than any that currently appears in the literature—different, less elegant, and in need of its own interpretation of historical change in the 20th century.[9]

Similarly, a long-run perspective casts considerable doubt on the argument, put forward quite frequently in the 1970s and 1980s, that unemployment rates have been rising because the demographic composition of the labor force has changed. According to this view, the upward creep in unemployment rates can be attributed, at least in part, to an increase in the proportion of women and youth in the labor force: since unemployment rates for these groups are relatively high, their growth has been pushing the statistics upwards.[10] But as Richard Krashevski has pointed out, there is nothing about the "intrinsic qualities" of these groups that guarantees high unemployment (1988, 290). Historically, moreover, unemployment rates among different demographic groups display a great deal of variety and change. Prior to the 1930s, for example, rates for men and women were nearly identical; the gap between the unemployment rates for teenagers and adults was much smaller than it became after World War II; and blacks in the turn-of-the-century North appear to have experienced relatively little unemployment because they were restricted to service occupations that happened to be fairly steady (Keyssar 1986, ch. 4). All of this implies that recent differences in unemployment among demographic groups are themselves the product of historical conditions and structures; as such, those differences cannot be viewed as independent causes of rising aggregate unemployment rates.

Indeed, the historical record suggests that recent analyses of the causes of unemployment have tended to be too narrowly conceived, too single-mindedly focused on locating specific mechanisms or institutions that may have prevented the labor markets from clearing, at least in a given year or set of circumstances. A long-run perspective on the problem offers fairly compelling evidence that the causes of unemployment are not likely to be found in such mechanisms. The problem of unemployment in the United States was not generated, or brought into being, by the Social Security Act of 1935, the Fair Labor Standards Act of 1938 (which mandated a minimum wage), or by unionization. The causal arrows, in fact, run in the opposite direction: those programs and institutions were the consequence of a social order, and a labor market, in which the insecurity of employment was already rampant. In terms of policy, there is no reason to expect that eliminating the minimum wage or unemployment insurance or even trade unions would exterminate unemployment or have much long-term effect on it.

The historical record suggests instead that the causes of unemployment are likely to be found—and fruitfully to be sought—in the fundamental dynamics and structures of our social and economic system. Unemployment has been an important presence in American society for 100 to 150 years, and it seems extremely unlikely to vanish in the foreseeable future. It appears, in sum, to be a problem that is characteristic of industrial, capitalist societies—or, at the very least, our industrial, capitalist society. Analyses that dwell exclusively on short-run, proximate causes are not only intrinsically ahistorical; they run the risk of being blind to some of the large issues.

In fact, the history of unemployment offers a fairly compelling case for resurrecting the venerable, and now much out-of-fashion concept of a "reserve army of labor" or "reserve army of the unemployed." In the late 19th and early 20th centuries (in contrast to the present), that concept was not very strongly identified with Karl Marx or with Marxist economic thought. Although Marx certainly offered one of the earliest and most developed expositions of its meaning, the phrase was widely deployed in the English-speaking world between the 1880s and the 1930s. Beveridge used the concept in his pathbreaking work, and American analysts such as Lescohier and Leiserson made it central to their Progressive-era studies.[11] "However prosperous conditions may be," concluded the pioneering, yet politically mainstream, Massachusetts Bureau of Statistics of Labor in 1911, "there is always a 'reserve army' of the unemployed" (Keyssar 1986, 72).

What the phrase signified was an acceptance, or recognition, of the fact that unemployment was a chronic (and permanent) presence in industrial, capitalist societies. The concept of a reserve army also implied that unemployment was generated by the normal functioning, rather that the malfunctioning, of the economy, that some "involuntary idleness" was necessary for capitalist economies to perform well and to grow. Marx himself, in *Capital*, tried to sketch out the dynamics that made this so, noting—as did state labor bureaus in Massachusetts and New York in the early 20th century—that capitalist economies seemed to demand the ability to throw "great masses of men suddenly on the decisive points without injury to the scale of production in other spheres" (I, 1967 [1887], 632). For such "masses" to be ever-present, of course, there had to be a reserve. (Marx, as well as other analysts, tried to delineate the different forms that these reserves could assume.) At the same time, employers in market economies seemed to demand the right to reduce the number of men and women they employed whenever they deemed such reductions to be necessary or desirable, which, incessantly and almost inescapably, transformed some active workers into members of a "reserve army" of labor.[12]

Whether there exists sufficient evidence to amply, and persuasively, document the multinational existence of a reserve army—as well as the dynamics that generate such a reserve—is an issue that extends beyond the scope of this essay. But it does seem clear that the concept fits reasonably well the broad outlines of the historical record in the United States. Just as the notion of a reserve army would predict, unemployment has been a continuous presence in American society for more than a century; only in wartime has the joblessness rate dropped to truly negligible levels (and the very fact that it does drop sharply in wartime would appear to confirm the presence of peacetime reserve). Just as Beveridge (and Marx, for that matter) would have predicted, economic growth has never "solved" the unemployment problem; high rates of growth have, on numerous occasions, coexisted with substantial unemployment. And unemployment rates in the United States have always varied from place to place, fluctuating locally more than nationally, as "masses of men" (and women) have sometimes here, and sometimes there, been thrown on the point of production—or thrown out of work. In effect, the concept of a reserve makes comprehensible (or explains) the omnipresence and durability of unemployment by characterizing the phenomenon as systemic in its origins and functional in its operation.[13]

One additional virtue of the idea of a "reserve army" is that it accepts the existence of unemployment as a given, as a point of departure for further research and inquiry. Theories of reserves not only fit the statistical record; they hypothesize the permanence of unemployment in capitalist economies. While neoclassical theory tends to treat unemployment as something that is not supposed to exist, the concept of a reserve army implies that involuntary joblessness, as a rule, will exist. Consequently, and in contrast to classical and neoclassical thought, theories based on the idea of a reserve do not treat the existence of unemployment (or the statistical record) as something that has to be explained or explained away.

The idea of a reserve army, then, has the operational advantage of circumventing or obviating debates about whether "involuntary unemployment" does or can exist. It also serves to refocus the research agenda, to pose old questions somewhat differently or to bring new questions to the fore. The key causal question, for example, ceases to be "why does unemployment exist?" (or "what causes unemployment?") and becomes "why is there more unemployment in some economic and historical circumstances than in others?" Or, in the words of Goran Therborn (1986), why are "some peoples . . . more unemployed than others?" Yet another variant would be: why do capitalist economies seem to require or generate larger reserves at some moments than at others? In addition, such a perspective encourages close scrutiny both of the composition of the reserve army and the ways in which individuals were recruited to membership in it (as well as how that has changed over time). In so doing, it would remove any moralistic overtones or hints of blame from inquiries into the social composition of the unemployed population. All of these issues, moreover, would be refocused in such a way as to demand the kind of multifaceted and multidisciplinary research that is likely to enhance our understanding of the problem. Labor markets do not necessarily behave like commodity markets; and unemployment is not a purely economic phenomenon.

Mobilizing the concept of a reserve army would, of course, have policy implications as well. With the issue of "voluntary" versus "involuntary" unemployment put aside, reducing the size of the reserves would again become a clear-cut goal of macroeconomic policy. Moreover, techniques that focused on the labor supply (through manipulating its size or through training programs) would likely be deemphasized since the problem of unemployment would be seen as stemming from the demand, rather than the supply, side of the equation. And considerable attention might well be drawn to two policy issues that have heretofore remained rather invisible: (1) What are the rules and principles according to which unemployment is, and should be, allocated in our society? (2) How should people who are unemployed—and thus carrying out an important, perhaps vital, economic function—be compensated?

Once one accepts the basic proposition that market economies inescapably generate unemployment, these two questions move to a prominent position in the arena of public dialogue; at the same time, they become more difficult to answer. If, for example, capitalism demands a reserve army and serving in that army is helping the economy, then a very strong argument can be made that an unemployed person should be paid his or her full salary.

If the past can serve as a guide (and historians have a vested interest in believing that it can), then it seems improbable that this proposal for resuscitating the concept of a reserve army will be embraced by mainstream economists. Whatever the merits (or lack thereof) of the idea itself, academic fields are not, in general, very receptive to suggestions that come from outsiders; more importantly, shifts in concepts in the social sciences tend to be linked to, and to reflect (if imperfectly), prevailing political currents. And in the world of the early 1990s, a world distinguished by the collapse of state socialist regimes in eastern Europe and the Soviet Union and by the ongoing conservative drift of politics in the United States, the concept of a reserve army, which has so often been linked with Marxism, seems unlikely to attract a new and large following. A pity, perhaps, but probably true.

On the other hand, it does seem likely that the terms, categories, and methods that have been utilized to analyze unemployment will change, and change significantly, in the not-too-distant future. There seems, unfortunately, to be an excellent chance that unemployment will be a far more serious problem in the 1990s than it was during the final years of the 1980s. The American economy appears to have opened the decade with a prolonged recession; unemployment rates in western Europe remain high; and the conversion to market economies in eastern Europe and the Soviet Union may well give a more dramatic visibility to the problem of joblessness than we have seen since the 1930s. (This seems to be happening already in Poland and in Hungary.) Such developments could well lend a sense of urgency to unemployment both as a social problem requiring policy initiatives and as a socioeconomic phenomenon that is not nearly as well understood as it could or should be. If, as may occur, that lack of understanding serves to inhibit the development of effective policies, then the existing intellectual frameworks could give way to different ideas and new approaches. And perhaps, just perhaps, as we approach the 100th anniversary of the first march of the unemployed on Washington, those ideas and approaches will be infused with an historical perspective.

Notes

1. For examples of these arguments and discussions of them, see: Darity (1981–82); Carmichael (1985); Tobin (1990, 3); Cain (1979, 29); Samuelson (1985, 3); Shapiro and Stiglitz (1985).

2. The earliest appearance in print of the term *unemployment*—of which I am aware—was in 1887; that appearance, in a publication of the Massachusetts Bureau of Statistics of Labor, is also the basis for the *Oxford English Dictionary*'s earliest recorded use of the term. The word *unemployed* took on its modern meaning (out of work and wanting or needing work) in the United States between the 1850s and the 1870s. For a more lengthy discussion of the history of the words, see Keyssar (1986, 3–5). Among the dictionaries consulted for current usage were: *The Random House Dictionary of the English Language*, second edition (1987); *Webster's New Twentieth Century Dictionary of the English Language*, second edition (1977); *The New College Edition of the American Heritage Dictionary of the English Language* (1979); and *The Oxford English Dictionary*, second edition (1989).

3. For discussions of these issues, see: Summers (1990, 227–285); Gordon (1987, 223–246); Gordon (1988, 117–123); McCombie (1985–86); Feldstein (1973, 5–6); Krashevski (1988, 291); Gordon (1989, 220–252); and Duboff (1977).

4. See the discussions of these issues in: Kiefer (1988, 646–679); Summers (1990, 3–108); Akerlof and Main (1981 1003–1012); (1980 885–893); Sider (1985, 461–471); Carlson and Horrigan (1983, 1143–1152); Cain (1979, 2–6); Norwood (1988, 284–288); Baker and Trivedi (1985, 153–174).

5. See, among other works, Lescohier's *The Labor Market* (1919); Beveridge's *Unemployment: A Problem of Industry* (1909); and Leiserson, "The Problem of Unemployment Today" (1916).

6. The historical account presented here is based largely on my own previously published work (Keyssar, 1986; 1987). Those interested in the history should also see: Garraty (1978); Salais, Baverez, and Reynaud (1986); Piore (1987); Romer (1986); and Lebergott's reply to, and discussion of, Romer's revision of Lebergott's historical unemployment series (1986).

7. For discussions of aggregate unemployment rates and the distribution of unemployment among different social groups, see Keyssar (1986, ch. 3, 4, and 10); (1987, 210–214). The claim that durations have increased is implicitly supported by the analyses of Summers and Clark (Summers 1990, 3–85) who argue that actual durations are much longer than those suggested by the CPS figures. The shifts that occurred in the distribution of unemployment seem to have been, at least in part, the consequence of the widespread, and often formal, adoption of seniority as the principle governing layoffs between the mid-1930s and the mid-1940s. This served to protect mature white, male workers while heightening the incidence of joblessness among various new entrants to the labor markets.

8. For examples of such arguments, see: Summers (1990, 316–322); Darity (1981–82); Feldstein (1973, 14–16; 30); Cain (1979, 29); Keeley and Robins (1985, 337–362); Ben-Horim and Zuckerman (1987, 386–390); Montgomery (1989, 170); Shapiro and Stiglitz (1985); Krashevski (1988, 292).

9. Cf. the discussion in Piore (1987). An augument that the causes of unemployment were significantly different before the 1930s than they are today would, of course, require identifying—among other things—a critical period during which the causal dynamics changed.

10. For discussions of these issues, see: Feldstein (1973, 7–12); Cain (1979, 25–28); Bowers (1981); Barrett and Morgenstern (1974); Krashevski (1988, 289–291); Duboff (1977, 12–25).

11. See the sources in note 5 above, Marx's discussion of the reserve army is in *Capital*, I, ch. 25.

12. A more ample discussion of the dynamics of a reserve is presented in Keyssar (1986, 72–74, 109–110). See also the discussion in Darity (1981–82).

13. See the discussions of these issues in Keyssar (1986, 39–76, 111–123, 299–307, 340–341). See also Summers (1990, 307–313) and Duboff (1977, 3–7, 15–22).

References

Akerlof, G.A., and Main, B.G.M. 1980. "Unemployment Spells and Unemployment Experience." *American Economic Review* (December): 885–893.

————. 1981. "An Experience-Weighted Measure of Employment and Unemployment Durations. "*American Economic Review* (December): 1003–1012.

Baker, G.M., and Trivedi, P.K. 1985. "Estimation of Unemployment Duration From Grouped Data: A Comparative Study." *Journal of Labor Economics* (July): 153–174.

Barrett, N.S., and Morgenstern, R.D. 1974. "Why Do Blacks and Women Have High Unemployment Rates?" *Journal of Human Resources:* 452–464.

Beveridge, W.H. 1909. *Unemployment: A Problem of Industry*. London: Longmans, Green and Company.

Ben-Horim, M., and Zuckerman, D. 1987. "The Effect of Unemployment Insurance on Unemployment Duration," *Journal of Labor Economics* (July): 386–390.

Bowers, N. 1981. "Have Employment Patterns in Recessions Changed?" *Monthly Labor Review* (February): 15–28.

Cain, G.G. 1979. "The Unemployment Rate as an Economic Indicator." *Monthly Labor Review* (March): 24–35.

Carlson, J.A., and Horrigan, M.W. 1983. "Measures of Unemployment Duration as Guides to Research and Policy: Comment. "*American Economic Review* (December): 1143–1152.

Carmichael, L. 1985. "Can Unemployment Be Involuntary? Comment." *American Economic Review* (December): 1213–1214.

Darity, W., Jr. 1981–82. "Beveridge and the New Search Unemployment." *Journal of Post Keynessian Economics* (Winter): 171–180.

Duboff, R. 1977. "Full Employment: The History of a Receding Target." *Politics and Society* 7(1): 1–26.

Feldstein, M. 1973. "The Economics of the New Unemployment." *The Public Interest* (Fall): 3–42.

Garraty, J.A. 1978. *Unemployment in History*. New York: Harper and Row.

Gordon, D.M. 1987. "Six-Percent Unemployment Ain't Natural: Demystifying the

Idea of a Rising Natural Rate of Unemployment." *Social Research* (Summer): 223–246.

———. 1988. "The Un-Natural Rate of Unemployment: An Econometric Critique of the NAIRU Hypothesis. "*American Economic Review* (May): 117–123.

Gordon, R.J. 1989. "Hysteresis in History: Was There Ever a Phillips Curve?" *American Economic Review* (May): 220–225.

Keeley, M.C., and Robins, P.K. 1985. "Government Programs, Job Search Requirements, and the Duration of Unemployment." *Journal of Labor Economics* (July): 337–362.

Keyssar, A. 1986. *Out of Work: The First Century of Unemployment in Massachusetts*. New York: Cambridge University Press.

———. 1987. "Unemployment Before and After the Great Depression." *Social Research* (Summer): 201–222.

Kiefer, N.M. 1988. "Economic Duration Data and Hazard Functions." *Journal of Economic Literature* (June): 646–670.

Krashevski, R. 1988. "What Is So Natural About High Unemployment?" *American Economic Review* (May): 289–293.

Lebergott, S. 1986. "Discussion." *Journal of Economic History* (June): 367–371.

Leiserson, W. 1916. "The Problem of Unemployment Today." *Political Science Quarterly* (March): 1–16.

Lescohier, D.D. 1919. *The Labor Market*. New York: Macmillan.

Liem, R. 1987. "The Psychological Costs of Unemployment." *Social Research* (Summer): 319–354.

Marx, K. 1967 [1887]. *Capital: A Critique of Political Economy*. New York: International Publishers.

McCombie, J.S. 1985–86. "Why Cutting Real Wages Will Not Necessarily Reduce Unemployment—Keynes and the 'Postulates of the Classical Economics.'" *Journal of Post Keynesian Economics* (Winter): 233–248.

Montgomery, E. 1989. "Employment and Unemployment Effects of Unions." *Journal of Labor Economics* (April): 170–190.

Norwood, J. 1988. "The Measure of Unemployment." *American Economic Review* (May): 284–288.

Piore, M.J. 1987. "Historical perspectives and the Interpretation of Unemployment." *Journal of Economic Literature* (December): 1834–1850.

Romer, C. 1986a. "Spurious Volatility in Historical Unemployment Data." *Journal of Political Economy*: 1–37.

———. 1986b. "Is the Stabilization of the Postwar Economy a Figment of the Data?" *American Economic Review* (June): 314–334.

———. 1986c. "New Estimates of Prewar Gross National Product and Unemployment."*Journal of Economic History* (June): 341–352.

Salais, R. Baverez, N., and Reynaud, B. 1986. *L'invention du Chomage: Histoire et transformations d'une categorie en France des annees 1890 aux annees 1980.* Paris: Presses Universitaires de France.

Samuelson, L. 1985. "Implicit Contracts with Heterogeneous Labor." *Journal of Labor Economics* (January): 70–90.

Shapiro, C., and Stiglitz, J.E. 1985. "Can Unemployment Be Involuntary? Reply. "*American Economic Review* (December): 1215–1217.

Sider, H. 1985. "Unemployment Duration and Incidence: 1968–82." *American Economic Review* (June): 461–473.

Solow, R.M. 1980. "On Theories of Unemployment." *American Economic Review* (March): 1–11.

Summers, L.H. 1990. *Understanding Unemployment*. Cambridge: MIT Press.

Tobin, J. 1990. "Current Controversy in Macroeconomics: The Four Schools." *Harvard Graduate Society Newsletter* (Fall): 5–9.

II HOW LABOR MARKETS REALLY WORK

3 THE IMPACT OF FORMAL ON-THE-JOB TRAINING *on Unemployment and the Influence of Gender, Race, and Working Lifecycle Position on Accessibility to On-the-Job Training*

Alfred J. Field
Arthur H. Goldsmith

The literature concerning the influence of race and gender on layoff likelihood (Blau and Kahn 1981) and wages (flanagan 1974; Corcoran and Duncan 1979; Blau and Beller 1984; Blinder 1973) reveals that after controlling for factors expected to influence personal productivity, differences persist between whites and blacks as well as males and females. These differences are often attributed, among other things, to discrimination, although culture may play a role, particularly with respect to unemployment differentials. However, it is possible that important personal characteristics likely to alter an individual's productivity, such as formal on-the-job training, have not been adequately accounted for. If a substantial correlation exists between formal on-the-job training, the missing variable, and some of the traditional set of variables used in wage and layoff equations,

The authors are indebted to Bob Lee, Tom Kniesner, Stuart Low, David Guilkey, William Darity Jr., and Jean Kimmel for helpful discussions and suggestions. They also thank Jean Kimmel for performing the computations. Grant support from the Liz Claiborne Foundation and the Institute for Research in the Social Sciences at the University of North Carolina is gratefully acknowledged. Author names are listed alphabetically.

conventional models are misspecified, resulting in biased coefficient estimates that possibly overstate the role of discrimination. Proxies such as tenure (Parsons 1972; Duncan and Hoffman 1979), job classification (Oi 1962; Mincer 1962; Rosen 1966) and wage growth (Lazear 1979a; 1979b) have been used as measures of on-the-job training. Although these proxies may appropriately represent *informal* on-the-job training, they are unlikely to accurately measure an individual's *formal* on-the-job training activities.

All on-the-job training, both informal and formal, entail skill accumulation through individual and/or group endeavors. However, informal training is concurrent with production, while formal training occurs away from the immediate production process. Thus, it is likely that different techniques of instruction are utilized in each type. For example, skills that necessitate text-aided learning are more commonly acquired in formal training programs. On the other hand, operational techniques entailing on-the-line instruction are better suited to the informal setting. Each type of training potentially affects productivity, but in different ways. Informal on-the-job training is acquired in a continuous fashion and is typically proxied by age, experience, and tenure (years with current employer). The primary purpose of such training is to improve worker performance on the current job given a particular technology. These measures do not capture the more intense but infrequent participation in formal on-the-job training that workers may undergo. However, formal on-the-job training typically imparts different skills to the workforce leading to new employment opportunities and thus may facilitate the adoption of alternative, potentially new technologies.[1]

It seems clear that people of the same age, experience, and tenure may possess significantly different skill levels as a result of differential formal on-the-job training activities. Unfortunately, no effort is made to account for this source of worker heterogeneity in current empirical work. Thus the existing research which attempts to measure both informal and formal on-the-job training with one variable (e.g., age, experience, tenure) is statistically flawed.

It is possible that differential accumulation of formal on-the-job training by gender and race, controlling for working life cycle stage, can influence (1) differences in layoff unemployment rates and (2) differences in wages. Differential accumulation of formal on-the-job training may occur due to discrimination based upon race, gender, age, and ethnicity.

Lazear (1979) argues that affirmative action narrows entry-level white–black wage differentials, but that discriminatory employers respond by denying blacks access to on-the-job training and thus reestablish the racial wage imbalance over time. He apparently believes that firms maximize both profits and utility, which may have a negative impact by female, black, and old status. But what are the facts? Unfortunately, up to now, *direct* data on the accumulation of formal on-the-job training have been unavailable, preventing these questions from being addressed properly.[2] Until formal on-the-job training is explicitly analyzed, labor economists will continue to have an incomplete, and possibly inaccurate, understanding of the key determinants of wages and layoffs.

The purpose of this chapter is to use recently available direct objective measures of formal on-the-job training to examine the influence of formal on-the-job training on the likelihood of experiencing a layoff. This exercise may be seen as an effort to refine our understanding of the role of human capital in generating job security. If formal on-the-job training significantly reduces layoff likelihood, then the impact of gender, race, and working lifecycle stage on: (1) the likelihood of participating in formal on-the-job training programs, and (2) the duration of these on-the-job training experiences for program participants will be investigated in an effort to address the role of formal on-the-job training in explaining race and gender unemployment differentials.[3] This portion of the analysis also tests one of the core precepts of human capital theory—that benefit and cost considerations motivate "early" accumulation—using formal on-the-job training data rather than formal education data (Becker 1962). Moreover, isolating the impact of gender and race on accumulation should shed light on the role of worker heterogeneity and institutional phenomena on current human capital accumulation.

The remainder of this chapter is organized as follows. The expected relation between formal on-the-job training and layoff experience, as well as previous efforts to examine the hypothesized relations, are discussed in the next section. In the third section the data used to develop direct measures of formal on-the-job training are discussed. The fourth section contains a presentation of the empirical analysis regarding the impact of formal on-the-job training on the likelihood of layoff. A discussion of the empirical analysis concerning the influence of gender, race, and working lifecycle stage on the likelihood of participating in formal on-the-job training programs appears in the fifth section, after which the influence of gender, race, and working lifecycle position on the duration of formal on-the-job training activities is examined. Concluding remarks appear in the final section.

Formal On-the-Job Training and Layoff Experience

To the extent that on-the-job training makes it more difficult for the firm to substitute other inputs for trained relative to untrained labor, the demand curve for trained labor vis-a-vis untrained labor will be more steeply sloped.[4] The labor demand curve for trained workers also will be more steeply sloped if on-the-job training acts as a signal of desirable worker characteristics (e.g., high motivation, good attitude, career oriented, trainability, adaptability). It is conventional to dichotomize on-the-job training into specific (e.g., nontransferable skills) and general (e.g., transferable skills) activities. However, it is important to recognize that both formal and informal training can contain elements of each type.

Suppose a firm hires untrained and trained workers at wages (possibly different) that are sticky downward in the short run.[5] Then a recession that is uniformly distributed across skill types (e.g. an equivalent fall in labor demand) will result in a typical untrained worker being more likely to be laid off than a typical trained worker due to the relative slopes of their demand curves. Thus, workers that participate in on-the-job training programs may be investing in employment stability as well as skill accumulation.[6] But again, what are the facts? Is there evidence to support the hypothesis of a positive relation between on-the-job training and employment security?

Unfortunately, efforts to examine the impact of on-the-job training on job security have been plagued by data limitations, especially the lack of availability of *direct* measures of on-the-job training. For example, some studies (Oi 1962; Mincer 1962; Rosen 1966) have employed the wage level as a measure of on-the-job training acquired. However, Parsons (1972) argues that the wage is a poor proxy since other factors that are difficult to control for also influence the wage rate. Parsons prefers to use tenure as a proxy for on-the-job training.

Indeed, following Parsons (1972), a tradition has been established in the literature of using tenure as a proxy for total on-the-job training (both formal and informal). For instance, Blau and Kahn (1981) report that greater tenure reduces the probability of layoff among young workers as expected. Moreover, evidence provided by Mincer and Jovanovic (1981) and Bartel and Borjas (1981) of rising wage-tenure profiles is interpreted as supporting the hypothesis of a positive relation between wages and on-the-job training.[7]

It is possible that job tenure merely acts as a signal of desirable worker characteristics that both reduce the likelihood of layoff and are positively associated with earnings. Some indirect evidence consistent with this view of tenure may be inferred from recent papers by Altonji and Shakotko (1985), Abraham and Farber (1986), and Marshall and Zarkin (1987) that find tenure has little or no effect upon wages once worker and job heterogeneity are appropriately accounted for. One possible explanation for this finding that casts further doubt on the usefulness of tenure as a measure of on-the-job training is that workers with limited mobility due to adequate, but not exceptional, performance are likely to be characterized by greater tenure. Consequently, greater tenure may reflect nothing more than loyalty and adequate performance which receive nonwage compensation.

Although tenure may perform reasonably well as a proxy for desirable personal characteristics, it may be a very imprecise measure of on-the-job training particularly *formal* on-the-job training. A worker's day is composed of time allocated to training and work. The proportions are likely to vary over the course of a week or month as well as over the years. In particular, early in a worker's tenure, during the probationary period, the day's activities are likely to be heavily weighted by training relative to work. At the end of the probationary period, most of the basic skills necessary to perform a job have presumably been acquired. Refinement of these basic skills may take place in the months, possibly years, that follow.

But at some point, as the worker's tenure with the firm increases, the worker's incentive to engage in training activities diminishes as does the firm's need for the worker to participate in such programs given the state of technology. Thus, a worker with 20 years of tenure is unlikely to have acquired four times as much total on-the-job training as a worker with five years of tenure. In fact, based on the characteristics of the job these workers perform, they may possess quite similar amounts of formal training. Parsons (1977, 217) appears to recognize the problems associated with the use of tenure as a proxy for both formal and informal on-the-job training since he argued:

> More careful consideration of the measurement of the independent variables in turnover regressions is warranted. The exploration for useful empirical measures of firm specific human capital should also be undertaken.

Clearly, the proxies that have been utilized as measures of on-the-job training are simply inadequate to permit a viable test of the linkage between formal on-the-job training and layoff experience. Our research attempts to eliminate this shortcoming in the literature by using *direct* measures of an individual's formal on-the-job training to examine the influence of formal on-the-job training on an individual's layoff experience.

The Data

The January 1984 Job Training Survey, designed by the Bureau of Labor Statistics (BLS) under contract with the Employment and Training Administration, which *supplements* the January 1984 Bureau of the Census Current Population Survey (CPS), provides a large nationally representative microdata sample that contains *direct* and objective formal on-the-job training information. Surprisingly, the unique training data generated by the supplemental survey have yet to be systematically analyzed.

The January 1984 CPS provides data on the employment and displacement experiences of workers age 20 years or older during the years 1979–1984. The Job Training Supplemental Survey provides information on an individual's occupational training experiences during 1982 and 1983. In order to investigate the impact of on-the-job training on the likelihood of layoff, as well as the impact of gender, race, and working lifecycle stage on the likelihood of acquiring formal on-the-job training, the data from the supplemental survey and the regular January 1984 CPS are merged.[8]

In the supplemental survey, respondents are asked "...if they ever attended a training program to obtain occupational skills on a job since January, 1982?" Respondents answering "yes" were asked the number of programs they participated in and the years during which they received on-the-job training. Additional questions focused on the nature of the training activity, the source of funding, and the length of participation in weeks. This data set facilitates, for the first time, construction of direct objective measures of an individual's formal on-the-job training activities.

Formal On-the-Job Training and Likelihood of Layoff

The training data begin in 1982, making it impossible to determine the role of on-the-job training, if any, in layoffs occurring prior to 1983. Therefore, individuals laid off in 1983 are included in the sample while those laid off from 1979–1982 are excluded. It is essential to recognizse that in this study only training engaged in prior to a layoff experience is relevant in measuring an individual's training level. It would be desirable to have an estimate of an individual's total stock of formal on-the-job training; however, the data only provide information on recent accumulation. Because an individual's stock of on-the-job generated skills both declines due to obsolescence associated with technological change and depreciates, the layoff retarding effect of formal on-the-job training is greatest for those skills acquired closest to the point at which a layoff decision is being made. Since recently acquired skills are likely to be the most important portion of the stock of skills relevant to the firm when making layoff decisions, the shortcoming of not being able to measure an individual's total stock of training skills is not serious in the context of examining the impact of on-the-job training on the likelihood of layoff. In essence, we are examining the influence of marginal as opposed to total formal on-the-job training on job security.

Theoretically the wage level would account for more distant acquisition of human capital in the form of on-the-job training. Unfortunately, wage data are unavailable and thus cannot be incorporated in the empirical analysis. Some of the compensation effects are presumably captured by occupation which is available and utilized.[9]

Hypotheses

A host of factors are expected to influence an individual's labor force status. These factors include human capital, accumulated both on and off the job, demographic characteristics, and job traits. Hypotheses concerning the relation between these factors and layoff status are explicitly specified in this section. Of particular interest is the relation between layoff experience and formal on-the-job training.

Human Capital

Formal On-the-Job Training. It is hypothesized that workers characterized by formal on-the-job training have a comparative advantage in job security over similar untrained or less trained workers in a world characterized by short-run wage rigidity. A test of this hypothesis is conducted by examining whether participation in a formal on-the-job training program is negatively related to the likelihood of layoff and by examining whether additional weeks of formal on-the-job training, for program participants, reduces the likelihood of layoff.

Formal Schooling. Individuals with more schooling are expected to have superior personal characteristics, including greater trainability, than their less-educated counterparts, *ceteris paribus*, an should experience greater employment stability.

Demographic Characteristics

Age. Older workers may be perceived as less productive and trainable than their younger counterparts, enhancing layoff likelihood. These deficiencies, if they exist, may accelerate with advanced age. On the other hand, older workers may possess greater stocks of informal on-the-job training, and be viewed as more conscientious, serious, and stable than their younger counterparts, *ceteris paribus*. In addition, accumulation of these traits may accelerate with age. If productive maturity and overall workplace knowledge are valued by the firm, aging may reduce the likelihood of layoff. As a result, the impact of aging on employment is ambiguous.

Race and Gender. A common perception is that the relatively high layoff unemployment rates experienced by nonwhites and women are caused by lower skill levels due to limited opportunities and intermittent labor force participation. Of course, another potential explanation is race and/or gender discrimination on the part of employers. Since education level, formal on-the-job training, and age (which may account for overt discrimination and/or experience) are controlled for in this study, a "simple" test of these discrimination hypotheses is conducted by: (1) examining if being nonwhite positively influences the likelihood of layoff, and (2) examining if being female positively influences the likelihood of layoff.

Marital Status. Married individuals may behave in a more mature and responsible fashion than unmarried individuals. If this is the case, and professional behavior is considered a desirable personnel characteristic, employers may be less willing to lay off married individuals than their unmarried counterparts, *ceteris paribus.*

Control Variables. Finally, employment characteristics such as industry, occupation, and geographical region are controlled for in the study. The distinction between full-time and part-time work is also accounted for.

Model Specification, Data Characteristics, and Empirical Procedures

In order to test hypotheses regarding the likelihood of layoff, probit analysis is used. The formal on-the-job training data are separated into firm- and nonfirm-financed training in order to account for possible differences in training content in the investigation of the impact of formal on-the-job training on layoff experience. Public-sector-funded formal on-the-job training is included in nonfirm-financed training. Although the context of these various training programs is unknown, it seems reasonable to presume than nonfirm-financed training relative to firm-financed training programs are relatively weighted toward the acquisition of general skills. In particular, the following layoff probability function is estimated.

$$P(L) = \mathrm{f}(DFIRMFIN,\ FIRMFIN,\ DNONFIRMFIN,\ NONFIRMFIN,\ SCHOOLING,\ AGE,\ AGESQ,\ WHITE,\ MALE,\ MARRIED,\ FULL,\ IND_i,\ OCC_j,\ REGION_k) \tag{1}$$

Variable definitions, means, and standard deviations appear in Table 1. Surprisingly, less than 5 percent of the sample received some form of formal on-the-job training. In particular, only 1.34 percent (245) received nonfirm-financed training while 3.1 percent (566) acquired some firm-financed training. Moreover, the typical nonfirm-financed training program participant accumulated 15.8 weeks of training while firm-financed training program participants acquired 5.4 weeks of training. The data in this survey suggest that while relatively few workers received formal on-the-job training of any kind, those that did acquired a considerable amount on average.[10]

Probit analysis entails coefficient estimation via a maximum likelihood procedure that yields coefficient estimates that are consistent and asymptotically normally distributed. Although it is impossible to perform exact hypothesis tests in a probit model, "pseudo-t" ratios are reported to indicate if a variable *influences* the dependent variable. In addition, a chi-square test may be performed to determine if the independent variables as a group exert an impact on the dependent variable.[11]

Results

The probit coefficients and their associated asymptotic t ratios are presented in Table 2. The estimated coefficients on the dummies for both nonfirm-financed (DNONFIRMFIN) and firm-financed training (DFIRMFIN) are negative and significant, as expected. In particular, the average individual that receives formal on-the-job training is less likely to be laid off than their average untrained counterpart. On the other hand, the amount (NONFIRMFIN, FIRMFIN) of formal on-the-job training appears to have no impact on the likelihood of layoff. In summary these findings suggest that it is the *incidence* of on-the-job training rather than the duration that diminishes an individual's likelihood of layoff.

Our results also reveal that there is no statistically significant difference, at the $\alpha = .1$ level, in the likelihood of layoff for workers receiving firm-financed and nonfirm-financed formal on-the-job training (see Appendix Table 1), although there is a substantial difference ($-.425$ versus $-.219$) in the magnitude of the coefficients.[12] Because the t value was large, .65, the decision was made to maintain a distinction between firm- and nonfirm-financed formal on-the-job training.

Individuals of any race with greater SCHOOLING and those individuals who were white were significantly less likely to be laid off, as expected. An interesting finding is that gender (MALE) and marital status (MARRIED) do not appear to influence the likelihood of layoff, whereas aging significantly reduces the likelihood of layoff. This finding may suggest the

Table 1. Variable Definitions, Means and Standard Deviations: Probit Model of Layoff

Variable		*Description*	*Mean*	*Standard Deviation*
DTRAINING	1	If laid off in 1983	.0281	.1653
	0	Otherwise		
DNONFIRMFIN	1	If participated in a nonfirm-financed formal on-the-job training program in 1982 or 1983 that is prior to most recent layoff	.0134	.1151
	0	Otherwise		
NONFIRMFIN		Total number of weeks of nonfirm-financed formal on-the-job training received in 1982 or 1983 that are prior to most recent layoff	15.8184	22.2299
DFIRMFIN	1	If participated in a firm-financed formal on-the-job training program in 1982 or 1983 that is prior to most recent layoff	.0309	.1730
	0	Otherwise		
FIRMFIN		Total number of weeks of firm-financed formal on-the-job training received in 1982 or 1983 that are prior to most recent layoff	5.3706	11.1509
SCHOOLING		Total number of years of schooling completed	13.4015	3.1478
AGE		Age in years	45.2479	17.7862
AGESQ		Age in years squared	2363.7008	1777.2842
WHITE	1	If race is white	.8239	.3809
	0	Otherwise		
MALE	1	If gender is male	.4562	.4981
	0	Otherwise		
MARRIED	1	If married	.8377	.3687
	0	Otherwise		

Variable		Description	Mean	Standard Deviation
FULL	1	If prelayoff job was full time (35 hours or more per week)	.4549	.4979
	0	Otherwise		
IND_i	1	If prelayoff industry of participation is industry *i* [*i* = 1, 2, . . . 10, where:		
		1 = mining	.0074	.0857
		2 = construction	.0419	.2004
		3 = transportation	.0467	.2109
		4 = wholesale	.1229	.3284
		5 = finance	.0399	.1959
		6 = private services	.0515	.2210
		7 = medicine	.0516	.2212
		8 = education	.0556	.2292
		9 = other professional services	.0193	.1377
		10 = public administration]	.0313	.1741
	0	If *i* = 11 (manufacturing)		
OCC_j	1	If prelayoff occupation is occupation *j* [*j* = 1, 2, . . . 5, where:		
		1 = trades	.0827	.2755
		2 = plant labor	.1070	.3091
		3 = services	.0839	.2772
		4 = technical assistants]	.2013	.4009
	0	If *j* = 5 (professionals and administrators)		
REG_k	1	If respondent resides in region *k* [*k* = 1, ... 4, where:		
		1 = Midwest	.2394	.4267
		2 = West	.2460	.4307
		3 = South	.3014	.4589
	0	if *k* = 4 (Northeast)		
TOTAL = 18,251				

Note: Means and standard deviations for these variables refer only to those workers receiving training. For GENTRAIN $n = 245$, and for SPETRAIN $n = 564$.

Table 2. Probit Model of Layoff: Expected and Estimated Coefficient Signs (Dependent Variable: DTRAINING)

Variable	*Expected Coefficient Sign*	*Estimated Coefficient*	*Standard Error*	*Asymptotic t*
DNONFIRMFIN	–	–.4258	.2893	–1.471*
NONFIRMFIN	–	.0058	.0073	.796
DFIRMFIN	–	–.2192	.1369	–1.600*
FIRMFIN	–	.0023	.0094	.248
SCHOOLING	–	–.0147	.0092	–1.598*
AGE	?	–.0171	.0099	–1.714*
AGESQ	?	.0051†	.0114†	.447
WHITE	–	–.0879	.0549	–1.598*
MALE	–	–.0403	.0500	–.806
MARRIED	–	.0135	.0592	.228
FULL	?	.9713	.0650	14.943*
MINING	?	.3685	.1559	2.363*
CONSTRUCTION	?	.3619	.0816	4.435*
TRANSPORTATION	–	–.2923	.0979	–2.985*
WHOLESALE	–	.0328	.0649	.505
FINANCE	–	–.4164	.1235	–3.371
PRIVATE SERVICES	–	.0354	.0843	.420
MEDICAL	–	–.3390	.1090	–3.109*
EDUCATION	–	–.5760	.1343	–4.288*
OTHER PROFESSIONAL SERVICES	–	–.2179	.1567	–1.391*
PUBLIC ADMINISTRATION	–	–.4400	.1403	–3.137*
TRADES	+	.0784	.0786	.997
PLANT LABOR	+	.2711	.0698	3.887*
SERVICES	+	.1562	.0854	1.829*
TECHNICAL ASSISTANTS	+	.0059	.0660	.090
MIDWEST	?	.0288	.0648	.444
WEST	?	.0937	.0632	1.482
SOUTH	–	–.0294	.0626	–.471
INTERCEPT	?	–1.7414	.2254	–7.724*

n = 18,251

($-2 \times$ log likelihood ratio) = 747.6

† = $\times 10^{-2}$

Significant at the $\alpha = .1$ level.

existence of workplace customs and seniority rules that protect older workers. On the other hand, it is possible that informal workplace knowledge and productive maturity, that are positively related to age, are valued by the firm and exceed the possible productivity retarding effects of advanced age and intransigence with respect to change. However, this effect declines with advancing age. Full-time work status exhibits a positive and significant influence on the likelihood of layoff relative to part-time work. This is consistent with the view that full-time workers are more costly to the firm.[13]

Seven of the ten industry dummies were significant, indicating that structural differences in the likelihood of layoff exists across industries. The estimated coefficients on the occupational dummies reveal that professional /administrative work is, in general, more secure than nonprofessional work and significantly so for plant laborers and service workers.

In summary, participation by employed workers in formal firm- and nonfirm-financed on-the-job training programs significantly reduces the likelihood of layoff. This finding suggests that differential accumulation of formal on-the-job training may explain a portion of the observed white/ black, male/female, and middle age/youth unemployment gaps.

Likelihood of Participating in Formal On-the-Job Training Programs

Principal Hypotheses

Accumulation of formal on-the-job training is the outcome of decisions made by both employers and employees. Each party is expected to consider its own costs and benefits to determine its optimal level of formal on-the-job training activity. Thus, the impact of gender, race, and working lifecycle stage on the likelihood of acquiring formal on-the-job training depends on how these factors influence both the costs and benefits of formal on-the-job training. Hypotheses concerning the relation between gender, race, and working lifecycle stage and the acquisition of formal on-the-job training are specified explicitly in this section.

Working Lifecycle Position. Workers in earlier stages of their working lifecycle have a larger present value of total benefits associated with formal on-the-job training than comparable workers at later stages in their working lifecycle simply because they have a longer remaining worklife ahead of them. Hence, workers in earlier stages of their working lifecycle are expected to have a greater propensity, *ceteris paribus*, to solicit opportunities to participate in formal on-the-job training programs. Similarly, expected firm benefits from training also decline with working lifecycle stage. Hence firms are more likely to offer training opportunities to workers in earlier stages of the worklife. Thus, advanced working lifecycle stage is expected to have a negative influence on an employee's likelihood of participating in formal on-the-job training.

Gender. Workers, male and female, are expected to be willing participants in formal on-the-job training programs as long as the perceived benefits exceed the costs. Both groups expect formal on-the-job training to increase personnel productivity and hence wages. In addition, formal on-the-job training may enhance vertical mobility (e.g., promotion) and reduce intermittency (e.g., spells in and out of the labor force) by sending positive signals regarding personal characteristics (e.g., motivation, trainability), thus easing reentry.

The impact of *informal* on-the-job training, as measured by experience, on earnings is smaller for women than for comparable men. To the extent that this relation also characterizes the accumulation of formal on-the-job training, the present value of direct monetary benefits experienced by women may be insufficient to cover the costs of a formal training program. This issue of smaller female wage effects for comparable on-the-job training only will be of concern to individuals that bear the costs of such training.

If firms bear the costs of formal on-the-job training they are expected to be concerned about the factors, including gender, that influence post-training firm benefits. For example, the career pattern of many married women tends to consist of three distinct stages: employment preceding childbirth, non- or part-time participation subsequent to the birth of their first child, followed by a full-time return to labor market participation.[14] In addition, wives have historically tended to "follow" husbands to the geographical location of their job.[15]

Because of these factors, women vis-a-vis men are more likely to experience intermittent labor supply. Even though the marriage age of women is rising, the percentage who marry is lower and the time out of the labor force due to child birth is declining. Female labor force participation is still more variable than that of other comparable men. Intermittency reduces the number of working periods within an individual's expected worklife, thus reducing the present value of the benefits associated with on-the-job training from the firm's perspective.

As noted above, cost-benefit analysis suggests that women are less likely than men to finance the accumulation of training on-the-job. In addition, firms are less likely to offer formal training opportunities to women, relative to men, due to gender-based statistical characteristics such as greater intermittency.

Firm prejudice against women may also reduce their likelihood of participating in training programs. Government anti-discrimination programs are intended to reduce such behavior. However, these programs tend to concentrate on reducing entry level male-female wage differentials. Lazear (1979b) suggests that firms whose managers acquire disutility from the employment of women for which they take compensation in the form of a gender pay differential may respond to this legislation by selecting alternative means of discrimination against women. For example, management could reduce the future opportunities to participate in on-the-job training programs for female employees.

A test of the hypothesis that women are less likely than men to participate in formal on-the-job training programs, controlling for working lifecycle stage, is conducted by examining the difference in the likelihoods of participation for both gender groups.

Race. There is no reason to believe the set of benefit-cost factors an individual considers when deciding whether to seek formal on-the-job training is race dependent. However, there is reason to believe that the monetary, and possibly nonmonetary, benefits of formal on-the-job training may vary by race. Studies by Blinder (1973), Corcoran and Duncan (1979), Flanagan (1974), and Williams (1984) reveal that after controlling for differences in personal characteristics, black workers, regardless of gender, still earn less than their white counterparts.

If blacks, relative to whites, also expect to receive a smaller wage increase due to formal on-the-job training accumulation, then in the case of nonfirm-financed training there is a level of program costs for which blacks are less likely to participate than their white counterparts. Of course, black and white workers may perceive that training not only increases the wage in a given job but it also enhances the probability of advancement to a higher job class. Given the scarcity of blacks in higher track jobs, relative to whites, black workers may perceive a greater likelihood of advancement through formal on-the-job training than their white counterparts perceive. Hence, formal on-the-job training may result in greater *expected* monetary benefits for black workers relative to whites. Consequently, the impact of race on the likelihood of participating in formal nonfirm-financed on-the-job training is ambiguous.

Since no direct costs are born by the worker in the case of firm-financed training any expected wage increase may be sufficient to encourage a worker to seek opportunities to acquire firm-financed on-the-job training. An indirect cost may be a decline in post-training worker mobility due to the wage differential that only exists as employment (with the current employer) continues.

In the case of formal firm-financed on-the-job training, businesses will be concerned about the factors, including race, that influence post-training firm benefits. For instance, the firm will be less inclined to offer blacks formal firm-financed on-the-job training if their labor force attachment is perceived as being intermittent relative to that of whites. Furthermore, turnover is higher and hence on-the-job training lower in "secondary jobs" relative to "primary jobs," and since blacks are disproportionately represented in secondary occupations, we would expect blacks to be less likely to participate in formal on-the-job training as a group.

Thus, in order to investigate if race discrimination plays a role in the acquisition of on-the-job training it is necessary to account for occupation. According to post-WWII data (Blau and Beller 1984), blacks have higher unemployment rates than whites. They also report that black males have lower labor force participation rates than white males, and are less likely to have worked full time all year for their entire work lives than white males.

However, a study by Blau and Kahn (1981) revealed that when job and personal characteristics are controlled for, blacks do not appear to have higher quit rates than whites. In spite of thsi finding firms still may perceive black workers to be less committed to the labor market. Therefore, firms would be more likely to offer formal firm-financed on-the-job training opportunities to white workers relative to black workers. The expectation of employers that black employees have higher quit rates may lead them to be less inclined to offer blacks training relative to comparable whites and thus possibly trigger a higher quit rate on the part of black workers. Of course, discrimination against blacks, even in the presence of government anti-discrimination legislation (Lazear 1979a), would reinforce the tendency of firms to prefer whites to blacks when providing formal firm-financed on-the-job training. Although such firms may experience a pecuniary loss in the form of profits forgone by practicing such behavior and restricting the quality of their labor force, this may be insufficient to prohibit discrimination because there is little evidence that the U.S. economy is competitive in the sense of profit rates being driven to the minimum acceptable level.

On the other hand, if government anti-discrimination programs result in preferential treatment of black workers by employers, blacks may be more likely to receive opportunities to acquire formal firm-financed on-the-job training than comparable whites. Hence, it is unclear whether blacks are more or less likely to participate in formal firm-financed on-the-job training programs than whites. A test of the hypothesis that blacks and whites have different likelihoods of engaging in formal on-the-job training is conducted by examining the impact of race on the likelihood of participation.

Model Specification, Data Characteristics, and Empirical Procedures

In order to test the aforementioned hypotheses regarding the impact of working lifecycle position, gender, race, and a host of control variables on the likelihood of participation in formal on-the-job training programs, probit analysis is used to estimate the following probability of participation functions.

$$\left.\begin{array}{l} P(DTRAINING) \quad (1) \\ P(DFIRMFIN) \quad (2) \\ P(DNONFIRMFIN) \quad (3) \end{array}\right\} = f(SCHOOLING, BLACK, MARRIED, FULL, GENDER\text{-}WORKING\ LIFECYCLE\ STAGE_i, IND_j, OCC_k, REGION_p)$$

Variable definitions, means, and standard deviations appear in Table 3. Notice, the second and third functions estimated reflect stratification of the data by source of training financing in order to account for possible differences in training content. Only 4.8 percent of the sample received some sort of formal on-the-job training.[16] In particular, only 1.72 percent (314 observations) received formal nonfirm-financed training while 3.32 percent (606 observations) acquired some firm-financed training.

An individual's working lifecycle is proxied by a set of five dummy variables based on age. Although the categories are subjective, they were chosen to conform with intuitive notions of working lifecycle stages such as "Early" middle-age workers, Stage III (e.g., age 31–40) and "late" middleage workers, Stage IV (e.g., age 41–55). The set of working lifecycle stage dummies are interacted with the gender dummy variable to yield a set of gender-working lifecycle stage dummies. These dummies are included in the models to isolate the impact of, (1) working lifecycle position, controlling for gender, and (2) gender, controlling for working lifecycle stage. These isolated effects are derived by examining differences in the likelihood of participation for specified sets of gender-working lifecycle stage dummy variable pairs.

Unfortunately, the influence of working lifecycle position and gender on the likelihood of participation in formal on-the-job training is confined to whites, since there are too few blacks that acquired formal on-the-job training to allow stratification by working lifecycle stage. However, the data do permit a comparison of the likelihood of participation by blacks as a group relative to whites. Results relating to the aforementioned specified

Table 3. Variable Definitions, Means and Standard Deviations: Probit Models of Formal On-the-Job Training Participation

Variable		*Description*	*Mean*	*Standard Deviation*
DTRAINING	1	If participated in a formal on-the-job training program in 1982 or 1983	.0479	.2136
	0	Otherwise		
DNONFIRMFIN	1	If participated in a nonfirm-financed formal on-the-job training program in 1982 or 1983	.0172	.1300
	0	Otherwise		
DFIRMFIN	1	If participated in a firm-financed formal on-the-job training program in 1982 or 1983	.0332	.1790
	0	Otherwise		
SCHOOLING	Number of years of schooling		13.5509	2.9887
BLACK	1	If race is black	.1012	.3016
	0	Otherwise		
MARRIED	1	If married	.8374	.3690
	0	Otherwise		
FULL	1	If prelayoff job was full time (35 hours or more per week)	.4643	.4987
	0	Otherwise		
MALE I	1	If male 20–25 years of age	.0612	.2396
	0	Otherwise		
FEMALE I	1	If female 20–25 years of age	.0653	.2470
	0	Otherwise		
MALE II	1	If male 26–30 years of age	.0518	.2217
	0	Otherwise		
FEMALE II	1	If famale 26–30 years of age	.0554	.2287
	0	Otherwise		
MALE III	1	If male 31–40 years of age	.0882	.2835
	0	Otherwise		
FEMALE III	1	If female 31–40 years of age	.0963	.2951
	0	Otherwise		

Variable		Description	Mean	Standard Deviation
FEMALE IV	1	If female 41–55 years of age	.1027	.3036
	0	Otherwise		
MALE V	1	If male more than 55 years of age	.0621	.2413
	0	Otherwise		
FEMALE V	1	If female more than 55 years of age	.0891	.2849
	0	Otherwise		
IND_j	1	If prelayoff industry of participation is industry j [$j=1, 2, \ldots 10$, where:		
		1 = mining	.0074	.0857
		2 = construction	.0423	.2014
		3 = transportation	.0468	.2113
		4 = wholesale	.1240	.3296
		5 = finance	.0404	.1969
		6 = private services	.0523	.2226
		7 = medicine	.0522	.2226
		8 = education	.0576	.2329
		9 = other professional services	.0196	.1385
		10 = public administration]	.0318	.1755
	0	If $j=11$ (manufacturing)		
OCC_k	1	If prelayoff occupation is occupation k[$k=1, 2, \ldots 5$, where:		
		1 = trades	.0834	.2765
		2 = plant labor	.1048	.3063
		3 = services	.0819	.2742
		4 = technical assistants]	.2046	.4034
	0	If $k=5$ (professionals and administrators)		
REG_p	1	If respondent resides in region p[$p=1, \ldots 4$, where:		
		1 = Midwest	.2576	.4373
		2 = West	.2156	.4112
		3 = South	.3088	.4620
	0	If $p=4$ (Northeast)		

Note: n = 17,283 (for all probit models).

hypotheses are reported in Tables 4 and 5. The complete results of the estimated participation functions, including the probit coefficients and their associated asymptotic *t* ratios, are presented in Appendix Table 2.

Results

The influence of working lifecycle stage on the likelihood of participation in formal on-the-job training is examined by considering the difference in the likelihood of participation between workers in stage IV of the working lifecycle and other working lifecycle cohorts, *ceteris paribus*. The results of this analysis for white males and white females are presented in Table 4.[17]

As expected, male and female workers in stage V of the working lifecycle are significantly less likely to participate in formal on-the-job training than workers in stage IV, *ceteris paribus*. In addition, among white males, workers in earlier stages of the working lifecycle were significantly more likely to receive formal on-the-job training than comparable workers in stage IV. Surprisingly, white women in earlier stages of the working lifecycle do not appear to have a significantly higher likelihood of engaging in formal on-the-job training than white females in stage IV. The lone exception is that stage III females are more likely to participate in formal nonfirm-financed on-the-job training than comparable stage IV women.

The results reported in Table 5 reveal that among whites gender does not typically appear to influence the likelihood of participating in formal on-the-job training. Only in the case of stage IV workers is there a significant difference in the likelihood of participation. Surprisingly, the results suggest that women in stage IV are *more* likely to receive formal on-the-job training than their male counterparts in stage IV.[18]

The estimated coefficient on the black dummy variable in all three of the participation functions estimated is insignificant. This suggests that blacks overall are no more or less likely to receive formal on-the-job training than comparable whites.[19]

Additional schooling significantly increased an individual's likelihood of participation in formal on-the-job training. Marital status does not appear to influence the likelihood of receiving formal on-the-job training.

As hypothesized, full-time employment had a positive and significant impact on the likelihood of acquiring formal firm-financed on-the-job training, while part-time work status exhibited no discernible impact on the likelihood of receiving nonfirm-financed training. The findings also suggest that occupation, industry, and region of employment influence the likelihood of participation.

Table 4. Working Life Cycle Differences in the Probability of Participating in Formal On-the-Job Training

		t-Statistic for Difference Between Comparison Groups in the Probability of Participating in Formal On-the-Job Training					
		All Training		*Nonfirm-Financed Training*		*Firm-Financed Training*	
Comparison Groups	*Expected Sign*	*Male*	*Female*	*Male*	*Female*	*Male*	*Female*
$\hat{\beta}$(STAGE I)– $\hat{\beta}$(STAGE IV)	+	2.18*	.40	.33	.72	2.44*	.10
$\hat{\beta}$(STAGE II)– $\hat{\beta}$(STAGE IV)	+	5.25*	.57	2.86*	.815	4.62*	.09
$\hat{\beta}$(STAGE III)– $\hat{\beta}$(STAGE IV)	+	6.04*	1.37*	3.78*	1.68*	4.80*	.75
$\hat{\beta}$(STAGE V)– $\hat{\beta}$(STAGE IV)	–	–2.91*	–4.20*	–1.64*	–2.47*	–2.56*	–3.22*

* Significance at $\alpha = .1$ level.
Stage I: individuals 20–25 years of age.
Stage II: individuals 26–30 years of age.
Stage III: individuals 31–40 years of age.
Stage IV: individuals 41–55 years of age.
Stage V: individuals more than 55 years of age.

Table 5. Gender Differences Amongst Whites in the Probability of Participating in Formal On-the-Job Training

		t-Statistic for Difference Between the Comparison Groups in the Probability of Participating in Formal On-the-Job Training		
Comparison Groups	*Expected Sign*	*All Training*	*Nonfirm-Financed Training*	*Firm-Financed Training*
$\hat{\beta}$ (MALE I) – $\hat{\beta}$ (FEMALE I)	+	1.11	−1.18	−.57
$\hat{\beta}$ (MALE II) – $\hat{\beta}$ (FEMALE II)	+	.30	.10	.48
$\hat{\beta}$ (MALE III) – $\hat{\beta}$ (FEMALE III)	+	−.70	−.54	−.57
$\hat{\beta}$ (MALE IV) – $\hat{\beta}$ (FEMALE IV)	+	−4.48*	−1.63*	−4.13*
$\hat{\beta}$ (MALE V) – $\hat{\beta}$ (FEMALE V)	+	−.23	.67	.86

* Significance at $\alpha = .1$ level.
Stage I: individuals 20–25 years of age.
Stage II: individuals 26–30 years of age.
Stage III: individuals 31–40 years of age.
Stage IV: individuals 41–55 years of age.
Stage V: individuals more than 55 years of age.

Duration of Formal On-the-Job Training

The subset of individuals that *actually* participated in formal on-the-job training may be used to examine the impact of working lifecycle stage, gender, and race on the *duration* of program participation. The set of variables used to investigate these hypotheses is identical to that used in examining the likelihood of participation. Moreover, the expected influence of these variables on the duration of formal on-the-job training is consistent with their expected effects on the likelihood of participation.

Empirical Procedures

To test the set of hypotheses specified earlier regarding the impact of working lifecycle position, gender, and race on the duration of formal on-the-job training accumulated, linear models were estimated by ordinary least squares. In order to account for the possibility of differences in the characteristics of the sets of individuals that participated in formal training programs and those that did not, the "corrected" inverse Mills ratio, calculated from the likelihood of participation equation, is included in the associated estimated duration equation. Interestingly, the estimated coefficient on the inverse Mills ratio in all of the formal on-the-job training duration equations was insignificant. This result suggests, unexpectedly, that there are no statistical differences in the characteristics of those that do and do not participate in formal on-the-job training. Consequently, it was dropped from the estimated equations, and the statistical nonlinearity of the recursive two equation system ensures identification. Thus, the following models were estimated.

$$\left.\begin{array}{l} TOTTRAIN \quad (4) \\ FIRMFIN \quad (5) \\ NONFIRMFIN \quad (6) \end{array}\right\} = f(SCHOOLING,\ RACE,\ MARRIED,\ FULL,\ GENDER\text{-}WORKING\ LIFECYCLE\ STAGE_i,\ IND_j,\ OCC_k,\ REGION_p)$$

Variable definitions, means, and standard deviations appear in Table 6.

The typical training program participant received 9.74 weeks of training, while nonfirm-financed training program participants accumulated 16.17 weeks of training and firm-financed training participants acquired 5.70 weeks of training. Appendix Table 4 presents mean weeks of participation by gender and working lifecycle position for various types of training. For instance, the average female in stage III of her working lifecycle who engages

Table 6. Variable Definitions, Means and Standard Deviations: Regression Models of the Extent of Participation in Formal On-the-Job Training

Variable	Description	All Training		Nonfirm-Financed Training		Firm-Financed Training	
		Mean	Standard Deviation	Mean	Standard Deviation	Mean	Standard Deviation
TOTTRAIN	total number of weeks of formal on-the-job training received in 1982 or 1983	9.739	18.021				
NONFIRMFIN	total number of weeks of non-firm formal financed on-the-job training received in 1982 or 1983			16.165	22.816		
FIRMFIN	total number of weeks of firm-financed formal on-the-job training received in 1982 or 1983					5.695	12.743
SCHOOLING	total number of years of schooling completed	15.025	2.322	15.300	2.414	14.977	2.294
BLACK	1 if race is black 0 otherwise	.068	.253	.057	.233	.072	.258
MARRIED	1 if married 0 otherwise	.796	.403	.778	.416	.813	.390
FULL	1 if prelayoff job was full 0 otherwise	.749	.434	.636	.482	.806	.396
GENDER-STAGE$_i$							
MALE I	1—if male stage I, 0—otherwise	.059	.236	.047	.212	.061	.240
FAMALE I	1—if female stage I, 0—otherwise	.091	.287	.108	.311	.084	.277
MALE II	1—if male stage II, 0—otherwise	.091	.287	.081	.273	.094	.292
FEMALE II	1—if female stage II, 0—otherwise	.080	.271	.088	.283	.075	.264
MALE III	1—if male stage III, 0—otherwise	.173	.378	.165	.372	.178	.383

FEMALE III	1—if female stage III, 0—otherwise	.165	.370	.205	.405	.150	.358
FEMALE IV	1—if female stage IV, 0—otherwise	.119	.324	.104	.306	.124	.330
MALE V	1—if male stage V, 0—otherwise	.004	.060	.007	.082	.002	.042
FEMALE V	1—if female stage V, 0—otherwise	.004	.069	.003	.058	.005	.072
IND_j	1 If prelayoff industry of participation is industry $j[j=1, 2, \ldots 10$, where:						
	1 = mining	.012	.109	.034	.058	.016	.124
	2 = construction	.046	.209	.037	.189	.047	.212
	3 = transportation	.076	.265	.034	.181	.096	.295
	4 = wholesale	.133	.339	.148	.356	.122	.328
	5 = finance	.083	.276	.074	.262	.091	.288
	6 = private services	.065	.247	.091	.288	.051	.219
	7 = medicine	.129	.335	.162	.369	.122	.328
	8 = education	.104	.305	.131	.338	.091	.288
	9 = other professional services	.036	.187	.044	.205	.033	.179
	10 = public administration]	.089	.285	.051	.219		
	0 If $j=11$ (manufacturing)						
OCC_k	1 If prelayoff occupation is occupation $k\,[k=1, 2, \ldots 5$, where:						
	1 = trades	.106	.308	.061	.239	.122	.328
	2 = plant labor	.065	.247	.071	.257	.059	.236
	3 = services	.106	.308	.145	.353	.087	.283
	4 = technical assistants]	.315	.464	.269	.444	.335	.472
	0 If $k=5$ (professionals and administrators)						
REG_p	1 If respondent resides in region $p[p=1, \ldots 4$, where:						
	1 = Midwest	.276	.447	.263	.441	.283	.451
	2 = West	.263	.441	.317	.466	.244	.430
	3 = South	.295	.456	.256	.437	.312	.464
	0 If $p=4$ (Northeast)						
	Total number (n)	870		297		573	

in formal nonfirm-financed training acquires 21.7 weeks of training. The data suggest that while relatively few workers received formal on-the-job training, those that did acquired on average a considerable amount. It is also possible that on-the-job training of an informal nature occurs to a much greater extent than formal on-the-job training.

Results

The regression coefficients and their associated *t* statistics for the factors expected to influence the duration of formal on-the-job training are presented in Appendix Table 3. Once again, only the results pertaining to specified sets of gender-working lifecycle stage dummy variable pairs on the duration of program participation are reported in the text.

The influence of working lifecycle position on the duration of formal on-the-job training participation is examined by evaluating differences in the duration of participation between stage IV workers and workers in other working lifecycle cohorts, *ceteris paribus*.

White male workers in earlier working lifecycle stages appear to acquire more weeks of training than their stage IV counterparts (Table 7). In four of the nine categories investigated, stage I and stage III vis-a-vis stage IV, the difference is significant for all but firm-financed male workers. Interestingly the results reveal that workers in a later stage of their working lifecycle who receive formal on-the-job training acquired an amount that is not statistically different than that received by the workers in stage IV. With respect to white females, working lifecycle position does not appear to influence the amount of training acquired. Surprisingly, among program participants there are no gender differences in the amount of training accumulated (Table 8).

The estimated coefficient on the black dummy variable in all of the duration of training equations is positive and significant (see Appendix Table 3). This finding surprisingly indicates that among training program participants blacks receive significantly more training than their white counterparts. Additional schooling significantly increased the amount of nonfirm-financed training but did not appear to influence the accumulation of firm-financed skills acquired on the job. Married individuals acquired significantly less formal nonfirm-financed training. Employment status does not influence duration of accumulation. The findings suggest that region, occupation, and industry of employment influence the duration of firm-financed training accumulated while only occupation appears to influence the extent of nonfirm-financed training.

Table 7. Working Life Cycle Differences in the Extent of Participating in Formal On-the-Job Training

Comparison Groups	*Expected Sign*	*t statistic for Difference between Comparison Groups in the Extent of Participation in Formal On-the-Job Training*					
		All Training		*Non-Firm-Financed Training*		*Firm-Financed Training*	
		MALE	*FEMALE*	*MALE*	*FEMALE*	*MALE*	*FEMALE*
$\hat{\beta}$ (STAGE I) – $\hat{\beta}$ (STAGE IV)	+	1.63*	.26	1.76*	−.21	1.19	.003
$\hat{\beta}$ (STAGE II) – $\hat{\beta}$ (STAGE IV)	+	1.02	.69	.87	1.13	.44	−.19
$\hat{\beta}$ (STAGE III) – $\hat{\beta}$ (STAGE IV)	+	2.18*	.56	1.81*	.61	1.11	−.20
$\hat{\beta}$ (STAGE V) – $\hat{\beta}$ (STAGE IV)	−	.25	−.12	.001	.24	.06	−.08

* Significance at $\alpha = .1$ level.
Stage I: individuals 20–25 years of age.
Stage II: individuals 26–30 years of age.
Stage III: individuals 31–40 years of age.
Stage IV: individuals 41–55 years of age.
Stage V: individuals more than 55 years of age.

Table 8. Gender Differences Amongst Whites in the Extent of Participating in Formal On-the-Job Training

Comparison Groups	*Expected Sign*	*t-Statistic for Difference Between the Comparison Groups in the Extent of Participating in Formal On-the-Job Training*		
		All Training	*Nonfirm-Financed Training*	*Firm-Financed Training*
$\hat{\beta}$(MALE I)–$\hat{\beta}$(FEMALE I)	+	.51	.63	.54
$\hat{\beta}$(MALE II)–$\hat{\beta}$(FEMALE II)	+	−.46	−.84	.17
$\hat{\beta}$(MALE III)–$\hat{\beta}$(FEMALE III)	+	.22	−.001	.54
$\hat{\beta}$(MALE IV)–$\hat{\beta}$(FEMALE IV)	+	−.68	.82	.49
$\hat{\beta}$(MALE V)–$\hat{\beta}$(FEMALE V)	+	−.01	−.35	.03

* Significance at $\alpha = .1$ level.
Stage I: individuals 20–25 years of age.
Stage II: individuals 26–30 years of age.
Stage III: individuals 31–40 years of age.
Stage IV: individuals 41–55 years of age.
Stage V: individuals more than 55 years of age.

Concluding Remarks

The 1981–1982 U.S. recession and increased international interdependence have led to renewed debate among policymakers, economists, and the public concerning the appropriate response to both domestically and foreign-produced displacement. Fairly comprehensive studies[20] have examined various aspects of this adjustment problem. All of these studies focus on the plight of workers displaced by changes in economic structure as well as rapid technological change, and analyze alternative public and private programs intended to facilitate worker adjustment. Not surprisingly, post-layoff training programs are a central component of many policy prescriptions, inasmuch as these programs have the capacity to reduce the severity of the dislocation problem.

On the other hand, the success of any policy, private or public, to mitigate *ex ante*, the problem of labor dislocation requires that policy makers have information regarding the alterable characteristics of workers that influence layoff status and/or reemployment. Because skill level is an alterable characteristic, it is unfortunate that little has been known about the effect of employed worker formal on-the-job training programs on the *future* likelihood of layoff.

This study reveals that participation by employed workers in formal firm- and nonfirm-financed on-the-job training programs significantly reduces the likelihood of layoff. These results suggest that *ex ante* policies aimed at skill enhancement via formal on-the-job training should facilitate a smoother adjustment process and possibly reduce the dislocation problem. In light of the fact that few workers appear to participate in employed worker formal on-the-job training programs, the potential of these programs to ease employment adjustment has gone largely untapped.

In light of the compensation and job security benefits expected to accompany the accumulation of formal on-the-job training, an interesting question is who participates in these training programs.

The literature on human capital accumulation suggests that advances in working lifecycle position should affect adveresely the likelihood of participation in formal on-the-job training. Our results for white males and females are consistent with this hypothesis. In addition, theoretical models of formal training accumulation suggest that males and whites are more likely to acquire training than comparable females and blacks. However, our results indicate that gender and race fail to influence significantly the probability of engaging in formal on-the-job training.[21] (The lone exception is that women in stage IV of the working lifecycle were more likely to participate in formal on-the-job training than their male counterparts).

Furthermore, among program participants, the extent of accumulation is significantly greater for blacks while being independent of gender and, in the case of females, working lifecycle stage. A number of possible explanations for these findings exist. For instance, women may use training as a vehicle to greater competitiveness in the labor market. The successful application of affirmative action programs in the training field also can account for these findings.

Notes

1. In this chapter we do not intend to present a theory of technological change based on alterations of the workforce skill level, although this is a reasonable hypotheses. We are simply illuminating potentially different characteristics of informal and formal on-the-job training. Indeed, in the empirical work, which spans a two-year period, we implicitly assume fixed technology.

2. For instance, one of the most noted studies of the economic impact of on-the-job training was conducted by Duncan and Hoffman (1979), using data from the Panel Study of Income Dynamics. The Panel asks workers about their *subjective* evaluation of the number of years of training needed to perform their job and their current level of *tenure*. Using this data, Duncan and Hoffman (1979) construct two measures of on-the-job training, one of which is continuous, "number of years of training completed," and one that is dichotomous, "still training." Number of years of training completed equals tenure as long as tenure does not exceed the subjective amount of training needed, and in this case "still training" is coded as one. If tenure exceeds the subjective evaluation, the number of years of training is simply the subjective value of training required and "still training" is coded zero. Although Duncan and Hoffman claim their measures are direct, they are clearly indirect, when using tenure as a proxy. When tenure exceeds the worker's perception of training necessary, their measures, although direct, are subjective. Furthermore, their measures reflect both *formal* and *informal* training. Using these measures of total training, they report that white males are more likely to participate in training and tend to receive substantially more training than females and blacks.

3. Malveaux (1984) argues that equalizing training opportunities, both formal and informal, is the key to minimizing racial unemployment differentials.

4. Hamermesh (1986) provides evidence that labor demand curves are more steeply sloped for classes of workers with greater skills, *ceteris paribus*.

5. See Kniesner and Goldsmith (1987) for a recent discussion of wage rigidity.

6. Changes in technology tend to alter the structure of the economy's demand for labor, reducing the relative demand for unskilled labor vis-a-vis more skilled workers. Such displacement is likely to result in greater unemployment for those with less on-the-job training, both formal and informal, because they are less mobile vertically (e.g., other jobs within the firm) and horizontally (e.g., jobs with different firms).

7. An important consequence of permanent job loss may be a reduction in the value of previous job tenure when reemployed. Empirical work by Neumann (1978), Kiefer and Neumann (1979), Hamermesh (1984), Podgursky and Swaim (1986), and Kletzer (1987) attribute the earnings loss associated with permanent job separation to be a loss of job specific skills.

8. The likelihood of layoff study is restricted to civilian, nonfarmer, nonteenagers, who are not self-employed and who participated in the labor force over the period 1979–1984.

9. Reynolds, Masters, and Moser (1987) examine data on annual earnings of U.S. male workers in various occupations at three points (1939, 1955, and 1981) in the postwar period. They report that the "rank order of incomes is about what one would expect" (p.198). In all three periods, professionals were at the top followed by salaried managers government officials, sales personnel, craft workers, clerical workers, operatives, and laborers.

10. The percent of U.S. workers engaged in formal on-the-job training is strikingly low in comparison to the level of formal training that appears to occur in developed western European countries. For instance, Germany, has a guaranteed formal training program of up to three years provided by the Employment Promotion Act of 1969 that most workers take advantage of. Moreover, according to Marshall and Briggs (1989) Germany is not out of step with training policies in other western European countries.

11. The appropriate test is -2 (log likelihood ratio) $\cong x^2(q)$, where q is the number of independent variables.

12. We also have examined the impact of formal on-the-job training on the duration of layoff unemployment. Since the data on unemployment duration are right censored, a hazard function that takes account of the censoring was specified and estimated to derive asymptotically consistent estimates of the impact of on-the-job training on unemployment duration. Of the 508 individuals in the sample experiencing a layoff, only 4 received formal nonfirm-financed on-the-job training, while 14 acquired some formal firm-financed on-the-job training. As a result, it is not possible to estimate the influence of nonfirm-financed on-the-job training on the duration of unemployment, while the findings with respect to firm-financed training should be considered suggestive. The results indicated that participation in firm-financed training significantly enhances the likelihood of existing unemployment which can be directly interpreted as reducing the duration of an unemployment spell.

13. Another factor contributing to this finding is that part-time workers on a lumpy work schedule may not view a decline in hours or an unexpected period of idleness as being laid off. If so, the group that experiences layoff is likely to be composed primarily of full-time workers.

14. For example, according to Mincer and Polachek (1974), the expected work life of an average women at age 20 was 27.2 years in 1980, while the average man at age 20 could be expected to work for 36.8 years in 1980.

15. See Polachek and Horvath (1977) for evidence to this effect.

16. In the study investigating the impact of formal on-the-job training on unemployment, only training prior to layoff is relevant. Thus, individuals that received training after a layoff experience as well as those that engaged in training during the same year as a layoff experience were not considered to have participated in training. Since we have no information indicating whether training came before or after a layoff experience during the same year, we assumed that it came afterward, biasing the case against training adversely impacting layoff likelihood. However, in the study of training participation, whether or not one engages in training is all that matters. Hence, a larger proportion of the sample is recorded as having engaged in formal on-the-job training in the training participation study.

17. The t statistics that appear in all of the tables concerning differences in dummy variable pairs are constructed as follows:

$$t = \frac{\hat{\beta}(Gender\text{-}WLCP)_i - \hat{\beta}(Gender\text{-}WLCP)_{i-1}}{\sqrt{\text{Variance } \hat{\beta}\{(Gender\text{-}WLCP)_i + \text{Variance } \hat{\beta}(Gender\text{-}WLCP)_{i-1} \pm 2 \text{ Covariance}\{\hat{\beta}(Gender\text{-}WLCP)_i), \hat{\beta}(Gender\text{-}WLCP)_{i-1})\}}}$$

where $WLCP$ denotes working lifecycle position.

18. Lazear (1979b) reports significantly higher wage growth for women in a study of young workers. He attributes this difference to greater accumulation of on-the-job training for women

relative to men. Our finding using direct data on *formal* on-the-job training only support the hypothesis that women are more likely to receive formal on-the-job training than comparable men during stage IV of the working lifecycle.

19. Based on his analysis of wage growth, Lazear (1979a) suggests that blacks accumulate less total (e.g., informal plus formal) on-the-job training than comparable whites. Our results using direct data on formal on-the-job training do not support the hypothesis that blacks are less likely to receive formal on-the-job training than whites.

20. Among the more notable of these studies are those completed by the Office of Technology Assessment (1986) and the recent study on Technology and Employment produced under the auspices of the National Academy of Sciences by Cyert and Mowery (1987).

21. The lone exception is that women in stage IV of the working lifecycle were more likely to participate in formal on-the-job training than their male counterparts.

References

Abraham, K., and Farber, H.S. 1986. "Job Duration, Seniority, and Earnings." National Bureau of Economic Research, Working Paper Series, No. 1819.

Altonji, J., and Shakotko, R. 1985. "Do Wages Rise with Job Seniority?" National Bureau of Economic Research, Working Paper Series, No. 1616.

Bartel, A.P., and Borjas, G.J. 1981. "Wage Growth and Job Turnover: An Empirical Analysis." In *Studies in Labor Markets*, National Bureau of Economic Research, ed. Sherwin Rosen, 65–90. Chicago: University of Chicago Press.

Becker, G.S. 1962. "Investment in Human Capital: A Theoretical Analysis. "*Journal of Political Economy* (Suppl.), 70(5), Part 2: 9–49.

Blau, F., and Andrea Beller, A. 1984. "Trends in Earnings Differentials by Sex and Race: 1971–1981." (Unpublished paper, University of Illinois.

Blau, F.D., and Kahn, L.M. 1981. "Causes and Consequences of Layoffs." *Economic Inquiry* 19(2): 270–296.

Blinder, A.S. 1973. "Wage Discrimination—Reduced Form and Structural Estimates." *Journal of Human Resources* 8(4): 436–455.

Coleman, 1987. "Unemployment Behavior: Evidence From the CPS Work Experience Survey." National Bureau of Economic Research.

Council of Economic Advisors. 1987. *Economic Indicators.* Washington, DC: U.S. Government Printing Office.

Corcoran, M., and Duncan, G. 1979. "Work History, Labor Force Attachment, and Earnings Differences Between the Races and Sexes. "*Journal of Human Resources* 14(1): 3–20.

Cyert, R.M., and Mowery, D.C., eds. 1987. *Technology and Employment: Innovation and Growth in the U.S. Economy.* Washington, DC: National Academy Press.

Duncan, G., and Hoffman, S. 1979. "On-the-Job Training and Earnings Differences by Race and Sex. *Review of Economic and Statistics* 61(4): 594–603.

Dynarski, M., and Sheffrin, S.M. 1987, "New Evidence on the Cyclical Behavior of Unemployment Durations." In *Unemployment and the Structure of Labor Markets*, K. Long and J.S. Leonard, eds. New York: Basil Blackwell.

Flaim, P. and Seghal, E, "Displaced Workers of 1979–1983: How Well Have They Fared?" U.S. Department of Labor Bureau of Labor Statistics, Bulletin 2240, Washington, DC.

Flanagan, R.J. 1974. "Labor Force Experience, Job Turnover and Racial Wage Differentials." *Review of Economics and Statistics* 56(Nov.): 521–529.

Hamermesh, D.S., 1984. "The Costs of Worker Displacement."National Bureau of Economic Research Working Paper Series No. 1495.

————. 1986, "The Demand For Labor in the Long Run." In *Handbook of Labor Economics*, Vol. I, eds. O.C. Ashenfelter and R. Layard. New York: Elsevier Science Publishers.

Jacobson, L.S. 1978. "Earnings Losses of Workers Displaced from Manufacturing Industries." In *The Impact of International Trade and Investment on Employment*, ed. William G. Dewald, Washington, DC: U.S. Department of Labor, Bureau of International Labor Affairs.

Kiefer, N.M., and Neumann, G.R. 1979. "An Empirical Job-Search Model, with a Test of the Constant Reservation Wage Hypothesis." *Journal of Political Economy* 87(1): 89–107.

Kiker, B.F., and Roberts, B. 1984. "The Durability of Human Capital: Some New Evidence." *Economic Inquiry* 22(2): 269–281.

Kletzer, L.G. 1987. "Job Tenure and Earnings After Permanent Job Loss." William College Working Paper.

Kniesner, T.J., and Goldsmith, A.H. 1987. "A Survey of Alternative Models of the Aggregate U.S. Labor Marker." *Journal of Economic Literature* 25(3): 1241–1280.

Lazear, E, 1979a. "The Narrowing of Black-White Wage Differentials ins Illusory." *American Economic Review* 69(4): 553–564.

————. 1979b. "Male-Female Wage Differentials: Has the Government Had Any Effect?" In *Women in the Labor Market*, Cynthia B. Lloyd et al., eds., 331–351. New York: Columbia University Press.

Malveaux, J. 1984. "Theoretical Explanations of the Persistence of Racial Unemployment Differentials." In *Labor Economics: Modern Views*, W. Darity, Jr., ed., 91–118. Boston: Kluwer Press.

Marshall, F.R. and Briggs, V., Jr. 1989. *Labor Economics: Theory, Institutions, and Public Policy,* 6th ed. Homewood, IL: Irwin.

Marshall, R.C., and Zarkin, G.A. 1987. "The Effect of Job Tenure on Wage Offers." *Journal of Labor Economics* 5(3): 301–324.

Maxwell, N.L., and D'Amico, R. 1986. "Employment and Wage Effects of Involuntary Job Separations: Male-Female Differences." *American Economic Review* 76(2): 373–377.

Mincer, J. 1962. "On-the-Job Training: Costs, Returns and Some Implications." *Journal of Political Economy* (Suppl.) 70(5), Part 2: 50–79.

Mincer, J., and Jovanovic, B. 1981. "Labor Mobility and Wages." In *Studies in Labor Markets*, Sherwin Rosen, ed., 21–63. National Bureau of Economic Research. Chicago: University of Chicago Press.

Mincer, J., and Polachek, S. 1974. "Family Investments in Human Capital: Earnings of Women." *Journal of Political Economy*. 82(2): 576–588.

Neumann, G.R. 1978. "The Labor Market Adjustments of Trade Displaced Workers: The Evidence from the Trade Adjustment Assistance Program." In *Research in Labor Economics*, Vol. 2, Ronald Ehrenberg, ed., 353–381. Greenwich, CT: JAI Press.

Office of Technology Assessment. 1986. *Technology and Structural Unemployment: Reemploying Displaced Adults*, OTA–ITE–250. Washington, DC: U.S. Government Printing Office.

Oi, W. 1962. "Labor as a Quasi-Fixed Factor of Production." *Journal of Political Economy* (Suppl.) 70(5), Part 2: 538–555.

Parnex, H.S., Gagen, M., and King, R. 1981. "The Incidence and Impact of Job Loss Among Long-Service Workers." In *Work and Retirement: A Longitudinal Study of Men,* H.S. Parnes, ed. Cambridge; MIT Press.

Parsons, D.O. 1972. "Specific Human Capital: An Application to Quit Rates and Layoff Rates." *Journal of Political Economy* 80(6): 1120–1143.

————. D.O. 1977. "Models of Labor Market Turnover: A Theoretical and Empirical Survey." In *Research in Labor Economics*, Vol. 1, Ronald Ehrenberg, ed., 185–223. Greenwich, CT: JAI Press.

Podgursky, M., and Swaim, P. 1986. "Job Displacement and Earnings Loss: Evidence from the Displaced Worker Survey." Working Paper, University of Massachusetts.

Polachek, S., and Horvath, F. 1977. "A Life Cycle Approach to Migration." In *Research in Labor Economics*, Vol. 1, Ronald Ehrenberg, ed. Greenwich, CT: JAI Press.

Reynolds, L.G., Masters, S.H., and Colletta H. Moser, C.H. 1987. *Economics of Labor*. Englewood Cliffs, NJ: Prentice-Hall.

Rosen, S. 1966. "Short-Run Employment Variation on Class 1 Railroads in the U.S., 1947–1963." Doctoral dissertation, University of Chicago.

Ruhm, C. 1987. "The Extent and Persistence of Unemployment Following Permanent Quits and Layoffs." Working Paper, Boston University.

Shapiro, D., and Sandell, S. 1985. "Age Discrimination in Wages and Displaced Old Men." *Southern Economic Journal* 52(1): 90–102.

Williams, R. 1984. "The Methodology and Practice of Modern Labor Economics: A Critique." In *Labor Economics: Modern Views*, William Darity, Jr., ed. Boston, MA: Kluwer Publishing.

Appendix Table 1

$$H_0: \quad \underset{(-)}{\hat{\beta}\,(\text{DNONFIRMFIN})} - \underset{(-)}{\hat{\beta}\,(\text{DFIRMFIN})} = 0$$

$$H_A: \quad \underset{(-)}{\hat{\beta}\,(\text{DNONFIRMFIN})} - \underset{(-)}{\hat{\beta}\,(\text{DFIRMFIN})} \begin{array}{l} > 0 - 1 \text{ tailed} \\ \neq 0 - 2 \text{ tailed} \end{array}$$

$$t = \frac{-.425 - (-.219)}{\sqrt{\text{Variance } \hat{\beta}\,(\text{DNONFIRMFINO}) + \text{Variance } \hat{\beta}\,(\text{DFIRMFIN}) \pm \text{Covariance}}}$$

$$t = \frac{-.425 - (-.219)}{\sqrt{.083 + .018 - .0013}} = -\frac{.206}{.315}$$

$t = .653$. Thus cannot reject H_0

Appendix Table 2. Probit Models of Formal On-the-Job Training Participation

	All Training (Dep. Var. = DTRAINING)		*Nonfirm-Financed Training (Dep. Var. = DNONFIRMFIN)*		*Firm-Financed Training (Dep. Var. = DFIRMFIN)*	
Variable	*Estimated Coefficient*	*Asymptotic t statistic*	*Estimated Coefficient*	*Asymptotic t statistic*	*Estimated Coefficient*	*Asymptotic t statistic*
SCHOOLING (+)	.055	6.48*	.062	5.11*	.046	4.76*
BLACK (−)	.087	1.13	.003	.02	.102	1.17
MARRIED (?)	−.034	−.68	−.083	−1.17	.028	.48
FULL (?)	.290	6.76*	.012	.21	.410	8.21*
MALE I (+)	.191	2.18*	.045	.37	.240	2.44*
FEMALE I (−)	.343	4.40*	.288	2.66*	.328	3.66*
MALE II (+)	.401	5.26*	.321	2.86*	.393	4.62*
FEMALE II (−)	.363	4.64*	.303	2.79*	.327	3.61*
MALE III (+)	.382	6.04*	.348	3.78*	.339	4.70*
FEMALE III (−)	.456	7.13*	.433	4.95*	.406	5.52*
FEMALE IV (−)	.303	4.48*	.162	1.63	.315	4.13*
MALE V (−)	−.597	−.29	−.412	−1.64	−.720	−2.56*
FEMALE V (−)	−.533	−.30	−.692	−2.18*	.376	2.09*
MINING (?)	.317	1.83*	−.093	−.25	.086	1.84*
CONSTRUCTION (?)	.137	1.49	.180	1.26	.388	4.66*
TRANSPORTATION (−)	.333	4.26*	.042	.30	.025	.34

WHOLESALE (–)	.097	1.54*	.209	2.33*	.370	4.25*
FINANCE (–)	.403	5.08*	.399	3.44*	.034	.36
PRIVATE SERVICE (–)	.179	2.28*	.344	3.30*	.436	5.55*
MEDICAL (–)	.512	7.42*	.567	6.12*	.170	2.06*
EDUCATION (–)	.263	3.68*	.350	3.62*	.171	1.39
OTHER PROFESSIONAL SERVICES (–)	.269	.25	.372	2.62*	.658	7.66*
PUBLIC ADMINISTRATION (–)	.598	7.42*	.276	2.12*	.186	2.39*
TRADES (?)	.160	2.26*	–.024	–.21	–.186	–2.15*
PLANT LABOR (?)	–.109	–1.47	.039	.37	–.041	–.50
SERVICES (?)	.072	1.05	.171	1.88*	.085	1.55
TECHNICAL ASSISTANT (?)	.076	1.56	.004	.06	.188	3.10*
MIDWEST (?)	.175	3.29*	.119	1.55	.134	2.13*
WEST (+)	.174	3.21*	.232	3.09*	.137	2.28*
SOUTH (+)	.121	2.29*	.074	.96	–3.289	–18.66*
INTERCEPT (?)	–3.144	–20.55*	–3.44	–15.72*		
Total number	17,283		17,283		17,283	
(–2 log likeliood ratio)	297.5		759.0		748.0	

* Significant at the $\alpha = .1$ level.

Appendix Table 3. Regression Models of the Extent of Formal On-the-Job Training

	All Training (Dep. Var. = TOTTRAIN)		*Nonfirm-Financed Training (Dep. Var. = NONFIRMFIN)*		*Firm-Financed Training (Dep. Var. = FIRMFIN)*	
Variable	*Estimated Coefficient*	*Asymptotic t statistic*	*Estimated Coefficient*	*Asymptotic t statistic*	*Estimated Coefficient*	*Asymptotic t statistic*
SCHOOLING (+)	.923	.19	1.212	1.67*	.106	.37
BLACK (−)	7.581	2.53*	20.902	2.90*	3.310	1.33*
MARRIED (?)	−4.473	1.28	−6.667	−1.76*	−.630	−.41
FULL (?)	1.083	.04	2.758	.89	.112	.08
MALE I (+)	5.188	.29	14.267	1.76*	3.427	1.19
FEMALE I (−)	4.869	.16	6.368	1.03	1.092	.46
MALE II (+)	3.678	.10	5.373	.87	1.003	.44
FEMALE II (−)	6.597	.11	13.777	2.34*	.334	.14
MALE III (+)	6.689	.19	9.040	1.81*	2.118	1.12
FEMALE III (−)	6.423	.16	9.048	1.91*	.315	.16
FEMALE IV (−)	2.886	.11	4.568	.82	1.040	.49
MALE V (−)	.755	.01	.019	.00	.840	.06
FEMALE V (−)	1.712	.03	10.211	.45	.382	.05
MINING (?)	−9.286	−.34	−45.410	−1.89*	6.534	1.47
CONSTRUCTION (?)	−2.350	−.18	−6.010	−.74	−1.382	−.50
TRANSPORTATION (−)	−6.639	−.22	−11.181	−1.39	−6.210	−2.92*
WHOLESALE (−)	1.114	.12	3.764	.73	−3.603	2.80*

FINANCE (−)	−.223	−.01	−5.180	−.73	−1.453	−.66
PRIVATE SERVICE (−)	−3.949	−.23	−4.925	−.85	−5.273	−1.96
MEDICAL (−)	2.080	.05	1.454	.20	−2.930	−1.46*
EDUCATION (−)	.456	.02	−1.034	−.20	−3.096	−1.41*
OTHER PROFESSIONAL SERVICES (−)	.207	.01	−0.404	−.07	−3.837	−1.21*
PUBLIC ADMINISTRATION (−)	.560	.01	6.511	.92	−3.974	−1.89*
TRADES (?)	9.372	.63	21.350	2.96*	5.016	2.45*
PLANT LABOR (?)	6.656	.62	13.564	2.22*	2.267	.87
SERVICES (?)	4.988	.71	.909	.18	5.731	2.58*
TECHNICAL ASSISTANT (?)	.186	.03	1.336	.33	.415	.30
MIDWEST (?)	−4.838	−.30	−1.087	−.26	−3.776	−2.25*
WEST (+)	−3.436	−.22	−2.453	−.60	−3.990	−2.30*
SOUTH (+)	−2.110	−.19	.462	.92	−.960	−.57
INTECEPT (?)	−14.300	−.04	−8.178	−.64	7.086	1.33
Total number						
n	870		297		573	
F	1.99		1.603		1.44	
R^2	.072		.153		.074	

* Significant at the $\alpha = .1$ level.

Appendix Table 4. Mean Weeks of Formal On-the-Job Training Received for Training Participants by Gender and Working Lifecycle Position

	All Training Mean	*Nonfirm-Financed Training Mean*	*Firm-Financed Training Mean*
MALE I	14.73	29.21	8.94
FEMALE I	9.18	14.47	5.64
MALE II	10.26	18.27	6.26
FEMALE II	11.22	21.71	5.21
MALE III	11.03	19.46	6.66
FEMALE III	9.39	15.56	5.32
MALE IV	6.44	6.92	6.99
FEMALE IV	6.67	11.66	5.00
MALE V	3.83	5.50	.50
FEMALE V	5.88	10.00	4.50

4 EMPIRICAL TESTS OF LABOR MARKET EQUILIBRIUM: AN EVALUATION

J. HECKMAN
T. MACURDY

For good reason there is widespread professional interest in the theory of unemployment. Unemployment in OECD countries is at an all-time postwar high. The unemployment rate in France has increased each year for the past 14 years. Mean durations of unemployment have increased in the United States over the past decade. The data indicate that measured unemployment is an important fact of economic life. However, the causes of the rise in unemployment are not clearly understood.

Numerous theoretical models have been set forth to explain the widely accepted "fact" of "excess supply" or "involuntary unemployment" in the labor market. A whole field of disequilibrium economics and disequilibrium econometrics has come into existence to explain or measure involuntary unemployment and the working of disequilibrium economies. A growing literature in microeconomics has emerged that examines the evidence in support of disequilibrium in the labor market.

In a concise and elegant monograph, Malinvaud (1984) summarizes the available empirical evidence. He concludes that "permanent market clearing is an untenable hypothesis," that "many . . . spells of unemployment are too long to result from the voluntary behavior of job seekers" and that the systematic widespread use of disequilibrium forecasting models provides "a very serious proof that the disequilibrium hypothesis is the correct one to make."

This chapter challenges the presumption that underlies this emerging empirical enterprise—that "equilibrium" or "disequilibrium" models of the labor market are testable against models constructed within the competing paradigm under credible conditions. We claim that the available empirical evidence is consistent with either point of view. One reason for this state of affairs is that equilibrium theories taken as a group are tautological even though a particular equilibrium theory may not be. A "soft protective belt" of *plausible* omitted (unobserved) variables always can be erected to rationalize any empirical outcome. To penetrate this belt requires much sharper disequilibrium theory, agreement on what constitutes an acceptable equilibrium theory, and better data than have appeared to date. At this stage, the choice between equilibrium and disequilibrium frameworks is made on the basis of prior beliefs and tastes in methodological programs, and not on the basis of empirical evidence.

In arriving at this conclusion, we take a much broader definition of equilibrium than just the naive Walrasian model. Disequilibrium is usually defined in a negative way—as the absence of an equilibrium. Most often, disequilibrium is defined as the absence of a classical Walrasian equilibrium. In all of its guises, disequilibrium theory is the absence of a theory or a mechanism to explain the observed state of affairs. Once a mechanism explaining an economy is developed, the labels of "equilibrium" or "disequilibrium" become irrelevant. For each mechanism producing unemployment and rationing workers to jobs, an appropriate policy for reducing the unemployment is indicated. The misleading aspect of recent discussions about "disequilibrium" is that a theoretically and empirically undefined concept is used to advocate certain macro policies.

The appropriate way to study unemployment is to understand labor market mechanisms. A search for mechanisms and not tests of disequilibrium is required to develop useful policies for lowering unemployment.

The plan of this chapter is to examine three widely cited empirical tests of equilibrium in the labor market. We demonstrate the fundamental ambiguity in the evidence obtained from these tests. Our objective is not to emphasize technical errors in the published work. Rather we seek to establish interpretive ambiguity. Under certain conditions which we will make precise, there are valid tests of the disequilibrium hypothesis. At issue is the credibility of these conditions and the robustness of the tests to plausible equilibrium alternatives. Also at issue is the inherent ambiguity about appropriate policy recommendations based on the evidence in support of disequilibrium.

Evidence in support of the disequilibrium point of view falls into three categories of studies: (1) those claiming to find evidence of constraints forcing workers off desired labor supply schedules; (2) those claiming that known estimates of labor supply elasticities are too small relative to known variability in wages for a market clearing model to describe the aggregate data; and (3) those claiming that unemployment spells are "too long" for unemployment to be a voluntary phenomenon. We review each argument in the stated order. The chapter concludes with a summary of our conclusions.

Unemployment as a Constraint

The essence of this approach to testing for disequilibrium is captured by the following one-period model of labor supply under perfect certainty that ignores all taxes, transactions costs, and transfers, and that assumes workers are free to supply as many hours as they desire at a known parametric wage W. Given observed additional economic characteristics X and defining ϵ as a variable representing unobserved characteristics relevant to labor supply, desired hours of work h derived from neoclassical theory are described by

$$h = h(W, X, \epsilon). \tag{1}$$

Ashenfelter (1979, 1980) uses this framework in his influential analysis.

Involuntary unemployment is said to exist if among persons of *identical* W, X, ϵ some are forced off of their supply function (1). Defining h^0 as observed hours of work, a labor market constraint is said to be operative if $h \neq h^0$. Letting $h - h^0 \equiv U_I$, we may write observed hours of work as

$$h^0 = (W, X, \epsilon) - U_I. \tag{2}$$

In this literature, the mechanism for determining the amount of involuntary unemployment experienced by the individual, U_I, is left unspecified. Operationally, U_I is in fact assumed to be fixed outside of the model and to be econometrically exogenous with respect to the arguments of h.[1]

For two reasons, reported hours of unemployment, U_R, may differ from U_I. First, persons who face constraints may drop out of the labor force so that they do not appear among the reported unemployed. Second, some unemployment may be voluntary, arising in response to incentives from government programs or as a consequence of voluntary mobility decisions. These considerations suggest the following empirical specification implemented by Ashenfelter:

$$h^0 = h(W, X, \epsilon) - \theta U_R \tag{3}$$

where $\theta = U_I / U_R$.

If all of the variables in equation (3) were known, regression evidence that $\theta = 1$ is said to indicate that all reported unemployment is involuntary unemployment. Evidence that $\theta = 0$ is said to indicate that all reported unemployment is voluntary. "U_R" should contribute nothing to the fit of the equation if there is no involuntary unemployment. Estimating a linear expenditure system version of equation (3) on aggregate data, Ashenfelter (1980) finds that $\theta = .5$ and concludes that 50 percent of reported unemployment is involuntary.

A test of $\theta = 0$ is a valid test of disequilibrium if ϵ is identical for everyone and W and X are known for everyone. Provided that the functional form of h is known, desired hours of work in an equilibrium setting are perfectly forecastable. Any discrepancy between desired and observed hours of work must be due to disequilibrium unemployment. To the extent that U_R *proxies* U_I, an estimated nonzero value of θ in equation (3) correctly indicates that there is disequilibrium in the labor market.

To the extent that W, X, or ϵ are measured with error (or not at all) and to the extent that measured unemployment depends on W, X, or ϵ, the test is compromised. If W, X, ϵ are measured with error (see Abowd and Card 1987 for recent evidence documenting the importance of measurement error), or are not measured at all, and if U_R depends on W, X, ϵ or variables that are correlated with them, U_R may contribute substantially to the fit of equation (3) because it proxies the true omitted variables. At issue, then, is the observability of the righthand-side variables in equation (1), and the plausibility of the concern about observability. "Omitted variables bias" or "measurement error" is always possible to invoke as an argument to discredit any empirical study. For this reason, it is not a compelling argument.

However, an equilibrium model with heterogenous agents provides a plausible, specific source of omitted variables which is central to equilibrium theories of the labor market. We focus on observability of W because more is known about it. In the remainder of this section we focus on the binary work—no work decision to simplify the exposition. Our discussion could easily be extended to handle interior solution cases and more general settings for the labor supply decision (e.g., uncertainty and lifecycle considerations), but little of analytical interest is gained by such extensions. In the binary case $U_R = h$ if the person doesn't work and $U_R = 0$ otherwise. If there is only one offered wage in the market as is postulated in the homogeneous agent paradigm adopted by many equilibrium and disequilibrium theorists, knowledge of that wage obtained by observing the wage of workers suffices to recover W. If wages are stable over time, using the wage in previous jobs to proxy the current wage is also appropriate. Both methods are used in the empirical literature on this topic—the latter in microeconomic studies of disequilibrium.

A large volume of research in labor economics in the past 15 years or so documents the presence of heterogeneity in wages over people at a point in time and over time for the same persons. Much of this heterogeneity is in unobservables. The R^2 of wage equations fit on commonly available micro-data rarely exceeds .30 for most demographic groups. The same is true for hours of work, unemployment, and job tenure equations. The sources of these unobserved differences are explored in numerous empirical and theoretical studies.

One major source of unobservables in equilibrium models arises from self-selection decisions by agents. If reservation wages (determined by nonmarket opportunities) exceed offered market wages, the offered wages are rejected and hence not observed. Precisely because the offered wage is not observed for the unemployed, we are free to pick any wage as the offered, but rejected, wage, for an unemployed person. In particular, we are free to choose a value of W (given X, ϵ) that makes U_I *identically zero* so that unemployment would contribute nothing to the fit of equation (2). In this sense unless a homogeneous agent model is invoked, the market clearing view is an irrefutable tautology, and tests against it have no power.

If offered wages are observed, but ϵ or X are not observed, the equilibrium theory is also tautologous. The reservation wage is that value of $W = W_R$ that solves

$$0 = h = h\ (W_R,\ X,\ \epsilon).$$

This implicit equation defines a function for W_R as a function of X, ϵ, provided that labor supply is not wage inelastic. Since X or ϵ are unobserved, we are free to pick values of those variables to rationalize an observed choice in hours of work as an equilibrium choice; that is, given any offered wage, we can rationalize observed hours of work by picking the reservation wage, or alternatively, X and ϵ, to set U_I in equation (2) identically to zero. Again within the testing framework advocated by Ashenfelter, the market clearing view is an irrefutable tautology, and tests against it have no power unless a homogeneous agent model is invoked. The central defect of the proposed test as viewed from a microeconomic perspective which recognizes the importance of heterogeneity is its dependence on the absence of crucial *plausible* unobserved variables that determine labor supply. If there are such variables, an equilibrium model can always be constructed to rationalize observed labor supply.

Another way to make this point notes that imputing the average wage of *workers* as the wage of nonworkers misspecifies the wage in equation (3) and compromises the proposed test unless both groups have the same average offered wage. Unemployment and nonemployment are virtually synonomous for prime-age males. Accordingly, U_R is a function of the discrepancy between the offered wage W and the reservation wage W_R. The probability that a prime-age male is unemployed is the probability that W_R exceeds W. Letting $f(W, W_R)$ denote the joint density of wages and reservation wages (assumed degenerate in a strong form of the representative consumer model), the probability of unemployment is

$$Pr(person\ unemployed) = P = \iint_{W_R \geq W} f(W, W_R)\,dW\,dW_R$$

and the expected wage of workers is

$$E(W \mid W > W_R) = \frac{\iint_{W \geq W_R} W f(W, W_R)\,dW\,dW_R}{\iint_{W \geq W_R} f(W, W_R)\,dW\,dW_R} = \frac{\iint_{W \geq W_R} W f(W, W_R)\,dW\,dW_R}{1 - P}.$$

Within a neoclassical framework that recognizes diversity in wage offers and nonmarket opportunities (as do theories of search and many theories of labor supply), the mean measured wage systematically depends on the probability of unemployment (P) in all but exceptional cases. Thus the *economics* of the neoclassical model suggests that in the presence of heterogeneous market wages, the wage in equation (3) is mismeasured for unemployed persons in a way that depends on U_R and, therefore, U_R (the mean of which is proportional to P) may contribute to the fit of h^0 even though there is no disequilibrium in the labor market.

Another way to make essentially the same point is to follow Lucas and Rapping (1969) and postulate that unemployment is one form of nonmarket time. Then we are entitled to write

$$U_R = U_R\,(W, X, \epsilon) \tag{4}$$

since the same constraints, preferences, and opportunities that determine h also determine U_R in their theory. If ϵ is unobserved, it is plausible that U_R

would contribute to the fit of equation (3) even if W and X were exactly measured because U_R proxies ϵ. A parallel story could be told if there were search unemployment as in the Burdett—Mortensen (1979) labor supply model. There are no plausible econometric exclusion restrictions (variables that would affect U_R and not h). Evidence of a statistically significant U_R in a regression estimate of equation (3) would merely indicate that there are unobservables common to hours of work and unemployment equations. Such a test has no power against an equilibrium alternative if worker heterogeneity is viewed as empirically relevant.

The issue here is deeper than the problem of missing data on offered wages. Even if data are available on individual perceptions of offered market and reservation wages, it would not be possible to use them to test whether unemployment is involuntary.

According to the disequilibrium point of view, a person is involuntarily unemployed if his/her reservation wage is less than his/her perceived market wage but the person is unable to work at that wage. Implicit in this view is the notion of inequity in the allocation of jobs. Identically situated persons have different market opportunities. Some unspecified mechanism prevents a person from obtaining a job at his/her perceived market wage. This view is more cogent if the list of acceptable jobs is restricted to those for which the agent is qualified. Otherwise any job (e.g., President of the United States) that the person would like to have but for which the person is unqualified would be a job from which a person is involuntarily excluded. Even with the argument amended to apply only to "relevant" jobs, the specification of the mechanism preventing the worker from obtaining desired jobs is critical. One needs to know the nature of the rationing mechanism in order to determine whether unemployment is involuntary. One must determine not only why the person is excluded from a desired job but also why the person does not accept a lesser wage above the reservation wage at some other job rather than become unemployed.

To make this discussion more specific, suppose unions raise wages above market clearing levels. Many persons would seek union jobs, and some rationing mechanism must be used to allocate the available jobs. Such rationing does not automatically translate into unemployment. Moreover, when it does, as in the Harris-Todaro (1970) model in which occupancy of the unemployment state makes it more likely for a person to obtain a rationed job in the future, it seems unnatural to define an unemployed person as being involuntarily unemployed unless she has no other options than employment in the rationed sector or unemployment. If, for some reason, jobs are allocated by a lottery, losers are "rationed" even though they may have voluntarily participated in the lottery and may continue to do so in the future.

It seems arbitrary to define losers as involuntarily unemployed while winners are voluntarily employed.

The data requirements for determining whether someone is involuntarily unemployed are staggering. They go well beyond knowing available market wages and reservation wages. One must know skill qualifications of persons and skill requirements of jobs. One must know why individuals become unemployed rather than taking less well-paying jobs that are available to them. Moreover, because in some statements of the theory, being involuntarily unemployed entails a perception of unfairness by the worker, one must measure the perceptions of workers about their market and nonmarket opportunities, which may differ greatly from reality. One must assess perceptions and intentions. One must assess market matching and sorting mechanisms. To make such assessments requires data with much more detail on perceptions of fairness and labor market equity than standard information on observed market transactions.

Even if it were possible to execute this empirical program, it is not clear what would be learned from it. Evidence in favor of equilibrium in the sense that people are ''on'' their labor supply curves does not imply any statement about social optimality or that we live in the best of all possible worlds. There may be many policy reforms and institutional and technological changes that could improve social welfare even if individuals are currently making privately optimal decisions given their preferences and constraints. (One example of such a reform might be elimination of legislation prohibiting certain types of economic activity.) Evidence against equilibrium in the sense that people are ''off'' their labor supply curves does not suggest an appropriate policy response until the mechanism by which individuals are forced out of equilibrium is understood. The equilibrium-disequilibrium dichotomy is ultimately a false one. The real issue is our current lack of understanding of labor market mechanisms allocating workers and firms.

Once a source of unemployment is understood, the mechanism for reducing it is obvious. For example, if wages are set ''too high'' as many disequilibrium theorists contend is the case, policies that reduce the real wage are indicated *if lower unemployment is desired*. Determining that the wage is too high is a nontrivial empirical task. Trade union policy or legislated minimum wages may make the wage too high. A full evaluation of optimal policy responses requires accounting for why the wage is too high if indeed that concept can be given precise empirical content, and who—if anyone—benefits from the current wage level. Then, and only then, is it possible to make an informed policy judgment.

In performing such a rigorous policy analysis, concepts such as ''disequilibrium'' play no role at all. This is so because once a mechanism determining unemployment is understood, *by construction* there is no role for unspecified ''shocks'' or ''disturbances'' that force people off their labor supply curves. This discussion underscores our contention that disequilibrium theory is the absence of a theory.

In the context of minimum wages as a cause of unemployment, a proper understanding of the causal mechanism goes beyond the observation that the wage is too high. It requires specification and measurement of the schemes by which work is rationed and the reasons why firms and workers do not take other actions to circumvent the ''artifically high'' wage. Posing the problem in this way suggests an appropriate data collection strategy to gain insight into the nature of unemployment, and highlights the theoretical and empirical sterility of ''disequilibrium'' economics which suggests no mechanisms and no data collection programs.

An Equilibrium Model to Rationalize The Data

''Labor supply elasticities are too small and wage variability too low for an equilibrium model to rationalize the data.'' This line of argument began with Hall (1980), was refined by Ashenfelter (1984), and is given a prominent role in Malinvaud's survey (1984). Stated most simply, it says that labor supply elasticities are too small and aggregate wage variability is too small for a neoclassical labor supply function to rationalize large fluctuations in employment and labor supply that are observed over business cycles.

Without qualification, the argument makes no sense. Adopting a log-linear specification of equation (1),

$$ln\ h = \alpha_0 + \alpha_1\ ln\ W + \alpha_2\ ln\ X + \epsilon, \tag{5}$$

a regression of $ln\ h$ on $ln\ W$ and $ln\ X$ fit on time series data always produces an estimate of α_1 that is of the right size to rationalize the data. An estimate of α_1 is what it is. One may quarrel with equation (5) as an appropriate functional form, and one amy question whether $ln\ W$ and $ln\ X$ are endogenous, and one may further question whether minimizing the sum of squares of prediction errors is the correct statistical fitting criterion. For any answer to these questions, an estimate of α_1 can be obtained that rationalizes the data.

A version of this argument that makes somewhat more sense relies on independent microevidence on α_1 to establish prior beliefs about ''reasonable'' magnitudes for ''the'' labor supply parameter. Both Hall and Ashenfelter present selective evidence from microdata on the magnitude of this key parameter.

Use of microeconomic evidence in macroeconomic studies has become an increasingly fashionable activity, especially attractive in light of the limited number of degrees of freedom in macro time series and also because recent macromodels have been formulated in terms of interpretable, microeconomic parameters. Yet, it is an enterprise fraught with danger especially for macroeconomists accustomed to thinking within the confines of a world with one type of person. At issue is the question of which of many possible micro labor supply parameters should be chosen to produce the desired macroparameter. This question makes no sense within a homogeneous consumer paradigm but is central once heterogeneity among agents is recognized. The answer to this question that recognizes the fruits of recent research in labor economics involves the choice of a macroparameter for each demographic group that most closely approximates the macrotheoretical parameter of interest *and* the choice of a procedure for aggregating the labor supply of different demographic groups.

As documented by Coleman (1984), much of the quarter-to-quarter cyclical variation in aggregate employed manhours comes through entry and exit of agents from the workforce. Although entry and exit decisions are ignored in homogeneous consumer models widely used in macroeconomics (for an exception, see Rogerson 1986), they are an important feature of business cycle labor force activity and they play a central role in modern labor economics. Accounting for heterogeneity in worker opportunities and outcomes, one must consider both microemployment and hours of work equations in forming priors about plausible macro labor supply parameters. Ashenfelter (1984) presents microevidence only for hours of work equations for continuously working prime-age white males. It is well known that the labor supply wage elasticity for this group is quite low. For this reason, Ashenfelter's claim that the microevidence suggests that *the* macro labor supply elasticity is "low" should be regarded as unsubtantiated.

Letting $E(h|h>0, W, Y)$ denote expected hours of work for workers, the aggregate labor supply function for a given W, Y is

$$E(h|W, Y) = E(h|h>0, W, Y)\, E(h>0|W, Y)$$

where the second term is the probability of employment. The aggregate labor supply elasticity is obviously larger than the labor supply elasticity reported by Hall and Ashenfelter:

$$\frac{\partial \ln E(h|h>0, W, Y)}{\partial \ln W}$$

(the derivative of the log of expected hours for workers) since the probability of employment is an increasing function of the wage.

Evidence cited in Killingsworth (1983) and Schultz (1980) indicates that participation or employment wage elasticities may be very high, especially for members of the secondary labor force. The available micro wage elasticities that account for entry and exit decisions are very large.

Even these labor supply parameters tend to understate the appropriate micro parameter values. Most of the available empirical participation and employment studies use current wage and income measures as regressors and do not distinguish between current and future wages. If leisure is a normal good and preferences are intertemporally separable, the effect of current wage innovation holding future wages constant is more positive than the effect of changing the entire wage profile by the same amount as the one period innovation (MaCurdy 1981). This suggests that properly specified lifecycle participation equations may be very wage elastic. The evidence reported in the one available lifecycle participation study (Heckman and MaCurdy 1980; 1982) suggests that future-wage-constant lifecycle employment and participation elasticities are very large.

In our view, the empirical evidence is not yet in on the claim that labor supply elasticities are too small for an equilibrium model to rationalize aggregate labor supply movements. Models of labor supply that recognize labor force entry and exit decisions show high wage elasticities (Alogouskoufis 1987). The small subset of participation models that also account for intertemporal substitution show even higher wage elasticities.

The empirical evidence presented to document limited aggregate wage variability is unconvincing. Variability in *offered* wages is not measured in the aggregate statistics unless it is assumed that all persons have the same offered wage or else that the offered wages of workers are the same as the offered wages of nonworkers. The evidence that is presented in support of the claim of limited wage variability is for straight-time hourly wages in manufacturing. Overtime premiums—which raise wages by 50 percent—and bonuses are excluded from the conventional statistics. When they are included, the measured wage shows considerable cyclical variability. Microeconomic evidence by Bils (1984), and Keane, Moffitt, and Runkle (1986) demonstrate that wages are variable over the business cycle.

Failure of any consistently aggregated labor supply model to explain aggregate labor supply fluctuations would be evidence in support of disequilibrium *provided that the specific equilibrium theory underlying this aggregated model is universally accepted*. This condition is unlikely to be realized. There is too much disagreement about alternative equilibrium labor supply models. Disagreements over the importance of expectations, the role of fixed cost, and so on, are chronicled by Killingsworth (1983). Ham's (1986) rejection of the Lucas–Rapping model of unemployment and his discussion of alternative equilibrium specifications makes this point clear. The large variety of possible microeconomic alternative equilibrium labor supply models that might fit the aggregate data constitutes a protective belt around equilibrium theory and effectively makes it a tautology. The absence of a precisely formulated disequilibrium alternative only reinforces this point.

Length of Unemployment Spells and Voluntary Unemployment

In a widely cited article, Clark and Summers (1979) claim that unemployment spells are "too long" for unemployment to be a voluntary phenomenon. On the basis of an analysis of unemployment durations, they conclude that job offers are scarce and that job creation strategies are required to solve the unemployment problem. (See also their 1980 policy paper.) Malinvaud cites complementary evidence by Salais (1980) that unemployment distributions follow a nonexponential, thick-right-tail distribution. As noted by Malinvaud, this implies that the probability of leaving unemployment decreases as a function of the time spent unemployed. It also means that some fraction of the population will remain unemployed for "a fairly long" period. Implicit in this view is that nonexponentially distributed unemployment spells with thick right tails imply labor market disequilibrium.

For four reasons, the stated conclusions do not follow from the data on unemployment durations presented by Clark and Summers.[2] First, evidence on long average unemployment spells is intrinsically ambiguous. It is consistent with bad market opportunities, good nonmarket opportunities or some combination of the two. Second, thick right tail duration distributions can arise from uncontrolled person specific unobservables—a purely statistical phenomenon well documented in the microeconomic literature on duration analysis. Such unobservables may originate from the demand side or the supply side. Third, the data utilized by Clark and Summers are intrinsically biased toward producing unemployment spells that on average are longer than those actually experienced in the population. Inadequate attention to the consequences of the sampling plan used to generate the data produces a statistical illusion. Fourth, and most basic, even if all of the empirical problems listed above could be solved and one could exactly measure both market and nonmarket opportunities confronting agents, there remains a fundamental ambiguity in interpreting the evidence in support of equilibrium or disequilibrium. We consider each of these arguments in turn.

Ambiguous Evidence on Spell Lengths

It is analytically useful to distinguish two issues that are frequently confused in the literature: (1) whether unemployment spells follow an exponential distribution and (2) what the length is of unemployment spells. An exponential distribution can generate long unemployment spells. We address our first point—the ambiguity of the evidence on long unemployment spells—by assuming an exponential unemployment duration model in order to simplify the exposition.

A variety of models of unemployment can be characterized by the following deliberately simplified framework. Wage offers (job offers) arrive at rate $\lambda\Delta t$ per period. The probability of two or more wage offers in interval Δt is negligible. Wage offers come from distribution $F(W)$. To simplify the argument, wage offers are assumed to be statistically independent of arrival times of the offers. An agent leaves unemployment if an offered wage W exceeds his/her reservation wage W_R. The probability that a person escapes unemployment in interval Δt is the probability of receiving an offer ($\lambda\Delta t$) times the probability that the offered wage exceeds the reservation wage ($= Pr(W \geq W_R) = 1 - F(W_R)$). This probability is the exit rate or hazard rate h. Then

$$Pr(\textit{person exits in interval } (t,\ t+\Delta t)) = h\ \Delta t = (\lambda\Delta t)\,(1 - F(W_R)).$$

In the limit as $\Delta t \to 0$, the time rate of change of the probability is

$$h = \lambda(1 - F(W_R)). \tag{6}$$

The density of unemployment durations is

$$g(t) = he^{-ht}$$

with mean $\frac{1}{h}$. The higher the exit rate h, the lower the mean spell of unemployment.

From the data on accepted wages collected for a group of persons with the same reservation wage it is possible to consistently estimate W_R using the minimum accepted wage if the number of persons in the group becomes large. From data on accepted wages it is possible to estimate the distribution of accepted wages:

$$F(W \mid W \geq W_R) = \frac{F(W) - F(W_R)}{1 - F(W_R)}, \quad W \geq W_R. \tag{7}$$

From data on unemployment spells, it is possible to estimate h. The inverse of mean completed spells consistently estimates h.[3] Market data on unemployment spells and accepted wages provides information on h, W_R, and $F(W|W_R)$. A high mean unemployment spell or low h is consistent with infrequent wage offers (a low λ) or a high refusal rate of job offers $F(W_R)$ or both. Market data on lengths of unemployment spells cannot be used to decide between the two explanations without invoking arbitrary and untestable restrictions (given data on only unemployment durations and accepted wages) about the shape of the offer wage distribution F.

The available data determine equation (7) and W_R. They cannot determine the lower tail area of F below W_R unless a functional form for F is assumed. Such an assumption is arbitrary. The most the data tell is the shape of the density $f(W)$ above W_R and not the shape or tail area of $f(W)$ below W_R (see Figure 1).

This implies that from observed unemployment spells, one cannot separate λ from $(1 - F(W_R))$. Evidence on long unemployment spells is thus intrinsically ambiguous. It is consistent with the interpretation that there are few market opportunities (low λ) or with the interpretation that there are good nonmarket opportunities (a high refusal rate $(1 - F(W_R))$ or some combination of the two. In light of this fundamental ambiguity it is inappropriate to conclude from the observation of long unemployment spells that job creation strategies (a higher λ) are required to solve the unemployment problem.

This is not to say that it is impossible to distinguish between these two interpretations if data on the arrival of job offers were available or if data on the distribution of wage offers were collected [see, for example, Blau (1986) or Holzer (1987)]. Either source of data enables one to decompose the hazard into its two components. However, data on lengths of unemployment spells alone are intrinsically ambiguous and are not a valid basis for policy analysis.[4]

Ambiguous Evidence on Thick-Tail Duration Distributions

Thick-tail, nonexponential, unemployment duration distributions of the sort noted by Malinvaud and Clark and Summers can arise from differences among people in h, the exit rate from unemployment. For example, if data are pooled on individuals from different markets with different arrival rates of job offers (λ) or with different wage offer distributions (F) or if people differ in their nonmarket opportunities so that W_R varies in the population, then h will differ among people. High-exit-rate persons leave the unempolyment pool faster than low-exit-rate persons. As the length of time unemployed increases, the average h of the *remaining* unemployed declines

Figure 1: Two wage densities that rationalize data on accepted wages basis for policy analysis.

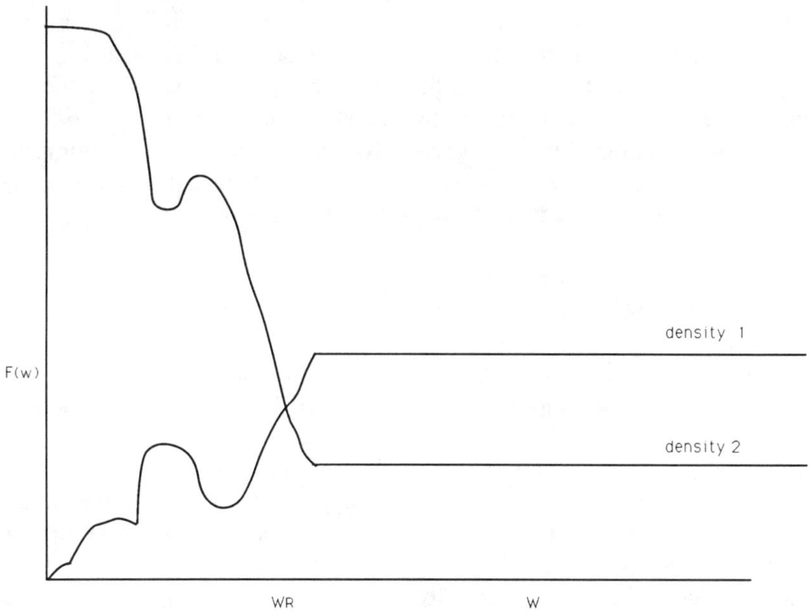

even though no person's h changes over time. This selective departure of persons from the sample is a dynamic form of selection bias that does not arise if all persons are alike but that naturally arises if they are not.

To take an extreme example, suppose that there are two types of persons: those with $h = 0$ who never exit unemployment and those with a high "h" who exit quickly. Let $1 - \pi$ be the proportion of movers ($h > 0$) and π the proportion of stayers. Unemployment dynamics is characterized by a rapid exit of high h persons from the pool of unemployed with the remaining pool being permanent stayers ($h = 0$). Such heterogeneity can account for the "thick-tail," "nonexponential" distributions noted by Malinvaud. In our extreme example, proportion π of the persons never leave the state of unemployment. The density of unemployment spells has a thick right tail. As the high h persons leave the pool of the unemployed, the average h of the remaining population declines. Evidence of a declining sample exit rate as unemployment duration increases does not imply that any single person's hazard rate is declining. It can be shown that population dispersion in h leads to a thick tailed, declining hazard (with spell length) distribution in less extreme cases as well.

Heterogeneity in h can arise from the demand side (dispersion in λ or F) or the supply side (dispersion in W_R not due to variations in demand). Thick-tailed duration distributions with declining population hazards convey no information about market equilibrium or disequilibrium or whether the source of the thick tails is due to bad market opportunities or good nonmarket opportunities. Data on market offers, job arrivals, and nonmarket opportunities are required in order to assess the sources of unobservables that give rise to observed thick-tailed duration distributions.

Length-Biased Samples

A technical error mars the work of Clark and Summers and related papers based on their methodology. The data utilized by them oversample long spells of unemployment. To see this, note that they sample CPS spells *in progress* at some survey date. Short spells completed before the survey data are underrepresented. Because of this sampling problem they oversample long spells and present an exaggerated description of the length of completed unemployment spells. The Appendix spells out the consequences of this sample selection bias more formally.

Clark and Summers analyze a deformed duration distribution that does not represent the population distribution of unemployment spells. Their findings of long unemployment spells may be a creation of their statistical procedures. Valid evidence on the true lengths of unemployment spells awaits more careful accounting for the effects of length-biased sampling on estimated unemployment durations.

Ambiguity of the Evidence

Even if one could surmount the empirical problems discussed above, a fundamental interpretive ambiguity remains. Implicit in the preceding discussion is the assumption that "demand factors" and "supply factors" (nonmarket opportunities) can be isolated. Yet the modern theory of equilibrium unemployment [e.g., Albrecht and Axell (1984) or Mortensen (1986)] emphasizes the joint determination of arrival rates, wage offer distributions, reservation wages, unemployment, and search strategies. In this context, a low arrival rate of job offers may well be an equilibrium outcome of a market in which there are many willing workers. A high reservation wage may reflect good demand-side opportunities. Naive policy recommendations based on "high reservation wages" or "low job arrival rates" that ignore the market determination of these economic constructs may be very misleading.

To isolate true demand and supply factors (exogenous characteristics and technology of firms and potential workers) requires digging deeper than "merely" isolating reservation wages, offered wages, and job arrival rates that are already difficult to recover. Within the confines of equilibrium theory, such "deep structural" parameters cannot be identified without making strong assumptions (see Flinn and Heckman 1982). As in the case of labor supply discussed in the second section, an infinite variety of equilibrium unemployment models can be generated to account for data on arrival rates, offered wages, and reservation wages. The "flexibility" of the equilibrium theory effectively converts it into a tautology. A protective belt of logically possible equilibrium alternatives and the absence of any clearly stated disequilibrium alternative make impossible a sharp test of disequilibrium in the labor market.

Summary and Conclusions

This chapter examines the conceptual and empirical foundations of recent tests of labor market disequilibrium. Three widely cited arguments are critically evaluated.

The first argument considers whether unemployment is a constraint. The test based on this argument is shown to be nonrobust to the introduction of plausible person—specific unobservables: offered market wages and reservation wages. Such unobservables are an essential feature of the equilibrium theory. When such variables are present, an equilibrium model can always be constructed that can rationalize any measured hours of work as being voluntarily chosen. Because the equilibrium theory is tautologically true when plausible person-specific unobservables are present, tests of disequilibrium based on measured labor supply and wage data have no power against an equilibrium alternative.

We also discuss the difficulty of defining and hence measuring involuntary unemployment. We demonstrate that even if data on offered and accepted wages were available, additional information is required on perceptions of opportunities and on fairness. Information on observed market transactions does not suffice.

We go on to note that disequilibrium theory is defined as the absence of an equilibrium theory. Whereas equilibrium theories specify a mechanism by which unemployment is determined, disequilibrium theories by their very nature do not specify a complete mechanism determining unemployment. Disequilibrium and incompleteness of the theory are synonomous.

The second argument in support of disequilibrium asserts that labor supply elasticities are too small and that wage variability is too small to account for observed movements in aggregate manhours. This argument requires micro estimates of labor supply elasticities that are not yet available. At issue is the choice of the "correct" labor supply elasticity to take to the macro data. Micro research on intertemporal labor supply decisions at the intensive and extensive margins is in its infancy. The little that is known suggests that intertemporal participation elasticities are large for secondary workers who constitute a disproportionately large share of the unemployed. Considerable evidence exists of micro wage variability—including 50 percent changes in wage rates when overtime schedules ar paid. Much further microanalysis is required for the second argument to carry any empirical weight, but the required research is empirically feasible.

For the second type of test to be convincing, agreement is required on the "correct" labor supply theory. But there is no such agreement currently, and none is likely to emerge. Indeed, if a specific equilibrium labor supply model failed to predict aggregate fluctuations, it would likely be discarded. The infinite variety of "plausible" alternative equilibrium models makes the equilibrium theory a tautology. Specific equilibrium models can be rejected. Equilibrium as an hypothesis is irrefutable.

The third argument—that unemployment spells are too long for unemployment to be a voluntary phenomenon—is unconvincing given plausible differences among agents in market and nonmarket opportunities. Long unemployment spells are consistent with the interpretation that there are good nonmarket opportunities or bad market opportunities. Data on wage offers and the rate of arrival of job offers are required to determine which interpretation is more appropriate.

Knowledge of the distribution of unemployment spells alone is uninformative. Thick-right-tail duration distributions may be a consequence of unobserved market and nonmarket opportunities, and are consistent with many alternative descriptions of the labor market. More refined analyses of the determinants of unemployment are required. Such analyses will be of great value in elucidating the "causes" of unemployment. Given the variety of alternative equilibrium models of unemployment, most of which are untested and many of which are fundamentally underidentified, we are skeptical that any rejection of equilibrium for a specific model (when possible) will be accepted as a valid general test of the disequilibrium hypothesis.

The ambiguity that is intrinsic in the proposed tests of labor market equilibrium suggests that the choice between equilibrium and disequilibrium paradigms must be made on the basis of criteria that are not strictly empirical. Intellectual esthetics favor the equilibrium point of view. Equilibrium theory suggests a variety of market mechanisms by which workers and firms are sorted although there is as yet little empirical evidence on such mechanisms. (We do not equate equilibrium with a naive Walrasian model.) The fact that equilibrium theory suggests such mechanisms and motivates empirical work on them is a powerful argument in its favor as a productive research paradigm. Disequilibrium theory is necessarily incomplete, and less of a stimulant to empirical research, because it does not articulate the mechanisms or institutional structures that prevent agents from completing mutually advantageous trades in the labor market nor does it explain how such mechanisms come into existence.

Even if a disequilibrium model could be constructed that would predict time-series data as well as, or better than, an equilibrium model, one would be uneasy about using a disequilibrium model to forecast the likely impact of new policy interventions not previously experienced or about forecasting critical turning points in thime series. The intrinsic incompleteness of specification that is the hallmark of disequilibrium models greatly undermines the confidence that one would be willing to place in disequilibrium forecasting models, no matter how good the fit of a model within a sample period.

Adopting the equilibrium point of view does not imply that any current state of the economy is an ideal state or that specific policies will not improve welfare. It simply requires the analyst to be specific about mechanisms that give rise to unemployment and to design policies and data collection strategies that account for such mechanisms.

Appendix: Length-Biased Sampling

To explore the consequences of the CPS sampling plan, suppose that the population density of completed unemployment spells is $g(t)$. It is useful to compare several random variables describing various durations. Let T be population completed unemployment duration. Let Z be the *sampled* completed unemployment duration. The distribution of Z is different from the distribution of T in such a way that the distribution of Z *overrepresents* long durations relative to their occurrence in the population. It is fruitful to decompose Z into two components: B—the portion of the sampled spell that occurrs before the interview date and A—the portion of the sampled spell that occurs after the interview date.

Suppose that the economic environment is stationary so that ρ persons become unemployed at each point in time. The fraction of each cohort still unemployed after t periods is $1 - G(t) = Pr(T > t)$, the probability of "surviving" in the unemployed state at least t periods.

Let 0 denote the interview date. The total stock of unemployed people at 0 is the set of survivors from all previous cohorts. Let this be S. Then

$$S = \rho \int_0^\infty (1 - G(l))dl$$

where we use the fact that a person unemployed l periods at 0 must have become unemployed l periods ago and have survived in that stage at least l periods. The stock unemployed t periods is $\rho(1 - G(t))$ (the survivors of the cohort starting unemployment t periods ago). Letting b be the length of an interrupted spell (for time spent unemployed before the spell is sampled), the density of unemployment spells of duration b as sampled at the interview date is

$$f(b) = \frac{\rho(1 - G(b))}{\rho \int_0^\infty (1 - G(l))dl} = \frac{1 - G(b)}{\int_0^\infty (1 - G(l))dl}.$$

This is the density of interrupted spell lengths. If the population mean exists ($E(T) < \infty$), the denominator is the expectation of T. (Integrate by parts.) Then the proportion of spells of length b sampled at time 0 is

$$f(b) = \frac{1 - G(b)}{E(T)}. \tag{A–1}$$

$f(b)$ is the density of *interrupted spells* sampled at time 0. Clark and Summers use data from $f(b)$ to estimate completed spell distributions. The density of *postsurvey* duration a (for "after") given that a person has been in the state b periods is

$$g(b + a | T > b) = \frac{g(b + a)}{1 - G(b)}, \quad a \geq 0.$$

Total sampled spell length is $z = b + a$. Then the density of z given pre-interview duration b is

$$g(z | T > b) = \frac{g(z)}{1 - G(b)}, \quad z \geq b. \tag{A–2}$$

The density of z is obtained by multiplying equations (A–1) and (A–2) and integrating out b, that is,

$$m(z) = \int_0^z g(z|T>b)\, f(b)\, db$$

$$= \int_0^z \frac{g(z)}{1-G(b)} \frac{(1-G(b))}{E(T)}\, db$$

$$m(z) = \frac{zg(z)}{E(T)} .$$

The density ($m(z)$) weights high z observations more than the population density of z, $g(z)$. If $g(t) = h\, e^{-ht}$,

$$m(z) = h^2 t\, e^{-ht} .$$

The mean of Z is *twice* the mean of T. The mean of the *interrupted spell* (sampled at 0) is exactly the mean of a population completed spell. (However, this result is special to the exponential. In the general case, the mean of the interrupted spell can be shorter or longer than the population mean of completed spells.) Note that this density has a thicker right tail (because of the t factor) than the underlying population exponential density.

As a consequence of the sampling plan used to generate their data, Clark and Summers analyze a thick-tail duration distribution that does not represent the population distribution of unemployment spells. Their finding of long unemployment spells is a creation of their statistical procedures and conveys no information about the functioning of the labor market. Valid evidence on the true lengths of unemployment spells awaits more careful accounting for the effects of length-biased sampling on estimated unemployment durations.

Notes

1. Presumably, U_I depends on the discrepancy between aggregate demand and aggregate supply. A richer economic model would make U_I depend on aggregate demand and supply variables as well as on explicit rationing mechanisms. Such considerations do not aid in securing econometric identification of the model because they rule out demand-side variables as instruments for U_I. See the discussion below in the text.

2. We note that the data used in their analysis are generated from hazards fit on the first few months of measured unemployment spells. They do not have data on the full distribution of unemployment durations nor do they adjust their estimates for the fact that parameter estimation error is present in their manufactured unemployment distributions.

3. This assumes no censoring. Modifications for censored data are known in the literature; see Kalbfleisch and Prentice (1980).

4. Eckstein and Wolpin (1987) demonstrate that in the equilibrium model of Albrecht and Axell (1984) it is possible to estimate λ and hence $1 - F(W_R)$ from unemployment duration

data. This result is not general. Flinn and Heckman (1982) prove that in an equilibrium matching model λ and $1 - F(W_R)$ are not identified even if duration data are supplemented with accepted wage data unless the wage offer distribution satisfies a "recoverability condition."

References

Abowd, J., and Card, D. 1987. "Intertemporal Labor Supply and Long Term Employment Contracts." *American Economic Review* 77(1): 50–68.

Albrecht, J, and Axell, B. 1984. "An Equilibrium Model of Search Unemployment." *Journal of Political Economy*, 824–840.

Alogouskoufis, G. 1987. "On Intertemporal Substitution and Aggregate Labor Supply." *Journal of Political Economy*. Birkbeck College, University of London, forthcoming.

Ashenfelter, O. 1979. "Unemployment as A Constraint on Labor Market Behavior." In *O. E. C. D., Structural Determinants of Employment and Unemployment*. Paris.

———. 1980. "Unemployment as Disequilibrium in A Model of Aggregate Labor Supply." *Econometrica* (April).

———. 1984. "Microeconomic and Macroeconomic Analyses of Labor Supply." *Journal of Monetary Economics*.

Blau, D. 1986. "An Analysis of Employed and Unemployed Job Search Behaviour." University of North Carolina.

Bils, M. 1984. "Real Wages over The Business Cycle." *Journal of Political Economy*.

Burdett, K., and Mortensen, D. 1979. "Labor Supply Under Uncertainty." In *Research in Labor Economics*, Vol. 2, ed. R. Ehrenberg, 109–157. Greenwich, CT: JAI Press.

Clark, K., and Summers, L. 1979. "Labor Market Dynamics and Unemployment: A Reconsideration." *Brookings Papers on Economic Activity*, 1: 13–72.

———. 1980. "Unemployment Reconsidered: The Real Problem is Concentrated, Long Term Joblessness." *Harvard Business Review* (November).

Coleman, T. 1984. "Essays on Aggregate Labor Market Business Cycle Fluctuations. Unpublished doctoral thesis, University of Chicago.

Eckstein, Z., and Wolpin, K. 1987. "Estimating A Market Equilibrium Search Model From Panel Data on Individuals." Unpublished manuscript, University of Minnesota.

Flinn, C., and Heckman, J. 1982, "New Methods For Analyzing Structural Models of Labor Force Dynammics." *Journal of Econometrics* 18: 115–168.

Hall, R. 1980. "Labor Supply and Aggregate Fluctuations." In *On The State of Macroeconomics*, K. Brunner and A. Meltzer, eds., Carnegie Rochester Conference Series: 12. Amsterdam: North Holland.

Ham, J. 1986. "Testing Whether Unemployment Represents Intertemporal Labor Supply Behaviour." *Review of Economics Studies* 53: 306–353.

Harris, J., and Todaro, M. 1970. "Migration, Unemployment and Development: A Two-Sector Analysis." *American Economic Review* 60: 126–142.
Heckman, J., and MaCurdy, T. 1980. "A Life Cycle Model of Female Labor Supply." *Review of Economic Studies.*
———. 1982. "Corrigendum." *Review of Economic Studies.*
Holzer, H. 1987. "Informal Job Search and Black Youth Unemployment." *American Economic Review*, 77(3): 446–452.
Kalbfleisch, J., and Prentice, R. 1980 *The Statistical Analysis of Failure Time Data.* New York: Wiley.
Killingsworth, M. 1983. *Labor Supply* Cambridge, England: Cambridge University Press.
Keane, M., Moffitt, R., and Runkle, M. 1986. "Cyclical Variation in Wages." Unpublished manuscript, Brown University; forthcoming, *Journal of Political Economy.*
Lucas, R., and Rapping, L. 1969. "Real Wages, Employment and Inflation." *Journal of Political Economy.*
MaCurdy, T. 1981. "An Empirical Model of Labor Supply in a Life Cycle Setting." *Journal of Political Economy* 89: 1059–1085.
Malinvaud, E. 1984. *Mass Unemployment.* Oxford, England: Basil Blackwell, Oxford University Press.
Mortensen, D. 1986. "Job Search and Labor Market Analysis." In *Handbook of Labor Economics*, Vol. 2, O. Ashenfelter and R. Layard, eds. Amsterdam: North Holland.
Rogerson, R. 1986. "Risk Sharing, Indivisible Labor and Aggregate Fluctuations." University of Rochester.
Salais, R. 1980. "Le Chomage: Un Phenomene de File d'attente." *Economie et Statistique.*
Schultz, T.P. 1980. "Estimating Labor Supply Functions For Married Women." In *Female Labor Supply: Theory and Estimation*, J. Smith, ed. Princeton., NJ: Princeton University Press.

5 LABOR MARKET SEGMENTATION THEORY: RECONSIDERING THE EVIDENCE

William T. Dickens
Kevin Lang

When asking questions about the labor market, particularly earnings determination, human capital theory is the most important tool in the economist's toolbox. However, there is an alternative—labor market segmentation theory. Labor market segmentation was advanced as an alternative to human capital theory by several authors in the early 1970s. After a brief period of popularity, it faded after influential critiques suggested that existing evidence did not differentiate between labor market segmentation and standard human capital theory (Wachter 1974; Cain 1976). In the last decade several important theoretical and empirical developments have generated a resurgence of interest in the theory.

We review these developments and conclude that labor market segmentation theory provides a good alternative to human capital theory and deserves an equivalent position in the economist's toolbox. When analyzing policy questions or when designing new explorations, economists

We would like to thank the usual group of little people without whose help this would have been done much sooner. We would also like to acknowledge the generous research support of the Institute of Industrial Relations at U.C. Berkeley.

should consider the implications of labor market segmentation theory. This opens a broad area of work—the application of labor market segmentation theory to several problems previously only analyzed from the standard perspective. We briefly consider some of these applications below.

Since labor market segmentation has often been accused of being untestable, we begin with a discussion of epistemology. In the second section we describe the essential elements and common attributes of labor market segmentation theories. The third section briefly describes the theoretical foundations of labor market segmentation theory—efficiency wage theory or the closely related literatures on rent sharing or rent extraction. The fourth and fifth sections present the evidence on labor market segmentation theory where we discuss first the evidence on the extent and origin of interemployer wage differences and then the explicit tests of dual market theory. The sixth section is a reply to criticisms of some of our early work on dual market theory. In particular, we return to the question of what makes a good theory and discuss our work in light of these criteria. The final section summarizes our arguments and briefly considers the implications of labor market segmentation theory for future work.

What is a Good Theory?

Economists are frequently hostile to discussions of epistemology. Tjalling Koopmans is almost apologetic in the introduction to his famous essay on methodology (1957) as were two of his eminent predecessors in the field (Harrod 1938; Robertson 1940). This hostility is unfortunate because it significantly undermines our ability to assess the significance of hypothesis tests in economics.

Economists are frequently naive falsificationists, holding the view that a bad theory is one that has been proved wrong. Similarly, a good theory is one that could be proved false, has been subjected to testing and has not yet been demonstrated to be false. This view is often associated with Karl Popper but represents an oversimplification of his position. Naive falsificationism leads economists to look for "definitive" tests of a theory. A "good" test is one that could definitively falsify a theory. To be definitive, a test must generate a result that is not explicable by the theory being tested. By the same logic, good theory is one for which a definitive test can be developed.

This position would be laughable if it did not inform seminar discussions and presumably influence research and publication decisions. It is also the position that has allowed many economists to dismiss labor market segmentation theory as untestable. While economists are apt to envy the scientist's ability to generate crucial experiments, the truth is that experiments are deemed crucial only with the hindsight of history. Lakatos (1978 86–87) reports,

> There were many experiments in the eighteenth century which were, as a matter of historico-sociological fact, widely accepted as "Crucial" evidence against Galileo's law of free fall, and Newton's theory of gravitation. In the nineteenth century there were several "crucial experiments" based on measurements of light velocity which "disproved" the corpuscular theory and which turned out later to be erroneous in the light of relativity theory. These "crucial experiments" were later deleted from justificationist textbooks as manifestations of shameful short-sightedness or even of envy. (Recently they reappeared in some new textbooks, this time to illustrate the inescapable irrationality of scientific fashions.) However, in those cases in which ostensibly "crucial experiments" were indeed *later* borne out by the defeat of the programme, historians charged those who resisted them with stupidity, jealousy, or unjustified adulation of the father of the research programme in question.

Experiments or hypothesis tests cannot be crucial because there is no theory that remains free of anomalies for long. Similarly, there is no result that cannot be explained by some modification of the theory which its proponents will claim is minor.[1]

If we cannot expect to reject theories with decisive tests, how then should we decide between theories? One plausible answer is that we should ask which theory is compatible with a wider range of "known facts" about the world. While attractive, this gives too much weight to theories that have been around for a long time. We can ask the question, If you wanted to go to San Francisco, would you prefer to be on a train 1,000 miles or 1,500 miles away? Everything else equal, we would prefer the train that was closer. However, if the train that is farther away is moving twice as fast, we may get to San Francisco sooner on that train. In short, as in may topics economists discuss, we care not only about levels but also about derivatives.

Indeed, since we expect to do economic research for a long time, the rate at which a research program is progressing and not its ability to explain known "facts" is of primary importance. Thus, the true test of a theory or research program is dynamic. A good theory generates excess empirical content that tends to be corroborated and expands the range it can explain without large adjustments. A regressive program is one that is continually being altered in the face of contradictory evidence.[2]

In our assessment, we, of course, do not ignore the importance of other criteria for assessing economic theories such as their simplicity (Occam's razor) or their mathematical elegance. These aspects of theories influence their treatment in other disciplines and affect our judgment of economic theories as well.

We will argue that in recent years labor market segmentation theory has been a very progressive research program. In contrast, human capital theory has required frequent modification to account for the empirical regularities generated by the labor market segmentation research program.

What Is Labor Market Segmentation Theory?

We identify two crucial elements of segmented labor market theory. First, the labor market can be usefully thought of as being made up several distinct segments with different rules for wage determination and employment policies. Second, access to jobs in at least some sectors at some times is limited in the sense that more people want jobs than there are jobs offered. Thus there may be queuing for these jobs either in the form of unemployment or job queues among employed workers or both.

While it is easy to state that labor market segmentation theory implies distinct segments, just what is meant by "distinct segments" is more difficult. Minimally, a number of important characteristics of the wage determination mechanism and the employment relation must be correlated so that segments can be characterized as regions in a space with dimension significantly smaller than the space of characteristics. In the extreme, dual market theory has been interpreted by some as implying that a wide range of job characteristics are all highly correlated so that jobs can be arrayed along one dimension and described adequately by their position along that dimension.

Many tests of dual market theory have operationalized the concept of segment with particular reference to the wage determination mechanism. Most of these studies find that there is a difference between the wage determination mechanisms in the primary and secondary sector. Furthermore, the differences are in accord with the descriptive literature on labor market segmentation. We will discuss these findings in greater detail below.

This aspect of the research helps to establish that labor market segmentation theory provides a good description of the income distribution and is therefore of heuristic importance. Although to summarize many characteristics of a job by its location in some classification system may be useful, it does not challenge the application of human capital theory to labor market problems. The reasons for segmentation may be important for understanding the form of the income distribution, but segmentation, as such, does not imply any market failure. Thus, Heckman and Sedlacek (1985) estimated a model of a segmented labor market consistent with a human capital view, and Heckman and Hotz (1986) propose such an interpretation for their finding that two equations fit the Panamanian income distribution better than one. The more fundamental criticism of human capital theory implied by labor market segmentation theory is that labor markets do not clear—that access to some sectors is subject to nonprice rationing.

All the early writers on labor market segmentation theory identified limited mobility among sectors as an important aspect of the theory. More significantly, they argued that there is a hierarchy of sectors, with access to the highest paying being the most difficult. Critics of labor market segmentation theory used the fact that during the economic expansion of the 1960s blacks were more likely to move into high-wage jobs than whites as evidence against reduced mobility (Schiller 1977). Smith (1989) revives this argument by showing that earnings rise more rapidly with experience among blacks than among whites. Leigh (1976) finds substantial and comparable earnings growth for blacks and whites, and suggests that this refutes the dual market hypothesis. On the other hand, Rosenberg (1976) and Carnoy and Rumberger (1980) find that minority workers are more likely to begin their career in the secondary sector and, having started there, are less likely to leave than are whites. These authors argue that this differential mobility supports dual market theory.

Thus authors on both sides confounded lack of mobility with barriers to entry. However, in the extreme no mobility between sectors could be consistent with complete barriers to entry or no barriers at all. If workers always enter the sector they prefer on their first job, there is no need for mobility among sectors. On the other hand, if whites can enter whichever sector they prefer, but blacks must queue for good jobs, blacks will be more likely than whites to move into good jobs.

Indeed, segmented labor market theory can explain an anomaly that has been largely neglected in the literature on race discrimination. The evidence is fairly strong that within cohorts, wages have risen more rapidly for blacks than for whites (Smith 1989). On the other hand, Lazear (1979) shows that within a job, wages rise less rapidly for blacks than for whites. This is precisely what would be expected if blacks were more likely to be employed in low-wage jobs with little return to seniority while queuing for good jobs.[3]

By shifting the emphasis from mobility to evidence for queues the question becomes much clearer. Evidence of excess supply in high-wage jobs, wage differences unrelated to ability or job quality (and perhaps related to other characteristics not suggested by human capital theory), and the fact that workers in low-wage jobs would prefer high-wage jobs for which they would qualify, all provide evidence of queues.

Since queues imply excess supply to high-wage jobs, they also imply some degree of wage rigidity at least in high-wage jobs. Thus theories of labor market segmentation require some form of wage rigidity. In contrast with macroeconomic "disequilibrium" models, wages may be somewhat flexible in the short run. Thus segmentation is consistent with cyclical fluctuations in the short run as long as wage differentials are maintained in the long run. Exactly the opposite is required for macroeconomic models that must explain temporary deviations from market clearing. Fortunately for labor market segmentation theory, models of long-run rigidity have proven far easier to develop than models of short-run rigidity.

We view the existence of segments with different wage-setting mechanisms and queues for high-wage jobs as essential elements of labor market segmentation theory. However, there are several other attributes common to many versions of labor market segmentation theory. The first of these is that the labor market can be usefully modelled as having two major segments—secondary and primary. The latter is often divided into a lower and an upper tier.

The primary sector consists of high-wage jobs with good working conditions, considerable opportunity for advancement within the firm, and substantial rewards for obtaining education and training. Labor relations are generally formalized either by a union contract or in an employment relations handbook. Company policy sharply circumscribes supervisors' authority. Because of the high wages, employees tend to stay on the job for a long time. Because of firms' investment in screening and training, firms tend to hold onto workers. Also, primary firms may insulate themselves from demand swings by contracting out the more volatile portion of demand.[4]

The sociological literature on segmentation builds on Averitt's (1968) work on the dual economy. Since tests of the dual economy model often rely on labor market data, it is natural to interpret them as tests of the dual labor market model. It is therefore important to understand the relation between the dual economy and the dual labor market.[5] The dual economy literature holds that firms (and in some cases entire industries) can be usefully thought of as being part of either the core or the periphery. Core firms are large successful firms with substantial monopoly power. They tend to have a high return on capital, have high labor productivity, pay high wages, and have higher capital/labor ratios and larger employment, value of output, and market share than other firms.

Core firms mainly offer primary employment. Security, janitorial or other low-skilled occupations may be organized as either primary or secondary jobs or may be contracted out. In peripheral firms there is a small layer of technical, skilled, or managerial labor with most employees being unskilled production workers. The canonical example is a small job shop in some durable goods industry. The owner/manager is likely a skilled machinist who owns some older machine tools. He hires unskilled workers at low wages to tend the machines and clean the shop. The typical fast-food franchise also fits the description, with an owner/manager overseeing the work of a many unskilled minimum-wage employees.

Some industries are dominated by core firms. Others have few such firms. Industries typically viewed as being core include construction, mining, durable goods manufacturing and some nondurable manufacturing, transportation, utilities, and FIRE. Agriculture, textiles and apparel, retail trade, and most services contain a higher concentration of peripheral firms.

Thus certain industries will tend to employ primary workers disproportionately and others, secondary workers. However, industry is not a perfect proxy for segment, and neither is occupation since very few occupations are exclusively made up of secondary workers. This caveat must be kept in mind when reviewing research that relies on these proxies. Before turning to a review of this literature, we discuss theories of labor market segmentation.

Labor Market Segmentation and Economic Theory

As noted above, the notion that technology may create sectors of the labor market with distinctly different characteristics is not particularly controversial. The biggest problem for labor market segmentation theory is explaining why high-wage employers would not lower their wages in the face of excess labor supply. This is related to but slightly simpler than trying to explain unemployment, because labor market segmentation theory need not explain why those who fail to find high-wage employment spurn low-wage employment.

Recent theories of involuntary unemployment fall under the rubric of efficiency wage, rent-extraction, or rent-sharing theories. Verbal descriptions of many, if not all, of these theories date back as far as Adam Smith. However, their recent formalization has generated widespread interest and increased our understanding of their policy and welfare implications. More complete descriptions of these theories and their merits can be found elsewhere (Yellen 1984; Katz 1986; Weiss 1991). We will briefly review their implications for labor market segmentation.

What distinguishes efficiency wage theory from more standard models is that labor productivity depends not only on workers' observable skills and the numbers of different types of workers employed but also on the wage those workers are paid. There are several explanations for why wages might directly affect productivity. In developing countries where the wage is close to the subsistence level, raising wages may improve workers' nutrition and make them more productive (Stiglitz 1976; Bliss and Stern 1978). This model is clearly irrelevant for labor market segmentation in developed economies.

Alternatively higher wages may facilitate worker discipline (Calvo 1979). Raising the wage makes being fired more costly. Shapiro and Stiglitz's (1984) presentation of this model has been highly influential. Similarly, raising wages deters quits (Salop 1979; Beaudry 1990). If the firm invests in screening, hiring, or training new workers, it may want to pay a premium wage to protect this investment. Both the discipline and the worker-retention efficiency wage models are subject to the criticism that firms can deter shirking or quits more profitably by having newly hired workers post a bond (Carmichael 1990). Dickens, Katz, Lang, and Summers (1989) and Lang and Kahn (1990) suggest several considerations that complicate the bonding solution and suggest why it may not be used in practice.[6]

The adverse-selection efficiency wage model assumes that firms cannot observe worker quality perfectly both before and after hiring, but that better workers have better paying alternatives elsewhere (perhaps in self-employment). Therefore, the unobserved quality of a firm's workforce will be an increasing function of the wage it offers (Weiss 1980). It can be shown that in equilibrium, different firms will pay different wages (Weiss 1990), but it has not yet been determined whether wages and firm characteristics should be related.

Recruiting models emphasize that it is costly for firms to have vacancies. Raising wages reduces the expected length of a vacancy (Weitzman 1989; Lang 1991; Montgomery 1991). It is possible that firms will specialize in making offers at different wages. Where particular firms choose to specialize may be determined by their technology. Unemployment arises because some workers may (randomly) receive no job offers.

Finally, workers' effort and productivity may depend on how fairly they believe they are being treated (Solow 1979; Akerlof 1984). In particular, workers may have expectations about what constitutes a fair wage and may expect to be paid according to that norm. Norms may differ across industries and across firms depending on the history, market structure, and technology of the firm or industry.

It has long been acknowledged that unions may raise workers' wages and that the union wage will be related to technology and market structure. It seems reasonable that firms wishing to avoid unionization may pay high wages to prevent unionization. Even without a formal union, worker collective action or the threat of worker collective action may raise wages. This is the theme of the rent-extraction/collective action/insider-outsider models (Dickens 1986; Lindbeck and Snower 1986).

In the expense preference or rent-sharing model (Heywood 1990), managers find their jobs are made easier by paying higher wages. Stockholders are unable to audit the true needs of the firm perfectly. Therefore managers hire overqualified workers and pay them high wages to make their own jobs more pleasant.

Our review of the empirical literature will demonstrate that these theories do not explain the empirical evidence equally well. However, labor market segmentation theory has come a long way in the last decade. It is no longer a set of observations in search of a formal theory. Instead its partisans have the problem of sorting through a host of promising explanations.

The Evidence Part I: Interemployer Wage Differences

In this section we consider evidence that there are large differences among employers in the wages paid apparently similar workers. This finding is obviously consistent with labor market segmentation but can be made consistent with human capital theory. We argue that examining additional predictions of the labor market segmentation and human capital models and considering the dynamic of their interaction strongly suggests that the market segmentation view should be preferred.

Economists have known for a long time that large wage differences may exist for workers doing similar work at different firms within the same city. Attention to these differences, their distribution across industries, similarity across occupations, and their persistence over time led a previous generation of labor economists and industrial relations specialists to conclude that worker bargaining power determined wages which were then greater than the opportunity cost of workers' time. However, that work left much to be desired. Since microdata were unavailable at the time the studies were done, they relied on aggregate data, allowing few controls for worker quality, geography, or differences in job characteristics.

The work was sufficiently flawed that labor economists trained in the '60s and '70s felt free to ignore it despite a brief revival of labor market segmentation theory in the early '70s. New evidence of interindustry and interemployer wage differentials generated using microdata in the early 1970s was easily dismissed by the critics of labor market segmentation theory as resulting from unobserved compensating differences (Cain 1976). Others suggested that such differences might be due to transitory demand for industry-specific skills so that such industry differences would disappear over time.

Spurred by the theoretical developments described in the last section, in the last decade several papers have revived the study of industry and employer wage differentials. By using microdata they go beyond the work of the '40s and '50s. By responding directly to the critics of labor market segmentation theory they go beyond the work of the '70s. The best known papers on interindustry wage differences (Dickens and Katz 1987a; 1987b; Krueger and Summers 1987; 1988; Katz and Summers 1989) and intra-industry wage variation (Groshen 1987; 1988a; 1988b) overlap considerably. This presentation follows Dickens and Katz's (1987b) analysis of the 1983 Current Population Survey (CPS) except where more recent evidence is available.

Among one-digit occupations, the standard deviation of log wages[7] across three-digit SIC industries ranges from .13 (clerical workers) to .37 (sales workers). Controlling for a wide range of worker attributes, state of residence and residence in an SMSA, has little effect on the dispersion of clerical workers' wages. However, it reduces the standard deviation of industry effects to .29 for sales workers. Thus controlling for nearly everything available in the CPS leaves substantial unexplained interindustry variation in wages. Even for clerical workers, an industry two standard deviations above the average would pay over 50 percent more than an industry two standard deviations below the average.

Not only are these differences large, they are persistent across time. Dickens and Katz (1987b) review a number of studies using aggregate data which show remarkable persistence in the interindustry wage structure going back to the late 1800s. Helwege (1987) uses census data going back to 1940 and controls for individual characteristics and geographic location. She finds that the correlation of the interindustry wage structure across time is even stronger when these controls are added. In addition to being correlated across time, interindustry wage differences are also correlated across space. Many studies have shown that average industry wages are correlated across countries (see Dickens and Katz 1987b). Lang, Marquez, and Romaguera (1989) found that Venezuelan wage differentials were more highly correlated with U.S. and Chilean differentials after human capital controls were added. Lucifora (1991) replicates many of the results of Dickens and Katz (1987b) using Italian data.

Slichter (1950) found that the average wages of skilled and unskilled workers were highly correlated across industries. However, he could not control for geography and worker characteristics. Also, the categories of skilled and unskilled are relative and may not be consistent across industries. Dickens and Katz (1987b) estimate the correlation of industry wages for different one-digit census occupations, controlling for the same wide range of variables described above, and find a median correlation of .79. Widely different occupations all show the same effect of being in a high-wage industry. For example, clerical workers and transportation equipment operatives have a correlation exactly equal to the median.

Given the similarity of industry wage patterns in so many dimensions, it becomes interesting to examine the correlates of industry wage differentials. Our inferences about the source of differentials might differ if they were associated with average worker quality and research and development rahter than industry concentration, capital/labor ratios, and profitability.

In fact, industry wage differentials are associated with all these and other factors. Dickens and Katz (1987a) show that there are large simple correlations between measures of industry wage surplus and the industry quit rate, labor productivity, average years of education, average job tenure, average age, percent of the workforce that is female, the layoff rate, the injury rate, hours worked per week, the ratio of the dollar value of total compensation to wages and salary, union coverage, firm size, concentration ratios, research and development expenditures, capital/labor ratios, percent production workers, profits as a percent of sales, profits per worker, and the rate of return on fixed capital. This is a long list that supports many interpretations.

As dual labor market theory and dual economy theory suggest, many job characteristics are highly correlated. Consequently, attempts to establish which relations are most important have been largely fruitless. The literature on the relation between industry wages and industry characteristics reveals little consistency (Dickens and Katz 1987a). Different data sets and specifications yield widely different results as to which variables are primary in explaining the differences. When Dickens and Katz perform their own analysis they find the same inconsistency. Only average education and profitability are consistently related to industry wages in all specifications. The high level of collinearity in the data makes it impossible to sort out the individual contribution of specific variables.[8]

Going below interindustry differences, Groshen (1987) finds large differences in wages across employers within industries which explain a substantial amount of individual wage variation. Her (1988b) paper demonstrates that these differences are quite persistent.[9] Groshen (1988a) reviews nearly two dozen studies finding similar results. Among them, Hodson (1983) matched individual and firm data and was able to control for many individual characteristics, while Evans (1960) and Conant (1963) found that standardized tests of clerical skills do not explain the interemployer variation in clerical wages.

Could these interindustry and interemployer differentials arise in markets that clear? Broadly, there are three possible market clearing-explanations for interemployer wage differences—transitory returns to industry specific skills, compensating differences for working conditions, or returns to unmeasured ability.

The first of these interpretations can be easily ruled out by the evidence showing strong correlations of industry and employer wage patterns over several decades. The second is not as easily dismissed. The similarity of industry wage patterns across countries suggests a technological explanation which would fit with compensating differences. However, a number of other aspects call this explanation into question. First, several studies have controlled for a wide range of job characteristics (see, for example, Krueger and Summers 1988). These studies find little or no effect on industry wage differences. If anything, industry wage differences are exacerbated by consideration of job characteristics. This would be consistent with industry wage differences giving workers larger incomes and job quality being a normal good. Second, since wage differentials are highly correlated across occupations, the compensating differentials explanation requires that job characteristics also be highly correlated. It is difficult to claim that industry-specific job characteristics are shared by secretaries and truck drivers.

The possibility that workers in high-wage industries receive a return on some unobservable skill is subject to the problem of explaining the similar wage differentials across occupations. Why would an industry that required highly skilled truck drivers also require highly skilled secretaries? Recall also that previous studies found that standardized tests of clerical ability cannot explain interemployer differences in clerical wages (Evans 1960; Conant 1963). There are additional problems this explanation must address.

Suppose that high-wage industries are industries that disproportionately employ high-quality workers. If this ability is useful in any industry, then when workers change industry, their wages should not change significantly. Several studies have examined this question. Except for Murphy and Topel (1987), all find that industry changers' wages increase or decrease by nearly the full amount of the difference between the average wages of the two industries (Krueger and Summers 1988; Blackburn and Neumark 1988; Gibbons and Katz 1989). Murphy and Topel find that industry switchers receive only about 30 percent of the difference between industries. However, their study has been replicated on a different data set by Gibbons and Katz (1989) who find that changers receive 75 percent of the average industry difference.

These results rule out a universally valued skill as the explanation for interindustry differences. However, it is possible that interindustry differences reflect a return to skills that are more valued in the high-wage industries. Indeed, it is hard to explain why high-skill workers would be concentrated in high-wage industries if their skills were not valued more highly there, although one might still expect more skill transferability than suggested by the results discussed above. Again, the high correlation of the wage patterns across occupations limits the types of industry specific skills that can be considered. The skill (or skills) must be valuable to both truck drivers and managers in the high-wage industry, but not to those in low-wage industries. It is not obvious what these skills would be, but perhaps the question can be finessed by assuming significant complementarities among different types of workers in a firm. Further, such job matching would be consistent with low quit rates in high-wage jobs. However, the existence of sorting does not mean that wages are market clearing. An employer forced to pay high wages by a union would at least partially offset the effect by using the higher wage to hire more able workers.

How much of the observed interindustry differences can be explained by unobserved ability? Murphy and Topel (1990) argue that if there is sorting on observed ability there should be at least as much sorting on unobserved ability since so much is unobserved to the econometrician. It is plausible that much of what is not observed by the econometrician is also not observed by the employer so that the Murphy-Topel assumption is not self-evident. Nevertheless, we will accept it for the purpose of discussion. They then examine the extent of sorting on observed ability and conclude that about 30 percent of the wage premium can be explained by matching and unobserved ability if marital status is treated as a measure of ability. A much smaller fraction is explained when sorting on education is examined. [10] The argument that marital status is a better measure of ability than education is rather strange. Marital status has not traditionally been treated as a human capital variable. Moreover, marital status may be determined by job status rather than vice versa. People may wait until they are established in a good paying job before they decide to marry and have a family.

One piece of evidence suggests that interindustry wage differences may be due, at least in part, to unobserved ability. Kletzer (1989) and Gibbons and Katz (1989) find that the wage differential in one's previous industry helps predict the wage on a new job after job displacement. That finding is predicted by the unobserved ability explanation and might not be anticipated from other perspectives. However, if one assumes that networks of connections or employer discrimination on the basis of nonpecuniary characteristics are important in access to good-paying jobs as some have argued (for example, Bowles and Gintis 1976), then this result is understandable.

In summary, the best remaining modification of human capital theory is one in which there are differential returns to unobserved skill across industries. It is consistent with or plausibly modifiable to be consistent with many of the facts about interemployer differences. It has generated one new finding but faces two major anomalies—the interoccupation correlations and the inability to explain the lack of sorting on the basis of observable human capital characteristics. Further, this version of human capital was reached after a series of modifications. Until recently, human capital theory ignored the possibility of interindustry wage differentials or dismissed them as being due to transitory skill premiums or compensating differences received by some workers in the industry. When documentation of these wage differentials became the focus of the revived labor market segmentation research program of the 1980s and the cross-occupation correlations were demonstrated, researchers first searched for a common source of compensating wage differentials (employment fluctuations) (Topel and Murphy 1987). When this failed to explain the evidence, they then tried to explain the differentials by the existence of unobserved abilities which were equally useful in all industries. The next step involved differentially valued unobserved ability and a job mobility model based on lifecycle considerations. Finally, we have reached the present modified human capital model. It remains to be seen whether the latest human capital model will prove to be a fruitful and progressive approach to industry wage differentials.

On the other hand, the labor market segmentation approach, while also suffering setbacks, has been much more progressive. If wage differences represent worker rents, we would expect differences in quit rates and application rates across industries with different wages.[11] Several studies have found a negative association between quit rates and wage premiums. Holtzer, Katz, and Krueger (forthcoming) find that application rates are higher in high-wage industries. While the market-clearing models can be made consistent with this result and the differentially valued ability model predicts it, the labor market segmentation models were the ones that generated the initial prediction.

The labor market segmentation model also predicts that individuals getting high-wage jobs should consider themselves lucky. The Boston working-class men interviewed by Wial (1988) clearly distinguished between good and bad jobs. Furthermore, most did not think that the good jobs went to the more able. Even those who held high-paying jobs generally attributed their having them to luck or to connections. To get a good job, even a nonunion one, workers felt they needed someone who would let them know when jobs were available so they would know when to apply. A friend or relative might also intercede with the person making the employment decision. Otherwise one needed to be phenomenally lucky to show up at the right time when jobs were being filled.

Similarly, the labor market segmentation model predicts that employers will give reasons other than ability for wage differentials. Fred Foulkes's (1980) managers did not see themselves as getting what they paid for in worker ability. He interviewed personnel directors at several large nonunion U.S. firms and concluded that paying enough to avoid unionization was the major consideration in determining pay. These managers relied heavily on industry wage surveys, even for workers for whom local wage surveys would have given more relevant information from a competitive labor market perspective.

While labor market segmentation theory is successful in making these predictions, without an explanation of why differentials arise, the power of the theory would be limited. The last decade has seen the development of a number of competing (efficiency wage) models which we discussed above. Some of these models do not fare much better than the market-clearing ones. The simple labor discipline and quits models have as much trouble explaining the high correlation of interemployer wage differences across different occupations as a market-clearing model. The adverse selection model and the employer search model are somewhat easier to fit with these findings. Wage norm models and rent-sharing or rent-extraction models predict these correlations. In fact, it was to test such models that Dickens and Katz (1987b) undertook their study. But, the wage norm theory has particular difficulty explaining the cross-national evidence. Why would the same wage norms prevail in such distinct countries as the former Soviet Union, Germany, Chile, Korea, Japan, and the United States? The rent-sharing and rent-extraction models are also challenged by this evidence. Why should the pattern of rent-sharing be so similar in such different economic systems? To believe that rent-extraction is the explanation for the inter-industry differences, one must believe that workers have substantial power even in very repressive systems.

This may not be that far-fetched. Goldman (1983) reports on a number of large organized labor actions in the former Soviet Union aimed at securing higher wages or better working conditions. These are overt actions. Doubtless, covert actions are even more plentiful in repressive societies. Mars (*Cheats at Work*, 1982) and Mathewson (*Restriction of Output Among Unorganized Workers*, 1969) describe numerous examples of such behavior in the United States.

Thus the labor market segmentation program has been very progressive. Plausible theories have been put forward, and evidence on interindustry wage differences has provided considerable support for those theories. Very little back-tracking has been necessary to explain the facts. Further evidence of the progressivity of the program follows.

Evidence Part II: Tests for Labor Market Segmentation

Many researchers (Gordon 1971; Buchele 1976a; 1976b; Oster 1979) have chosen to test labor market segmentation theory by factor-analyzing data on industries, occupations, or individuals. These studies find that the majority of the systematic variance can be explained by one or two factors, and nearly all by four or five. Furthermore, in all the studies one of the two factors that "explain" the most standardized variation fits with the descriptive literature on dual labor markets. Job and worker characteristics associated with the primary sector load positively on the factor while characteristics associated with the secondary sector load negatively. Therefore, although the dual market distinction may not be the only relevent distinction, it is clearly in important one. There does seem to be a high degree of association between different job and worker characteristics so that the dimensionality of these characteristics can be usefully reduced, as labor market segmentation theory suggests.

Two other approaches are to look for differences in the wage determination mechanism between different labor market segments and to look for barriers to mobility between the sectors. Most studies have used a priori classification systems, often derived from factor analysis of industry or occupation data. Studies taking this approach have usually been supportive of the view that there are different wage determination mechanisms in the different sectors. Examples of such studies include Osterman (1975), Carnoy and Rumberger (1980), Buchele (1976a; 1976b), Rosenberg (1976), Wright (1979), Beck, Horan, and Tolbert (1978), Heckman and Sedlacek (1985), and Heckman and Hotz (1986).[12] However, Zucker and Rosenstein (1981), Bibb and Form (1977), Hodson (1977), and Tolbert, Horan, and Beck (1980) find little support for the dual market typology, and even the supportive studies are not free of anomalies.

Furthermore, all these studies, except the two by Heckman and his co-authors, fail to account for the endogeneity of an individual's labor market segment. This is Cain's (1976) main criticism of this work. Figure 1 illustrates the problem. If we arbitrarily divide a single market into high- and low-wage sectors, with most workers in the high-wage sector, the estimated equations will tend to fit the dual market typology. Returns to education (or other measures of ability) will be lower in the low-wage "secondary" sector, and

Figure 1: Hypothetical Scatter Plot—Standard Human Capital Theory

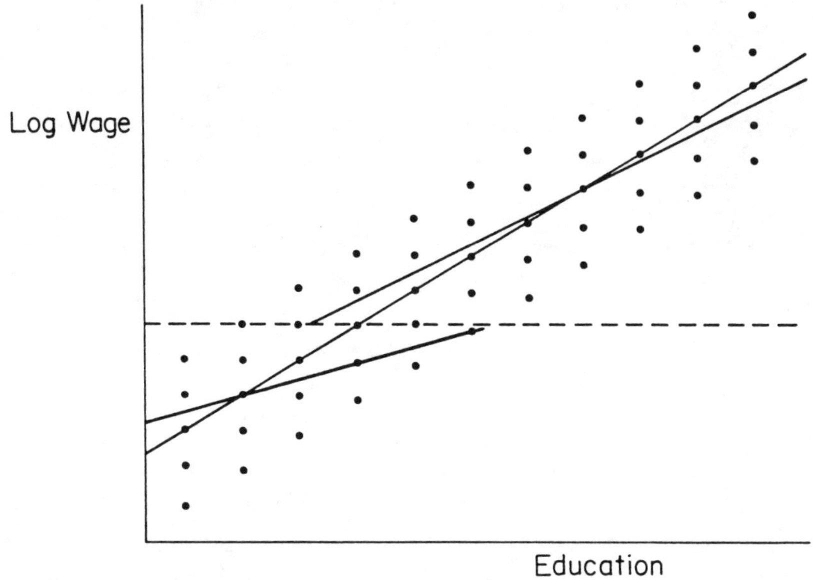

that wage equation will lie generally below the "primary" sector equation. One solution is to use a priori classification systems but to correct for the sample selectivity bias in estimating separate equations. This is the approach taken by Heckman and Sedlacek and Heckman and Hotz. However, dual market theory suggests that it is difficult to determine a priori who is in which sector. Recall from our discussion above that even within the same firm (let alone industry), there may be both primary and secondary workers. Furthermore, since some job titles such as operative are broad and many "secondary" occupations are treated like lower-tier primary jobs in some firms, occupational classification systems are suspect. Thus it is appropriate to treat sector as unknown.

In a series of papers we have implemented a technique that allows us to estimate the wage equations for unobserved sectors simply by postulating the number of sectors and the determinants of sector attachment. Dickens and Lang (1985a) is the first paper to present this approach. We turn to a description of that procedure now.

Consider how we might proceed if people's earnings potential could be summarized by a single observable trait—for example, education—and an unobserved trait that was uncorrelated with education. In that case we could

Figure 2: Hypothetical Scatter Plot—Dual Market Theory

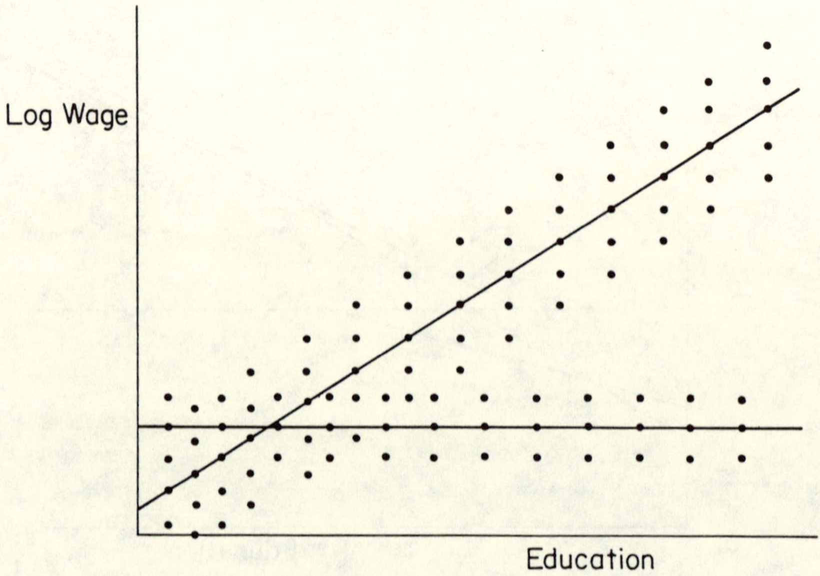

plot a scatter diagram of log wages and education. The standard view of the labor market holds that such a scatter diagram should resemble Figure 1. From dual market theory we would expect a scatter diagram similar to Figure 2. A straightforward test of the theories would therefore entail plotting the scatter diagram and assessing whether it corresponds to either the human capital model or the dual market model.

Two problems complicate such an approach. First, wages are determined by many observable characteristics other than education. To control for all variables simultaneously, we would have to plot a scatter diagram for each subgroup in the sample. As the number of other variables increased, the number of observations on each diagram would decrease considerably. With a reasonable number of controls, the number of diagrams and the sparseness of observations would certainly make it impossible to discern any pattern. Second, even if we were able to plot all the scatter diagrams, we would still lack a formal mechanism for testing the hypotheses. Each researcher could decide for him/herself whether the diagrams correspond more nearly to the predictions of human capital or dual market theory. These problems can be resolved by the use of the formal methods described in the following paragraphs.

Figure 3: Hypothetical Scatter Plot—Human Capital Theory with Non-Linear Wage-Education Relation

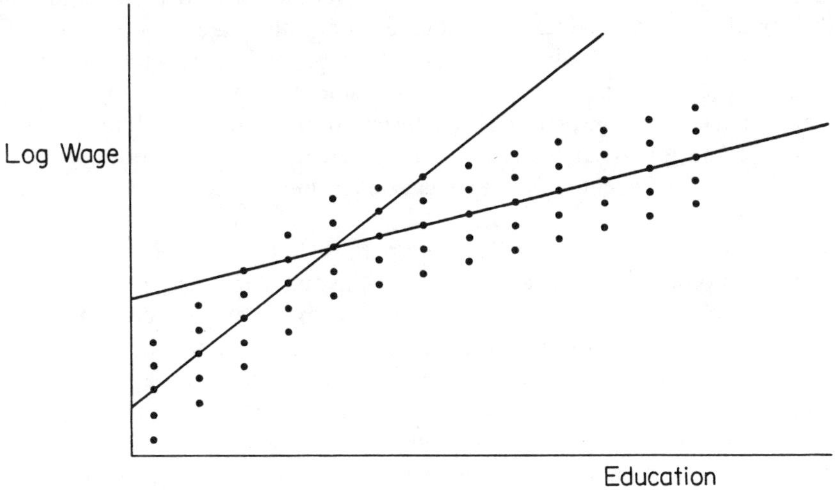

The question of whether a plot looks more like Figure 1 or 2 can be rephrased: do two wage equations fit the data significantly better than one, and do the best-fitting equations fit the predictions of the dual market hypothesis? We can imagine fitting first one and then two lines by hand to Figure 2. To compare the explanatory power we might, for example, compute the distance from each point to the closest line. The reduction in the sum of squares going from one line to two would be much larger for Figure 2 than for Figure 1.

Of course, two equations having more explanatory power than one is not, by itself, a test of the dual market hypothesis. For example, two equations might have significantly more explanatory power than one for a scatter diagram such as Figure 3. However, there is no identifiable secondary market. Thus, in addition to requiring two equations to have significantly more explanatory power than one, we also require the best-fitting lines to have characteristics consistent with the dual market hypothesis. To correspond to the predictions of dual market theory, one wage equation should be upward sloping in schooling and experience. The other equation should be nearly flat with respect to human capital variables and below the other at most points. Since we are dealing with a sample of adult males, we also expect that there will be fewer observations associated with the low-wage line.

Formally, we may fit two wage equations using maximum likelihood techniques. Since we do not know a priori with which wage equation to compare an individual, we estimate a switching model with unknown regimes. To do this we must specify two wage equations and a third equation that predicts sector attachment, and estimate all three equations simultaneously. Since the single-equation model is nested in the switching model, we may test the hypothesis that the two-equation model fits significantly better than the single-equation model by comparing the log-likelihood values for the two models. If we reject the single-equation hypothesis, we may examine the coefficients of the two wage equations to see if they fit the dual market hypothesis.

The results of our 1985a study were remarkably consistent with the dual market typology. Two wage equations fit the data considerably better than one with a chi-squared statistic of 177. A conservatively constructed 1 percent critical value is 29.14.[13] Furthermore, the estimated parameters of the two wage equations and the switching equation fit perfectly with the predictions of the dual market typology. One equation shows large and significant returns to education and experience. The other shows absolutely no returns. The switching equation showed, consistent with the dual market typology, that those who lived in cities, were married, and were white were more likely to be found in the primary sector.

Given the remarkable consistency of these findings with the dual market typology it is interesting to ask what the problem was with earlier studies that used a priori classification systems. As noted above, it seems likely that all these systems misclassify many workers. Prima facie evidence of this is presented by Zucker and Rosenstein (1981). Correlations among classification schemes that divide industries into core and periphery sectors are relatively weak, ranging from 57 percent to 83 percent agreement for the four taxonomies they studied. The degree of disagreement is striking when one considers that if each study had assigned people to the sectors randomly but in the same proportions as in the actual studies, the level of agreement would have ranged from 40 percent to 50 percent. Obviously systems based solely on industry will disagree considerably with those based solely on occupation since many occupations are common to many if not all industries. Do any of these systems come close to identifying the sectors correctly?

To answer this question we need to apply the switching equation technique to a very large data set so that we can accurately estimate the fraction of primary and secondary sector workers in the detailed industries and occupations used in the a priori classification systems.

The data used for this study are drawn from the 1983 Current Population Survey. All male heads-of-households between 20 and 65 years of age who were employed, reported that they normally worked more than 20 hours a week, earned more than the minimum wage, and for whom data on wages[14] and all independent variables were available were included in the sample. We limited ourselves to individuals who were in their fourth or eighth interview month. Screening on this basis left us with 48,411 observations. The sample was restricted to men because of the substantially different nature of many women's jobs and the difficulty of fitting them into the dual market typology. In particular, pink collar jobs have many characteristics of both primary and secondary jobs. The other restrictions ensure that if a secondary sector is identified by the analysis, it consists of more than part-time earners or those with transient labor market attachment.

We begin by estimating our original model with the modifications that experience squared is included in the wage equations and that experience and its square are included in the switching equation.[15] As can be seen in Table 1, this does not significantly alter the results. The first column of the table gives ordinary least squares (OLS) estimates, while the second through fourth columns give the primary sector, secondary sector, and switching equation estimates. As in our previous work, the primary sector equation is similar to that obtained using OLS estimation. The returns to education and experience are somewhat higher in the primary sector than in the OLS equation and the black-white wage differential somewhat lower. In contrast to our previous work, we can reject the hypothesis of no black-white wage differential in the primary sector. In the secondary sector there is no return to schooling and a perverse effect of experience. There are also somewhat surprisingly large effects of living in an SMSA and never having been married on secondary sector wages. The chi-squared statistic for the test of the hypothesis that only one wage equation is needed to describe the data is 2,368. The hypothesis can be rejected at any conventional level.[16]

These results continue to be strongly supportive of the dual market view. Therefore, we now turn to misclassification error in previous studies. Our estimation technique entails calculating a probability of being in each sector for each worker. These estimates are in some sense ex ante. Having estimated the wage equations, we can recompute the probability that each individual is attached to the primary sector. The two probabilities have very different interpretations. The probability calculated in the course of the estimation technique is the ex ante probability that the worker will end up in the primary or secondary sector. However, ex post, each worker is either in the primary sector with probability one or in the secondary sector with probability one. The ex post probability we calculate is therefore a measure of our ignorance—how certain we are that this individual is in the primary sector. Thus, if we estimate that an individual has a 99 percent probability of being in the primary sector, we are reasonably certain that he is in the primary sector.

Table 1. Parameter Estimates for Single and Dual Labor Market Models

Variable	*OLS Coef.*	*Switching Model* *Primary*	*Secondary*	*Switching*
CONSTANT	0.730	0.720	1.146	−0.315
	(0.014)	(0.086)	(0.107)	(0.137)
SMSA	0.109	0.078	−0.330	0.445
	(0.004)	(0.018)	(0.030)	(0.035)
NEVER MARRIED	−0.106	−0.057	0.397	−0.577
	(0.007)	(0.027)	(0.048)	(0.006)
SCHOOL	0.069	0.077	0.005	0.018
	(0.001)	(0.001)	(0.006)	(0.007)
WHITE	0.158	0.127	−0.321	0.515
	(0.007)	(0.023)	(0.045)	(0.054)
EXPERIENCE	0.030	0.030	−0.025	0.048
	(0.001)	(0.002)	(0.005)	(0.006)
EXPERIENCE SQUARED/100	−0.046	−0.041	0.066	−0.107
	(0.001)	(0.005)	(0.010)	(0.012)
STANDARD ERROR	0.418	0.347	0.772	*
COVARIANCE WITH SWITCHING ERROR		−0.028	0.775	–
LOG LIKELIHOOD	−26467		−25283	

* The standard error of the switching equation is normalized to one.
Figures in parentheses are standard errors.

If we estimate that he has a 50 percent probability of being in the primary sector, we have no information about sector of attachment. Therefore, to describe the composition of an industry or occupation we calculate the proportions of workers in that industry or occupation whom we can accurately classify as being in the primary sector or as being in the secondary sector and the proportion for whom sector of employment cannot be accurately ascertained.

Tables 2 and 3 show the breakdown of sector attachment for several industries and occupations. The three columns next to each category show the percent of people in that category who had a 0–30 percent probability of being in the secondary sector (secondary workers), a 30–70 percent probability (?s), and 70–100 percent probability (primary workers). The

Table 2. Composition of Industry Employment

Industry	*Secondary*	*?*	*Primary*
Agriculture, Forestry and Fisheries	25.29	36.39	38.32
Mining	2.07	8.64	89.29
Construction	3.75	13.12	83.13
Nondurable Manufacturing			
Food and Kindred Products	5.60	16.50	77.90
Tobacco	8.52	13.80	77.68
Textile Mill Products and Apparel	6.97	26.11	66.92
Paper and Applied Products	2.27	7.11	90.62
Printing, Publishing and Allied Ind.	7.83	11.12	81.05
Chem., Petrol., Coal, Rub. and Plastic	2.76	10.33	86.91
Leather and Leather Products	12.35	30.70	56.95
Durable Manufacturing			
Lumber, Wood and Furniture	9.33	26.14	64.53
Stone, Clay, Glass and Concrete Prod.	3.59	14.92	81.49
Primary Metals	2.26	7.20	90.54
Machinery and Equipment	2.42	7.74	89.84
Transportation	6.27	10.53	83.20
Communications (Except Telephone)	9.69	15.52	74.79
Utilities and Telephone	1.40	5.01	93.59
Wholesale	6.94	14.50	78.56
Retail (Except Eating, Drinking and Liq.)	13.35	21.60	65.06
Eating & Drinking Places, Liquor Strs.	29.29	32.11	38.60
Finance, Insurance and Real Estate	7.06	11.73	81.20
Business and Repair Services			
Advertising, Research and Computers	2.75	6.05	91.21
Services to Bldgs and Personnel Supply	24.21	24.12	51.67
Detectives and Protective Services	48.66	17.83	33.51
Repair and Services N.E.C.	8.35	20.31	71.34
Personal Services	23.94	26.88	49.18
Entertainment and Recreational Services	18.75	22.91	58.34
Profesional and Related Services			
Offices of Health Professionals	9.69	7.05	83.26
Hospitals and Health Services N.E.C	11.33	18.04	70.63
Nursing, Child and Residential Care	26.61	22.09	51.30
Education and Related Institutions	15.51	15.29	69.19
Other Profesional Services	2.79	5.78	91.43

Table 3. Composition of Employment by Occupation

Occupation	*Secondary*	*?*	*Primary*
Managers and Professionals (except those below)	3.44	5.83	90.73
Therapists and Physicians' Assistants	11.81	16.34	71.85
Post-Secondary Techers and Librarians	9.73	7.53	82.74
Economists*	0.00	4.71	95.29
Other Teachers	19.15	16.11	64.74
Social, Recreational and Religious Workers	36.41	20.16	43.43
Writers, Artists, Entertainers and Athletes	7.54	11.08	81.37
Technical, Sales and Administrative Support Occupations			
Health Technologists and Technicians	5.69	15.87	78.44
Technologists and Technicians Except			
Health Sales	2.10	6.95	90.95
Retail	22.68	23.61	53.72
Other Than Retail	6.68	11.67	81.65
Administrative Support			
Super., Comp. Op. and Secretaries	4.23	11.65	84.13
Information Clerks	19.24	17.00	63.76
Messengers, Office Machine Operators, Mail, Rate, Personnel, Library and Bookkeeping Clerks	18.38	22.09	59.53
Bank Clerks	26.09	29.19	44.72
Other	5.97	16.64	77.39
Service Occupations			
Protective Services (except guards)	16.04	0.00	83.96
Guards	39.05	22.87	38.08
Food Preparation and Service	34.29	34.07	31.64
Health Service Occupations	23.94	44.93	31.13
Cleaning, Household and Personal Services	24.61	28.09	47.31
Farm, Forestry and Fishing Occupations	27.42	37.57	35.01
Precision Production, Craft and Repair Occupations			
Mechanics and Repairers	3.72	13.05	83.23
Construction Supervisors	2.10	6.22	91.68
Construction Trades (except supervisors)	3.26	13.45	83.29
Extractors, Plant and System Operators, Craft Supervision and Inspection and Metal Crafts	2.07	7.38	90.55
Other Precision Production	5.14	19.15	75.70

Occupation	*Secondary*	*?*	*Primary*
Operatives (except textile, apparel and furnishings)	4.33	15.09	80.58
Operatives (textile, apparel and furnishings)	9.60	36.98	53.42
Transportation and Material Moving Occupations			
Motor Vehicle Operators	10.08	19.68	70.24
Rail and Water Transportation	5.46	8.45	86.09
Material Moving Equipment Operators	3.99	15.74	80.27
Handlers, Equipment Cleaners, Helpers, and Laborers			
Garage Workers, Vehicle Washers and Packers	20.07	39.39	40.55
Others	10.56	21.82	67.62

* Based on small number of economists in sample.

results are substantially in accord with descriptive work on the dual market. Agricultural workers, retail sales workers, and service workers are more likely to be associated with the secondary market. Most manufacturing workers are very likely to be in the primary sector, but textile and apparel workers are not. Also, more secondary workers can be found among operatives in manufacturing than among the skilled crafts. One notable attribute of these tables suggests why past studies have often produced anomalous and inconsistent results. None of the industries or occupations examined is identifiable as being entirely secondary. It seems that even in those industries or occupations which are substantially secondary, there are many people who are probably primary workers. This finding is not an artifact of our choice of industries or occupations for this table. It was true of all occupations and industries for which there were enough people in our sample to be confident of the composition estimates. With over 48,000 people, this was nearly all two-digit categories and many three-digit categories.

A large number of classification schemes have been used in previous research. The large degree of misclassification which is inherent in a priori schemes suggests that one reason for the inconsistency of results across studies may be varying degrees of inaccuracy. To cast light on this possibility, we review four industrial classification schemes (Beck, Horan, and Tolbert 1978; Tolbert, Horan, and Beck 1980; Bibb and Form 1977; Hodson

1977) and one occupational classification scheme (Osterman 1975). We chose these studies because Zucker and Rosenstein (1981) have reanalyzed the industrial schemes, permitting a direct comparison of their results and because the analysis in Osterman is comparable to that used by Zucker and Rosenstein.

Zucker and Rosenstein compare the classification shemes frist by examining the average characteristics of workers in each sector. Of the 17 characteristics examined, Beck, Horan, and Tolbert's classification system produced the anticipated differences in means for 12, Tolbert, Horan and Beck's for 9, Bibb and Form's for 7, and Hodson's for 6. In addition, Zucker and Rosenstein estimated separate earnings equations for each sector for the four classification schemes. Beck, Horan, and Tolbert's (1978) system was the only one that produced significantly different results in the two sectors. Thus among the industrial classification schemes, Beck, Horan, and Tolbert's performed somewhat better than the others, followed by Tolbert, Horan, and Beck, Bibb and Form, and Hodson.

Studies that have used occupational classifications have generally been more supportive of dual market theory (Rosenberg 1976; Osterman 1975). In particular, Osterman estimates sharply differing wage equations for the primary and secondary sectors, and the differences correspond to the predictions of dual labor market theory.

Table 4 presents our estimates of the true distribution of workers in each of the five studies' "sectors." Our results suggest that all four schemes are broadly consistent with the data. Sectors classified as periphery or secondary contain a higher fraction of secondary workers and fewer primary workers. However, all four schemes also misspecify many workers. Thus it is not surprising that the evidence generated by using these classification systems is so mixed.

Osterman's occupationally based classification scheme does a much better job than the industrial schemes of dividing workers between sectors, although there is substantial misspecification. It nevertheless appears that his results are strongly supportive of the dual labor market hypothesis because his classification scheme is more accurate than those used by other researchers. Furthermore, the two schemes used by Beck, Horan, and Tolbert, which performed marginally better in Zucker and Rosenstein's comparison, perform slightly better than the other two systems here. Both have fewer primary workers misclassified as being in the periphery, and more secondary workers who are correctly classified.

Is it surprising that two equations fit the wage distribution significantly better than one? Several critics of our approach have suggested that it is not. They argue that the standard OLS wage equation is too simple to be

Table 4. Comparison of Dual Labor Market Classification Systems

	Secondary	*?*	*Primary*
BECH, HORAN AND TOLBERT (1978) INDUSTRIAL CLASSIFICATION			
	Secondary	*?*	*Primary*
Core	4.97	10.63	84.39
Periphery	14.19	22.66	63.14
BIBB AND FORM (1977) INDUSTRIAL CLASSIFICATION			
	Secondary	*?*	*Primary*
Core	3.38	10.04	86.58
Periphery	11.29	17.37	71.32
HODSON (1977) INDUSTRIAL CLASSIFICATION			
	Secondary	*?*	*Primary*
Core	3.05	9.69	87.27
Periphery	12.02	18.42	69.56
State	1.33	6.01	92.66
TOLBERT, HORAN AND BECK (1980) INDUSTRIAL CLASSIFICATION			
	Secondary	*?*	*Primary*
Core	3.52	9.69	86.80
Periphery	14.98	21.97	63.03
OSTERMAN (1975) OCCUPATIONAL CODING SYSTEM			
	Secondary	*?*	*Primary*
Upper Tier, Primary	8.81	8.32	82.87
Lower Tier, Primary	5.48	12.31	82.21
Secondary	20.42	27.77	51.81

taken seriously. In particular, the error term is known to be heteroskedastic. These critics suggest that if we tested our dual market specification against a more general single equation model with heteroskedastic errors, we would no longer reject the single market model.

We have now done this (Dickens and Lang 1987). In that paper we estimated a 22-parameter single equation model (our dual labor market model had 21 parameters). Eleven of the parameters were coefficients of the wage equation, including terms for: a constant, dummies for residing in an SMSA, never having been married, and race and measures of years of schooling, years of schooling squared, years of labor market experience, experience squared, and interactions between schooling and experience, race and schooling, and race and schooling squared. the same 11 terms were also allowed to describe the heteroskedasticity—a very general model. Several other specifications were tried. This one fit best. The predicted distribution based on the general heteroskedastic single equation model was then compared with the true wage distribution. The model is rejected at any conventional level of significance. Even this very general model fails to track the true distribution of wages. It predicts fewer low-wage workers and many more middle-wage workers than are observed. It also tracks the upper tail poorly.

How well does the dual market model do in the same test? With one less degree of freedom, the dual market model fits the empirical distribution sufficiently well that one cannot reject it at the 5 percent level. It is possible to reject the model at the 10 percent level, but only because the dual market model is unable to predict the bunching of wages at values of $7.50 and $10.00 an hour. Other than that, the theoretical distribution implied by the dual market model conforms to the empirical distribution quite closely.

All of the studies described above are restricted to studying the labor market experience of men. A failing of the dual market approach has been our inability to extend it to women. We anticipated this, and consequently our early work excluded women. The pink-collar sector fits neither the description of the primary or the secondary sector. Like the secondary sector, such jobs are typically "dead end." Therefore, one would expect little return to experience. On the other hand, such jobs tend to be concentrated in large primary firms, and education may help women obtain better jobs within the pink-collar sector. This is close to what Friedberg, Lang, and Dickens (1988) find. Nearly all women are located in a women's sector with little return to potential experience but with substantial returns to education.

So what does it mean if two equations fit better than one? The existence of two sectors with different wage-setting mechanisms is fundamental to dual market theory, but it is not incompatible with human capital theory. Neoclassical economics tends to emphasize models that are continuous and therefore tractable in calculus. However, if the technology were sharply discontinuous in the way suggested by Piore (1980b), no fundamental assumptions of mainstream economics would be violated. In this case, individuals would choose the sector of employment that maximized the expected present value of their lifetime utility.

The second tenet of dual market theory, that primary sector jobs are rationed, is less compatible with human capital theory. Dual market theory maintains that individuals cannot always choose the sector that they prefer. Some workers who would prefer to be employed in the primary sector cannot find jobs there. On the face this seems likely. Who would prefer to work in the secondary sector when his/her wages would be substantailly lower than in the primary sector throughout his/her work-life? For example, given the results in Table 1, an average, white, married city-dweller with a high school education would start out earning $4.61 an hour more in the primary sector and continue to earn at least that much more throughout his career. Even an average unmarried nonwhite who lived outside a SMSA—for whom the primary/secondary difference is minimized—would earn more in the primary sector for his entire career if he had more than a high school education. The same person with a ninth grade education would be earning more in the primary sector in less than five years. A similar person living in an SMSA would always be paid more in the primary sector.

Some people might prefer the nonwage characteristics of the secondary market. However, descriptions of the secondary sector are unanimous in maintaining that the nonpecuniary aspects of secondary employment are inferior to those in primary employment, making this unlikely. Nonetheless, secondary employers may be less concerned with lateness and absenteeism and the work pace may be slower in secondary jobs. Therefore, it is worthwhile to consider another test.

To implement this test we need to postulate a mechanism for allocating workers between the sectors in the absence of rationing. In our 1985a paper we assumed that experience in one sector raises wages in the sector more than it raises wages in the other sector. We also assumed that workers will behave so as to maximize utility over their lifetime. Utility was assumed to be increasing with the net present value (*NPV*) of lifetime income. Assuming further that workers are perfectly informed about job characteristics and that preferences about the nonpecuniary aspects of jobs do not change over their lifetime, workers will choose one sector and stay there permanently.

If the nonpecuniary characteristics of the two sectors were similar, workers would pick the sector that yields the highest lifetime income. To allow for differences in how workers perceive the nonpecuniary value of secondary employment, we assume that workers will choose primary sector employment if the log of the *NPV* of their income stream in the primary employment exceeds the log of the *NPV* of secondary employment by more than an amount *C*—the additive inverse of the compensating differential for secondary employment. We may write the probability that a worker is employed in the primary sector (denoted *P*) as

$$P = Pr\{ln(NPV_p) - ln(NPV_s) > C\} \tag{1}$$

where the subscripts *p* and *s* denote primary and secondary. To model the *NPV* in the two sectors, we write the two wage equations:

$$ln(W_p) = XB_p + Ya_p + e_p; \tag{2}$$

$$ln(W_s) = XB_s + Ya_s + e_s, \tag{3}$$

where X is a vector of individual characteristics, Y is years of job experience, W_p is the wage received in the primary sector, e_p is a normally distributed error representing unobserved characteristics affecting the primary sector wage, and B_p and a_p are parameters. The terms W_s, e_s, B_s, and a_s are similarly defined for the secondary sector. Approximating the length of the individual's working life by infinity, and using equations (2) and (3), equation (1) becomes

$$P = Pr\{X(B_p - B_s) + e_p - e_s + C' > 0\}, \tag{4}$$

where

$$C' = ln((d - a_s)/(d - a_p)) - C, \tag{5}$$

and d is the discount rate.

If we assume that C' is equal to a constant (C'') plus a normally distributed error term which is independent of X and d (i.e., people's preferences with respect to the nonpecuniary aspects of employment and their discount rates do not vary with observable characteristics (X)), we may test the hypothesis that people choose their sector of employment to maximize their utility. We do this by estimating an equation to determine sector membership and testing the hypothesis that the coefficients on the Xs are equal to $B_p - B_s$, or that the B_ws in

$$X(B_p - B_s + B_w) + C'' + e_p - e_s + e_w \tag{6}$$

are equal to zero.

Alternatively, we might assume that experience is equally valuable in both sectors independent of the sector in which the person worked. In that case people with free choice will, at each point in time, choose the sector that maximizes their utility. In that case equation (6) becomes

$$X(B_p - B_s + B_w) + C'' + Y(a_p - a_s + a_w) + e_p - e_s + e_w \tag{6'}$$

where Y may be either experience or a vector of experience and experience squared, and the as are conformable vectors of parameters.

It may be reasonable to assume that preferences for the nonpecuniary aspects of primary or secondary employment are related to some observed worker characteristics. If so, at least some of the B_ws would be different from zero even if workers can choose the sector in which they are employed. In this case we may be able to find some Xs that should not be related to tastes, or to suggest the direction of their effects. We propose specific tests of this type below.

An intuitive explanation of this approach uses the example of race. Suppose that the lines fitting the scatter diagram in Figure 2 were the same for blacks and whites. Suppose further that the distribution of education were the same for the two groups, but that a higher proportion of blacks than of whites were scattered around the lower line. Under these circumstances, we would conclude that either blacks are less averse to secondary employment than are whites, or that blacks face discrimination in obtaining primary jobs. Supplementary evidence would support the latter explanation.

We have no strong expectations regarding the effect that living in an SMSA, having experience, or never having been married has on tastes for secondary sector employment. However, there is no reason to believe that blacks will be less averse than whites to the working conditions in the secondary sector. Indeed, auxiliary evidence discussed in Dickens and Lang (1985a) suggests that the opposite may be true. Also we expect more educated workers will be indifferent or more averse to secondary employment than other workers. Therefore, we limit ourselves to testing the relation between the wage and the switching coefficients for education and race. In our 1985a paper we test this hypothesis excluding experience from the switching equation and reject it at the .01 level. Here we include experience and experience squared in the switching equation to allow for mobility between the sectors. Again we reject the hypothesis of free choice between the sectors at the .01 level.[17]

A potential problem with our test for queuing is that we include union members in our sample. Not surprisingly nearly all are found in primary sector jobs (see Dickens and Lang 1985b). One might argue that it is no surprise that there are queues for union jobs, and that may be all we are seeing. To answer this objection we estimated a three-equation switching model with one known regime (union) and two unknown regimes (nonunion primary and secondary) (Dickens and Lang 1988; 1986). We found that even with the union sector treated separately there were distinct nonunion primary and secondary sectors with similar characteristics to those found in previous studies. Furthermore, nearly all workers would earn more in the primary sector than in the secondary sector. The test for barriers between the nonunion primary and secondary sector confirms their existence—particularly for blacks. Thus the existence of queues for primary jobs in our previous work is not solely the result of including union members in our sample.

Finally, these tests are only as good as our distributional assumptions. If there are substantial departures from normality in the distribution of the unobservables, then the tests are invalid. In this regard the goodness-of-fit test described above is quite encouraging. That the implied distribution of wages from the model, assuming normality for the errors, fits the true distribution so well suggests that the normality assumption may be a good one.

A Reply to Some Critics

Heckman and Hotz (1986), while presenting finding consistent with the dual market view for Panamanian males, have criticized our work as being uninformative. They make four specific points: (1) that there may be more than two sectors so the test for free choice may be invalid because the model is misspecified; (2) that we do not adequately account for nonpecuniary differences between the sectors; (3) that because of costs to mobility between the sectors, the decision rule for sector choice is misspecified; and (4) our assumption of joint normality of the unobservables in the model may be incorrect. They also note "in passing" that the likelihood ratio statistic we use to test the null hypothesis of only one sector is not theoretically valid. As noted in footnote 3 of our 1985a paper and in note 13 here, despite the theoretical problem defining the distribution of the test statistic, Monte Carlo evidence cited in Goldfeld and Quandt (1976) suggests that our approach provides a conservative test of the null hypothesis. Given the size of the test statistic relative to this apparently conservative critical value (well over 50 times the .01 significance level), the data overwhelmingly reject the restrictions of the single market model. The exact distribution of the test statistic simply is not an issue here.

As Heckman and Hotz note, points 1, 2, and 4 were all discussed in the 1985a paper. Point 3 is wrong. The version of the model we tested in our 1985a paper assumed that there were sector specific skills and thus costs to mobility. Above we have replicated that test as well as one that assumes no costs to mobility. Nonetheless, the more general criticism that the choice model may be misspecified is valid. The estimation of a more complicated model which allowed for limited transferability of skills between sectors proved intractable.

Points 1 and 2 have no bearing on our first concern—whether the dual market model provides a better description of the wage distribution than the standard single market model. Point 4 does, and as described above, we (Dickens and Lang 1987) subjected our original model to a goodness-of-fit test and showed that not only do we fail to reject the distributional assumptions at the .05 level but also that the dual market model significantly outperforms a complex single sector model with a very general error distribution and one more parameter.

All four points are of more concern to the interpretation of the test of free choice. Heckman and Hotz, in their second point, claim that our tests require us to assume that race and schooling have no effect on tastes for secondary employment. In fact, we argue on the basis of auxiliary evidence that more educated workers and blacks are likely to have a greater preference for primary employment. This expectation is not confirmed. In any case, our 1985a paper notes that an alternative interpretation of our test is that blacks, more educated workers, or both prefer secondary jobs. More generally, their arguments can be interpreted as saying that the null hypothesis of free choice may be rejected either because it is false or because of errors in the empirical specification or the auxiliary hypothesis used to derive the theoretical prediction. We accept this criticism, but point out that it is applicable to any empirical hypothesis test. It is, therefore, possible to reject all empirical tests as uninformative. Indeed Heckman and Hotz come close to this position when they accept that human capital theory is also untestable.

We believe that the way to view the question is not to reject the testability of theories. Instead we must recognize that no test can ever be viewed as definitive except with the hindsight of history. As we discussed above, this problem is not unique to dual market theory, economics, or even the social sciences. It is always possible to reinterpret the results of any test to make them consistent with another theory. However, when a theory motivates a long string of tests and comes through them with as little need for revision as labor market segmentation theory has, the theory deserves attention. It has proved itself to be a fruitful path for research. It is not any one test, but the weight of the evidence, particularly the dynamic context of the evidence, that suggests that labor market segmentation theory deserves serious attention.

Conclusion

Labor market segmentation theory has been very progressive. In the early '70s factor analytical tests of the descriptive power of the segmentation perspective were remarkably successful. Most of the early studies of differences in wage determination mechanisms were successful. Problems with inconsistency in the results of these studies have been shown to be due to inadequate a priori classification schemes. When the early studies were challenged for their problems with sample selectivity bias, later studies showed that even after corrections for this problem the differences in the wage determination mechanisms persist. Early empirical work showed patterns of mobility between the sectors consistent with descriptive work. Furthermore, in our work on dual markets we have developed considerable evidence suggesting the existence of barriers to mobility between the sectors. In response to critics we have shown that the dual market model provides a much better description of the income distribution than does a highly augmented human capital model. The examination of interindustry wage differences in the last decade has also provided a long string of successes for the labor market segmentation perspective.

In comparison, the human capital perspective has not fared well. Although highly progressive for much of the '60s and '70s, the human capital program has become quite regressive in recent years. The challenges of the evidence generated by the labor market segmentation perspective have left advocates of human capital theory stretching to explain anomalous results. Attempts to empirically verify patched versions of the theory have generally not been successful. Sample selection bias did not explain the differences in the wage determination mechanisms between the primary and secondary sectors. Helwege (1987) found that failure to control for human capital did not explain the intertemporal correlation of interindustry wage differences. Several attempts to find evidence that interindustry wage differences are due to unobserved ability have been unsuccessful.

The success of labor market segmentation theory both in the theoretical and empirical domain, particularly its relative success in predicting the outcome of studies undertaken in response to criticism of previous work, deserves recognition. Labor market segmentation theory should be taken seriously by economists.

What does this mean? Labor market segmentation theory should be given at least equal consideration with human capital theory when economists are analyzing policies or planning tests of economic hypotheses. What are the effects of increasing school quality on worker productivity or the effects of job training? What are the welfare costs and benefits of unemployment insurance? What are the benefits of trade and industrial policies? These questions may have markedly different answers from the two perspectives.

The application of labor market segmentation theory to new problems will not be easy. Labor market segmentation theory is still in its infancy. Much work remains to build and expand the theory. If economists are to take labor market segmentation theory seriously, they will need to develop the theory further. In particular, the nature of the wage determination mechanism in different sectors needs to be established. We still face a wide range of theories that can explain interemployer wage differences and queuing. Since they have different policy implications, it is important to sort them out.

The relation of labor market segmentation to race discrimination is another area that deserves study. Our examinations give inconsistent results on the relative importance of wage and employment discrimination in the two sectors. It would be interesting and important to understand these results. Furthermore, extensions of the labor market segmentation model to capture the nature of women's labor markets would allow us to address more convincingly how much progress women have made in the last two decades.

Finally, models of labor market segmentation are closely related to models of unemployment. These models are natural vehicles for examining questions about the composition and distribution of unemployment and its likely response to active labor market policies. However, first we need to answer some basic questions about unemployment. How much unemployment is caused by workers queuing for primary sector jobs? How much is the result of jobs churning in the secondary sector? What are the roles of layoffs and recall in the unemployment process? The development and application of labor market segmentation theory poses an exciting challenge to economists wanting to understand how the labor market works.

Notes

1. The flat earth theory still has proponents who are adept at explaining why apparently contradictory evidence really conforms with the theory. As recently as 15 years ago an organization calling itself the "Defenders of the Geocentric Universe" published their own newspaper, *The Brayhian Debater*, which offered rationalizations of their views.

2. Even this criterion (most often identified with Imre Lakatos) has its critics. Paul Feyerabend, for example, argues that many research programs now viewed as progressive have had regressive periods and that it is inappropriate to prefer one over another on the basis of its past performance. We accept the point that second and higher derivatives matter in determining who will get where they are going first. However, in the absence of information on higher order derivatives we still prefer the train that, projecting current rates, will seem to arrive first.

3. While waiting in secondary jobs, blacks experience few wage increases. Since more blacks are in secondary jobs, their within-job growth rate is smaller than for whites. However, since fewer whites start out in the secondary sector, few experience the large wage growth as they move from the secondary to the primary sector. Consequently, overall black wage growth is higher.

4. Rebitzer and Taylor (1991) provide a formal model of such behavior.

5. Our presentation follows our recollections of lectures given by Piore to his graduate labor class at Massachusetts Institute of Technology in the mid-1970s.

6. Carmichael (1990) also has criticized these models for not being able to predict the

correlates of high wages. While this is true of the original models, simple intuitive elaborations eliminate this problem. For example, if in the shirking model firms face a continuum of workers with different unobservable costs of effort and the cost of shirking to the firm is proportional to the cost of the machines people work with, then the efficiency wage will depend on the cost of the machines. This could explain the correlation of wages with capital/labor ratios discussed below.

7. Standard deviations of the natural log of wages can be roughly interpreted as percentages.

8. Of course, this is exactly the sort of "reduction in the dimensionality of job characteristics" that labor market segmentation theory requires. We discuss this evidence at greater length below.

9. Leonard (1989) shows that this is not true of the electronics industry in California's Silicon Valley. In this new industry firm relative wages are quite volatile.

10. They conclude that all of the interindustry difference can be explained by the combination of sorting and unobserved ability. This is because by their estimates only about 30 percent of interindustry differences cannot be attributed to common unobserved ability. (See the discussion of this evidence above.)

11. It is possible to create compensating difference models with both these properties. Our argument is not that these findings are incompatible with such models, only that one would not expect them a priori.

12. Most of these studies use specially created a priori classification systems based on industry and/or occupation codes. Heckman and Sedlacek (1985) contrast the wage determination mechanism in manufacturing versus the rest of the economy, and Heckman and Hotz (1986) divide workers into primary and secondary sectors on the basis of their earnings.

13. Since some of the parameters of the dual market model are not identified when the single equation model is imposed as a constraint, the distribution of the test statistic is unknown. However, the Monte Carlo tests of Goldfeld and Quandt (1976) suggest that setting the degrees of freedom equal to the number of constraints plus the number of unidentified parameters yields a conservative test using the chi-squared distribution.

14. For salaried workers, wages are computed by dividing weekly earned income by normal hours of work.

15. Experience is measured as Age – (Years of schooling + 5).

16. See note 13 for a qualification concerning the nature of the test.

17. We have also estimated a version of the model using these data where experience and experience squared were not included in the switching equation. There, too, the hypothesis of free choice was rejected (see Dickens and Lang 1985b).

References

Akerlof, A. 1984. "Gift Exchange and Efficiency Wage Theory: Four Views." *American Economic Review* 74: 79–83.

Averitt, R.T. 1968. *The Dual Economy*. New York: Norton.

Beaudry, P. 1990. "Entry Wages Signalling Futures Wages: A Foundation to Turnover Models of Unemployment." Mimeo, Boston University.

Beck, E.M., Horan, P.M., and Tolbert, C.M. 1978. "Stratification in a Dual

Economy: A Sectoral Model of Earnings Determination." *American Sociological Review*, 43: 704–720.

Bibb, R., and Form, W.H. 1977. "The Effects of Industrial, Occupational and Sex Stratification on Wages in Blue-Collar Markets." *Social Forces* 55: 974–996.

Bliss, C.J., and Stern, N.H. 1978. "Productivity, Wages and Nutrition, 1: The Theory." *Journal of Development Economics* 5: 331–362.

Bowles, S., and Gintis, H. 1976. *Schooling in Capitalist America*. New York: Basic Books.

Buchele, R., 1976. "Jobs and Workers: A Labor Market Segmentation Perspective on the Work Experience of Young Men." Unpublished doctoral dissertation, Harvard University.

Cain, G. 1976. "The Challenge of Segmented Labor Market Theories to Orthodox Theory." *Journal of Economic Literature* 14: 1215–1257.

Calvo, G. 1979. "Quasi-Walrasian Theories of Unemployment." *American Economic Review* 69: 102–107.

Carmichael, H.L. 1990. "Efficiency Wage Models of Unemployment: An Overview." *Economic Inquiry* 28.

Carnoy, M., and Rumberger, R. 1980. "Segmentation in the U.S. Labor Market: Its Effects on the Mobility and Earnings of Whites and Blacks." *Cambridge Journal of Economics* 4: 117–132.

Conant, E.H. 1963. "Worker Efficiency and Wage Differentials in a Clerical Labor Market." *Industrial and Labor Relations Review* 16: 428–433.

Dickens, W.T. 1986. "Wages, Employment and the Threat of Collective Action by Workers." NBER working paper.

Dickens, W.T., and Katz, L.F. 1987a. "Industry Wage Differences and Industry Characteristics." In *Unemployment and the Structure of Labor Markets*, K. Lang and J.S. Leonard, eds., Oxford: Basil Blackwell.

———. 1987b. "Industry Wage Differences and Theories of Wage Determination." NBER Working Paper 2271.

Dickens, W.T., and Lang, 1985a. "A Test of Dual Labor Market Theory." *American Economic Review* 75: 792–805.

———. 1985b. "Testing Dual Labor Market Theory: A Reconsideration of the Evidence." NBER Working Paper 1670.

———. 1986. "Labor Market Segmentation and the Union Wage Premium. NBER Working Paper 1883.

———. 1987. "A Goodness of Fit Test of Dual Labor Market Theory." NBER Working Paper 2350.

———. 1988. "Labor Market Segmentation and the Union Wage Premium, The Review of Economics and Statistics.

Dickens, W.T., Katz, L., Lang, K., and Summers, L. 1989. "Employee Crime, Monitoring, and the Efficiency Wage Hypothesis." *Journal of Labor Economics* (July).

Edwards, R.C. 1975. "The Social Relations of Production in the Firm and Labor Market Structure." In *Labor Market Segmentation*, R. Edwards, M. Reich, and

D.M. Gordon, eds. Lexington, MA: D.C. Heath.

Evans, R. Jr. 1960. "Worker Quality and Wage Dispersion: An Analysis of a Clerical Labor Market in Boston." *Industrial Relations Research Association Proceedings.*

Foulkes, F. 1980. *Personnel Policies in Large Nonunion Companies.* Englewood Cliffs, NJ: Prentice-Hall.

Friedberg, R., Lang, K., and Dickens, W.T. 1988. "The Changing Structure of the Female Labor Market, 1976–1984." *IRAA 41st Annual Proceedings.*

Gibbons, R., and Katz, L.F. 1989. "Learning, Mobility, and Inter-Industry Wage Differences." NBER Working Paper 3182.

Goldfeld, S.M., and Quandt, R.E. 1976. "Techniques for Estimating Switching Regressions." In *Studies in Non-Linear Estimation.* Cambridge, MA: Ballinger.

Goldman, M.I. 1983. *U.S.S.R. in Crisis.* New York: W.W. Norton.

Gordon, D.M. 1971. "Class, Productivity and the Ghetto." Unpublished doctoral dissertation, Harvard University.

Groshen, E.L. 1987. "Sources of Wage Dispersion: The Contribution of Inter-Employer Differentials Within Industry." Mimeo, Federal Reserve Bank of Cleveland.

————. 1988a. "Why Do Wages Vary Among Employers?" *Federal Reserve Bank of Cleveland Economic Review*, 19–38.

————. 1988b. "Do Wage Differences Among Employers Last?" Mimeo, Cleveland Fed.

Harrod, R.F. 1938. "The Scope and Method of Economics." *Economic Journal* 48: 383–412.

Heckman, J.J., and Hotz, J.V. 1986. "An Investigation of the Labor Market Earnings of Panamanian Males: Evaluating the Sources of Inequality." *Journal of Human Resources* 21: 507–542.

Heckman, J.J., and Sedlacek, G. 1985. "Heterogeneity, Aggregation and Market Wage Functions: An Empirical Model of Self Selection in the Labor Market." *Journal of Political Economy* 93: 1077–1125.

Helwege, J. 1987. "Interindustry wage Differentials." Mimeo, UCLA.

Heywood, J.S., 1990. "Imports and Domestic Wages: Is the Relationship Consistent with Expense Preference Behavior?" Mimeo, University of Wisconsin-Milwaukee.

Hodson, R.D. 1977. "Labor Force Participation and Earnings in the Core, Peripheral and State Sectors of Production." Unpublished Masters thesis, University of Wisconsin–Madison.

————. 1983. *Workers' Earnings and Corporate Economic Structure.* New York: Academic Press.

Holzer, H.J., Katz, L.F., and Kreuger, A.B. 1988. "Job Queues and Wages: New Evidence on the Minimum Wage and Inter-Industry Wage Structure." Princeton University Industrial Relations Section Working Paper 230.

Katz, L.F. 1986. "Efficiency Wage Theories: A Partial Evaluation." *NBER Macroeconomics Annual, 1986.* Cambridge, MA: MIT.

Kletzer, L. 1989. "Returns to Seniority After Permanent Job Loss." *American Economic Review* 79: 536–543.

Koopmans, T. 1954. *Three Essays on the State of Economic Science*. New York: McGraw-Hill.

Kreuger, A., and Summers, L. 1987. "Reflections on the Inter-Industry Wage Structure." In *Unemployment and the Structure of Labor Markets*, K. Lang and J.S. Leonard, eds. Oxford: Basil Blackwell.

Kreuger, A., and Summers, L. 1988. "Efficiency Wages and the Inter-Industry Wage Structure." *Econometrica* 56: 259–293.

Lakatos, I. 1978. *The Methodology of Scientific Research Programmes*, Vol. I. Cambridge: Cambridge University Press.

Lang, K. 1991. "Presistent Wage Dispersion and Involuntary Unemployment." *Quarterly Journal of Economics* 106: ??.

Lang, K., and Dickens, W.T. 1988. "Sociological and Neoclassical Perspectives on Segmented Labor Markets." In *Industries, Firms, and Jobs,* G. Farkas and P. England, eds. New York: Plenum Press.

Lang, K., and Kahn, S. 1990. "Efficiency Wage Models of Unemployment: A Second View." *Economic Inquiry* 28: 296–306.

Lang, K., Marquez, G., and Romaguera, P. 1988. "Theories of Wage Determination: Lessons from Chile and Venezuela." Mimeo, Boston University.

Lazear, E. 1979, "The Narrowing of Black-White Wage Differentials Is Illusory." *American Economic Review* 69: 553–564.

Leigh, D.E. 1976, "Occupational Advancement in the Late 1960s: An Indirect Test of the Dual Market Hypothesis." *Journal of Human Resources* 11: 155–171.

Leonard, J. 1989. "Wage Structure and Dynamics in the Electronics Industry." *Industrial Relations* 28(2): 251–275.

Lindbeck, A., and Snower, D.J. 1986. "Wage Setting, Unemployment, and Insider-Outsider Relations." *American Economic Review* 76: 235–239.

Lucifora, C. 1991. "Inter-industry and Occupational Wage Differentials." Mimeo, Universita' Cattolica di Milano.

Mars, G. 1982. *Cheats at Work: An Anthropology of Workplace Crime*. London, Boston: Allen & Unwin.

Murphy, K.M., and Topel, R. 1987. "Unemployment, Risk, and Earnings: Testing for Equalizing Wage Differences in the Labor Market." In *Unemployment and the Structure of Labor Markets*, K. Lang and J.S. Leonard, eds. Oxford: Basil Blackwell.

Murphy, K.M., and Topel, R. 1990. "Efficiency Wages Reconsidered: Theory and Evidence." In *Advances in the Theory and Measurement of Unemployment*, Y. Weiss, ed. London: Macmillan.

Oster, G. 1979. "A Factor Analytic Test of the Theory of the Dual Economy." *Review of Economics and Statistics* 61: 33–51.

Osterman, P. 1975. "An Empirical Study of Labor Market Segmentation." *Industrial and Labor Relations Review*, 28: 508–523.

Piore, M.J. 1980a. "Dualism as a Response to Flux and Uncertainity." In *Dualism and Discontinuity in Industrial Societies*, S. Berger and M.J. Piore, eds. New York: Cambridge University Press.

————. 1980b. "The Technological Foundations of Dualism." In *Dualism and Discontinuity in Industrial Societies*, S. Berger and M.J. Piore, eds. New York: Cambridge University Press.

Rebitzer, J.B. and Taylor, L.J. 1991. "A Model of Dual Labor Markets When Product Demand is Uncertain." *Quarterly Journal of Economics* 106: ??

Robertson, D. 1940. *Essays in Monetary Theory*. London: King.

Rosenberg, S. 1976. "An Empirical Test of the Dual Labor Market Hypothesis." Unpublished manuscript, Williams College.

————. 1980. "Male Occupational Standing and the Dual Labor Market." *Industrial Relations* 19: 34–49.

Salop, S.C. 1979. "A Model of the Natural Rate of Unemployment." *American Economic Review* 69: 117–125.

Schiller, B.R. 1977. "Relative Earnings Mobility in the United States." *American Economic Review* 74: 433–444.

Shapiro, C., and Stiglitz, J.E. 1984. "Equilibrium Unemployment as a Worker Discipline Device." *American Economic Review* 75: 433–444.

Slichter, S. 1950. "Notes on the Structure of Wages." *Review of Economics and Statistics* 80–91.

Smith, J.P. 1989. "Career Wage Mobility." In *The Question of Discrimination*, S. Shulman and W. Darity, Jr., eds. Middletown, CT: Wesleyan University Press.

Solow, R. 1979. "Another Possible Source of Wage Stickiness." *Journal of Macroeconomics* 1: 79–82.

Stiglitz, J.E. (1976). "The Efficiency Wage Hypothesis, Surplus Labor, and the Distribution of Income in L.D.C.s." *Oxford Economic Papers* 28: 185–207.

Tolbert, C.M., Horan, P.M., and Beck, E.M. 1980. "The Structure of American Economic Segmentation: A Dual Economy Approach." *American Journal of Sociology*, 85: 1095–1116.

Wachter, M.L. 1974. "Primary and Secondary Labor Markets: A Critique of the Dual Approach." *Brookings Papers on Economic Activity* 3: 637–680.

Weiss, A. 1980. "Job Queues and Layoffs in Labor Markets with Flexible Wage Expectations." *Journal of Political Economics* 88: 526–538.

————. 1990. *Models of Unemployment, Layoffs, and Wage Dispersion*. Princeton: Princeton University Press.

Weitzman, M. 1989. "A Theory of Wage Dispersion and Job Market Segmentation." *Quarterly Journal of Economics* 104: 121–138.

Wial, H.J. 1988. "The Transition from Secondary to Primary Employment: Jobs and Workers in Ethnic Neighborhood Labor Markets." Unpublished doctoral dissertation, Massachusetts Institute of Technology.

Yellen, J.L. 1984. "Efficiency Wage Models of Unemployment." *American Economic Review Papers and Proceedings* 74: 200–205.

Zucker, L.G., and Rosenstein, C. 1981. "Taxonomies of Institutional Structure: Dual Economic Reconsidered." *American Sociological Review* 46: 869–884.

III RACE, DISCRIMINATION, AND COMPETITION

6 LABOR MARKETS AND RACIAL INEQUALITY

Jeremiah Cotton

Among the major theoretical undertakings of mainstream labor economics in the recent past has been the attempt to explain why racial differences in wages and employment arise and, more importantly, why they have persisted for so long. This is a project of the utmost urgency if capitalism is to be defended as a system in which individual rewards are distributed equitably commensurate with individual contributions to the production process.[1] The one explanation for these differences, put forward in one form or another by both orthodox and heterodox analysts, that complicates matters for this salutary view of capitalism, is discrimination. If it can be established that factors which are perfectly substitutable in production can and do receive differential compensation solely on the basis of the possession or lack of possession of some extraneous characteristic, then the claim that competitive capitalist markets are the most efficient orchestrators of the economic activities of self-interested individuals would have to be relinquished.[2] The resulting prices and quantities appearing in labor and product markets would reflect neither the true values nor optimal amounts of the resources employed and goods produced.

The reluctance of the neoclassical defenders of capitalism to accept discrimination as a significant factor in the generation of differential labor market outcomes by race is buttressed by their rendering of the concept of market competition. In their interpretation labor markets, like the rest of the economy, are subject to the workings of competitive forces that would, in the fullness of time, purge them of any external impediments such as discrimination. If racially distinct workers of equal ability are paid different wages or hired at different rates, the profit-making opportunities created thereby would attract entrepreneurs for whom profits are the sole consideration. They would forthwith take advantage of the situation by hiring away the underpaid and underutilized workers, produce the market output at lower cost, undersell the discriminators, and eventually drive them from the market. Given such an inevitability, the occurrence of discrimination cannot, therefore, be anything other than a short-run phenomenon. In the long-run the economic survival of the discriminators would be in serious jeopardy.

In several illuminating papers William Darity, Jr., and Rhonda Williams (Darity 1989; Darity and Williams 1985; Williams 1987) maintain that it has not been the essentially static neoclassical version of competition taken alone that has ultimately led to the undoing of discrimination as an explanation for racial inequality in capitalist labor markets; rather, it has been the dynamic Austrian notion of competition wherein the main emphasis is on the special faculty of the profit-seeking entrepreneur to overcome all obstacles that bar the way to economic gain. The existence of such entrepreneurs guarantees that wage and employment differentials among equally productive workers not only cannot be maintained under conditions of neoclassical perfect competition but neither can they exist for long in imperfectly competitive markets. For whatever the imperfection, the resourceful Austrian profit-maximizer, undaunted, will find a way around the barrier and turn the situation to account.

The major contribution made by Darity and Williams to this debate, however, is their contention that labor market discrimination is quite compatible with conceptualizations of market competition other than those delineated by neoclassical and Austrian economics. They argue that discrimination can endure indefinitely in both classical and Marxist formulations of competition. In neoclassical and Austrian competition it is the ability of labor to move more or less freely across all sectors of the economy that brings about the equalization of wages in all sectors and guarantees the elimination of long-run wage differences between equally productive black and white workers. By contrast, in classical and Marxist competition the tendency is toward the equalization of profit rates, not wage rates. The former is brought about by movements in finance capital. Whether racial wage differences exist, therefore, has no bearing on the attainment of long-run equilibrium. In classical competition discrimination can persist because

> . . . rigidities, imperfections, barriers to entry by firms, and the like are irrelevant to the existence of competitive conditions so long as it is possible for rates of return to equalize everywhere [Darity 1989, 355].

Marx's view of competition, however, was qualitatively different from the classical notion in a number of important details. For one thing, like Austrian competition, it focused on the process by which equilibrium is attained rather than solely on the characteristics of the equilibrium state itself. For another, it was "evolutionary" in the sense that the postulate of fierce competition between capitalists over surplus labor and therefore surplus value led, paradoxically, to increasing concentration of capital in monopoly forms:

> The evolutionary nature of Marxist competition simply means that competition gives rise to monopolies, but monopoly is not the antithesis of competition. Centralization (the redistribution of existing capital) intensifies and advances competition, which is manifested in the flow of capital between branches of industry. Marx's capitalist winners consolidate and concentrate; they can exclude the losers and consolidate their positions for long stretches of time [Darity and Williams 1985, 259–260].

Darity and Williams then conclude that what works for capital in establishing and maintaining its monopoly positions under Marxist competition can also work for labor in maintaining discriminatory barriers to entry and therefore wage differentials:

> We extend Marxist competition to labor powers. Workers can also concentrate and consolidate, particularly by ethnicity or race. Via control of training, evaluation, information, and the definition of jobs, winners in early rounds of labor market competition can insulate themselves from the most recent recruits to the wage labor force. [Darity and Williams 1985, 259–260].

Both in the classical and Marxist solutions discrimination is restored as a credible explanation for persisting differential economic outcomes by race. Those who would therefore defend capitalism against charges of giving aid and comfort to racism must encamp on the theoretical terrain provided by the neoclassical explanation of inequality shored up here and there by the tougher Austrian notions. However, the closer examination of the development and deployment of both explanations that follows reveals flaws that are all but fatal to both as arguments for capitalism as a disinterested arbiter of values.

The general acknowledgment by orthodox analysts of the role played by discrimination in labor market outcomes by race began with the publication of Gary S. Becker's *The Economics of Discrimination*, the work that in effect set the neoclassical terms of debate on the issue. Assuming perfectly competitive labor markets and employing the vocabulary of utility theory, discrimination was conceived by Becker as a "taste" that originated outside of the market. It was indulged when employers, either exercising their own predilections or accommodating those of their employees or customers, chose to hire whites rather than equally qualified blacks and would hire the latter only if they were prepared to accept lower pay for the same job performed by the former, or a lower-paying job altogether. Becker assumed that the resulting measured differences in wages between white and black workers were pecuniary compensation for the disutility suffered by the discriminator as a consequence of economic association with blacks.

This, however, is precisely the situation that is made to order for the nondiscriminatory, profit-driven entrepreneurs adumbrated in neoclassical competition and fully realized in the Austrian framework. Neither the current position of the discriminators nor the existing discriminatory wage differentials could long survive the adjustment process set in motion with the coming of these profiteers. The discriminators might be able to continue in business with an all-white workforce, but differences in wages between their white employees and black workers of equal skill employed elsewhere would perforce disappear.

Thus, the inadequacy of the Becker model as a "theory" of discrimination was made manifest by its inability to explain how discriminatory wage differentials could long endure, given the assumptions of the model.

The need for a long-run explanation was apparent and pressing, however, since racial wage differentials had been observed in practically every significant labor market over the long history of black-white wage labor in the United States. Moreover, subsequent to the advent of Becker's model in the late 1950s, numerous empirical studies of racial wage and earnings differentials were undertaken in which analysts attempted to control for differences in so-called productivity or human capital factors that were assumed to generate legitimate differences in wages. In most of these studies, only a relatively small portion of the wage and earnings gaps was explained by human capital attributes. The remaining unexplained residuals were interpreted by many as at least upper-bound estimates of labor market discrimination, tacitly recognizing thereby that such residuals could also reflect the influence of other factors that might have been omitted from the equations.

Not everyone, particularly not many neoclassicists, was convinced of this interpretation of the residuals. In a well-known survey article, Cain stated their position:

> If, according to neoclassical theory, workers of equal productivity should receive equal wages, and they do not, then it is natural to expect the defenders of the theory to question whether productivity was really equal; specifically, whether the personal productivity factors are completely enumerated and accurately measured [Cain 1976, 1235].

In support of this observation Cain reported the results of a longitudinal study by Hall and Kasten (1973) that attributed the lack of labor market progress among young black males to their "pre-labor market endowments." This was the substance of the neoclassical response to the matter of the residuals. On the one hand, they tended to back away from the notion of equal black-white productivity characteristics, thereby at once attributing the presence of the residuals to model misspecification and underscoring the importance of human capital differences. On the other hand, they suggested that some underlying characteristics acquired outside the market and peculiar to blacks were largely responsible for their labor market plight, and these were going unmeasured.[3] The presumed characteristic or endowment accounting for the residuals that is now becoming increasingly popular among defenders of the neoclassical faith is culture. I will return to a consideration of both the human capital and culture arguments subsequently.

In the first wake of the collapse of the Becker model a number of economists who labor in the neoclassical vineyard were not yet ready to abandon the assumption of equally productive blacks and whites. They abandoned instead the assumption of perfect competition and sought the explanation for persisting racial wage and earning differences between equally productive workers in some form of market imperfection.[4] The most widely noted of these revisions traced the cause of long-term discriminatory wage differentials to employers' risk-averse behavior rather than any bias against blacks.

As the story goes, employers simply do not have very reliable information about the true productivity of blacks, and the costs associated with the risk of hiring them in the absence of such information are nontrivial. Rather than bearing these costs themselves, employers pass them along to blacks in the form of lower wages or lower hiring rates.

This lack of information may be evident in employers' negative subjective evaluations of blacks, that is, they may, albeit mistakenly, believe that blacks are less productive than whites. Even when blacks and whites are known, for example, to have the same amount of schooling, employers may discount the quality of black schooling. There also could be an objective basis for these beliefs. It may be that tests designed to measure worker skill are less accurate for blacks than for whites. In the former case the employer, relying on stereotypical perceptions, uses race as a riskless, cost-free signal that screens out blacks, and in the latter case the test itself screens blacks out. The result is the same in either event: equally able blacks receive lower remuneration for their ability not because the employer has a taste for discrimination but rather because the employer has a rational desire to minimize costs.[5]

But given the other competitive assumptions underlying this formulation, all that is required to erode the racial wage differentials generated in the first case is for less risk-averse or more perceptive enetrepreneurs who recognize the inherent profitability in the situation to enter the market, hire away the underestimated, undercompensated blacks, and set in motion the process that will ultimately lead to the economic demise of the stereotypers. The second case presents no problem either: profit-sensitive entrepreneurs should devise and employ tests that more accurately gauge the productivity of blacks. Suffice it to say, the candidates most willing and able to take up these tasks are the farsighted entrepreneurs anticipated in the Austrian concept of competition. But even in the kinder, gentler neoclassical version, as long as no barriers to entry exist, the wage differentials that result from these forms of statistical discrimination cannot long endure.

Another even less fruitful direction taken in the search for market imperfections that would sustain long-run racial wage differentials was the appeal to product market monopoly. A number of highly arguable conditions must hold, however, for the monopoly explanation to be defensible. Principal among them, as several commentators have maintained, would have to be the ability of the monopolist to prevent nondiscriminators from buying out the business.[6] Inasmuch as there are few companies of any consequence that are so closely held, this assumption is not promising. Moreover, since unexploited money profits would exist in such an industry, the specter of the barrier-breaching Austrian entrepreneur would always hang over it. Even if the monopoly operated under the aegis and control of the government so that it could indulge in discrimination without loss of its permitted profit levels, the industry would still be ripe for takeover by entrepreneurs skillful enough to devise ways to circumvent or dilute government control.

Swinton (1978) proposed an imperfectly competitive model characterized by "a hierarchical structure of jobs in the labor market based on differential wages" and collusive behavior by white workers aimed at ensuring their control over the upper hierarchy of good-paying jobs. White workers are able to impose their will on employers by threatening "increased wage demands'' or ''reduced efficiency'' or ''decreased work effort'' if equally qualified blacks are given the same access to the good jobs that whites are given. Racial wage differentials can be maintained indefinitely in this environment as long as the analysis is delimited by the neoclassical version of competition and the attendant flaws that can impair its full expression, factor market monopolies being among them. However, in the fullness of time, not even the barriers thrown up by coalitions of white workers would frustrate Austrian entrepreneurial ingenuity. Somehow, someway, the Austrian entrepreneur will take advantage of profit opportunities in the discrimination-ridden, white-worker-dominated industries—whether by forming countervailing coalitions of industry employers willing to face down white workers, or by setting up rival firms staffed exclusively with the abundant numbers of qualified but underemployed blacks, and whites who are willing to suppress their racial biases and brave the potential ostracism by more prejudiced whites in order to secure training and job opportunities.

The rigid wages, job hierarchies, and dominance by white workers depicted in Swinton's model are, however, consistent with much of the current realities of today's labor markets. In this respect Swinton's model cuts closer to the bone than any previous attempts at explaining long-term discrimination within the neoclassical framework. The stance taken in this article, however, is that this state of affairs is not the result of some ''imperfection'' or deviation from an ideal competitive norm, but rather it characterizes competitive capitalism in its best working order.

Keep in mind it was the inability of many orthodox theorists to reconcile long-run labor market discrimination with the neoclassical version of competition, coupled with the lackluster performance of the imperfectly competitive solutions, that ultimately led them to lay aside the troublesome assumption of equally productive workers and emphasize instead, racial differences in the acquisition and possession of characteristics that determine individual productivity. This was a more satisfying and orderly state of affairs since it paved the way for the restoration of the much revered, perfectly competitive milieu in which the marginal productivity theory could flourish.

As the defenders of capitalism advocated, workers now received the value equivalent in wages and earnings of that portion of total output created by their labors. The quality and quantity of their contribution, and hence their wages, were in direct proportion to the quality of their individual skills and the quantity of their individual efforts. These two hypotheses were elaborated in the intertwined theories of human capital investment and labor-leisure choice. Whereas the theory of marginal productivity stood as the demand-side guarantor of the essential fairness of capitalist labor markets, the two latter theories constituted the supply-side defense. If blacks on average earn less than whites, it is because blacks on average contribute less to the production processes than whites due to their lower investments and holdings of human capital, their generally higher reservation wages, and their greater preference than whites for leisure or nonmarket activities.

The large unexplained residuals from empirically generated racial wage equations were therefore assumed to be mostly artifacts of an omitted variable problem. On this account, it might appear to researchers that blacks and whites possess equal productivity endowments, but this is because important differences between the groups are left out of consideration. Specifically ignored in these empirical studies is the greater black predilection for "leisure" over "labor" evidenced by, among other things, the lower labor force participation rates of blacks and their greater willingness to accept government transfer payments and other nonmarket income sources as alternatives to market work.

As with Becker's and other subsequent neoclassical demand-side discrimination models, these two supply-side rejoinders were based on individual tastes of utility-maximizers—"tastes for market work." These tastes were presumed to be formed outside the labor market in the home or community, or, in other words, in the culture or subculture of the individual worker.

The suggestion that the residuals might be reflections of unmeasured tastes or cultural differences became even more appealing in the light of the evidence from the 1960s, 1970s, and 1980s. As Tables 1 and 2 show, although black and white educational attainment narrowed consistently and considerably over these decades, the same pattern was only partially realized when it came to income differences. In 1963, for example, the median educational attainment for black males 25 years and over was 3.2 years less

Table 1. Black-White, Male-Female Median Years of School Completed, Selected Years

Year	*Black Males*	*White Males*	*Years Difference*	*Black Females*	*White Females*	*Years Difference*
1963	8.8	12.0	3.2	9.4	12.1	2.7
1969	9.9	12.3	2.4	10.3	12.2	1.9
1979	12.1	12.7	0.6	12.1	12.5	0.4
1989	12.4	12.8	0.4	12.4	12.7	0.3

Sources: U.S. Bureau of Census, *Current Population Reports*. "Money Income of Households, Families and Persons in the United States," Series P-60 various years.

Table 2. Black-White, Male-Female Median Income Ratios

	Black-White Male Ratios		*Black-White Female Ratios*	
Year	*Full-time Workers Income Ratios*	*All Workers Income Ratios*	*Full-time Workers Income Ratios*	*All Workers Income Ratios*
1963	.64	.52	.62	.67
1969	.66	.58	.80	.84
1979	.73	.63	.92	.92
1989	.69	.60	.90	.80

Sources: U.S. Bureau of Census, *Current Population Reports,* Series P-60, "Money Income of Households, Families and Persons in the United states," various years.

than that of their white counterparts. By 1989, it was only 0.4 years less, having declined in each of the intervening decades. The decline in the educational gap between black and white females was similar. While differences in income between black and white full-time and all workers decreased over the 1960s and 1970s, they started to widen again during the 1980s. For example, for every $1 of income a white male full-time worker had in 1963, his black male counterpart had 64 cents. By 1969, it had risen slightly to 66 cents; in 1979, it was up to 73 cents. By the end of the '80s, however, it had fallen to 69 cents.

Not only did the black-white unemployment gap not narrow during these periods, but, with one exception, it steadily grew larger. In Table 3, an inspection of the decade-by-decade changes in the black-white, male, female, and teenage unemployment ratios reveal that, except for the male and female ratios during the 1960s, all the ratios increased over time.

Table 3. Black-White Unemployment Ratios, Selected Years

Year	*Black/White Male Ratios*	*Black/White Female Ratios*	*Black/White Teen Ratios*
1963	2.23	1.93	1.95
1969	2.12	1.86	2.25
1979	2.31	2.08	2.37
1989	2.77	2.44	2.42

Sources: Economic Report of the President, February 1989 and U.S. Bureau of Census, *Employment and Earnings* 37(1), January 1990.

Table 4. Black-White Unemployment Rates by Educational Attainment for Persons 16 to 24 Years of Age, Selected Years

	1970		*1979*		*1985*	
	Black	*White*	*Black*	*White*	*Black*	*White*
Less than four years high school	24.1%	15.0%	32.0%	16.5%	41.5%	23.6%
Four years of high school	16.8	8.9	21.7	8.5	29.4	9.8
One to three years of college	13.8	7.4	13.6	5.8	20.4	6.3
Four or more years of college	n.a.	6.8	18.2	4.0	18.2	4.8

Source: U.S. Department of Labor, *Handbook of Labor Statistics*, Bulletin 2340, Table 63, August 1989.

This situation posed an extraordinary dilemma for the human capital explanation and made the need for an additional explanation imperative. If increasing acquisition of education by blacks—and especially by young blacks, among whom relative educational advances were the greatest—was the reason why racial wage differentials decreased in the 1960s and 1970s, why did it not have the same salutary effect on racial unemployment differentials during the same period? As Table 4 shows, in 1970 the unemployment rate for young blacks, 16 to 24 years of age, with one to three years of college, was higher than that of young whites with just a high school education (13.8 percent vs. 8.9 percent). An even more dramatic disparity existed in 1979 when young blacks with four years or more of college had a higher unemployment rate than young white high school dropouts (18.2 percent vs. 16.5 percent). In 1985, the last year for which data comparable to previous years exist, the unemployment rate for young black college graduates was almost twice that for white high school graduates.

It is extremely difficult to accept the conclusion that the increasing acquisition and possession of human capital endowments by blacks can have a significantly positive effect on black-white relative incomes, earnings, and wages, but none on unemployment rates. If they are the major determinants of the former, as the theory implies, why don't they also influence the latter? Furthermore, if they are not capable of influencing the one, then their status as a principal determinant of the other is also open to question.

On the demand side of the labor market the human capital claim has it that employers, recognizing that blacks were accumulating more human capital and becoming more productive, had begun to pay them wages that were increasingly comparable to white wages. Why, then, would employers not carry this recognition over into their hiring decisions as well? On the supply side of the market it might be supposed that blacks' tastes for market work have been changing over time, and this is responsible for their growing accumulations of human capital and the attendant increases in their relative earnings. But the question still remains as to why the effects of these changing tastes and behaviors are not also reflected in changes in relative employment and unemployment rates. This is no small inconsistency.

The answer for some has been the argument that what is actually being observed are the separate labor market experiences of different classes of black workers. The relative earnings gap is closing for the educated black middle class as well as for a considerable segment of the better-trained black working class. What these dreary unemployment statistics essentially depict is the plight of the so-called black urban underclass. The overwhelming majority of the latter come into the labor market with few job skills and unreasonably high earnings expectations, or "reservation wages." They consequently pass up a number of jobs that are commensurate with their limited abilities because they do not pay enough. The costs of being unemployed for extended periods incurred by these blacks are largely defrayed by relatively generous and accessible government transfer programs such as public assistance or unemployment insurance.

The first problem with this view is the fact that the unemployment gap is not peculiar to the relatively uneducated but rather, as Table 4 shows, appears to exist at all educational levels. Nor is this gap strictly confined to the young. For individuals 25 to 64 years of age in 1985, the black-white unemployment ratio for those with four years of high school was 2.13; for those with one to three years of college it was 2.72; and for those with four or more years of college it was 2.57.

Second, the notion that many in the black lower classes are voluntarily unemployed because of their refusal to accept lower-paying work is suspect because it neglects evidence that many of these jobs are being increasingly suburbanized and made inaccessible to urban workers. It also overlooks data indicating that rather than being undereducated or underqualified, many workers, black and white, have more education and skills than the jobs they hold require. This overqualification phenomenon, however, affects blacks more adversely than whites. In 1980, for example, over one-third of employed black males and over one-fourth of employed black females were overeducated for the jobs they were doing. By comparison less than one-fourth of white males and one-fifth of white females were similarly overqualified.[7] The existence of these large overqualification rates further undermines what faith one might be inclined to place in the human capital investment model. Its inability to explain racial unemployment differentials greatly limits its usefulness as a strategy on which either policymakers or blacks themselves can rely in attempting to improve their lot.

But more importantly, the apparent failings of the human capital explanation threatens the integrity of the underlying marginal productivity theory and hence the integrity of capitalism itself. Darity rightly noted that "in a world where unemployment is a persistent condition, it is not clear how much validity the lineal predecessor of modern human capital theory, the marginal productivity theory of distribution, can have" (1982, 85).

Thus, a more fundamental explanation for black-white differences in labor market outcomes other than that provided by human capital theory alone was needed and the cultural explanation was a ready candidate. It had already been foreshadowed in a number of the subsidiary variables favored, if not employed, by many human capital theorists: for example, motivation, work commitment, and especially family background. Moreover, it was compatible with and could be encapsulated in the modern utility notion of "tastes" or "preferences." The adoption of the culturalogical argument, therefore, did not require a great deal of adjustment.

The substance of the argument proceeds along the following lines. Some cultures place a higher premium than others on so-called middle-class values such as hard work, self-reliance, and the postponement of present in favor of future consumption, such as establishing savings accounts, undertaking investments in education and occupational training, and so on. Market work is considered in these cultures to be the principal route out of poverty and toward economic advancement. Consequently, substantial amounts of the resources and efforts of the family, community, and group are devoted to preparing and disciplining the young for their coming careers in the labor market. Thus, in these cultures strong tastes or preferences are formed for human capital accumulation and market work.

By contrast, members of other cultures are more present-oriented, more fatalistic, and inclined to leave the future to chance. They do not attach great value to activity, work included, that involves an extensive sacrifice or investment of current time and resources. Families formed in the relatively precarious environments created by such attitudes are generally poor and ill equipped to pass on to their children much useful knowledge about how to get ahead in the marketplace. Not surprisingly, those entering the labor market with these proclivities and handicaps generally earn low wages and register high unemployment rates.[8]

Even individuals who appear to have acquired, or who start out with, the same amount of education or training but who come from these two disparate cultural backgrounds may end up on different rungs of the economic ladder. The added drive, motivation, and self-confidence imparted by the one culture will amplify the employment and earnings effects of the education or training acquired by its members. Therefore, in cases where there do not appear to be any differences in the traditional measures of human capital, and yet wage, earnings, or employment differences occur, culture is the omitted variable.

Once again it is the evocation of the Austrian entrepreneur that lays bare the theoretical flaw in the differential cultural argument, just as it did in the case of differential treatment or discrimination. Darity and Williams have insisted that Austrian entrepreneurs would immediately recognize that there are profits to be made in markets for cultural attributes even as there were in discriminatory markets.

> ... if some groups possess cultural attributes that enhance their performance in an environment where market exchange is a major aspect of social life, then we would expect incentives to emerge for members of the culturally advantaged group to transfer those attributes to less favorably endowed groups. The "new" cultural variant of the human capital theory presumes a persistence of market-valued cultural differences that is at odds with the conception of competition that undermined the theoretical persistence of market discrimination.
> ... Either Austrian entrepreneurs can undercut both market discrimination and cultural differentiation, or they can do neither [1985, 257–258].

Whenever profits are in the offing, whether on the demand-side of the market as with discrimination or on the supply-side in the case of cultural differences, the Austrian entrepreneur can be expected to intervene. The attempt, therefore, to rescue the human capital explanation for long-run racial earnings and employment differences by appeal to culture falters, and the matter is left still in doubt.

This is not the only shadow to be cast over the culture/taste/human-capital nexus. Robert Cooter and Peter Rappaport (1984) have resurrected an interpretation of "utility" espoused at the turn of the century by economists such as Alfred Marshall, A.C. Pigou, and Edwin Cannan that is incompatible with many of the implications of the modern neoclassical utility theory that lies at the roots of the human capital/labor-leisure choice theoretic. Instead of utility as the expression of a psychic, subjective desire, preference, or taste, utility was understood in objective terms as "material welfare," or the satisfaction of material needs such as food, housing, and health care.

The modern notion of utility as a subjective preference was then termed "ophelimity," while the term "utility" itself was reserved for the concept of material welfare.[9] Cooter and Rappaport observed that "the difference between utility and ophelimity is thus the difference between 'socially useful' and 'desired'" (1984, 515). The former is indisputably an economic category and in principle can be measured and therefore compared across individuals and groups. The latter is, as its modern adherents contend, incomparable, and is more reminiscent of a psychological than an economic category. Whether person A is better fed or better clothed or receives better health care than person B can be fairly readily discerned and their relative states compared. Whether person A desires or would enjoy a particular level of consumption or economic activity more or less than person B is a matter of the relative intensities of their individual preferences, and these are not susceptible of either cardinal measure or interpersonal comparison.

Although individuals are driven by desires and preferences to fulfill economic goals, the satisfaction of basic material needs through the acquisition of basic necessities generally takes precedence over all other motivations for economic activity. The Cooter-Rappaport explication of this point is worth quoting at some length:

> The material welfare school made a distinction among the *types* of satisfactions that could be derived from goods. Indeed, goods, the motives for acquiring them and the satisfactions yielded by their consumption were arranged in a hierarchy that proceeded from the "purely economic" or "material" at one end to the purely noneconomic or nonmaterial at the other. It was stressed that there was no hard-and-fast line separating the economic part of the scale from the noneconomic, although the extremes were clearly distinguishable. The material end of the hierarchy was concerned with survival and health. The goods that fell most securely within the purview of material welfare economics were food, "clothing, house-room and firing," followed by rest. These were dubbed "necessaries" by Marshall. As one proceeded further along the hierarchy, one came to "comforts" and "luxuries," whose material content was less certain [1984, 513].

The "tastes" to which modern utility theory refers and on which the structure and content of an individual's preference function is assumed to be based may very well be influenced strongly by their particular cultural environment or set of cultural experiences. But these are not the tastes that a given level of economic activity is primarily undertaken to satisfy. First and foremost it is the tastes derived from the material welfare function and shaped by physical and economic needs common to all cultures that determine the amount of economic activity an individual will pursue. In pursuing "purely economic" goals, the maximization of utility as material welfare rather than as ophelimity is the rule.

This is the fundamental flaw at the heart of labor-leisure choice theory: instead of linking the choice of how much market work an individual will pursue to meet material needs, it invokes tastes predetermined by nonmarket factors as the basis for choice. But individuals of whatever race or culture make decisions on how much labor to supply (and thus how much income and goods to obtain) on the basis of their material welfare needs, not on an idiosyncratic, cultural attitude toward work. Therefore, tastes for market work based on material welfare considerations can be expected to be similar across cultures.

The majority of studies on the tastes or attitudes toward work of blacks and other poor people have found no racial differences in work attitudes; several even suggested that blacks had stronger work commitments than whites.[10] A long-term social-psychological study conducted by Goodwin concluded that:

> Poor people—males and females, blacks and whites, youths and adults—identify their self-esteem with work as strongly as do the nonpoor. They express as much willingness to take job training if unable to earn a living and to work even if they were to have an inadequate income. They have, moreover, as high life aspirations as do the nonpoor and want the same things, among them a good education and a nice place to live. This study reveals no difference between poor and nonpoor when it comes to life goals and wanting to work. [1972, 80].

Findings such as these call into question the notion from job search theory that the high reservation wages of low-skilled blacks is a major factor in their high rates of unemployment. Indeed, if poor blacks want to work even if earnings are "inadequate," they must have relatively low, not high, reservation wages.

These are serious, perhaps even fatal, blows, with wide forebodings. If human capital theory comes under a cloud, so also does the marginal productivity theory of income distribution, on which the demand for labor in labor markets is based. It is one of the main pillars of the neoclassical capitalist defense. According to marginal productivity theory, irrespective of demographic identity, workers are hired in accordance with, and paid the wage equivalent of, their marginal product. The quantity and quality of this product—worker productivity—depends on the quantity and quality of the worker's stock of human capital. How much human capital workers will acquire depends in turn on their tastes for market work. These tastes are formed outside of the market and, in some recent views, are the products of the cultures from which workers spring.

These relationships begin to unravel, however, when first the cultural bases of the so-called tastes for market work are put out of commission.

This occurs on theoretical grounds with the coming of the Austrian entrepreneurs and the reclaiming of utility as an objective concept. It occurs on empirical grounds as account is taken of the historical effect of social class as the intervening variable in explaining differential cultural success (see note 8). Next, the human capital argument comes apart as evidence mounts that individuals from different racial groups with roughly identical stocks of human capital are persistently hired at different rates and paid different wages. This, of course, is wholly incompatible with predictions based on the neoclassical and especially the Austrian assumptions underlying the human capital model. It also lays open to question the human capital-productivity-wage/employment link.

Some on the periphery of the neoclassical orthodoxy have always entertained doubts about the strength of this link. One of the earliest statements of this skepticism was contained in Ivar Berg's 1970 book whose title said it all: *Education and Jobs: The Great Training Robbery*. Medoff and Abraham (1981) studied the personnel records of the white male managers and professionals of a large U.S. corporation to determine whether the high relative earnings of the more experienced managers and professionals could be justified on the basis of their relatively greater productivity. Although some consider their experience measure weak, Medoff and Abraham's conclusion—that productivity differences played a substantially smaller role in determining the associated earnings differences than a human capital explanation would have predicted—is highly suggestive.

If, over long periods of time, some workers are not paid or hired on the basis of their actual or potential productivity but rather on the basis of an extramarket characteristic such as race, then naturally marginal productivity theory has little or no explanatory power; neither do the competitive assumptions that underlie it have any basis in reality. The first to fall is Austrian economics since its tenets are the foremost guarantors of the marginal productivity payoff. Not far behind is neoclassical competition with its emphasis on labor mobility.

Given these failings, we are forced to look elsewhere for an explanation for persisting racial economic differences. In order to understand how these differences are generated and maintained, we must start from a point much closer to reality than either the neoclassical-cum-Austrian theory of human capital, or Becker's so-called theory of discrimination. We must go quite a step beyond Becker and recognize that race permeates the conscious and unconscious thought and decision-making processes of the overwhelming majority of the individuals in this society. Furthermore, distinctions and preferments based on race are routinely made at every level of social, political, and economic activity. Racial group identification and allegiances are extremely strong and cuts across class, gender, and ethnic lines.

Marcus Alexis (1973), though writing in the neoclassical tradition, had it right when he modeled the utility function of white employers with the incomes of white workers as one of its arguments. Although he did not appreciate it, the full spectrum of utility, from "ophelimity" to "material welfare," was affected. But why would white employers choose to forgo profits in order to maximize the incomes of white workers? What is in it for them? With the relinquishment of the neoclassical version of market competition, white employers may not have to forgo profits at all but can overpay whites with the proceeds from the underpayment of blacks. But more importantly, as Alexis implies, the overpayment of white workers can be thought of as an investment in the maintenance of the white power structure. As long as white workers can be placated with preferments over blacks, they will guard and defend the status quo that has the white capital-owning class at the pinnacle of the economic pyramid. This is certainly a material welfare consideration.

Furthermore, many white workers in their turn have the incomes of black workers among the arguments of their ophelimity and material welfare functions. With respect to the latter they largely see any economic advances made by blacks as a threat to and diminution of their own economic prospects. They benefit materially from the barriers to black economic mobility, and particularly resist and fear any form of affirmative action that would remove these barriers.

It is practically an article of faith among some Marxists—the work of Michael Reich (1981) being a leading statement—that white workers suffer economic losses as a result of discrimination against blacks. This view is strongly challenged by other radical economists who argue that white workers in effect band together, either in unions or through other institutional organs, to monopolize the better job and employment opportunities. In a recent empirical study, Shulman (1990) found that racial inequality generally improved the employment opportunities of white males and females in 1969 and 1979. The author himself has conducted a number of studies of racial wage differentials in which estimates were made of the amount by which whites are overpaid and blacks underpaid (see Cotton 1985; 1988).

It may, therefore, be concluded that discrimination is economically beneficial both to white employers and white workers and is thereby endogenous to the labor market earnings- and employment-generating processes. Becker's so-called tastes for discrimination are brought to the labor market as an expression of ophelimity, but they are reinforced and reproduced as a result of the material welfare benefits derived from their implementation.

The environment in which these inequalities take place is best described by the Marxist notion of competition. Most workers desire and seek employment in the sectors of the economy dominated and controlled by large corporations, business aggregates, and government bureaucracies, among whom the drive to consolidate and concentrate is intense. The neoclassical competitive assumption is therefore unrealistic, appearing to serve more of an apologetic rather than an analytic function.

Labor market outcomes are generated in a racially collusive, oligopolistic environment where white employers and white workers are mutually benefitted by the underpayment and underutilization of black workers. It not only satisfies nonpecuniary, psychic needs, or tastes for racial ascendancy over blacks but confers pecuniary, materials advantages as well. These psychic tastes for discrimination are inextricably bound up with the material. At bottom they serve to justify and legitimate the past and current treatment of blacks and to sanctify the material benefits derived from it.

Most white Americans take pride in portraying themselves as members in good standing of a fair, open, meritocratic, social melting pot where devotion to the work ethic and self-improvement through education and training are the keys to economic upward mobility accomplished through self-discipline. They are defensive about charges that they reap unwarranted benefits from racial discrimination. Instead, even if they admit the existence of past discrimination, they maintain that it has presently been eliminated and that any remaining black-white disparity is due to whites' greater skills and commitment to market work. The theories of human capital investment and labor-leisure choice, based as some would have it now on culturally determined tastes for market work and played out in an impartial, competitive milieu, are useful articulations of this fictive outlook.

The apparent association between the narrowing of black-white labor market earnings up to the 1980s and the narrowing of the black-white educational attainment gap is taken as strong, prima facie evidence of the general relevance of the outlook. Some who admit the role of past discriminatory practices in the determination of black outcomes attribute much of the recent convergence in earnings to government's intervention and correction of labor market failures by the enforcement of the antidiscrimination laws enacted in the civil rights legislation of the 1960s (see Freeman 1973a; 1973b; 1978). These efforts are thought to be central to the opening of opportunities for blacks to acquire human capital. This, too, was a demonstration of the essential fairness of the capitalist system.

While government intervention was no doubt instrumental in forcing white employers to cease or moderate some of their more egregious practices of wage and job discrimination, and these curtailments were probably a major reason for the closing of the wage gap that started in the 1960s, this view tends to overlook or minimize the fact that it was black demands, sit-ins, mass demonstrations, civil disobedience, and street riots that compelled government to take action. The government did not act on its own initiative, nor was action taken solely to redress past and current social and economic wrongs against blacks. The government, acting beacuse of black-initiated social conflict, had as its goal to "save the Republic," as it were, by cooling out black protests, restoring civil order, and preserving a reasonable facsimile of the status quo ante.

The downplaying of conflict and the portrayal of government as the great reconciliator in this context was crucial for discrediting the need for fundamental, revolutionary change. The neoclassical paradigm was well suited to carry this forward, assuming as it did a society and economy in which the harmonious interests of disparate classes and groups lead to smooth, conflict-free equilibria, with the state acting when necessary as a sort of referee or arbiter, guaranteeing that all will be well.

Although the passage and enforcement of the antidiscrimination laws of the 1960s no doubt contributed materially to the diminution of wage discrimination and thereby to the narrowing of the wage gap, it appears to have done little to affect the long-term patterns of employment discrimination. Indeed it appears that even the effects on relative wages have begun to wear off since the wage gap started to open again in the late 1970s and 1980s (see Bradbury and Browne 1986; Cotton 1989).

It could be argued that employers who no longer found it feasible to exercise their discriminatory tastes through wage differentials switched to reducing employment opportunities for blacks. Some evidence is consistent with this hypothesis. The ratio of black-white male labor force participation rates was fairly constant up to 1960, varying betwen .993 and .998. It fell from .990 to .980 between 1961 and 1966, and then began a more pronounced fall over the next ten years, reaching a low of .893 in 1976, after which it started to rise somewhat and stood at .926 in 1988. Similar changes over the same periods are detectable in the female ratios, though black female labor force participation rates were uniformly higher than those of white females. In 1962 the black-white female ratio was 1.308, and by 1988 it had fallen to 1.033.

Although the evidence on black-white adult unemployment rates is not as clear, since the increase in the relative rates did not begin in earnest until about 1975, the teenage rates do exhibit the feature common to the labor force participation rates: the ratio of black-white teenage unemployment rates started to increase dramatically after 1964, the year of the first major piece of civil rights legislation.

Employment discrimination is easier to get away with than wage discrimination. It is more difficult for an employer, having already hired a black worker, to justify paying her or him a different wage for the same job being done by a white worker than it is simply to not hire the black in the first place. When it comes to employment, the employer can always claim an inability to find a "qualified" black. Moreover, most of the good jobs in the primary sector of the labor market are filled through the networks of those already on the job, and these networks are mainly controlled by white workers. Furthermore, with the shift of more and more jobs out of the reaches of black communities, there are fewer black job candidates to confront.

Racial employment and wage differences have persisted over time because labor market discrimination has persisted over time. And labor market discrimination has persisted because racism is still an American social affliction, the true "tangle of pathology," Becker could not acount for this long-term persistence because he assumed, first, that discrimination was a pre-market taste that conferred psychic but not pecuniary benefits on the discriminator; and, second, that all of this was taking place under the regime of neoclassical perfect competition. All attempts to patch Becker up by dropping the competitive assumption failed also because they too were unable or unwilling to recognize that discrimination is an endogenous as well as exogenous labor market variable.

The human capital model also has been unable to explain the enduring differentials because it implicitly assumes that tastes for work, like those for discrimination, are formed outside of the market and that whites, by virtue of their greater investments in human capital, reveal a greater taste for market work than blacks. The human capital model comes with the neoclassical competitive assumption built in since it derives its analytic power from marginal productivity theory. The human capital model appears able only to explain wage, but not employment, differences. Even its ability with respect to the former is questionable since there are several competing, equally plausible explanations for narrowing wage differences observed in the 1960s and 1970s.

Even without these internal flaws, however, the human capital model would collapse into a discrimination model because the differential acquisition by race of the characteristic it prizes most dearly, education, is determined by discriminatory practices in the larger society. Moreover, on-the-job training, perhaps the most relevant productivity characteristic, cannot be acquired until one is employed already. As Darity has pointed out:

> If differences in human capital are largely attributable to actual work experience, one would have to find an explanation *other than* human capital differences to isolate how workers distribute themselves across entry points to careers.If job-specific skills are learned on the job, then human capital theory itself does not explain income inequality; rather, the processes that allocate persons across jobs are more fundamental. [1982, 84].

The apparent inability of neoclassical labor economics to explain satisfactorily the persistence of racial differences in employment and earnings leaves capitalism open to the charge of being both an inefficient as well as inequitable economic arrangement. Capitalist labor markets send out false signals about labor values, thereby misallocating human resources, and curtailing market accessibility and maldistributing market incomes. This arises because capitalist labor markets are characterized for the most part by collusive arrangements between cabals of white workers and white capitalist employers. These arrangements yield both psychological and material benefits to both parties. White workers have effective control of the best jobs and occupational slots in the economy, and white employers are assured of a relatively docile, system-defending workforce. All of these developments appear to be consistent only with the Marxist view of competitive capitalism. Mainstream neoclassical labor market theory, on the other hand, appears to be built on a series of assumptions that function less to explain the nature and operation of the forces at play in capitalist labor markets than to defend the outcomes in those markets from capitalism's critics.

Notes

1. E.K. Hunt (1979, 374) identified three articles of faith that constitute the neoclassical ideological defense of capitalism:

> (1) the marginal productivity theory of distribution, which pictured competitive capitalism as an ideal of distributive justice, (2) the 'invisible hand' argument, which pictured capitalism as an ideal of rationality and efficiency, and (3) the faith in the automatic, self-adjusting nature of the market, which demonstrated that the principal functions of government should be to enforce contracts and to defend the powers and privileges of private property.

Hunt went on to observe that all three propositions are interrelated, forming a mutually consistent whole in which the adoption of any two necessarily implies the adoption of the third. Each of these propositions, of course, has been challenged by critics from both without and within the neoclassical tradition. Indeed it was Keynes himself, a stout believer in marginal productivity theory and the allocative efficiency of the market, who urged the abandonment of the assumption of the self-correcting market in order to rescue capitalism from self-destruction. The theory of marginal productivity has been assailed as a not-so-subtle apologia for the distribution of income emanating from capitalist markets and resulting in great wealth for a few and poverty or near poverty for many.

2. Shulman and Darity (1989) called the perspective that endorsed capitalism by rejecting discrimination as an explanation of racial economic inequality "methodological individualism." This is the analytical method employed by most mainstream economists and reflects their belief in the efficacy of the invisible hand doctrine as it applies to racially unequal market outcomes. Methodological individualism

> ... presumes that economic institutions are structured such that society-wide outcomes result from an aggregation of individual behaviors. If individuals act on the basis of pecuniary self-interest ... then labor market dynamics dictate equal treatment for equal individuals regardless of ascriptive characteristics such as race [p. 2].

Those who consider discrimination to be "symbiotically connected to the socioeconomic dynamics of the (capitalist) marketplace" are called "methodological structuralists." They believe that market outcomes are determined by the relative economic sway of competing groups:

> Racial discrimination, in this view, is an inherent feature of our economic system. Competition is either not powerful enough to offset the group dynamics of identity and interest, or it actually operates so as to sustain discriminatory behaviors [p. 3].

3. Darity commented on both of these tendencies in an important critique of the human capital argument:

> To retrieve the elegant world (of perfect competition and still explain the existence of racial wage differentials, economists relaxed Becker's original assumption that blacks and whites have the same abilities. They restored the first assumption and dropped the second assumption of the original Becker model. Where the third assumption, the postulate of exogenous white prejudice, was retained, it affected the processes determining black and white levels of ability—processes normally characterized as lying outside the marketplace. This yielded the substance of the human capital approach to black-white earnings inequality [1982, 77–78].

One early precursor of this human capital approach was the suggestion by Welch (1967) that rather than being perfect substitutes, because of their unequal educational attainment blacks and whites have different skills and are therefore complements in production.

4. There does not appear to be general agreement even among neoclassical theorists themselves about all of the elements that constitute the ideal state of neoclassical competition. Some economists make a distinction between "pure" and "perfect" competition, while others seem to use the terms interchangeably. According to those who care, perfect competition is more exacting than pure competition. The latter assumes (1) a large number of price-taking buyers and sellers, (2) a standardized product, (3) freedom of market entry and exit, and (4) free movement of resources. Perfect competition incorporates all of the pure competition assumptions and adds a fifth: perfect knowledge or information; or, as one pair of writers described the fifth assumption:

> The participants in the market have *perfect knowledge* [emphasis in the original]. Consumers know prices; producers know costs; workers know wage rates; and so on. In addition, everyone has complete knowledge of the future [Maddala and Miller 1989, 284].

See also Eckert and Leftwich (1988) and Bronfenbrenner and associates (1990). Chamberlin (1933) required only the first two assumptions for his definition of "pure" competition. Stigler (1957) called his version of the concept "market competition," and eliminated free entry-exit and free mobility of resources. Since he claims that the industry will not be in long-run equilibrium, it is not clear how market competition differs from short-run perfect competition. Maddala and Miller go on to contend, however, that perfect knowledge is not peculiar to perfect competition since "one can argue that full knowledge of prices is easier to achieve under monopoly than under a system with a large number of firms" (1989, 284).

5. The principal statements of these "statistical discrimination" models are to be found in McCall (1971), Phelps (1972), Arrow (1972a; 1972b; 1973), Spence (1973). For a somewhat, but not altogether, skeptical survey of these models, see Aigner and Cain (1977). For thorough skepticism, see Darity (1982).

6. For a discussion and critique of product market monopolies as sources of long-run racial wage discrimination, see Morgan Reynolds (1973) cited in Darity (1982), and Armen A. Alchian and Reuben A. Kessel (1962) cited in Cain (1976).

7. From the United States Commission on Civil Rights report, *Unemployment and Underemployment Among Blacks, Hispanics and Women*, Clearing House Publication 74 (November 1982), Table 2-1, p. 5.

8. Among labor economists, one of the most insistent proponents of the culture thesis is Thomas Sowell. His favorite example of a successful culture is that of the Jews. In one of his earliest works on the subject he states that "(t)he Jews were among the most successful—if not *the* most successful—of American minorities . . ." (1975, 70). Along with other culture adherents, Sowell cites the economic and social advances made by Jewish immigrants after their arrival on these shores from eastern Europe at the turn of the century. They came penniless and poor, and were often the victims of discrimination; yet because of a cultural value system that esteemed and encouraged hardwork, thrift, self-discipline, and self-investment in education and training, they managed to overcome the obstacles to economic success that still stymie blacks. The reasons for the differences in economic outcomes between the two groups are to be found in their respective cultural value systems. To further substantiate the culture-not-race explanation, Sowell regularly adduces the case of West Indian immigrants to the United States who, black themselves and therefore susceptible to the same discriminatory treatment as native-born blacks, tend to outperform the latter on most economic indicators. The West Indian culture, like that of Jews and unlike that of native-born blacks, places a high value on hard work and a well-developed future orientation.

Critics, however, have pointed out that what Sowell and others of like mind omit altogether from these comparisons is consideration of the differences in the initial social class backgrounds from which Jews, West Indians, and native-born blacks spring. In addition, Steinberg also notes the timing of Jewish immigration:

> . . . all immigrant groups started out on the bottom. In point of fact, ethnic groups in the United States come out of very different historical and material circumstances, and therefore different outcomes may only reflect different beginnings. Secondly, depending on the time of their arrival and the patterns of settlement, immigrant groups encountered different opportunities, as well as different external obstacles to their economic advancement [1981, 83].

With respect to West Indians, Darity and Williams raised the question as to why those who immigrated to the United States did well while those who immigrated to Great Britain or stayed at home in the Islands did not? They cited researcher Nancy Foner who reported

> . . . that the Jamaicans who moved to London were of a lower socioeconomic background than their highly educated and skilled counterparts in New York City, the difference a function of respective British and U.S. immigration policies. The central point remains unaltered. West Indians in Britain and those still at home in the Caribbean share the same national culture with West Indians in the United States, but they did not share the same prior class position [1985, 259].

As for their relative discriminatory treatment, Darity and Williams cited researcher Faye Arnold who stated

> . . . that despite a common racial identity, West Indians and native blacks did not face similar patterns of discrimination. The West Indians were viewed as "exceptional" among blacks by the larger white population, as veritable "black Englishmen" [1985, 259].

9. According to Cooter and Rappaport, it was Vilfredo Pareto who first coined the term "ophelimity" to refer to the preference that modern analysts now call utility.

10. See Katzell and associates (1970), and Corcoran and Duncan (1979). This is not a surprising result from the material welfare perspective since the fewer resources one has and therefore the greater one's material welfare needs, the more attached one is to activities that will satisfy those needs.

References

Aigner, D.J., and Cain, G.G. 1977. "Statistical Theories of Discrimination in the Labor Market." *Industrial Labor Relations Review* 30 (January): 175–186.

Alchian A.A., and Kessel, R.A. 1962. "Competition, Monopoly, and the Pursuit of Pecuniary Gain." In *Aspects of Labor Economics: A Conference of Universities—National Bureau for Economic Research Committee*, 156–175. Princeton, N.J.: Princeton University Press.

Alexis, M. 1973. "A Theory of Labor Market Discrimination with Interdependent Utilities." *American Economic Review* 63 (May): 296–302.

Arnold, F. 1984. "West Indians and London's Hierarchy of Discrimination." *Ethnic Groups* 6: 47–64.

Arrow, K. 1972a. "Models of Job Discrimination." In *Racial Discrimination in Economic Life*, A.H. Pascal, ed., 83–102. Lexington, MA: D.C. Heath.

————. 1972b. "Some Mathematical Models of Race in the Labor Market." In *Racial Discrimination in Economic Life*, A.H. Pascall, 187–204. Lexington, MA: D.C. Heath.

————. 1973. "The Theory of Discrimination." In *Discrimination in Labor Markets*, O. Ashenfelter and A. Rees, eds., 3–33. Princeton, NJ: Princeton University Press.

Becker, G.S. 1957. *The Economics of Discrimination*. Chicago: University of Chicago Press.

Berg, I. 1971. *Education and Jobs: The Great Training Robbery*. Boston: Beacon Press.

Bradbury, K.L., and Browne, L.E. 1986. "Black Men in the Labor Market." *New England Economic Review* (March/April): 32–42.

Bronfenbrenner, M. et al. 1990. *Economics*, 3rd ed. Boston: Houghton Mifflin.
Cain, G.G. 1976. "The Challenge of Segmented Labor Market Theories to Orthodox Theory: A Survey." *Journal of Economic Literature* 14: 1215–1257.
Cooter, R. and Rappaport, P. 1984. "Were the Ordinalists Wrong About Welfare Economics?" *Journal of Economic Literature* 22: 507–530.
Corcoran, M. and Duncan, G. 1979. "Work History, Labor Force Attachment, and Earnings Differences Between the Races and Sexes." *Journal of Human Resources* 14: 3–20.
Cotton, J. 1985. "A Comparative Analysis of Black-White and Mexican-American-White Male Wage Differentials." *The Review of Black Political Economy* 13: 51–69.
————. 1988. "On the Decomposition of Wage Differentials." *The Review of Economics and Statistics* 70: 236–243.
————. 1989. "Opening the Gap: The Decline in Black Economic Indicators in the 1980s." *Social Science Quarterly* 70: 803–818.
Darity, W., Jr. 1982. "The Human Capital Approach to Black-White Earnings Inequality: Some Unsettled Questions." *Journal of Human Resources* 17: 72–93.
Darity, W., Jr., and Williams, R.M. 1987. "Peddlers Forever?: Culture, Competition, and Disderation of Racial Earnings Inequality." *The Review of Radical Political Economics* 19: 1–15.
————. 1989. "What's Left of the Economic Theory of Discrimination?" In *The Question of Discrimination*, Steven Shulman and William Darity, Jr., eds., 335–374. Middlebury, CT: Wesleyan University Press.
Eckert, R.D., and Leftwich, R.H. 1988. *The Price System and Resource Allocation*, 10th ed. Chicago: The Dryden Press.
Foner, N. 1979. "West Indians in New York City and London: A Comparative Analysis." *International Migration Review* 13: 284–297.
Freeman, R.B. 1972. "Changes in the Labor Market for Black Americans, 1948–72." *Brookings Papers on Economic Activity* 1: 67–132.
————. 1973. "Decline of Labor Market Discrimination and Economic Analysis." *American Economic Review* 63: 280–286.
————. 1978. "Black Economic Progress After 1964: Who Gained and Why." National Bureau of Economic Research Working Paper No. 282.
Goodwin, L. 1972. *Do the Poor Want to Work?: A Social-Psychological Study of Work Orientations*. Washington, DC: The Brookings Institution.
Hall, R.E., and Kasten, R. 1973. "The Relative Economic Success of Blacks and Whites." *Brookings Papers on Economic Activity* 3: 781–795.
Hunt, E.K. 1979. *History of Economic Thought: A Critical Perspective*. Belmont, CA: Wadsworth Publishing Co.
Katzell, R., et al. 1970. "The Job Attitudes of Workers from Different Ethnic Backgrounds." U.S. Dept. of Labor Research Report Contract No. 41-8-006-34.
Maddala, G.S., and Miller, E. 1989. *Microeconomics: Theory and Applications*. New York: McGraw-Hill.
McCall, J.J. 1972. "The Simple Mathematics of Information, Job Search, and Prejudice." In *Racial Discrimination in Economic Life*, A.H. Pascall, ed.,

205–224. Lexington, MA: D.C. Heath.

Medoff, J.L., and Abraham, K.G. 1981. "Are Those Paid More Really More Productive?: The Case of Experience." *Journal of Human Resources* 16: 186–216.

Phelps, E.S. 1972. "The Statistical Theory of Racism and Sexism." *American Economic Review* 62: 659–661.

Reich, M. 1981. "The Statistical Theory of Racism and Sexism." *American Economic Review* 62: 659–661.

Reich, M. 1981. *Racial Inequality: A Political-Economic Analysis*. Princeton, NJ: Princeton University Press.

Reynolds, M. 1973. "Economic Theory and Racial Wage Differentials." Institute for Research on Poverty Discussion Paper 1974–73, University of Wisconsin.

Shulman, S. 1990. "Racial Inequality and White Employment: An Interpretation and Test of the Bargaining Power Hypothesis." *The Review of Black Political Economy* 18: 5–20.

Sowell, T. 1975. *Race and Economics*. New York: McKay.

Spence, A. M. 1973. "Job Market Signaling." *Quarterly Journal of Economics* 87: 355–374.

Steinberg, S. 1981. *The Ethnic Myth: Race, Ethnicity, and Class in America*. New York: Atheneum.

Stigler, G. 1957. "Perfect Competition Historically Contemplated." *Journal of Political Economy* (February): 1–17.

Swinton, D. 1978. "A Labor Force Competition Model of Racial Discrimination in Labor Markets." *The Review of Black Political Economy* 9: 5–42.

Welch, F. 1967. "Labor Market Discrimination: An Interpretation of Income Differences in the Rural South." *Journal of Political Economy* 75: 225–240.

Williams, R.M. 1987. "Capital, Competition, and Discrimination: A Reconsideration of Racial Earnings Inequality." *The Review of Radical Political Economics* 19: 1–15.

7 RACIAL INEQUALITY AND RACIAL CONFLICT: RECENT DEVELOPMENTS IN RADICAL THEORY

Rhonda M. Williams

Introduction

It is clearly too early to identify definitively the economic, political, and cultural parameters that future generations will accord significance when they reconstruct the histories of the 1970s and 1980s. Nonetheless, I am willing to venture an educated guess: the turbulent dynamics of racial conflict will emerge as a pervasive theme. One can easily imagine interdisciplinary collaborations aimed at reconstructing the relationship between the the emergence of the New Right and the demise of the moral vision of the Civil Rights movement. Or we might witness scholarly treatises that attempt to connect the climactic resurgence of neoconservative discourse on the pathology of urban African-Americans to the shift in federal spending from transfer programs to militarization during an era of rising income inequality, indebtedness, economic growth, and increasingly publicized racist violence on university campuses and urban streets.

Future generations of political economists also will find that matters of race permeated theoretical, empirical, and policy debates of the era. Perhaps they will trace the profession's theoretical and empirical debates, which range from the triumphant claims in the 1970's that racial earnings inequality was headed the way of the dinosaur to a 1980s fascination with hypothesized relationships between transfer programs, marriage rates, labor supply, and racial gaps in family income. The students of our students will find no shortage of readings on either the viability of labor market discrimination in competitive capitalist economies or the role of racial ethnic culture in enhancing and retarding economic achievement. And their computer searches will reveal extended debates on the theory and empirical consequences of federal antidiscrimination policy.

If they are attuned to the diversity of economic paradigms and methods, our professional descendants also should discover that the late 1970s and 1980s witnessed the revitalization of radical research on class and race. Political economists have been debating racial politics, reassessing the saliency of Marxism for understanding and eliminating racism and sexism, and reexamining white workers' "interest" in perpetuating discrimination. These are the debates that orient and anchor this chapter.

Unlike their neoclassical counterparts, radical economists believe that labor market discrimination can and does persist in a competitive capitalist economy. However, radical theorists disagree as to the precise nature of this process. This chapter presents alternative Marxist conceptualizations of how race shapes and is shaped by the process of competitive capital accumulation. At the most general level, it challenges leftists to accord greater significance to the social processes that have created a racialized U.S. working class. On a more concrete plane, this chapter examines alternative explanations of how capitalism reproduces racism.

For example, the "divide-and-conquer" camp argues that discrimination divides white and black workers and thereby reduces their power vis-a-vis capitalist employers. Their perceptions notwithstanding, most white workers are hurt by discrimination. It divides workers in general, and white workers suffer from lowered wages, low levels of unionization, and regressive social policy. An opposing perspective proposes that racism's consequences are both multifold and historically contingent: racial identification can unify white ethnics, provide a cultural context for group competition, and thereby establish a means to reduce competition from nonwhites. White workers can thus benefit from reduced job competition, enhanced occupational mobility, and higher employment probabilities.

The second section critiques the analysis of racial inequality developed in Gordon, Edwards, and Reich's *Segmented Work, Divided Workers* (1982).[1] I began with Gordon and colleagues for two reasons. First, the authors take as their charge a theme of longstanding concern to leftist intellectuals and activists—that is, the historical emergence of a politically and culturally divided U.S. working class. Their analysis accords centrality to "social structures of accumulation," the institutional environment within which capitalist accumulation occurs. The conclusion: the U.S. working class remains divided largely because of objective divisions among workers in their production experiences.

Second, the social structures of accumulation (SSA) model has emerged as a highly visible radical explanation of the rise and demise of the post-World War II profit boom (see Bowles, Gordon, and Weisskopf 1983; 1986; 1987; 1989). Casual empiricism suggests that nonradicals are more familiar with Bowles, Gordon, and Weisskopf than with other Marxists. Their work is a potential bridge between neoclassical and radical paradigms. The section following summarizes Weisskopf, Bowles, and Gordon's radical macroeconomic extension of the early SSA model. The "power and profits" research moves their agenda beyond the perimeter of microeconomic profit making to the social, political, and cultural environment in which it occurs—the "outer limits" of the social structure of accumulation. However, this research program consistently and problematically marginalizes the shifting form and content of racial conflict.

Robert Cherry (1988; 1990) recently has emerged as a vocal critique of Weisskopf and colleagues' analysis of racial inequality's impact on profits and the rate of accumulation. In so doing, he calls our theoretical and historical attention to the ongoing radical debates regarding white workers' and capitalists' gains and losses from discrimination. The succeding section critically evaluates Cherry's contribution, including his characterization of "neo-Marxist" theories as fundamentally "nationalist" in orientation. I argue that Cherry both underestimates the economic bases of conflict between black and white workers and misconstrues his opposition. The conclusion speculates that his misreading of those radicals he brands neo-Marxist is rooted in a failure to consider seriously race's centrality in the shaping of U.S. culture and politics.

Race, Segmentation, and Social Structures of Accumulation

Segmented Work, Divided Workers explains present-day black workers' disproportionate concentration among the low-waged and unwaged as rooted in the post-World War II era.[2] Allegedly, black men and women worked beyond the pale of the capitalist factory until the first world war. Thereafter, African-Americans became a valued low-wage labor supply to peripheral manufacturing industries and service sector capitalists. By 1970, 60 percent of employed African-Americans worked in secondary jobs. Boston's (1988) cross-section analysis of the 1983 Current Population

Survey (CPS) data identified 55.5 percent of African-American workers in the secondary sector.[3]

Critics of segmentation theory continue to challenge its fundamental tenets. Friedman (1984) summarized challenges to segmentation theory's empirical and conceptual commitment to the dual economy tradition. Nolan and Edwards (1988) argued that Gordon and colleagues construct a simplified conceptualization of capital accumulation that reduces all crisis and change to capitalists' efforts to impose surplus labor time through systems of labor control. Other possible sources of crisis, such as changes in the organic composition of capital, are excluded from the argument. Botwinick (1988) challenges Gordon and associates's commitment to a monopoly capital paradigm, and still others (Wilkinson 1981; Albelda 1985) challenge their periodization of systems of labor control.

This section extends and expands upon these earlier critiques of sementation theory. I contend that SWDW's efforts are deeply marred by substantive historical inaccuracies and a failure to address the social construction of racialized communities in the formation of the U.S. working class. Both white subordination of African-American workers and racial divisions in the working classes long predate the era of labor market segmentation.[4]

Segmented Work, Divided Workers periodizes the U.S. economic history according to structural changes in the organization of labor markets and processes. These production relations are constituent components of a "social structure of accumulation," the institutional arrangements that make possible sustained and expanded capital accumulation. Successful capital accumulation presupposes the formation of institutions and relations which ensure capitalists' control over workers' labor power. Class conflict conditions the formation, consolidation, and decay of SSA's.

Gordon and colleagues identify three historical transformations of class relations. The "era of proletarianization," from 1840 to 1890, demarcated the establishment of wage labor relations in the U.S. economy. Class conflict in the late 19th century resulted in the "homogenization," or deskilling, of labor between 1890 and World War II. The current (decaying) social social structure of accumulation signalled the "segmentation" of workers into primary and secondary jobs between the 1940s and the 1970s.

As Albelda (1985) observed, Gordon and associated offer an important disclaimer that forewarns readers interested in their theorizing about race: their concern is the capitalist (wage labor) sector. Hence,

> We should repeat our earlier caution that this book focues on the capitalist sector of the economy. Many of the important national political-economic issues of the nineteenth century—the conflicts over the extension of the transportation system,

tariffs, slavery, and Reconstruction in the South ... involved the expansion of the capitalist system into non-capitalist areas. Despite their evident significance for U.S. history as a whole, these events lie outside our perimeter here. Thus, for example, we touch only tangentially on the emancipation of the slaves and the Civil War ... [1982, 245].

A host of phenomena thus lie beyond the perimeter: the young nation's struggle to reconcile slavery and its libertarian ideals; racism as a political and cultural bond between whites of different class and national-ethnic cultures; Reconstruction and the solidification of agrarian-based and state-supported white supremacy; the daily renewal and generational reproduction of the white working class, to name but a few. The perimeter excludes the labor of numerous communities of color, from Chinese workers and Chicano agricultural peons in the West, to enslaved African-Americans and their formally free postbellum kin. Gordon and associates' study takes as given the boundary between "free" and "unfree" laborers.[5] It therefore substantiates Albelda (1985) and Glenn's (1985) claims: in the United States, workers *always* have been segmented into race specific labor processes.[6]

Gordon and associates' footnote reveals more than the descriptive boundaries of their work; it contains the seeds of an important analytic premise. These authors believe they can meaningfully analyze the development of 19th century class relations in abstraction from the political economy and ideology of white supremacy. They therefore purport to explain both the historical transformation of wage-labor relations between white male capitalists and workers, and the development of a culturally and politically divided 19th century working class, as processes largely unmediated by race.

SWDW's presentation thus implies that social relations and cultural practices beyond the perimeter do not mediate those within. Hence they can provide comprehensive explanations of the dynamics of class relations within the wage-labor sector in abstraction from an analysis of the political, economic, and ideological processes that determined workers of European heritage would be free and African-American workers would be unfree. Recall the authors' desire to explain the political and cultural fragmentation of the U.S. working class. Their decision to begin with a perimeter, rather than posing the construction of the perimeter as a phenomenon to be explained, is a case of puting the analytic cart before the horse.

An alternative approach would take as problematic the divisions between enslaved blacks and formally free whites, and would begin by posing questions about the political construction of free and unfree labor. For example, is there a relationship between the racialized class and sexual exploitation of enslaved black workers, on the one hand, and the formation of the 19th century industrial working class on the other? How did the class conflicts over the termination of slavery affect the conditions under which African-Americans entered or were pushed from wage-labor markets?

One way of demonstrating the theoretical necessity of exploring the division between the waged and unwaged is to examine in greater detail the consequences of not problematizing this boundary. Gordon and associates' discussions of black workers during the eras of proletarianization and homogenization are a logical starting point. Passages on both "blacks" and "women" provide the needed text.[7]

When discussing African-Americans during the era of proletarianization, the authors observe that

> . . . the integration of blacks into the modern working class, made possible by the demise of slavery, . . . properly belongs to the history of the twentieth century [1982, 56].

A description of young New England women as wage laborers in textile mills during the initial proletarianization of labor reads ". . . the earliest manufactures did draw upon those—mainly girls and single women—who were assigned the spinning and, (to a lesser extent) the weaving within New England households" (1982, 71). After documenting women's limited participation in manufacturing during the period of homogenization, Gordon and associates observe the increase in women's employment as clerical workers:

> As late as 1900, women accounted for less than one-quarter of clerical and kindred worker; by 1930, their proportion of clerical employment had increased to over half [1982, 151].

Following the authors' observation that most employed women worked either as teachers, clerical workers, saleswomen in the retail sector, or domestic/personal service workers (thus describing an aspect of gender-based occupational segregation), we read that "this occupational segregation meant that most employed women had not yet been affected by the job differentiation among ethnic and racial groups that was beginning to develop throughout the corporate capitalist sector" (1982, 151). Finally, the discussion of blacks and the homogenization of labor includes two significant observations: "Employers' use of blacks as strikebreakers in the North began in the 1890's in the coal mines," and "In the North, free blacks had traditionally worked as craft workers and had enjoyed relatively free income and occupational opportunities." (1982, 152).

When placed in a richer historical context, these passages demonstrate the theoretical problems generated by an analysis that refuses to interrogate fully the processes and relations that determine the perimeter between waged labor and nonwaged labor. Consider, for example, Gordon and associates' discussion of the women and children in the New England textile mills. As Harley (1978) documents, the mill experiment was a white enclave. Mill workers were young, single, white women from poor families in dire financial straits (Matthaei 1982, ch. 7). White hostility toward free blacks precluded their employment in manufacturing, capitalist labor demand notwithstanding. Goldin (1981) observes that the antebellum construction of white-only employment sectors included children. While white female household heads sent their children into Philadelphia's textile mills, their black counterparts could not and sought employment themselves.

If we examine the racial segmentation of early 19th century "women's work" through the filter of dominant antebellum cultural assumptions, the emergence of the mills as a white enclave is hardly surprising. As Fredrickson (1981) richly documents, the assumption that the United States was meant to be a homogeneous white nation, peopled primarily by Anglo-Saxons and their racial kin, anchored national ideology in the late 18th century (Fredrickson 1981, 145). Moreover,

> ... the practical purpose of the Declaration was more to assert the right of a particular "homogeneous" community to self-determination than to establish a haven of freedom and equality for all types and varieties of people ... White Americans of the post-revolutionary era may have recognized a similar right for other such communities, but they reserved the option of applying tests of cultural and racial compatibility to those who sought admissions to their own ranks ... all nonwhites were, from the beginning of nationhood, regarded as "aliens" of the unassimilable kind. [Fredrickson 1981, 145]

Carby's (1987) examination of "the cult of true womanhood" demonstrates that the antebellum discourse of white supremacy also was deeply gendered. As the dominant ideology that defined the boundaries of acceptable female behavior between the 1820's and the Civil War, the "cult" proscribed piety, purity, submissiveness, and self-sacrificing domesticity. The ideology of womanhood dictated that a woman's character could be read from her external appearance; hence the social validation of softness, delicacy, and fairness of complexion. Carby observes that popular novels of the era constructed dark-complexioned black woman as the moral opposites of their fair-haired, blue-eyed heroines. Black women thus existed outside the bounds of true womanhood, and "black womanhood" signified an absence of piety, the presence of overt sexuality, and taboo sexual practices (Carby 1987, 32).

Antebellum ideological parameters thus defined black women as lascivious creatures who could, by no stretch of the imagination, satisfy the the mill community's desire for workers of "good moral character." Chattel slavery's profoundly gendered constituting ideology mitigated against free black women's employment in manufacturing. Neither Yankee farm girls nor their employers embraced racial integration of the mill workforce, and the presence of adequate supplies of poor whites substantially reduced the economic costs of employers' adhering to the norms of white supremacy.

Free black women in New England worked outside capitalist manufacturing as maids, servants, washerwomen, and seamstresses for pay lower than that of their formally waged white counterparts. In Gordon et. al.'s, language, they were not part of the "capitalist sector." Yet we cannot explain their exclusion from this sector without going beyond the perimeter. In order to explain black women's absence form the mills—that is, the location of the perimeter—we must engage the racially coded constructions of womanhood. Only an analytic framework that foregrounds the early 19th century cultural practices that produced racial and racialized (and racist) communities and individuals can accomplish this task.

Free black *women* clearly did not enjoy free income and occupational opportunites. What about African-American *men*? It is quite likely that, in the urban North, black men were well represented among the ranks of skilled craftsmen during the first few decades of nationhood; however, this experience was short-lived (Foner 1974, ch. 1). Again using Philadelphia's large black population as a case in point, DuBois (in 1899) documented white immigrants' successful displacement of African-American tradesmen from their crafts between 1820 and 1890. The formation of "white only" unions came in wake of numerous recurring race riots involving immigrants and black migrants from the South:

> So intense was the race antipathy among the lower class, and so much countenance did it receive from the middle and upper class, that there began, in 1829, a series of riots directed chiefly against Negroes, which recurred frequently until about 1840, and did not wholly cease until after the [Civil] war [DuBois 1967, 26–27].

The white and black populations in Philadelphia county increased 174 present and 12 percent, respectively, between 1840 and 1870. DuBois attributes this growth differential to the legacy of the race riots.

Beyond Philadelphia, racial job competition between European immigrants and blacks flourished throughout the North during the era of proletarianization. Irish immigrants in search of employment used mob violence to force African-Americans out of canal, construction, and service jobs in the Northeast during the 1840s and 1850s (Litwack 1961, 157–165).

Moreover, white capitalists begain deploying black strikebreakers well before the 1890s. As early as 1855, New York employers imported black male laborers to break a white longshoremen's strike. During the Civil War, race riots exploded in Chicago, Detroit, Cleveland, Albany, Brooklyn, and Boston when capitalists recruited African-American men to replace striking Irish waterfront workers.[8] Between 1882 and 1900, white workers initiated at least 50 strikes to protest the hiring of blacks (Hill 1984). Whereas Gordon and associates assert that strikebreaking commenced in the 1890s, the historical record suggests that it may have *peaked* in the 1890s!

Segmented Work, Divided Workers' discussion of women workers in the early 20th century also warrants careful scrutiny. The authors claim that the social division of labor by gender worked in opposition to the emergence of a race-ethnic division of labor among women. They report that 79 percent of employed, nonagricultural female employees worked as teachers, clerical workers, sales workers, apparel industry operatives, and service workers in 1930. Yet as early as 1900, women's work displayed considerable racial and ethnic concentration. Black and Asian women were disproportionately concentrated in agriculture. However, farm work lies outside the perimeter.

Yet even within the domain of nonfarm wage labor, Matthaei (1982) reports African-American women's continued exclusion from the mills, and the concentration of native-born (but not immigrant) white women in stenography, typing, and sales. Matthaei also documents the ethnic segregation of immigrant white women. Cotton and woolen mills employed Italians, English, Welsh, and Irish. Bohemians, Russians, and Italians dominated cigar factories. The female huckster was most likely Italian or Russian (Matthaei 1982, 224–229)[9]. Her portrait of a turn-of-the-century, industry-based, race-ethnic division of labor among working-class women clearly undermines Gordon et. al.'s characterization of women's work.

In Southern textile mills and food processing and garment factories in the West, intrafirm racial divisions of labor were the norm. Mexican-American food processing and garment laborers worked in the most arduous and lowest paid jobs those industries offered, and worked apart from white women. Durham's tobacco factories enforced a rigid racial division of labor for white and black women workers as early a 1900.[10] In the cotton mills, foreign and native-born white women performed the actual manufacturing, while black women worked as laborers, machine scrubbers, and waste gatherers.

What, then, are we to make of the authors' "perimeter," and more generally, their history of race and ethnic relations within the working class? The authors' claim that free Northern blacks enjoyed unfettered occupational choice in the 19th century cannot be sustained for women or men. Their research on the gender division of labor seriously misrepresents the extent to which sex-typing obliterated race-ethnic divisions among women at the level of production during the so-called era of homogenization. Although their research makes visible the changing contours of the gender division of labor among whites, and corporate capital's efforts to racially "divide and conquer" working men at the turn of the century, it obscures the racial division of labor among women and the deep roots of race-specific job competition among white immigrants, native whites, and African-Americans.

At the heart of SWDW's inadequate analysis of the working class in the 19th century lie two related conceptual problems. First, because their construction of the "working class" excludes unwaged workers, the authors do not explore the cultural and social processes that construct the political divisions between free and unfree labor, waged and unwaged workers. The failure to undertake this analysis seriously undermines their theoretical project, and leads them to see segmentation simply as a 20th century development among waged workers.

Second, Gordon and associates do not include the social construction of racial and ethnic selves as constitutive of the relationships between capital and labor in the 1800s. Thus their history does not consider as problematic the extent to which the development of racial and ethnic consciousness among native and immigrant whites conditioned relations between and within classes, and constructed the contested boundaries between the high waged, the low waged, and the unwaged.[11] The fourth section elaborates on this assertion.

Power, Profits, and the Post-War Political Economy

Segmented Work, Divided Workers does not acknowledge a longstanding relationship between capitalism's labor processes/systems of control and white supremacy. Only in the 20th century does race appear within the "inner boundary" [that which "divides the capital accumulation process itself (the profitmaking activities of individual capitalists) from the institutional (social, political, legal, cultural, and market) context within which it occurs" (Gordon 1982, 25)] of a social structure of accumulation. Race also remains largely peripheral to the theorizing of a prolific radical cadre that has expanded the SSA paradigm to explain the rise and demise of U.S. post-World War II profitability.

I refer here to the research produced by Thomas Weisskopf, Samuel Bowles, and, again, David Gordon (1983; 1986; 1987; 1988; 1989).[12]

During the 1980s, Weisskopf and associates joined the army of economists (radicals and nonradicals) trying to explain the rise and decline in post-World War II U.S. corporate profitability. For Weisskopf and associates, the level and stability of profits condition the rate of capital accumulation (investment), which, in turn determines the rate of economic growth. Thus, "as profits go, . . . so goes the economy" (Gordon, Weisskopf, and Bowles 1987, 44).

In sharp contrast to the neoclassical definition of profit as payment to a scarce productive input, the authors define profits as "a deduction from net output made possible by the power of the capitalist class over other economic actors with which it deals." Although their work does not employ value theoretic categories, Bowles and associates conceive of themselves as working well within the Marxist tradition.[13]

In keeping with the SWDW analysis, Bowles and associates explain the rise and fall of after-tax corporate profitability in the United States in terms of a social structure of accumulation—in this case, the postwar SSA. Earlier works (1983; 1986) identified three institutional relationships that determined U.S. nonfinancial capital's ability to exercise power over other economic agents:

1. A "capital-labor accord" assured management control over corporate decisionmaking. Unions (after purging their leadership of Communists) would maintain a relative "labor peace" in return for productivity-pegged rising real wages.
2. "Pax Americana" established an open economy with favorable terms of trade for U.S. capitalists.
3. The limited "capital-citizen" accord established political arrangements to moderate the excesses of an economy ordered by capital accumulation. State managers would use macroeconomic policies, transfer programs, and public investment to make the nation safe for accumulation and secure citizen support for capitalist-led development.[14] (Recently, Gordon and associates have added a fourth component to the postwar SSA model: the "moderation of inter-capitalist rivalry," which refers to U.S. capital's relative dominance of domestic markets in the first two postwar decades.)

According to Gordon and company, the capital-labor accord, Pax Americana, the capital-citizen accord, and the moderation of global inter-capitalist competition fostered a period of sustained capitalist profitability between 1948 and 1966. Thereafter, each pillar of the SSA began to crumble. The availability of nonwage income weakened employers' hold over workers by reducing the "cost of job loss," thereby creating a climate in which unionized workers became increasingly restive about work intensity and safety. Workers within the accord were more likely to strike and quit. Pax Americana wavered in the face of the Bay of Pigs, Vietnam, and, of course, the change in terms of trade wrought by OPEC in the early 1970s. As consumer and environmental movements challenged the capital-citizen accord, European and Japanese capital challenged U.S. worldwide market shares. The net effect: a post-1966 decline in corporate profitability, explained and econometrically tested in the authors' SSA framework.[15]

What does all of this have to do with racial conflict and inequality in the working class? Apparently very little. Most of Bowles and associates' theoretical and empirical studies do not formally address white racial domination and black challenges thereto. Ergo, profitable capital accumulation and white supremacy are largely separable phenomena. We do get a glimpse of the authors' vision of race and the social structure of accumulation in *Beyond the Wasteland*, which notes that African-Americans were not primary beneficiaries of the capital-labor accord. Blacks manifested displeasure with the distributive injustice of the growth coalition in the Civil Rights and Welfare Rights movements.[16] The subsequent expansion of Great Society programs increased the costs of maintaining the SSA and contributed to the undermining of the postwar corporate system. Although Bowles and associates formally acknowledge the significance of these struggles, they describe the social movements as "outside" the accord.

Rethinking Capital Accumulation and the Reproduction of Racial Inequality

Weisskopf and associates' analysis of the macroeconomy thus suggests the relative autonomy of white supremacy and capital accumulation. Their "macro" analysis thus mirrors the "micro" labor process analysis presented in *Segmented Work, Divided Workers*. An earlier section argued that political and cultural relations (constructed by, but not reducible to, class processes) defined the subset of social subjects who clashed within the perimeter. A similar critique can and must be made here.

Gordon and associates argue that most African-Americans neither participated in nor directly benefitted from the capital-labor accord. This is beyond dispute. What's missing from the analysis is an examination of the relationship between the institutionalized white supremacy of civil society process and black workers' exclusion from the full benefits of both the citizen and capital-labor accords. The postwar social structure of accumulation did not intitate white racial domination; it did, however, change its form.

For example, Weisskopf and associates' claim that the government committed itself to at least "a margin of economic security for all Americans" is highly questionable. Until the black liberation struggles of the 1950s and 1960s—and therefore well into the life of the accords and the emergence of the modern welfare state—state and local governments continued unchallenged their decades-old practices of racial repression and segregation. In keeping with the needs of local landowners, Southern states routinely excluded black women from the AFDC rolls.[17]

At the federal level, public expenditures and programs had race-specific impact. The 1949 National Housing Act subsidized the suburbanization of whites, but not blacks. The 1954 Housing Act's "urban renewal" program accorded primacy to the needs of universities, downtown businesses, and hospitals. Urban renewal destroyed black homes and settlements. State-financed urban planners then deposited the refugees from "renewed" areas in segregated public housing. Meanwhile, the Highway Act of 1956 supported the construction of freeways in every major city. These highways connected the emerging white suburbs, and/or were planted as "buffers" to protect white neighborhoods from expanding ghettoes. (Wacquant 1989).

Bowles and associates' ode to state benevolence is incomplete and may be connected to their conceptualization of the Civil Rights movement as a black protest against exclusion from the growth coalition. The authors do not mention the movement's explicit critique of state-sanctioned white supremacy, that *other* longstanding capital-citizen accord that made possible both the politics of urban removal and black workers' disproportionate exclusion from the "growth coalition."

Robert Cherry (1988; 1990) similarly is dissatisfied with this cadre's theorizing on race. His focus is Bowles and associates' formulation of the relationship between race and accumulation. Cherry chastizes Marxists for failing to incorporate race (and gender) into their analysis of capital accumulation. According to Cherry, this failure has created fertile ground for the emergence of (so-called) "neo-Marxist" theories that challenge the theoretical saliency of Marxism to the struggles against racism and sexism. Cherry's critique connects three dimensions of Gordon and associates' research: (1) their understanding of the demise of the capital-labor accord; (2) their propensity to discount the profitability of discrimination to capitalists; and (3) their latent support of what he alternatively identifies as "nonclass" or "neo-Marxist" theories of discrimination.

Gordon and colleagues claim that dominant corporate capital accepted the accord but workers broke it as the cost of job loss declined. Moreover, white male workers benefitted from wage growth in primary sector employment at the expense of excluded blacks (males and females) and white women,[18] who could only challenge the accord from beyond its boundaries.

Cherry (1989) suggests an alternative explanation:

> The profit boom may have had more to do with superexploiting a growing female and divided labor force than any capital-labor accord. Second, the breakdown of the accord may have resulted from the *weakness* of disadvantaged groups. Seeing the profits which could be made from low-wage female workers and a racially divided southern work force, capitalists may have decided that the accord was too costly to maintain.

In other words, *capitalists* broke the accord and were not committed to ever-rising wages. Thus production worker wages in the durable goods sector grew at a declining rate in the 1950s. Interregional wage comparisons show that wage increases (adjusted for regional differences in industries) in the South were comparable to those in the Midwest between 1954 and 1967. In light of the South's strong antiunionism, these data challenge the notion that wage growth among the beneficiaries of the accord surpassed the gains of those outside the core.

Moreover, Cherry challenges Bowles et. al.'s thesis that the immediate postwar period was a boom era. Close examination of the authors' graph (1983, 96) shows that profit rates between 1948 and 1957 were not much higher than in the 1970s (although profit expectations, as proxied by Tobin's q, rose steadily). This indicates that it is only during the subperiod 1958–66—the years after unionized workers received their largest wage gains—that profit rates are high. Industrial capitalists therefore had ample reason to pursue cost-reducing strategies in the early 1950s—which leads us to Cherry's fourth counterpoint.

Cherry's survey of management studies leads him to challenge the notion that corporate America largely accepted unionized manufacturing; what appeared to be an acquiescence to unions was a pragmatic adaptation to the higher costs of union busting. By 1952, corporate America had begun to pursue its "southern strategy." Accordingly, in the durable goods sector between 1955 and 1967, employment grew by 73.9 percent in the South, but only 4.6 percent in the Midwest. Many of the "New South's" manufacturing workers were white and black women. The former tended to be older, married women with blue-collar husbands; many of the latter were shifting out of domestic employment and into manufacturing.

Cherry's evidence paints a different scenario: capitalists' profits rose because of their successful exploitation of workers excluded from the capital-labor accord: "the crucial accommodation made by unions was to allow corporations unlimited exploitation of disenfranchised workers." He locates the profit boom in manufacturers' Southern strategy, mechanization, subcontracting to nonunion firms, and relocation overseas, all of which facilitated declining rates of wage increases for unionized white men. Manufacturers shifted South, began work intensification, and reduced investment in Northern plants.[19] According to Cherry, it is corporate capital that broke the so-called "accord," and did so well before the mid-1960's. Union leaders were content to pursue economic gains for a predominantly white membership.

Cherry's documentation of the industrial capital's Southern strategy supports the thesis that the racial boundaries of the social division of labor are a contested terrain in the U.S. economy. The integration of more Southern blacks into manufacturing as "free" workers occurred when capitalists needed new and cheaper labor upon which to ground new rounds of capital accumulation. Capital's pursuit of profit shapes and reshapes the racial division of labor. Organized and race-conscious white workers are not simply passive bystanders., On the contrary, their short-term political choices mediate capitalist strategy.

However, Cherry's argument does not stop here. He also asserts that white men's gains in the Northern, unionized primary sector were temporary. The accord of the 1940s gave way to declining rates of wage growth in the 1950s, soon to be followed by the speed-ups in the 1960s and the capital relocations, union-busting, plant closings, and declining real wages in the 1970s and 1980s. Here is Cherry's (1990) challenge to Gordon and associates' support of "nationalist/nonclass" theories of discrimination:

> Nationalist views suggest that white male workers can benefit from the suppression of women and blacks. The alternative view claims to the contrary, that the suppression of disenfranchised workers was responsible for the undermining of benefits attained by white male workers. It was the *weakness* of disenfranchised workers which provided the economic incentive for capitalists to break the accord.

Thus white male unionists set the stage for their own undoing.

What exactly are these so-called "nationalist" theories of discrimination, and how do they differ from between the "class-based" theories of discrimination, which Cherry embraces? Beginning with the latter—as articulated by Syzmanski (1976), Roemer (1979), and especially Reich (1981)—discrimination generates racial income inequality. This inequality separates and creates discord within the working class, thereby reducing workers' collective strength and enhancing capitalists' bargaining power. Employers thus maintain earnings differentials between comparable workers, and competitive market structures (here using a neoclassical notion of competition) reproduce racial earnings inequality.

Reich's cross-section estimations emerged as the 1980s empirical cornerstone of the class-based theorists. Reich results show that greater racial income inequality (as measured by family income) increases income (class) inequality among whites, lowers white earnings, and decreases government per capita spending on social services. Thus, capitalists gain from racial inequality, but most white workers lose.

Cherry (1988; 1989) describes an opposing radical camp as "nationalists" with neo-Marxist roots. According to Cherry, nationalist theorists (including Baron 1975; Bonacich 1976; Bowles, Gordon, and Weisskopf 1983; Shulman 1984; and Williams 1987) trace their lineage to Baran and Sweezy's *Monopoly Capital* (1966) according to which capitalism is now in its "monopoly capital" stage. Under monopoly capital, large capitalists have achieved sufficient market power so as to have overcome the need to reduce costs. Monopoly capitalists no longer "need" racism to discipline dominant white labor, reduce unit labor costs, and sustain profits. To the extent that discrimination raises white wages, those costs are offset by the benefits of a large and relatively inexpensive reserve army of black labor. White male workers thus benefit from racial domination.

Cherry's assessment of the so-called "neo-Marxists" is profoundly problematic on several counts.[20] Although Baron (1975) largely discounts the cost-benefit calculus of discrimination, other theorists who critique Cherry and Reich ground their models in an analysis of costs and profits. Consider Bonacich (1976), who traces the origins of a racially "split" U.S. labor market to chattel slavery. She was among the earliest observers to connect the more than two-to-one black-white unemployment ratios (which now seem commonplace, but emerged after 1940) to the racial implications of the New Deal legislation. Bonacich argues that after the new labor laws limited the extent to which capitalists could deploy black workers as strikebreakers against unionizing whites, capitalists pursued alternatives to high-cost labor. She thus explains the post-1940 rise in black unemployment as a consequence of capital's aformentioned strategies of relocation overseas, employment of undocumented workers, and automation.

Her analysis is clearly class-theoretic. Furthermore, Bonacich anticipates Cherry and Albelda (1985) in describing capital's relocation and automation as strategic responses to high-wage, unionized, white-male labor. Surely this is not the analysis of someone who thinks that capitalists are no longer concerned about costs!

Cherry's reading of Shulman (1984) is equally mysterious. Shulman's theoretical discussion is based on a detailed analysis of competition and costs:

> Competition creates incentives to minimize costs. If costs are not minimized, then prices must be raised and/or profits reduced, resulting in a loss of market share. It is exactly because discrimination is alleged to raise the costs of production that competition is supposed to erode it. *But, if costs also increase as a consequence of ceasing discrimination, competition wil have the opposite effect* [1984, 115; emphasis added].

Shulman recognizes the social nature of production and the reality of racism in the working class: capitalists who challenge the prerogatives of white labor face the prospect of costly and productivity-disrupting changes. When unemployment is nonzero, the costs of ending employment discrimination may increase as racially identified white workers engage in cartel-like behavior to maintain job security. Shulman's (1990) most recent work directly undermines Reich, and demonstrates that increased racial income inequality increases white male and female employment prospects in 1970 and 1980.

Shulman's research points to a serious shortcoming in both Cherry and Bonacich's analyses. Bonacich proposes that government-provided transfer income and a militant black consciousness (black workers reject low-wage unemployment) contribute to the black-white unemployment gap, but does not consider the possibility of intraworking class conflicts over the distribution of employment. Cherry, like Reich, fails to address substantively the significance of the reserve army of the employed when evaluating the economics of discrimination. His theoretical and empirical discussions emphasize the wage distribution, but accord only minimal attention to the distribution of *work*.

This omission is particularly paradoxical in light of Cherry's class-based approach. In the first volume of *Capital*, Marx identified capital's endless reproduction of a reserve army of the unemployed as "The General Law of Capital Accumulation." Contemporary Marxists provide analyses of capital arguing that the divisions between the employed and unemployed, the waged and unwaged (e.g., homemakers, students, children), and so on, are political divisions that condition the balance of power within the working class (see Rubery 1978; Cleaver 1979, ch. 3; R. Williams 1987; 1989; Darity 1989). Politically divided workers sometimes pursue a recomposition of working class power that enhances collective class strength against capital. However, workers struggling to secure a stable living standard under capitalism also confront the spectre of unemployment and a shifting wage hierarchy. Variations therein fan the flames of job competition and confound the construction of long-term class-based politics.

Herein lies the rub: white workers can improve their employment and earnings prospects if they can periodically insulate themselves from nonwhite job competition. Cherry (like Bonacich) is absolutely correct to note that U.S. manufacturers sought less organized workers shortly after the capital-labor accord was established and have accelerated that search in the past two decades. What he fails to consider is the possibility that capitalists, most of whom are white in the United States, frequently have been willing to place white workers, male and female, at the head of the labor queue in the postwar economy. Their willingness to do so does not indicate a disregard for costs. On the contrary, it is the presence of nonzero white unemployment and white workers who define community in racial terms that can turn discrimination into good economic sense.[21]

Shulman's (1984) empirical analysis of the cyclical variablity of racial unemployment ratios and differences is significant here: prior to 1970, black unemployment was more cyclically sensitive than white unemployment. During the 1970s and early 1980s, however, black workers benefitted less and less with each recovery. During Reagan's first term, black workers (men and women) experienced employment losses during an upswing! Williams' (1990) investigation of the racial distribution of employment reduction between 1980 and 1985 in select manufacturing industries lends support to Shulman's thesis that employment discrimination escalates during times of rising unemployment. She finds that African-American workers suffered disproportinately large employment losses in several significant industries. Racial identification thus cuts both ways: it divides white from nonwhite, but it can also serve to assimilate and mobilize white workers and can make capitalists pay handsomely for disregarding racial solidarity.

Job competition also ranges across the wage hierarchy and is rooted in workers' quests to secure preferred niches in the occupation-industry matrix. Contrary to Cherry's claim, Darity and Williams (Darity and Williams 1985; Williams 1987, 1991; Darity 1989) deploy an explicitly Marxist conceptualization of competition that connects interindustry wage differentials between comparable workers to the heterogeneity of capital itself. In their models—which explicitly are not rooted in the monopoly capital tradition —competition between capitals creates inter- and intrasectoral differences in productivity that can become both the basis for wage differentials between comparable workers and job competition among workers seeking high wages. Competition between capitals thus provides a foundation for a job competition that reaches beyond workers' struggles to avoid unemployment. Inter- and intraindustry wage and occupational hierarchies also are contested domains.

Conclusion: What's Race Got To Do With It?

This chapter problematizes leftist understandings of race and capital accumulation. At a more concrete level, it also challenges leftists wedded to the notion that racial inquality is best conceptualized as the outcome of a capitalist strategy to "divide and conquer" the working class. Shulman's (1990) assessment neatly summarizes the prevailing critique:

> Discrimination indeed divides the working class, and it is plausible that white workers suffer wage losses as a result. However, racism also unifies whites by giving disparate ethnics a common identification. It is conceiveable that racial discimination can benefit whites in some ways (e.g., employment) but hurt them in others (e.g., wages), benefit them in the short term but hurt them in the long term, benefit their bargaining position in one set of historical circumstances but hurt it in another.

Together with Darity and Williams, Shulman's research calls attention to discrimination's distributional complexities—a complexity concealed by perspectives that measure white workers' gains solely in terms of their income relative to capital, but overlook absolute white incomes and employment levels.

Cherry's observation that white workers' postwar wage gains were temporary must not be shunted aside. White workers may well be purchasing their relative racial advantages at the price of increasing vulnerability to capital. However, as the current period demonstrates, that vulnerability also derives from capital's global mobility and the cost-cutting imperatives of never-ending capitalist competition.

Racial solidarity does not provide white workers with permanent immunity to capital's periodic onslaught. Rather, white solidarity offers contingent and contested benefits. In the current period of declining real wages and stagnant family incomes, being white may buy less in absolute terms. Yet when we view white workers' income and employment prospects relative to those of their African-American counterparts, being white still pays.

This chapter suggests the need to reconsider why the "divide-and-conquer" analysis holds such sway among contemporary radical economists. Beyond the legacy of class determinism, one possible explanation is the simplicity of the implied political agenda: a united workforce can more easily thwart, minimize, or even end capitalist exploitation. However, if racially dominant workers seek to climb, rather than smash, the wage hierarchy, then the practice of racial solidarity in the pursuit of income and employment stability has, at the very least, a contingent rationality. It is not, of course, a rationality that fosters the sort of multiracial, militant, working-class partnerships that characterized the CIO drives of the 1930s and early 1940s. It has, however, proved to be a highly resilient and practical rationality—one deeply rooted in the white supremacist culture of European immigrants and their descendants.

A second factor seems to be a commitment to a strictly delimited understanding of "agency" and "interest"—that is many leftists still insist that as co-workers, blacks and whites have a common interest, grounded in the social relations of production. The notion that one's class position determines his/her self-understanding, consciousness, and agency in the world has strong foundation in the Marxist tradition. Yet a variety of social theorists—many of whom embrace a Marxist heritage—continue to challenge this position.[22]

If radical economists want to explain race-ethnic (and nonracially based) divisions within the U.S. working class, they must seek to understand how workers come to define themselves and give meaning to their world, which means we must pay attention to structural and cultural meaning-making activities. We must engage the processes which, in conjunction with the never-ending recomposition of the wage-employment hierarchy, constitute subjects who define "class" objectives in starkly racial terms.

Most radical economists seem loathe to engage seriously white supremacy's longevity and significance in the modern world. The very notion that racism somehow "divides" workers implies the existence of some halcyon bygone days when European immigrants and enslaved Africans understood themselves as members of a common community. And indeed, this may have been the self-understanding of the indentured black and white servants laboring side by side in the 17th century. As Lerone Bennett (1975) reminds us, white workers had to learn racism.

And they have learned it. "Race" has been deeply constitutive of North American economic, cultural, and political life for 300 years. The coexistence of racially demarcated "unfree" and "free" workers is older than the nation itself, and has provided the historical foundation for generations of racially infused cultural, economic, and political struggles. "Whiteness" has been a cultural lynchpin in the process of European immigrants' acculturation as "Americans" (see Hill 1984; 1989).

Leftists seeking to articulate race and class face no small challenge. They must struggle within a political domain heavy with the successes of a right-wing discourse and politics which has racially coded inter- and intraclass politics.[23] The time-honored invocation of white workers' economic interests in joining hands with their black and Latino sisters and brothers clearly obscures the complexity of distributional issues illuminated in this chapter. Moreover, it clearly remains mired in a class reductionism that assumes an a priori subjectivity and understanding of "interests."

Beyond the smooth terrain of economic determinism lies the rocky path of working-class communities deeply rooted in racialized self-understanding. Perhaps it is time for leftists to confront, in a creative, non-reductive, and nonessentialist fashion, the intransigence of racial meanings and politics in our social order. There seems to be no place to run. Leftists who hide from the political significance of racialized working-class communities run the danger of political obsolescence.

Notes

1. Hereafter, I often abbreviate *Segmented Work* ... as SWDW.

2. "The more recent patterns of economic life for black workers began to crystallize during and after World War II." (Gordon, Edwards, and Reich 1982, 206).

3. However, Boston's operationalization of segmentation differs from that of Gordon and colleagues. Hence comparisons should be made with caution. Boston defines primary jobs as those requiring specific training; Gordon and associates use a combination of job and industry characteristics to define the segments. Dickens and Lang (1987) document a dramatic decline in total secondary employment in the 1970s, and corresponding substantial decline in nonwhite male and black female employment in the secondary sector. However, their estimation technique involves a radical departure from the fundamental tenets of segmentation theory. More concretely, their switching regime model defines segments in terms of the attributes of workers, rather than jobs and/or industries.

4. This chapter thus builds upon and extends the earlier works of Albelda (1985) and Glenn (1985).

5. Morgan (1981) describes "unfree labor" as "a variety of forms of labor from [chattel] slavery through indentured labor to present-day European migrant labor 'contract' arrangements." Unfree workers are coerced into a particular labor process with a specific owner of the means of production; once in their contract, they have negligible opportunities to terminate the same. I know of no one who would object to defining enslaved Africans (or indentured Africans and Europeans of the 17th century) as unfree labor. However, economists do disagree as to the "unfreedom" of sharecroppers and tenant farmers. Ransom and Sutch (1977) and, more recently, Jaynes (1986) argue that anti-enticement laws, convict labor, and debt bondage institutionalized the unfreedom of former slaves. Higgs (1980) is less convinced of the efficacy of laws and ordinances. More recently (Higgs 1989), he emphasizes the role of the state in keeping blacks isolated and ignorant, on the one hand, and failing to protect black lives and property, on the other, as important factors in creating their relative immobility. Amid disagreement, there is a consensus that state policies are crucial in the production and reproduction of the free/unfree distinction.

6. I thus am in substantive agreement with Boston (1988, 115) that "in a more real sense, one can say that the segmentation of black labor began with the institution of African slavery in America."

7. Under "blacks," one can find passages on wage labor (p. 56), the homogenization of

labor and strikebreakers (pp. 152–153), job segregation (p. 174), migration from the South (p. 153), segmentation of labor by race (pp. 206–210), and in core versus periphery firms (pp. 190–192). Under "women," we find employment and the structure of labor markets (pp. 93–94), initial proletarianization (pp. 67–73), labor market homogenization (pp. 120–121), occupational segregation (pp. 150–152, 174), and segmentation (pp. 204–206).

8. Capitalists' recruitment of black workers as strikebreakers is documented by Spero and Harris (1968, ch. 1), and Foner (1974, ch. 1). Neither source appears in Gordon and associates' bibliography.

9. Her data come from Census "Special Reports."

10. See Glenn (1985) for a discussion of Chicana workers in the West, and Janiewski (1985, ch. VI) for tabulations of the race-gender division of labor in tobacco.

11. Hill (1984; 1989) has written extensively on exactly this topic: the extent to which the embracing of "whiteness" became a core value for successive waves of immigrants, and the relationship between this ideological move and white racism within the working class during the past 150 years.

12. Because the authors rotate the order of their names, articles and books are listed under Gordon, Weisskopf, and Bowles.

13. Gordon and associates argue that their theoretical approaches to class, competition, and the international economy place them within the Marxist community. Radical theorists remain divided as to the theoretical significance of Marx's labor theory of value. Shaikh (1987a) and Steedman (1987) provide a recent summary of the core of this debate; see also Roberts (1988). Explanations of crises in capital accumulation also reflect differences between those who do and those who do not embrace value-theoretic categories (e.g., the organic composition of capital; productive versus unproductive capital). Shaikh (1987b; 1987c), for example, argues that the post-World War II period has been characterized by a secular decline in the rate of profit (adjusted for capacity utilization) which has, in turn, been driven by the rise in the value composition of capital. Productivity decline is thus an effect, not a cause, of crisis. Shaikh's references to race and social movements suggest he believes that crisis exacerbates capitalists' "divide-and-conquer" efforts. This chapter connects with these debates in the following section.

14. The "capital-citizen accord" is best conceptualized as the emergence and consolidation of the post-World War II managerial state which "began trying to smooth the rough edges of the market economy without compromising the reign of profits as a guide to social priorites" (Bowles et al. 1983, 77). The authors identify three aspects of an expanded state. First, public managers committed themselves to the reduction of macroeconomic instability, via automatic stabilizers and military spending. Second, government spending provided secure markets, infrastructure, and education, all of which subsidized capital accumulation. Third, through the welfare state, the government (allegedly) committed itself to at least a margin of economic security for all Americans.

15. Bowles and associates' regressions increasingly focus on time-series analyses of profit rates and Tobin's q. The open economy, linear input-output model, and estimations are presented in Bowles, Gordon, and Weisskopf (1986); additional results are presented in Bowles, Gordon and Weisskopf (1989). The latter article also concisely defines the measures of capital's power: the cost of job loss, an index of worker resistance, trade power, index of government regulation, capital's tax share, and product market tightness.

16. Bowles and associates (1983, 85–87). The authors do not explain the origins of these different movements; rather, they simply assert that protests against the racism (and sexism) and distributive injustice of the growth coalition "emerged" through social movements.

17. Perhaps this is what the authors have in mind with the note (p. 78) that social insurance objective were tempered by the need to preserve discipline in low-wage labor markets.

18. Cherry frequently juxtaposes "women and minorities." The problem here is an old one: race and gender are not conceptual substitutes. For example, Cherry does not address the extent to which some working-class white women benefitted materially from their male kin's access to primary sector jobs. Although these women often were not "independent" wage workers, they nonetheless had access to a higher standard of living than did excluded black workers and their families.

19. As Cherry observes, his analysis concurs with those of Albelda (1985) and Smith (1987), who also have identified capital's pursuit of automation, foreign labor, and nonunion domestic labor. Albelda also describes the expansion of the female-based service and state sectors.

20. For the sake of brevity, and in light of who remains active in the debates, I will focus on Shulman, Bonacich, Williams, and Darity. A thorough response to Cherry's lumping together of Marxist feminist theories of partriarchy and the oppositional camp's analysis of racial conflict between gendered blacks and whites requires another essay.

21. In his relatively unheralded but fascinating study of black factory workers in a Midwest industrial suburb, Bruce Williams (1987) documents a complex nexus of race and class relations within the community and the factory. In keeping with the Shulman-Darity-Williams models, his research describes a community that experienced a significant increase in the black population during the late 1970s. In "Promac" (a fictitious name), Williams discovered an intramanagerial conflict over the employment of African-Americans. Although the Equal-Employment-Opportunity-Commission oriented labor relations specialists were able to hire black workers (thus giving Promac the reputation as a "black plant"), they were effectively opposed by the "old guard" managers in the manufacturing division. The old guard was successful in withholding training and therefore opportunities for upward mobility from black workers. Key members of the manufacturing division expressed a pronounced "aversion" to blacks, and expressed serious concern about recruiting skilled whites to such a black plant. Skilled white workers, on the other hand, complained of bonus schemes that allowed black operatives to earn wages equal to or slightly in excess of their own. Thus, although blacks were in the plant, management and labor collaborated in transforming blacks into a noncompeting group.

22. Nelson and Grossberg (1988) provide an overview of recent developments of Marxist-inspired social theory.

23. Howard Winant (1990) provides a threefold typology of rightist projects: the far right, the new right, and the neoconservatives. He argues that all three projects articulate class issues in racial terms, and challenges leftists to articulate racial issues in class terms. His article has inspired the tone of my concluding remarks.

References

Albelda, R. 1985. "'Nice Work If You Can Get It': Segmentation of White and Black Women Workers in the Post-War Period." *Review of Radical Political Economics* 17(3): 72–85.

Baran, P., and Sweezy, P. 1966. *Monopoly Capital*. New York: Monthly Review Press.

Baron, H. 1975. "Racial Domination in Advanced Capitalism: Theories of Nationalism and Divisions in the Labor Market." In *Labor Market Segmentation*, R. Edwards, M. Reich, and D. Gordon, eds. Lexington, MA: D.C. Heath.

Bennett, L., Jr. 1975. *The Shaping of Black America*. Chicago: Johnson Publishing Company.

Bonacich, E. 1976. "Advanced Capitalism and Black/White Race Relations in the United States: A Split Labor Market Interpretation." *American Sociological Review* 41: 34–51.

Boston, T.D. 1988. *Race, Class, and Conservatism*. Boston: Unwin Hyman.

Botwinick, H. 1988. "Wage Differentials and the Competition of Capitals: A New Explanation for Inter- and Intra-Industry Wage Differentials Among Workers of Similar Skill. Doctoral dissertation, New School For Social Research.

Bowles S., Gordon, D.M., and Weisskopf, T. 1983. *Beyond the Wasteland: A Democratic Alternative to Economic Decline*. New York: Anchor Press/ Doubleday.

————. 1986. "Power and Profits: The Social Structure of Accumulation and the Profitability of the Postwar U.S. Economy." *Review of Radical Political Economics* 18(1, 2): 132–167.

————. 1988. "Social Institutions, Interests, and the Empirical Analysis of Accumulation: A Reply to Bruce Norton." *Rethinking Marxism* 1(3): 44–58.

Bowles, S., Gordon, D.M., and Weisskopf, T. 1989. "Business Ascendancy and Economic Impasse: A Structural Retrospective on Conservative economics, 1979–87." *Journal of Economic Perspectives* 3(1): 107–134.

Carby H. 1987. *Reconstructing Womanhood: The Emergence of the Afro-American Woman Novelist*. Oxford: Oxford University Press.

Cherry, R. 1988. "Shifts in Radical Theories of Inequality." *Review of Radical Political Economics* 20(2, 3): 184–189.

————. 1989. *Discrimination: Its Impact on Blacks, Women, and Jews*. Lexington, MA: D.C. Heath.

————. 1991. "Race and Gender Aspects of Marxian Macroeconomic Models: The Case of the Social Structure of Accumulation." Science and Society SS(1): 60–78.

Cleaver, H. 1979. *Reading Capital Politically*. Austin, TX: University of Texas Press.

Darity, W.A., Jr. 1989. "What's Left of the Economic Theory of Discrimination?" In *The Question of Discrimination: Racial Inequality in the U.S. Labor Market*, S. Shulman and W. A. Darity, eds. Middletown, CT: Wesleyan University Press.

Darity, W.A., Jr., and Williams, R.M. 1985. "Peddlers Forever?: Culture, Competition, and Discrimination." *American Economic Review* 75(2): 256–261.

Dickens, W.T., and Lang, K. 1987. "Where Have All the Good Jobs Gone: Deindustrialization and Labor Market Segmentation." In *Unemployment and the Structure of Labor Markets*, K. Lang and J. Leonard, eds. New York: Basil Blackwell.

DuBois, W.E.B. 1933. "Marxism and the Negro Question." *Crisis*. 45: 103–104, 118.

———. 1967 [1899]. *The Philadelphia Negro: A Social Study*. New York: Schocken Books.

Foner, P.S. 1974. *Organized Labor and the Black Worker, 1619–1973*. New York: Praeger Publisher.

Fredrickson, G. 1981. *White Supremacy: A Comparative Study in American and South African History*. Oxford: Oxford University Press.

Friedman, S. 1984. "Structure, Process, and the Labor Market." In *Labor Economics: Modern Views*, W.A. Darity, Jr. ed., 175–218. Boston: Kluwer-Nijhoff.

Glenn, E.N. 1985. "Racial Ethnic Women's Labor: The Intersection of Race, Gender, and Class Oppression." *Review of Radical Political Economics* 17(3): 86–108.

Goldin, C. 1981. "Family Strategies and the Family Economy in the Late Nineteenth Century: The Role of Secondary workers." In *Philadelphia, Work, Space, Family, and Group Experience in the Nineteenth Century*, T. Hershberg, ed. 277–305. New York: Oxford University Press.

Gordon, D., Edwards, R., and Reich., M. 1982. *Segmented Work, Divided Workers: The Historical Transformation of Labor in the United States*. Cambridge: Cambridge University Press.

Gordon, D.M., Weisskopf, T.E. and Bowles, S. 1987. "Power, Accumulation and Crisis: The Rise and Demise of the Postwar Social Structure of Accumulation." In *The Imperiled Economy—Book I: Macroeconomics from a Left Perspective*, R. Cherry, C. D'Onofrio, C. Kurdas, et al., eds. New York: Union for Radical Political Economics.

Harley, S. 1978. "Northern Black Female Workers; Jacksonian Era." In *The Afro-American Woman: Struggles and Images*, S. Harley and R. Terborg-Penn, eds. Port Washington, NY: Kennikat Press.

Higgs, R. 1980. *Competition and Coercion: Blacks in the American Economy, 1865–1914*. Chicago: University of Chicago Press.

———. 1989. "Black Progress and the Persistence of Racial Economic Inequalities, 1865–1940." In *The Question of Discrimination: Racial Inequality in U.S. Labor Markets*, W.A. Darity, Jr., and S. Shulman, eds. Middletown, CT: Weslyan University Press.

Hill, H. 1984. "Race and Ethnicity in Organized Labor." *Journal of Intergroup Relations* 13(4): 5–49.

———. 1989. "Race, Ethnicity, and Organized Labor: The Opposition to Affirmative Action." In *The Question of Discrimination. Racial Inequality in U.S. Markets*, W.A. Darity, S., and S. Shulman, eds. Middletown, CT: Wesleyan University Press.

Janiewski, D.E. 1985. *Sisterhood Denied: Race, Gender, and Class in a New South Community*. Philadelphia: Temple University Press.

Jaynes, G.D. 1986. *Branches Without Roots: Genesis of the Black Working Class in the American South, 1862–1882*. Oxford: Oxford University Press.

Litwack, L.F. 1961. *North of Slavery; The Negro in the Free States, 1790–1860*. Chicago: University of Chicago Press.

Marx, K. 1967. *Capital*, Vol. I. New York: International Publishers.

Matthaei, J. 1982. *An Economic History of Women in America: Women's Work, the Sexual Division of Labor, and the Development of Capitalism*. New York: Schocken Books.

Morgan, G. 1981. "Class Theory and the Structural Location of Black Workers." *Insurgent Sociologist* 10: 21–34.

Nelson, C. and Grossberg, L., eds. 1988. *Marxism and the Interpretation of Culture*. Urbana: University of Illinois Press.

Nolan, P. and Edwards P.K. 1984. "Homogenise, Divide, and Rule: an Essay on *Segmented Work, Divided Workers*." *Cambridge Journal of Economics* 8: 197–215.

Ransom, R.L., and Sutch, R. 1977. *One Kind of Freedom: The Economic Consequences of Emancipation*. Cambridge: Cambridge University Press.

Reich, M. 1981. *Racial Inequality: A Political-Economic Analysis*. Princeton: Princeton University Press.

Roemer, J.E. 1979. "Divide and Conquer: Microfoundations of a Marxian Theory of Wage Discrimination." *Bell Journal of Economics* 10.

Roberts, B. 1988. "What Is Profit?" *Rethinking Marxism* 1(1): 136–151.

Rubery, J. 1978. "Structured Labor Markets, Worker Organization, and Low Pay." *Cambridge Journal of Economics* 2.

Shaikh, A. 1987a. "The Poverty of Algebra." In *Alternatives to Economic Orthodoxy*, R Albelda, C. Gunn, and W. Waller, eds. Armonk, NY: M.E. Sharpe.

————. 1987b. "The Falling Rate of Profit and the Economic Crisis in the U.S." In *The Imperiled Economy—Book I: Macroeconomics from a left Perspective*, R. Cherry, C. D'Onofrio, C. Kurdas, et al., eds. New York: Union for Radical Political Economics.

————. 1987c. "The Organic Composition of Capital." In *The New Palgrave: A Dictionary of Economic Theory and Doctrine*, J. Eatwell, M. Milgate, and P. Newman, eds. London: Macmillan.

Shulman, S. 1984. "Competition and Racial Discrimination: The Employment Effects of Reagan's Labor Market Policies." *Review of Radical Political Economics* 16(4): 111–128.

————. 1990. "Racial Inequality and White Employment: An Interpretation and Test of the Bargaining Power Hypothesis." *The Review of Black Political Economy* 18(3): 5–20.

———— and W. Darity Jr. eds. *The Question of Discrimination* Middletown, CT: Wesleyan University Press 1989.

Spero, S.D., and Harris, A. 1972 [1931]. *The Black Worker: The Negro and the Labor Movement*. New York: Antheum.

Steedman, I. 1987. "Value, Price, and Profit." In *Alternatives to Economic Orthodoxy*, R. Albelda, C. Gunn, and W. Waller, eds. Armonk, NY: M.E. Sharpe.

Syzmanski, A. 1976. "Racial Discrimination and White Gain." *American Sociological Review* 41.

Wacquant, L.J.D. 1989. "The Ghetto, the State, and the New Capitalist Economy." *Dissent* (Fall): 508–520.

Wilkinson, F., ed. 1981. *The Dynamics of Labor Market Segmentation*. London: Academic Press.

Williams, B. 1987. *Black Workers in an Industrial Suburb: The Struggle Against Discrimination*. New Brunswick: Rutgers University Press.

Williams, R.M. 1987. "Capital, Competition, and Discrimination: A Reconsideration of Racial Earnings Inequality." *Review of Radical Political Economy* 19(2): 1–15.

———. 1990. "Beyond 'Bad Luck': The Racial Dimensions of Deindustrialization." Washington, DC: Joint Center for Political Studies.

———. 1991, forthcoming. "Competition, Discrimination, and Differential Wage Rates: On the Continued Relevance of Marxian Theory to the Analysis of Earnings and Employment Inequality." In *New Approaches to Economic and Social Analyses of Discrimination*, R. Cornwall and P. Wunnava, eds. New York: Praeger.

Winant, H. 1990. "Postmodern Racial Politics: Difference and Inequality." *Socialist Review* 20(1): 121–147.

IV CULTURE, ETHNICITY, AND POVERTY

8 CULTURE AND HUMAN CAPITAL: THEORY AND EVIDENCE OR THEORY VERSUS EVIDENCE?

Stephen A. Woodbury

The economic analysis of wages took a variety of new turns during the 1980s, but none more important than the reinterpretation of wage gaps that were once viewed as discriminatory. At the beginning of the '80s, wage gaps between minority groups and whites that could not be explained by differences in observable characteristics—such as years of schooling or experience in the labor market—were widely attributed to discrimination. By the end of the decade these *unexplained wage gaps* were being viewed as a reflection of underlying unobservable differences in human capital or "culture".

There could hardly be a more significant change in our view of black-white (or Hispanic-non-Hispanic) wage gaps. Admitting the possibility of discriminatory wage gaps opens the door to enactment and enforcement of antidiscrimination policies of various kinds.[1] Attributing all wage gaps to differences in "culture"—this term will need to be defined—suggests a natural order to the existing structure of wages. Culture evokes an image of something that should not be disturbed: would we want to impose policies that might diminish the uniqueness or heritage of a racial or ethnic group, even if doing so would bring higher earnings to that group?

My goal in this chapter is to appraise the degree to which existing empirical evidence can resolve the controversy over interpreting unexplained wage gaps. The first section provides a heuristic treatment of what has become the traditional approach to analyzing wage gaps among various groups of workers. The section also develops the cultural interpretation of unexplained wage gaps and examines some relatively new evidence on the wages of American blacks who are the descendants of British West Indians. In the second section, I review a more recent strand of the literature—that on immigrants—to see whether such an examination can narrow the scope for debate. The final two sections offers my attempt to sort through the possible sources of this wage gap controversy, and to suggest that the rise of culture as an explanator of wage gaps is a degenerate response to an empirical problem that has arisen in the human capital framework.

Wage Gaps and Their Decomposition

Two related analytical devices have proven themselves to be indispensable to analyzing wage gaps among various groups of workers. The first is the human capital wage function (often called the "earnings function"), as developed most fully by Jacob Mincer (1974). The second is a decomposition of the total (or gross) wage gap between two groups of workers into "explained" and "unexplained" components. Since this decomposition first appeared in articles published almost simultaneously by Alan Blinder (1973) and Ronald Oaxaca (1973), it has come to be known as the Blinder-Oaxaca decomposition.[2]

Mincer's Human Capital Wage Function

Mincer (1974) provided a specific functional form that links a worker's wages to the number of years of schooling completed by the worker, the worker's experience in the labor force, and a number of other variables.[3]An important aspect of Mincer's work is to show that years of work experience—as approximated by a worker's age minus the number of years of schooling minus five (the age at which schooling usually begins)—is a better predictor of wages than is age. Mincer interprets the importance of the relationship between wages and experience as suggesting the importance of postschool investments in human capital, and does so in way that many have found convincing.

For present purposes, however, it is enough to think of Mincer's wage function as a black box that transforms individuals' observable traits into a predicted level of wages. We might take the observable traits of a randomly chosen white male worker—his years of schooling, labor market experience, tenure on current job, location, occupation and industry of employment, and so on—and pour them into a hopper at one end of the black box. Out the other end of the black box would come a predicted level of wages. The black box into which the white male worker's traits would be poured would ordinarily be specific to white men; there may exist different black boxes giving different relationships between wages and individual traits for women, blacks, Hispanics, Asians, and so on.

The Blinder-Oaxaca Decomposition: Estimating Discrimination

Mincer's wage function has provided a widely used and powerful framework for analyzing wage gaps among various groups of workers. Suppose the mean wages of white male workers were observed to be $14,988 in 1979, and the mean for black male workers were $9,604.[4] The gross wage gap in percentage terms is about 45 percent.[5] Is this gap fully the result of labor market discrimination against blacks, or can part of it be attributed to other factors?

The answer provided by Blinder (1973) and Oaxaca (1973) was that, indeed, some of the gross wage gap may be attributable to factors other than discrimination. That is, the gross wage gap can be viewed as "explained" in part by observable differences between whites and blacks that we might expect to lead to differences in productivity. If black workers have on average fewer years of schooling or postschool work experience than do whites, then we could expect blacks' earnings to be lower than whites'.

But by how much? Blinder and Oaxaca provided an elegant answer that allows a quantitative decomposition of the gross wage gap into "explained" and "unexplained" components. If we pour the characteristics of the average white male worker into the hopper of the white-male Mincer black box, we will get in return the average observed wages of white men. We already know this was $14,988 in 1979, and it will be useful to refer to it as W_w. We could do the same for black male workers—pour the characteristics of the average black male worker into the black-male Mincer black box and get the average observed wages of black men. This was $9,604 in 1979, and we can refer to it as W_b. These figures and the notation are summarized in panel A of Table 1.

Now perform one more experiment. Pour the characteristics of the average black male worker into the hopper of the *white*-male Mincer black box. What will come out is an estimate of the wages of black men *if the*

Table 1. Wages and Wage Gaps for Black and White Male Workers, 1979

Panel A: Actual and Adjusted Wages

Group	*Geometric Mean*	*Logarithmic Mean*
White Men (W_w)	\$14,988	9.615
West Indian black men adjusted by white men's wage function (W^*_{bwi})	\$13,947	9.543
West Indian black men (W_{bwi})	\$12,456	9.430
Black men adjusted by white men's wage function (W_b^*)	\$11,626	9.361
Black men adjusted by West Indian black men's wage function (W_b^{**})	\$ 9,977	9.208
Black men (W_b)	\$ 9,604	9.170

Panel B: Gross and Adjusted Wage Gaps

Groups Compared	*Proportional Gross Wage Cap*	*Proportional Adjusted Wage Gap*	*Proportion of Gross Gap Explained*	*Proportion of Gross Gap Unexplained*
1. Black men/white men	.45 ($lnW_w - lnW_b$)	.26 ($lnW_w - lnW_b^*$)	.58 (.26/.45)	.42 [(.45–.26)/.45]
2. West Indian black men/white men	.19 ($lnW_w - lnW_{bwi}$)	.07 ($lnW_w - lnW_{bwi}^*$)	.37 (.07/.19)	.63 [(.19–.07)/.19]
3. Black men/West Indian black men	.26 ($lnW_{bwi} - lnW_b$)	.22 ($lnW_{bwi} - lnW_b^{**}$)	.85 (.22/.26)	.15 [(.26–.22)/.26]

Source: Woodbury and Bettinger (1991, Table 4).

labor market had treated them as it treats white men. This imputed wage is often referred to as an *adjusted wage* because it has been adjusted to reflect what blacks would have earned if their observable characteristics (aside from skin color) received the same return as did whites' observable characteristics. Call this adjusted wage W_b^*. Most studies that have performed the experiment described have found that W_b^* is somewhere between W_w and W_b. That is, if the labor market treated black workers as it does white workers, the average black worker would earn more, but would still earn less than the average white worker.

When Douglas Bettinger and I performed this experiment using data from the 1980 Census of Population, we found that black men would have earned $11,626 in 1979—instead of just $9,604—if their wages had come out of the white-male Mincer black box (Woodbury and Bettinger 1991). So if black men had been treated as white men in the labor market, the wage gap would have been 26 percent (this is the *adjusted* wage gap), rather than 45 percent (the gross wage gap).[6] This decomposition is summarized in Table 1 (see row 1 of panel B).

The implication is that 58 percent (26 percent out of 45 percent) of the gross wage gap can be "explained" by differences between blacks and whites that are observed. The remaining 42 percent of the gross wage gap would disappear if blacks' observed characteristics received the same return in the labor market as do whites' and is said to be "unexplained." (See again row 1 of panel B in Table 1.)

The interpretation of this "unexplained" portion of the wage gap is at issue. Blinder, Oaxaca, and many who have followed them have interpreted the unexplained wage gap as largely discriminatory, and have suggested that it offers a measure of the degree of direct labor market discrimination.[7] Blinder (1973, 439) refers explicitly to the unexplained portion of the wage gap as the "portion of the differential attributable to discrimination."[8]

Oaxaca goes still further and links the unexplained wage gap to Gary Becker's (1971) theory of discrimination, in which discrimination is conceptualized as the gap between the pay of favored workers (whites) and the pay of discriminated-against workers (blacks) who are perfect substitutes in production. This gap, which Becker calls the market discrimination coefficient (MDC) equals $(W_w/W_b) - (W_w'/W_b')$, where W_w and W_b are the actual wages paid to white and black workers, and W_w' and W_b' are the wages that would be paid in the absence of discrimination (Becker 1971, 17). Hence, the MDC is the gap that remains after subtracting from the gross wage gap (W_w/W_b) the portion of the gap that can be attributed to differences in productivity (W_w'/W_b'). Oaxaca's argument is that the actual wage of white workers gives an approximation to W_w' (that is, whites' wages would not change if there were no discrimination), and that the Mincer wage function gives an estimate of the wage that black workers would receive absent discrimination (that is, W_b* gives an empirical estimate of W'_b).[9] It follows that the unexplained wage gap is an estimate of Becker's market discrimination coefficient.[10]

An Alternative Interpretation: Culture

In the early 1980s a different interpretation of the unexplained wage gap was suggested by Thomas Sowell (1980; 1981; 1983) and Barry R. Chiswick (1983a; 1983b). Sowell's work contains a variety of subtleties and does not lend itself to simple characterization. But his basic argument is that the unexplained wage gap gives a poor estimate of the degree of discrimination because it confounds two effects, neither of which is directly observed: the effects of discrimination and the effects of what he calls "culture." As Sowell puts it, "Whether in an ethnic context or among peoples and nations generally, much depends on a whole constellation of values, attitudes, skills, and contacts that many call a culture and that economists call 'human capital'" (Sowell 1981, 282). In this view, there could be an unexplained wage gap either because of discrimination or because of unobserved characteristics of individuals that vary systematically by ethnicity—that is, culture. Since culture is correlated with labor market productivity, the unexplained wage gap does not measure discrimination at all. Rather, the unexplained wage gap gives a measure of how a worker's unmeasured "values, attitudes, skills, and contacts" influence his or her earnings.

Independently, Barry R. Chiswick (1983a; 1983b) published two articles challenging the usual Blinder-Oaxaca interpretation of the unexplained wage gap and supporting the cultural interpretation. One of Chiswick's articles (1983b) offers an analysis of the wages (and rates of return to schooling) of Jews compared with non-Jews.[11] His basic finding is that when one pours the observable characteristics of Jews into the Mincer black box for non-Jews, the wage level predicted for Jews is about 16 percent *lower* than the level actually observed. That is, Jews are observed to do better in the labor market than one would predict, based on the wage function for non-Jews. The literal Blinder-Oaxaca interpretation of this finding would have to be that Jews have received *favorable* discrimination, which makes little sense in view of known patterns of past discrimination against Jews. Chiswick's alternative interpretation is that "shared aspects of the historical, cultural, and religious experiences of American Jews . . . are responsible for their labor market success" (Chiswick 1983b, 334). In other words, Jews possess a culture and unobserved human capital that enhances their success in the labor market.

Chiswick further finds that the wages of Jews increase more per year of schooling and per year of labor market experience than do the earnings of non-Jews—that is, the rates of return to schooling and experience are higher for Jews. Chiswick's interpretation of this finding is *not* that Jews simply have a greater "taste" for schooling that induces them to obtain more schooling, but rather that:

> [C]ultural characteristics . . . enable Jews to acquire more units of human capital per dollar of investment. For example, Jews may learn more in school or on the job because of supplemental training received in the home or in the Jewish community prior to or concurrent with schooling. Or, it may be that there are cultural characteristics that enable Jews to be more productive in the labor market with the human capital embodied in them [Chiswick 1983b, 334].

Chiswick's other article (1983a) analyzes the wages of native-born American men of Chinese, Japanese, and Philippine origin. The findings of this research echo the main conclusion of the research on Jews: first, when one pours the observable characteristics of Chinese into the Mincer black box for whites, the wage level predicted for Chinese is about the same as the level actually observed. Second, when one pours the observable characteristics of Japanese into the Mincer black box for whites, the wage level predicted for Japanese is only about 4 percent greater than the level actually observed. Finally, when the observable characteristics of Filipinos are poured into the Mincer black box for whites, the wage level predicted for Filipinos is about 18 percent higher than the level actually observed. The Blinder-Oaxaca interpretation of these findings would be that there is no wage discrimination against Chinese-Americans, wage discrimination of 4 percent against Japanese, and wage discrimination of 18 percent against Filipinos.

But Chiswick's interpretation is different. Given that Chinese and Japanese (as well as Filipinos) have experienced clear discrimination in the United States, it is surprising that Chinese and Japanese workers have the same (or nearly the same) earnings as native-born white Americans. That is, Chiswick implicitly expects unexplained differentials for Chinese and Japanese that are larger than those estimated. The implication is that Chinese-American and Japanese-American workers have somehow overcome the effects of the discrimination they have experienced. That is, they have a culture that is favorable to success in the labor market. Chiswick concludes as follows:

> [I]t is incorrect to assume that racial minority status in the United States and racial discrimination per se result in lower observed levels of earnings, schooling, employment, and rates of return from schooling. More care may be needed in attributing to racial discrimination the disadvantageous outcomes for other, less successful racial and ethnic minorities [Chiswick 1983a, 212].

In a review of one of Sowell's books, Chiswick (1984) has summarized Sowell's (and to some degree his own) critique of the empirical literature on discrimination. Chiswick first questions "the extent to which discrimination can account for the observed differences in the behavior and economic outcome of racial and ethnic groups." Noting that some minorities in the United States—such as Chinese, Japanese, and Jews—have been economically successful in spite of discrimination, he writes:

> Surely these successful minorities have not been the beneficiaries of favorable discrimination nor could discrimination by them explain their achievements! Some other factor (or factors) must be responsible for the achievements of the successful groups. Could the absence of this factor (or factors) rather than discrimination be primarily responsible for the disadvantages of the less successful? Could the residual in the estimation techniques be dominated by the missing factor (factors) rather than by discrimination? [Chiswick 1984, 1159].

Chiswick's questions are not entirely rhetorical, and the remainder of his review can in fact be read as a critique of Sowell's vagueness in specifying what is meant by culture.

But the implication of the critique offered by Sowell and Chiswick is clear: the unexplained wage gap between white and black workers is dominated not by discrimination, but by omitted variables that help determine productivity and pay. If we could observe these omitted variables and include them in the wage function, we would find that the unexplained wage gap between blacks and whites would drop or even vanish. The view underlying this position is strictly neoclassical: workers are paid according to the dollar amount that the marginal worker is responsible for adding to the employer's revenues, and there is no room for discrimination.[12]

West Indians: A Case in Point?

Sowell has buttressed his case that culture—not discrimination—is at the root of the wage gap between blacks and whites by arguing that at least one group of blacks has overcome the effects of discrimination. These are West Indian blacks—that is, blacks who immigrated from the British West Indies and the descendants of those immigrants. Sowell has shown that in 1969, the average family income of West Indian blacks was 94 percent of the national average family income. But black families as a whole had just 62 percent of national average family income (Sowell 1978, 41–48, 389–415).

Sowell suggests that a distinct West Indian culture is responsible for the relative success of West Indians: "While not racially distinct from American Negroes, West Indians have had a different cultural background and have remained socially distinct from the other blacks around them" (Sowell 1981, 216). The chief elements of this cultural difference are that West Indians "had generations of experience in individual reward for individual effort, [and] faced a wider occupational range than American Negroes" (Sowell 1978, 46). According to Sowell, West Indians are significant because "their very different background makes them a test case of the explanatory importance of color, as such, in analyzing socioeconomic progress in the American economy and society, as compared to the importance of the cultural traditions of the American Negro" (Sowell 1978, 42).

How robust is the evidence on the success of West Indians? Table 1 (rows 2 and 3 of panel B) summarizes the rather mixed findings of a study that used 1980 Census of Population data on native-born American blacks of West Indian ancestry (Woodbury and Bettinger 1991). Consider first a comparison of West Indian black men with white men in 1979. The average wages of West Indian blacks (W_{bwi}) were $12,456, and the average wages of whites (W_w) were $14,988. This implies a gross wage gap of 19 percent. How much of this gross wage gap can be explained? Pouring the characteristics of the average West Indian black into the Mincer black box for white men gives adjusted wages of West Indian blacks (W_{bwi}*) of $13,947. It follows that the adjusted (or explained) wage gap between West Indian blacks and whites is 7 percent. This implies that only 37 percent of the gross wage gap can be explained by observable characteristics of workers. The other 63 percent must be attributed either to discrimination against West Indian blacks, or to a disadvantageous West Indian culture. (The decomposition is shown in Table 1, row 2 of panel B.)

Note that the gross wage gap between West Indian blacks and whites is less than half the gross wage gap between other blacks and whites. But less of the gross wage gap between West Indian blacks and whites can be explained: only 37 percent compared with 58 percent of the gross wage gap between other blacks and whites.

Consider next a comparison of black men (not of West Indian ancestry) with West Indian black men. The average wages of blacks (that is, non-West Indian blacks, W_b) were $9,604, whereas the average wages of West Indian blacks (W_{bwi}) were $12,456. The gross wage gap is 26 percent. How much of this gross wage gap can be explained? Pouring the characteristics of the average black worker into the Mincer black box for West Indian blacks gives adjusted wages of blacks (W_b**) of $9,977. (The double-asterisk notation implies that the wages of blacks have been adjusted not by the white wage function, but by the West Indian wage function.) Hence, the adjusted wage gap between blacks and West Indian blacks is 22 percent, and nearly all (85 percent) of the gross wage gap between blacks and West Indian blacks can be explained by observable characteristics (see Table 1, row 3 of panel B).

To summarize, we have two principal findings. First, West Indian blacks earn more than other blacks mainly because they have more of the observable characteristics (such as schooling and labor market experience) that enhance wages, not because of unmeasurable human capital in the form of culture. Second, West Indian blacks earn less than whites not because they have *less* of those measurable characteristics than do whites, but either because they are discriminated against or because their culture is disadvantageous. Why do observable traits explain most of the wage gap between West Indian blacks and other blacks, but less than 40 percent of the wage gap between West Indian blacks and whites? One answer is that black workers, whether or not they are West Indian, are treated similarly in the labor market—that is, both receive discriminatory treatment. Another is that both are culturally disadvantaged. But this latter answer contradicts the notion that West Indian blacks have a culture that gives them an edge in the labor market, and suggests that a group that is alleged to have overcome the effects of discrimination really has not.

In short, the results suggest that the culture of West Indian blacks, which is thought to have led to success in the labor market, plays a limited role in explaining the wage gap between West Indian blacks and *either* whites or other blacks. West Indians' higher wages are the result of more schooling and other measurable factors that are expected to enhance wages. If culture explains relatively little, then discrimination based on color may explain more.

There is, of course, room for disagreement with this interpretation. One could argue that West Indian blacks get more schooling because they come from a culture that values schooling. The implication would be that acquisition of observable traits that enhance wages is part of culture, and that part of the explained wage gap could be attributed to culture. This point raises two sets of related issues that will be discussed below. The first is the issue of direct market versus premarket discrimination, which pertains to whether characteristics such as years of schooling can be attributed to discrimination. The second is a methodological issue called the colligation problem, which pertains to where it is best to "cut into" a set of social phenomena that we are trying to understand.

Wages of Black Immigrants

Another possible way of untangling the controversy over culture and human capital is to gather different kinds of evidence. For example, data on the wages of immigrants and native-born workers could be examined, and comparisons could be drawn between workers of the same race or ethnicity who come from different cultures. Do workers from different cultures— the immigrants—experience different outcomes than native-born workers? Do immigrants overcome barriers in the labor market more readily, or in a way that would suggest that discrimination can be surmounted? In fact, the study of immigrants' wages has become something of a growth industry in recent years, although whether such work can shed light on the degree to which discrimination plays a role in the labor market has been controversial.[13]

Assimilation and Cohort Effects

The pioneering study of immigrants' wages is by Barry Chiswick (1978), which is grounded in the human capital theory and makes explicit use of Mincer's wage function. The innovation in Chiswick's work is to ask a different question about wage gaps than had been asked before: if the labor market treated an immigrant as it treats a native-born worker, how much would that immigrant earn? In this case we pour the characteristics of the average immigrant into the Mincer black box for native-born workers to see what the immigrant would earn if treated as a native. In notation similar to that used above for white and black workers, we could denote the actual wages of native-born workers as W_n, the actual wages of immigrants as W_i, and the adjusted wages of immigrants (that is, the wages that the average immigrant would receive if his/her earnings were determined by the native-born wage function) as $W_i{}^*$.

Chiswick's work generated much interest when it was published (and has been controversial since) because it provides estimates of how the wages of immigrants grow as they become "assimilated" into the U.S. labor market.[14] With data on immigrants' times of arrival in the United States, we could ask what would be the wages of a cohort of immigrants if those wages were determined by the Mincer black box for native-born whites. This would mean pouring the characteristics of immigrants who arrived in time period t (1975–1980, for example) into the Mincer black box for native-born workers. The difference between the actual wage of cohort t of immigrants (W_{it}) and the adjusted wages of cohort t ($W_{it}{}^*$) would be an unexplained wage gap that would tell us the wage disadvantage of having immigrated during period t.

Table 2. Unexplained Wage Gaps between Immigrant Groups and Native-Born White Workers, by Year of Immigration

	Year of Immigration					
Immigrant Group	*1975–80*	*1970–74*	*1965–69*	*1960–64*	*1950–59*	*Pre-1950*
1. English-second-language whites	−26.6	−8.5	−1.0	2.4	4.1	3.6
2. English-only whites	4.0	1.8	8.9	3.8	4.2	5.1
3. West Indians blacks	−48.2	−27.3	−25.1	−25.9	−12.9	−26.9
4. Non-West Indian blacks	−72.7	−49.2	−36.2	−23.9	−40.4	−23.0
5. Asians	−47.5	−20.7	−12.1	−8.1	−10.8	−13.2
6. Hispanics	−44.8	−24.6	−18.7	−10.5	−7.5	−5.6

Source: Woodbury and Bettinger (1991, Table 6).

When such unexplained wage gaps have been constructed for successive cohorts of immigrants, what is usually seen is that the longer a cohort has been in the United States, the smaller is the unexplained wage gap. Row 1 of Table 2 reproduces some unexplained wage gaps that Bettinger and I generated for white male immigrants who spoke English as a second language using Chiswick's method (Woodbury and Bettinger 1991, Table 6). They show that the wage gap between white English-second-language immigrants who arrived during 1975–1980 and demographically comparable white male native-born workers was about −27 percent. That is, these newly arrived immigrants earned 27 percent less than they would have if their wages came out of the Mincer black box for white native-born workers. But the gap between white English-second-language immigrants who arrived before 1965 and comparable native-born workers was between 2 and 4 percent. These long-term immigrants earned *more* than comparable native-born whites.

The unexplained wage gaps in row 1 of Table 2 can be interpreted as the time path of wage gaps between a given cohort of immigrants and comparable native-born workers. That is, the recently arrived immigrants whose wages were 27 percent below those of comparable natives in 1980 could expect to draw even with comparable natives within 15 years. This is Chiswick's "dynamic" interpretation (as Borjas has called it), and the rationale given for the shrinkage of the gap is that immigrants become "assimilated": the longer they remain in the United States, the more human capital they accumulate. This makes good sense in the case of immigrants whose second language is English—their English language skills improve the longer they are in the United States and their wages improve accordingly.[15]

Borjas (1985; 1991) has criticized the dynamic interpretation of the profile of unexplained wage gaps, in essence because it requires that the Mincer wage function include all determinants of wages, omitting no relevant variable. This is a tall order: there may be unobserved differences between immigrants who arrived during the late 1970s and those who arrived during the early 1960s.[16] If these so-called *cohort effects* exist, then there is no reason to suppose that the late-1970s arrivals will have the same experience as the early-1960s arrivals. They could do better or worse because their basic capacities to perform well in the labor market differ.

The problem with the "dynamic" interpretation of the profile of wage gaps can be seen clearly in row 2 of Table 2. These are unexplained wage gaps between native-born white workers and white immigrants *whose only language is English*. What the gaps show is that English-only white immigrants earn between 2 and 9 percent *more* than comparable native-born whites from the day they set foot in the United States. No clear pattern of wage growth is discernible in the gaps shown in row 2. Does this mean that there is no assimilation effect for workers whose only language is English? Or does it mean that there is an assimilation effect and that the capacity of recent cohorts of English-only white immigrants to perform in the labor market is greater than that of earlier cohorts? (That is, many years of assimilation were required before the pre-1950s cohort did as well as—or better than—natives, but recent cohorts do as well immediately.)

Borjas (1985; 1988; 1991) has attempted to separate the assimilation and cohort effects by examining two successive cross-sections of data on immigrants. By examining the wages of a group of immigrants in 1970 and reexamining the wages of the same group in 1980, he draws inferences about underlying differences between various groups of immigrants.

The Possibility of Discrimination

There is, however, a third possible component of the unexplained wage gaps between immigrants and native workers: the impact of discrimination. Consider the literal interpretation of the wage gaps shown in Table 2. The figure -26.6 in row 1 of Table 2 implies that a white English-second-language immigrant who arrived during 1975–1980 earned 26.6 percent less than a demographically similar native-born worker. This interpretation is literal and uncontroversial.

But it should be clear that this unexplained wage gap mixes three effects. The first is the assimilation effect (or absence of assimilation in newly arrived immigrants), which can be interpreted as a human capital deficit that will erode as the cohort of immigrants becomes assimilated into the U.S. labor market. This is the effect that Chiswick has focussed on. The second is the cohort effect, which results from unobserved "culture" (or human capital) that does not change over time. Borjas has emphasized this effect; although he does not refer to it as culture. And the third is the effect of discrimination. If there were any discrimination against a group of immigrants—because of race, different appearance, accent, or any other reason—it could show up only in the unexplained wage gap. So there are three effects mixed up in the wage gaps shown in Table 2, and what we appear to have is so much hash.

Borjas has rejected the notion that unexplained wage gaps between immigrants and natives have a discriminatory component, and denies that anything about discrimination can be inferred from studies of immigrants. He argues that:

> . . . earnings differentials between the various national-origin groups and natives can be understood in terms of economic and political characteristics of the source countries and the United States. . . . In addition, several recent studies provide strong evidence that systematic discrimination against Hispanics or Asians (the two dominant groups in recent immigrant waves) is not an important aspect of the American labor market [Borjas 1990, 129–130].

These two statements can be read together as an affirmation that culture (cohort effects) and assimilation effects, rather than discrimination, lie at the root of wage gaps between immigrants and natives. In fact, the first statement reflects the results of a rather elegant theory that Borjas has developed and that is worth reviewing.[17]

Borjas develops the idea that there is an immigration market. Individuals in all countries are looking for the best available opportunities, and if there is a net advantage to be gained by moving from one country to another (and if it is possible), then a worker will move. It follows from such reasoning that migrant flows will be nonrandom and that migrants themselves will have predictable traits.

Borjas gives special attention to factors that determine whether a country attracts skilled or unskilled immigrants. He argues that there is a close relationship between the skill levels of immigrants and the degree to which skills are rewarded in both the country of origin and the host country. In some countries, skills and education receive a relatively high return, whereas in others they receive a lower return. Generally, the countries in which skills are highly rewarded are countries in which income distribution is relatively unequal, as in many developing countries.

Borjas shows that we should expect to see migration of highly skilled workers from countries where skills are poorly rewarded to countries where skills are well rewarded. Conversely, we should expect to see migrations of unskilled workers from countries where skills are well rewarded to countries where skills are less well rewarded. These expectations tend to be confirmed by the evidence Borjas presents on immigrant flows to the United States (Borjas 1990, ch. 7, for example). In particular, we would expect immigrants from relatively egalitarian western European countries to be highly skilled. Also, we would expect immigrants from developing countries, where income distribution is highly unequal, to be relatively unskilled.

Borjas's is by far the most sophisticated argument linking the wages of immigrants to their skills. It provides a rationale for believing that unexplained wage gaps between native workers and immigrants in fact reflect unobserved differences in productivity, rather than factors such as discrimination.

But the argument cannot wholly dispose of the notion that immigrants experience discrimination in the U.S. labor market—and consequently lower wages—because they are members of a racial minority. Indeed, Borjas relies in part on evidence from studies of discrimination against native-born workers to conclude that discrimination against Hispanics and Asians "is not an important aspect of the American labor market," and therefore that unexplained wage gaps between natives and immigrants do not include a discriminatory component. It should be noted that some labor economists would dispute Borjas's characterization of the evidence on discrimination against Hispanics. Particularly in the case of black immigrants, there is little if any prior evidence to suggest that wage gaps are uncontaminated by discrimination.

Wage Gaps Between Immigrants and Natives

To repeat, the unexplained wage gap between a cohort of immigrants and natives mixes three effects: an assimilation effect, a cohort effect, and a discrimination effect. It is important to keep these three possibilities in mind in examining rows 3 through 6 of Table 2, which show profiles of unexplained wage gaps for four groups of minority immigrants. In each case, the average characteristics of the cohort of immigrants are substituted into the Mincer wage function of native-born whites. The percentage gap between this imputed wage (W_{it}*) and the observed wage for the cohort of immigrants (W_{it}) is shown in Table 2.

It is clear that both groups of black immigrants fare worse than any other group of immigrants, including Asians and Hispanics. That is, the unexplained wage gaps are generally smaller for white, Asian, and Hispanic immigrants than for either group of black immigrants. These differences are especially pronounced when comparisons are made across groups who arrived before 1970.

It is striking that unexplained wage gaps are generally larger for West Indian black immigrants than for Asian and Hispanic immigrants, virtually all of whom speak English as a second language and come from cultures that have fewer English roots than the West Indies. The wage gaps fail to suggest that West Indians are a group of immigrants who come from an especially favorable culture or who have large stocks of unobserved human capital.

Rather, three alternative interpretations of the West Indians' wage profile suggest themselves. The first is that West Indians may be negatively self-selected; that is, the West Indians who immigrate to the United States are unskilled and have low earnings capacity. This would fit Borjas's theory of the market for immigrants, in that West Indians come from developing countries that tend to export workers from the low tail of the skill distribution. A possible problem with this interpretation is that it does not explain why West Indians' performance is as bad (or worse than) that of Asians and Hispanics, who we would expect to be negatively self-selected by the same reasoning.

A second possible interpretation is that West Indians come from a culture that gives them a disadvantage in the U.S. labor market. But our prior expectations, based on historical and institutional information, are that West Indians come from an advantageous cluture.

The third interpretation is that West Indian immigrants experience greater labor market discrimination than nonblack groups of immigrants. Consider first West Indian immigrants who arrived during the 1970s (that is, the 1970–1974 and 1975–1980 cohorts in Table 2). These recently arrived West Indians have wage gaps that are similar to those of recently arrived Asians and Hispanics (about 45 to 48 percent). This is surprising because the West Indians presumably have an English-language advantage over the Asians and Hispanics. It seems plausible that discrimination based on the color of

West Indians eliminates West Indians' English-language advantage relative to Asians and Hispanics. This is, the English-language advantage of West Indians is offset by the effects of discrimination against them. Recently arrived *non*-West Indian blacks have larger wage gaps than West Indians because, in addition to experiencing racial discrimination, they lack English-language skills that West Indians possess.

Consider next the older cohorts of West Indian immigrants (the 1965–1969, 1960–1964, 1950–1959, and pre-1950 cohorts in Table 2). Older cohorts of West Indian immigrants no longer possess an English-language advantage compared with Asian and Hispanic immigrants. The Asians and Hispanics have acquired English and have "assimilated" to some degree, but the West Indians still face discrimination. Hence, the wage gaps for West Indians are larger than for either Asians or Hispanics. Older non-West Indian immigrants still have the largest wage gaps of all.

This third interpretation, which includes the effects of discrimination, admittedly minimizes the importance of cohort effects. But currently available data are inadequate to allow estimation of cohort effects for black immigrants.[18] It would be unwise to be unprepared to revise one's views in light of future evidence, but it seems both plausible and consistent to include discriminatory effects in the interpretation of Table 2's immigrant wage gaps.

Characteristics of the Controversy

When I was a graduate student (and still idealistic), I attempted to classify economic controversies into five groups: empirical, logical, interest, ideological, and methodological (Woodbury 1979). Empirical controversy arises out of disagreement over "what is," or over how action x will influence outcome y. Presumably, an empirical controversy could be resolved through progress in economic measurement and modelling—that is, through the progress of economics as a normal science.[19]

Logical controversy occurs when the arguments of one or both parties to a debate fail to adhere to the rules of logic, or when ideas are incompletely formed or poorly expressed. Joan Robinson (1973) once argued that logical controversy is inexcusable and should not occur, although her notion presupposes that there is agreement about the rules of logic and what constitutes complete and clear argument.

Interest controversy arises when the material interests of two parties are at odds. Ideological controversy occurs when systems of ideas that express different social and moral philosophies—or different ideas about what social relations should exist—are at odds. These two may be related, but I would maintain a distinction between them.

Methodological controversy, which may be that most difficult form of controversy, can be defined in several ways. It can be seen as growing out of different answers being given to the same question without regard to empirical findings, out of different questions being directed toward the same set of social issues, or out of conflicting ideas about what is the proper way to go about doing social science.

Classification schemes are inevitably flawed, and this one is no exception. In particular, it has the drawback (among others) that we could spend more time arguing about what kind of controversy we have on our hands than on trying to understand the issues.

It is safe to say that the controversy over interpreting the unexplained wage gap has elements of all five types of controversy. Arguments over whether the unexplained wage gap over- or underestimates the true degree of discrimination smack of empirical controversy. Labor economists who have adhered mainly to the discriminatory interpretation of the unexplained wage gap readily admit that omitted variables could bias upward the estimate of discrimination that the unexplained wage gap yields. For example, Ashenfelter and Oaxaca (1987, 323–324) note that "no economist can make the appropriate guarantee that there is no specification error [in a wage equation]. . . . [A]n economist will be more or less convinced by the findings of a particular nonexperimental study according to how well it is done!" And now starts the debate over what makes a well-done nonexperimental study. This battle, which could be viewed as a part of normal science, has barely been joined.

There are surely examples in this controversy of incomplete logic and argument that could be clearer. Chiswick's (1984) implied criticism of Sowell's fuzziness in defining "culture" points to one possible example. The reluctance of those who adhere to the Blinder-Oaxaca interpretation to spell out the extent to which omitted variables are in fact a problem could be viewed as another. So the controversy may have a logical element.

Material interest also could be at stake in the debate over interpreting the unexplained wage gap. Arguments that discrimination has had no adverse impact on wages tend to justify longstanding social relations. Admitting adverse wage impacts could open the door to changed social relations—to changed job rights and possibly to changed opportunities for hiring and promotion.[20]

Although it seems unlikely that the economists involved in this controversy have a direct material stake in its outcome, they could be representative of parties who do. Sowell's strong antipathy to affirmative action, which he argues is inevitably a preferential policy that leads to racial quotas, is clearly interwoven with his equally strong belief that groups that have been discriminated against can and should succeed without such preferential policies: "The central presumption behind 'affirmative action' quotas ... is that systematic patterns ('representatin') show either intentional actions ('discrimination') or, at the very least, the consequences of behavior by 'society' at large—rather than actions for which the group in question may be in any way or to any degree responsible, or patterns arising from demographic or cultural causes, or statistical artifacts" (Sowell 1980, 256).[21]

But Sowell's and other economists' involvement in the debate over culture has a tone that suggests the importance not of material interest but rather of ideology and methodology. I suspect that many—Marxists especially—would view the controversy over interpreting the unexplained wage gap as mainly ideological. Such a view also has much to support it. A controversy is ideological to the extent that it involves a clash of systems of ideas that express different views of what social relations should exist. How could a controversy over whether discrimination has measurably adverse effects on wages lack a whiff of ideology? Few aspects of social relations are more basic than hierarchy, and discrimination is a reflection of implicit or explicit social hierarchy.

But I would venture the opinion that the controversy over interpreting the unexplained wage gap—which is largely a controversy among economists—has at lease as strong an element of methodological controversy. Here is a situation where two groups of highly regarded economists—both mainstream!—look at the same or similar evidence and come to dramatically different conclusions. One group wants to ask questions about (and measure) the degree to which racial and ethnic minorities have suffered discrimination, the other wants to ask questions about why some minorities that have suffered discrimination have succeeded nonetheless. Where one group sees the impact of discrimination, the other sees the influence of culture and unobserved human capital. It would be hard to concoct a better example of methodological controversy.[22]

The Colligation Problem

Like other controversies in economics, the interpretation of unexplained wage gaps involves a "colligation problem." As economic historian Jonathan Hughes (1970) has defined it, a colligation problem is a problem of sorting out which factors in an analysis are to be treated as exogenous and which as endogenous. In short, it is the problem of deciding where it is reasonable to "cut into" a set of "causally connected prior events and still produce a believable. . . . analysis" (Hughes 1970, 30).

The analysis of discrimination poses a classic colligation problem. Do we treat variables such as schooling and experience as predetermined and exogenous, implying that all workers face the same opportunities and incentives to gain schooling and experience? In other words, do we ignore premarket discrimination, which impedes workers from gaining the measurable traits that human capital theory suggests will enhance wages? Or do we treat these variables as part of the problem, and analyze premarket as well as direct labor market discrimination? Moreover, if we choose to focus only on direct market discrimination, how do we decide where premarket discrimination ends and direct market discrimination begins? For example, do we treat a worker's occupation as an exogenous premarket variable, or as variable that is the outcome of a direct market process in which discrimination may intervene?[23]

It would be convenient if the existence of a colligation problem told us what kind of controversy we might be dealing with. But the colligation problem can be an underlying factor in any of the five kinds of controversy outlined above.

Implicit in the specification of the Mincer wage function is a resolution (at one level) of the colligation problem that faces anyone who wants to treat discrimination in an empirical context. The resolution is also implicit in the use of the Blinder-Oaxaca decomposition, which takes specified individual characteristics as given and does not purport to offer an analysis of how or why an individual acquired those characteristics before arriving in the labor market. The decision to focus on direct market discrimination, and choices about which factors to treat as premarket, imply a view of what factors are beyond the reach of analysis—and perhaps of policy as well.[24] Few would argue that these decisions are made in a way that is free of prior belief, subjective judgment, or factors that are beyond the control of a researcher. In short, these are decisions that are bound to lead to one or another kind of controversy.

Culture, the Colligation Problem, and Human Capital Theory

The rise of culture as an explanator of wages in the human capital framework implies a different level of resolution of the colligation problem. Whereas before, the argument was basically about whether to treat one or another measurable characteristic as exogenous or endogenous, here the argument is about whether to consider culture, which cannot be observed, as the exclusive explanator of unexplained wage gaps.

The cultural interpretation is not an inherent part of the traditional human capital approach, which embodies two notions: that wage gaps arise mainly (but not necessarily exclusively) because of productivity gaps, and that there are systematic relationships between observed characteristics like schooling (among others) and productivity.

In its extreme form, the argument underlying the cultural interpretation is that, in fact, all wage gaps are the result of productivity gaps. Any wage gap that cannot be attributed to measurable correlates of productivity should be attributed to unobserved human capital or culture. Damage to wages from discrimination is ruled out by assumption. If a culturalist observes a wage gap that cannot be attributed to an observable factor that is believed to be related to productivity, then that unexplained wage gap is attributed to culture and other forms of unobserved human capital.

This leads to a basic objection to the cultural interpretation of wage gaps: it eliminates adverse wage impacts of discrimination by assumption rather than through empirical, historical, or institutional analysis. In other words, grafting culture onto the human capital model empties human capital theory of empirical content, and closes it to criticism or refutation. Culture is not something that can be observed, and no one has argued that the relationship between culture and wages could be measured. Far from strengthening the human capital approach, the use of culture to explain any otherwise unexplained wage gap undermines and makes a mockery of it.[25]

A somewhat different objection to admitting culture to the human capital framework is that doing so throws the framework into chaos by stressing the importance of an unobserved variable. If culture is systematically related to productivity and wages, but we cannot measure it or include it in the wage function, how do we interpret our estimated returns to schooling and experience? They are now contaminated by omitted variable bias.[26]

It is clear that some differences among workers are difficult or even impossible to measure. But as long as these differences are random, they pose no particular difficulty for estimating the wage function or rates of return to schooling and experience. The proper response to omitted variables is not to give them a collective name, like culture, especially when we believe there may be systematic relationships involved. Rather, a serious response in an empirical context is to improve measurement or methods of estimation.

Both of these objections suggest that culture as an explanator of wages can be viewed as an unnecessary and even deleterious appendage to human capital theory, rather than part of the basic approach. Two additional bits of evidence also support this view. The first is the presence of Gary Becker as a key figure in the development of both the theory of human capital (Becker 1975) and the economic theory of discrimination (Becker 1971), and the observation that the two theories are by no means incompatible. Why, then, have some empiricists felt it necessary to find ways to assume away discrimination? A second additional bit of evidence is at the empirical level. Implementation of human capital theory has focused on estimating rates of return to schooling and labor market experience, but the approach has been pragmatic, and limitations of data frequently admitted. Mincer's statement is indicative: "The positive relation between an individual's schooling and his subsequent earnings . . . is by no means direct or simple. . . . [S]chool is neither the only nor necessarily the most important training ground for shaping labor market productivities" (Mincer 1974, 1). Such statements hardly preclude the existence of labor market impacts of discrimination. The problem may be that such statements also leave the door open to such empirically empty concoctions as culture as the exclusive explanator of otherwise unexplained wage gaps.

Theory and Evidence or Theory Versus Evidence?

How do we weigh the two competing claims that have occupied this essay: on one hand, that unexplained wage gaps measure discrimination; on the other, that they measure unobserved differences in culture or human capital between groups of workers—differences that "should" (in some sense) give rise to wage gaps?

I have attempted two critiques of the cultural interpretation of unexplained wage gaps. The first is empirical and relies on evidence about the wages of two groups of black workers in the U.S. labor market: native-born American blacks of British West Indian ancestry and West Indian immigrants (see the first two sections). The second critique is methodological in that it appeals to ideas from the logic of verification (see the previous section).

Can evidence on native-born workers of West Indian ancestry and on West Indian immigrants narrow the scope for disagreement over the importance of discrimination? The evidence summarized in Table 1 shows that native-born blacks of West Indian ancestry have higher wages than do other native-born blacks mainly because they possess more of the observable characteristics that are generally believed to enhance productivity. Table 1 also shows that a relatively small part of the wage gap between West Indian blacks and whites can be explained by West Indians' lack of those observable characteristics. I interpret these findings together as suggesting that blacks—West Indians and others alike—experience adverse wage effects of racial discrimination. But an adherent of the cultural interpretation of unexplained wage gaps could always object that both West Indian and other native-born blacks suffer from an adverse culture or lack of human capital that cannot be observed.

What about the evidence on West Indian immigrants? Again, I believe that a consistent and plausible interpretation of the unexplained wage gaps in Table 2 is that black immigrants experience wage discrimination as a result of their color. But Table 2's results are open to multiple interpretation, and other researchers could reasonably (or unreasonably) disagree with the interpretation that I find most plausible.

Controversies like this one cannot be resolved by empirical evidence that has more than one possible interpretation. As long as evidence is equivocal, different observers with different priors will be able to interpret the same finding as favorable (or at least not unfavorable) to their view. The quality of evidence, like beauty, is in the eye of the beholder, and occasionally the quality of evidence is judged by its correspondence with what one already believes.

The criticism of the cultural interpretation in the previous section (which I have called methodological) is perhaps more direct. Put simply, the idea that culture is an important determinant of wages poses two serious problems for human capital theory. First, adding culture—which is clearly unobservable—to the human capital framework empties the theory of empirical content, makes it virtually irrefutable and throws into question whether it should be taken seriously as a scientific framework for research. Second, to suggest that a truly important variable has been omitted from the wage function throws the interpretation of the coefficients of the wage function into serious doubt. Both of these problems suggest that mainstream labor economists should be loathe to admit the notion of culture to the human capital framework. It is ironic that economists who have both adhered to and been innovators within the human capital framework have also unwittingly developed an interpretation of wage gaps that undermines that framework.

The idea that discrimination has had adverse impacts on wages needs to be taken seriously, as does the idea that empirical work on wages and wage gaps must improve to account for more of the correlates of productivity and wages. The solution is not to declare that unobserved wage gaps are the result entirely of either culture or discrimination. Rather, one solution—

perhaps the only productive approach—is to develop improved data and empirical methods, and to specify carefully the relationships between wages and the variables that are believed to enhance productivity.

This prescription—to develop improved data, empirical methods, and theory—admittedly views the culture controversy as mainly empirical. It implies that the controversy can be resolved through theoretical and empirical progress—in short, through the progess of normal science. There are at least two problems with this view. First, it may seem rather trite—how many studies conclude with the admonition that better data and methods must be developed? Second, and more to the point, viewing this controversy as empirical may be overly optimistic, naive, or simply wrong. I argued in the previous section that the controversy has logical, interest, ideological, and methodological aspects, which suggests that it may be impervious to more or improved evidence. So how can I hope for progress through improved theory, data, and empirical methods?

Perhaps one should not. The problem, of course, is that the growth of knowledge and the resolution of controversies have defied understanding.[27] Accordingly, it is difficult and perhaps pointless to prescribe a path for the resolution of a controversy.

This handwringing notwithstanding, I would not mind going on record as a believer in the value of further empirical work, even if it betrays me as a naive optimist. The logical, interest, ideological, and methodological aspects of controversy have no resolution, and there must be better ways to occupy our time than in the sort of circular, unending, ultimately unproductive arguments that mark these aspects of controversy. "Normal science," which in economics has come to mean the specification and estimation of models of behavior, is as good an occupation as any, and one can always hope.

Notes

For encouragement to take on this topic (as well as for comments on related work) I thank the editor, William Darity, Jr. I am also grateful to my colleagues at Michigan State and the Upjohn Institute for discussions of the issues treated here, and to Susan Pozo, David Shapiro, Hal Sider, and James Stewart.

1. The link between acknowledging the existence of discrimination and the formulation of policy is weak and difficult to characterize. For example, Thomas Sowell clearly recognizes the existence of discrimination, but strongly disapproves of affirmative action as a remedy. See also the treatment of alternative policies by Masters (1975, ch. 6).

2. Both have come to be a useful and durable devices in the analysis of discrimination, and their use has not been restricted to the pages of economics journals. As Bloom and Killingsworth (1982) show, they have been used extensively in litigation.

3. Mincer develops his function with reference to *annual earnings*, not hourly wage rates. For convenience, I will refer to "wages," "wage gaps," and "wage functions" throughout this chapter, with the understanding that the data involved generally refer to annual earnings.

4. These figures come from Woodbury and Bettinger (1991), in which we analyze data from the 1980 Census of Population. Throughout, the means reported are geometric means, and wage gaps are measured as the difference of the logarithmic means of wages between two groups of workers (mean of natural logarithm of group 1's wages minus mean of natural logarithm of group 2's wages). None of the conclusions drawn depends on the use of geometric (as opposed to arithmetic) means, or on the use of logarithmic differences to calculate wage gaps.

5. Again, this is the mean of the natural logarithm of white wages minus the mean of the natural logarithm of black wages: $ln(\$14{,}988) - ln(\$9{,}605) = 9.615 - 9.170 = 0.445$, or about 45 percent. Note that this approximately equals the percentage differential based on the average of white and black wages: $(\$14{,}988 - \$9{,}604)/(\$14{,}988 + \$9{,}604/2) = \$5{,}384/\$12{,}296 = 0.438$.

6. The adjusted wage gap is calculated as $ln(\$14{,}988) - ln(\$11{,}626) = 9.615 - 9.361 = 0.254$, or about 25 percent. Alternatively, $(\$14{,}988 - \$11{,}626)/[(\$14{,}988 + \$11{,}626)/2] = \$3{,}362/\$13{,}307 = 0.253$.

7. Cain (1986) gives an excellent selective review of the empirical studies.

8. Similarly, Oaxaca (1973, 704) writes, "The effects of discrimination are approximated by the residual left after subtracting the effects of differences in individual characteristics from the overall wage differential."

9. This would be an incorrect supposition if white workers benefit from positive discrimination; see Darity (1989, 366).

10. See also Ashenfelter and Oaxaca (1987) on the correspondence between Becker's theory of discrimination and the unexplained wage gap.

11. Chiswick's analysis is especially clever because it infers (apparently successfully) whether a worker is a Jew in a sample in which religion was not directly reported. The problem is that the Census Bureau does not ask questions about religion in its surveys, so some indirect way of inferring whether a worker is a Jew must be found. Chiswick notes that in the 1970 Census, individuals were asked whether a language other than (or in addition to) English was spoken in the home where they grew up. Those who responded that Yiddish, Hebrew, or Ladino was spoken at home are presumed to be Jewish. But this procedure can only identify whether someone is a Jew if he is the offspring of immigrants or is himself an immigrant. So Chiswick restricts the sample he analyzes to workers who are native-born but had one or both parents born abroad (that is, to second-generation workers). This restriction yields groups of Jews and non-Jews who should be reasonably comparable, except for religion. Chiswick estimates that his method of identifying whether a worker is a Jew properly identifies as Jewish about 60 percent of all second-generation Jews. It is possible that the findings would be different if data on the religion of all workers (rather than only second-generation workers) were available, so that wages of all Jews and non-Jews could be compared.

12. As the critique by Darity (1982) makes clear, the use of culture does not require the use of the notion of an unexplained wage gap. Moreover, the notion of culture predates the work of Sowell that I have relied on, and clearly predates the work of Chiswick. I have focused on the unexplained wage gap in the present discussion of culture both as a reflection of recent developments in the literature and to fix ideas.

13. Steinberg (1989, 267), in his excoriating attack on the cultural approach, has challenged the use of research on discrimination that uses data on immigrants as "more spurious scholarship extolling cultural virtue." In contrast, the approach taken here is that such research need not conclude that culture is important and discrimination unimportant.

14. It might be objected that the term "assimilation" implies that immigrants lose their cultural identity and adopt the characteristics of American culture in becoming integrated into the labor market. That connotation is not necessarily implied in this context, and Borjas often uses the term "aging" instead of assimilation to denote the effect of years in the United States on immigrants' earnings.

15. See McManus (1985), Kossoudji (1989), and Bloom and Grenier (1991) for treatments of the relationship between English-language proficiency and the wages of immigrants.

16. There may also be differences in the degree to which different cohorts and ethnic groups of immigrants experience discrimination. As discussed below, Borjas dismisses these possibilities.

17. These ideas were originally developed in Borjas (1987; 1991). For a clear and accessible discussion, see Borjas (1990, ch. 1 and 7).

18. Results presented by Borjas (1985) suggest a secular decline in the capacity of immigrants to perform well in the labor market. (Borjas refers to this as a decline in immigrant "quality.") But the profile of wage gaps for English-only white immigrants presented in Table 2 (row 2) suggests just the opposite—that successive cohorts of immigrants have been increasingly capable of doing well in the labor market. For similar findings and interpretation, see Woodbury (1991).

19. The idea of "normal science" comes from Thomas Kuhn (1970), and has been both developed and criticized by Lakatos (1973). For a lucid discussion of the ideas of Kuhn and Lakatos in the context of economics, see Caldwell (1982). The view of economics as a traditional science should not be accepted uncritically. See, for example, David Colander's (1991) recent critique.

20. It is worth reiterating, however, that the linkage between the acknowledgment that discrimination exists and policy is indirect (see note 2 above).

21. Sowell is an advocate of equal opportunity as opposed to affirmative action, which he views as a policy of preferential treatment. See, for example, his *Civil Rights: Rhetoric or Reality*? (Sowell 1984).

22. In one sense, this debate is *not* an especially good example of methodological controversy. The analytical tools used by both parties to this dispute are virtually the same. They agree on the types of data that are (or would be) useful, and they agree that Mincer's human capital wage function is an elegant (and surely the best available) framework in which to analyze workers' earnings. Often, methodological controversy is characterized by disagreement over what is the best way to go about "doing" social science—as in the case I looked at some years ago (Woodbury 1979)—but that does not seem to be the case here.

23. See Cain (1986; 1991) for lucid discussions of the problems of treating experience and occupation as exogenous, particularly in the context of estimating discrimination by gender. Variables that are usually treated as predetermined include quantity and quality of schooling, learning resources available to children at home, and various factors in the socialization of an individual. There has been little discussion in the economic literature of whether these variables should be treated as endogenous or exogenous.

24. There have been efforts to enrich the Blinder-Oaxaca approach to endogenize factors that are treated as exogenous in the standard approach; see, for example, Brown, Moon, and Zoloth (1980), and Robinson and Wunnava (1989).

25. A further implication is that attributing any unexplained wage gap to culture turns human capital theory and the estimation of wage gaps into a rather pointless exercise. If we already believe that wage gaps are wholly the result of differences in human capital and cannot be discriminatory, then why decompose the gross gap into explained and unexplained components?

26. The conviction expressed by Becker (1975), that estimated rates of return to schooling reflect true social rates of return, also suggests the view that unobserved correlates of productivity are random and pose no problem for estimation.

27. See the excellent and comprehensive discussion of methodology and the growth of knowledge in Caldwell (1982).

References

Ashenfelter, O., and Oaxaca, R. 1987. "The Economics of Discrimination: Economists Enter the Courtroom." *American Economic Review* 77 (May): 321–325.

Becker, G.S. 1971. *The Economics of Discrimination*, 2nd ed. Chicago: University of Chicago Press.

———. 1975. *Human Capital*, 2nd ed. Chicago: University of Chicago Press.

Blinder, A.S. 1973. "Wage Discrimination: Reduced Form and Structural Estimates." *Journal of Human Resources* 8 (Fall): 436–453.

Bloom, D.E., and Grenier, G. 1991. "The Earnings of Linguistic Minorities: French in Canada and Spanish in the United States." National Bureau of Economic Research Working Paper No. 3660.

Bloom, D.E., and Killingsworth, M.R. 1982. "Pay Discrimination Research and Litigation: The Use of Regression." *Industrial Relations* 21 (Fall): 318–339.

Borjas, G.J. 1985. "Assimilation, Changes in Cohort Quality, and the Earnings of Immigrants." *Journal of Labor Economics* 3 (October): 463–489.

———. 1987. "Self-Selection and the Earnings of Immigrants." *American Economic Review* 77 (September): 531–553.

———. 1988. *International Differences in the Labor Market Performance of Immigrants*. Kalamazoo, MI: W.E. Upjohn Institute for Employment Research.

———. 1990. *Friends or Strangers: The Impact of Immigration on the U.S. Economy*. New York: Basic Books.

———. 1991. "Immigration and Self-Selection." In *Immigration, Trade, and the Labor Market*, J.M. Abowd and R.B. Freeman, eds., 29–76. Chicago: University of Chicago Press.

Brown, R.S., Moon, M., and Zoloth, B.S. 1980. "Incorporating Occupational Attainment in Studies of Male Female Earnings Differentials." *Journal of Human Resources* 15 (Winter): 3–28.

Cain, G.C. 1986. "The Economic Analysis of Labor Market Discrimination: A Survey." In *Handbook of Labor Economics*, Vol. I, O. Ashenfelter and R. Layard, eds., 693–785. Amsterdam: North-Holland.

———. 1991. "The Uses and Limits of Statistical Analysis in Measuring Economic Discrimination." In *The Economics Discrimination*, Hoffman E., ed., 115–144. Kalamazoo, MI: W.E. Upjohn Institute.

Caldwell, B.J. 1982. *Beyond Positivism: Economic Methodology in the Twentieth Century*. London: George Allen and Unwin.

Chiswick, B.R. 1978. "The Effects of Americanization on the Earnings of Foreign-Born Men." *Journal of Political Economy* 86 (October): 897–921.

———. 1983a. "An Analysis of the Earnings and Employment of Asian-American Men." *Journal of Labor Economics* 1 (April): 197–214.

———. 1983b. "The Earnings and Human Capital of American Jews." *Journal of Human Resources* 18 (Summer): 313–336.

———. 1984. "Review of *The Economics and Politics of Race*, by Thomas Sowell." *Journal of Economic Literature* 22 (September): 1158–1160.

Colander, D. 1991. *Why Arent't Economists As Important As Garbagement?* Armonk, NY: M.E. Sharpe.

Darity, W.A., Jr. 1982. "The Human Capital Approach to Black-White Earnings Inequality: Some Unsettled Questions." *Journal of Human Resources* 17 (Winter): 72–93.

———. 1989. "What's Left of the Economic Theory of Discrimination?" In *The Question of Discrimination*, S. Shulman and W.A. Darity, Jr., eds. Middletown, CT: Wesleyan University Press.

Hughes, J. 1970. *Industrialism and Economic History*. New York: McGraw-Hill.

Kossoudji, S.A. 1989. "Immigrant Worker Assimilation: Is It a Labor Market Phenomenon?" *Journal of Human Resources* 24 (Summer): 494–527.

Kuhn, T. 1970. *The Structure of Scientific Revolutions*, 2nd ed. Chicago: University of Chicago Press.

Lakatos, I. 1973. "Falsification and the Methodology of Scientific Research Programs." In *Criticism and the Growth of Knowledge*, I. Lakatos and A. Musgrave, eds., 91–196. Cambridge: Cambridge University Press.

Masters, S.H. 1975. *Black-White Income Differentials: Empirical Studies and Policy Implications*. New York: Academic Press.

McManus, W.S. 1985. "Labor Market Assimilation of Immigrants: The Importance of Language Skills." *Contemporary Policy Issues* 3 (Spring) 77–89.

Mincer, J. 1974. *Schooling, Experience, and Earnings*. New York: Columbia University Press and NBER.

Oaxaca, R. 1973. "Male-Female Wage Differentials in Urban Labor Markets." *International Economic Review* 14 (October): 693–709.

Robinson, J. 1973. *Economic Heresies*. New York: Basic Books.

Robinson, M.D., and Wunnava, P.V. 1989. "Measuring Direct Discrimination in Labor Markets Using a Frontier Approach: Evidence from CPS Female Earnings Data." *Southern Economic Journal* 56 (July): 212–218.

Sowell, T. ed., with the assistance of Collins, L.D. 1978. *Essays and Data on American Ethnic Groups*. Washington, DC: Urban Institute.

Sowell, T. 1980. *Knowledge and Decisions*. New York: Basic Books.

———. 1981 *Ethnic America*. New York: Basic Books.

———. 1983. *The Economics and Politics of Race: An International Perspective*. New York: William Morrow.

———. 1984. *Civil Rights: Rhetoric or Reality?* New York: William Morrow.

Steinberg, S. 1989. *The Ethnic Myth: Race, Ethnicity, and Class in America*, expanded ed. Boston: Beacon Press.

Woodbury, S.A. 1979. "Methodological Controversy in Labor Economics." *Journal of Economic Issues* 13 (December): 933–955.

———. 1991. "Earnings of Black Immigrants: Implications for Racial Discrimination." In *New Approaches to Economic and Social Analyses of Discrimination*, R. Cornwall and P. Wunnava, eds., 295–330. New York: Praeger.

Woodbury, S.A., and Bettinger, D.R. 1991. "Culture, Human Capital, and the Earnings of West Indian Blacks." Manuscript, Michigan State University (Department of Economics) and W.E. Upjohn Institute for Employment Research.

9 LABOR ECONOMICS AND PUBLIC POLICY: DOMINANCE OF CONSTRAINTS OR PREFERENCES?

E. Michael Foster

This chapter considers the way in which economists—specifically labor economists—treat preferences and how it influences their understanding of poverty and the poor. This discussion contends that the idea that the poor are different—that is , have deficient preferences—has influenced American antipoverty policy and has been an essential part of the academic literature on poverty. *It maintains that this notion—indeed, a strong version of this notion—is implicit in modern analyses of labor supply.*

The first section documents the importance of preferences in the poverty literature. Particular attention is paid to the culture of poverty and underclass literatures. The second section examines revealed preference methodology, while the third considers this practice in the context of othodox analyses of labor supply and of racial differences in wages and employment. This section concludes that the explanation for the former in labor economics involves many of the same themes one finds in the poverty literature. A proposed solution involves incorporating preferences directly, and the final section examines attempts to do so.

Preferences and the Poverty Literature

What does it mean to be chronically poor? Unlike most things that microeconomists study, poverty status is not a choice variable: individuals do not chose to be poor or nonpoor. Rather, families are counted as poor depending on whether their income (given family size) is sufficient to purchase a minimally nutritous diet. Family income and composition reflect past and present choices about fertility, family structure, labor supply, and education. To be chronically poor, therefore, means to make "bad" choices consistently (e.g., turning down jobs at the "appropriate" wage) or to be unable to overcome a bad choice in the past (i.e., leaving school).

Modern microeconomic models individual choice as reflecting constraints and preferences. One can model chronic poverty as reflecting the persistence of certain constraints or preferences: individuals remain poor because their options remain limited or their decision-making poor.[1] One can sort poverty theories according to their emphasis on one explanation or the other:

> A number of different views have been advanced about the causes of poverty and the appropriate solutions. One view holds that poverty is a result of people having inadequate job skills and few opportunities to use the skills they do possess, and that the solution lies in increasing job skills through training programs, or in increasing job opportunities through a vigorous, expanding economy. Another holds that poverty results from certain attitudes, or an entire set of values and beliefs held by poor people—that there is a "culture of poverty" (Duncan, 1984, 33).

Constraint arguments often go further than citing a lack of opportunity for the poor. Quite frequently, these arguments see poverty as serving a purpose in the capitalist system: the existence of poverty, for example, makes sure that "dirty" (dangerous, temporary, and/or menial) work is done. By providing an alternative source of workers, it may also give employers leverage over their employees. In short, the success of the successful is tied to the failure of others.

Constraint-oriented analyses often involve a shift in focus away from the individual toward classes (or groups based on race or place of residence) and the relations between them. These arguments focus, for example, not so much on which blacks succeed but why minorities fail at such high rates. As Wright (1979) notes,

> To say that classes constitute "positions" implies . . . that there are "empty places" in the social structure which are filled by individuals. The analysis must be understood as the analysis primarily of such empty places, and only secondarily of the actual individuals who fill the slot [pp. 20–21].

Implicit in this perspective is the assumption that either preferences are distributed randomly or their importance is secondary. They have little effect on the process by which individuals find their place in the social structure. Implicit is the assumption that were the nonpoor faced with the options of the poor, they would make similar choices.

The alternative perspective is that the poor have different (i.e., deficient) attitudes or preferences.[2] This premise has obvious policy implications and is the focus of this discussion. If the poor have deficient attitudes, then merely changing constraints will not reduce poverty. If the poor have little regard for the future, for example, then better financial aid will not increase college attendance. The notion that the poor have deficient attitudes has had an important place in American culture and in the academic poverty literature.

Poverty in American Culture

Americans have traditionally viewed economic success or failure as reflecting—and revealing—an individual's character. Citing a variety of studies, Wilson (1988) demonstrates that Americans place far mor emphasis on individual characteristics (like "lack of thrift or proper money management", "lack of effort", "lack of ability or talent") than on structural explanations (like "failure of industry to provide jobs").[3] Furnham and Lewis (1986) summarize research showing that this emphasis is much stronger than in other industrialized countries.

The notion that the poor are different—that is, have different attitudes—has shaped American social policy. In periods where the poor are seen as strapped by constraints, the generosity of poverty programs increases. The programs of the Great Depression, for example, focused on the disabled, the orphaned, the widowed, and the abandoned. Poverty, in other words, was seen as reflecting one's constraints (e.g., bad luck). Similarly, the (structural) poverty of Appalachia is cited as having strongly shaped the origins of the Great Society.[4] In periods where the poor are perceived as deviant (e.g., as preferring to "cheat" the system rathar than work), welfare policy is reshaped and restricted. To some extent this was true during the Nixon administration, and the notion that the poor are different can be seen in current discussions of welfare reform and dependency.

The idea that the poor have different attitudes has had a strong influence on academic discussions of the poor since poverty was "rediscovered" in the 1960s. Most prominent was the culture of poverty debate in the 1960s, but more recently, the underclass literature contains many of the same themes. The next section briefly considers the former, while the following addresses the underclass literature in detail.

The Culture of Poverty

The most prominent—and explicit—source of the idea that the poor have different values and attitudes can be found in the culture of poverty literature of the 1960s: of particular prominence are *Five Families: Mexican Case Studies* and *La Vida: A Puerto Rican Family* by Oscar Lewis (1959; 1966a) and *The Other America* by Michael Harrington (1962).[5] Here we see the key feature of the culture of poverty: "the culture of poverty is not a phrase that refers to the absence of economic or social goods [i.e., to constraints]; it is not just a matter of economic deprivation" (Sarbin 1970, 31). While the culture of poverty literature is rather diverse (and, at times, ill focused), one can still distill three distinguishing features: "concentrated deprivation and neighborhood characteristics closely linked to poverty and welfare; intergenerational transmission of poverty and welfare; attitudes and values different among the poor, especially in areas on concentrated poverty" (Ellwood 1989, 7). The culturally poor have a specific psychological profile:

> The poor tend to be fatalistic ... [and are] resigned to the degrading and unpleasant conditions in which they live. The culture of poverty is marked by a present-time orientation—a tendency to seek gratification in the present and not worry about the future. Long-range plans and goals are secondary to pleasurable pursuits in the present [Furnham and Lewis 1986, 77].

These attitudes are manifested in behaviors as well. Lewis, for example, placed great emphasis on family structure as a key element of the culture of poverty.[6] The behavior of one's neighbors is also important. The culture of poverty contained a strong sense of isolation: the poor are isolated from the values of the middles class. The culture of poverty implies that "the poor are separate and different, not only economically but also intellectually and emotionally. ... The poor fell cut off from the sources of power in society" (Furnham and Lewis 1986, 76, 77).

This perspective does recognize that the culture of poverty may have its origin in the structure of economic relations. Some writers emphasized this more than others. For example, Leibow (1967) noted,

> Many similarities between the lower-class Negro father and son (or mother and daughter) do not result from "cultural transmission" but from the fact that the

> son goes out and independently experiences the same failures, in the same areas, as his father. What appears as a dynamic, self-sustaining cultural process is, in part at least, a relatively simple piece of machinery which turns out, in rather mechanical fashion, independently produced look-a-likes [p. 233].[7]

In fact, Wilson (1988) distinguishes Leibow (1967), Clark (1965), Rainwater (1970a), and Hannerz (1970) as "liberal field studies," more careful in method than Harrington and Lewis. This distinction, however, is too strong. Both Harrington and Lewis recognized the structural origins of the culture of poverty. In the October 1966 issue of *Scientific American*, Lewis spelled out the structural context of his argument. He explained that the culture of poverty was endemic to the free-enterprise, prewelfare stage of capitalism. He argued that it was common in colonial societies but would be unlikely to develop in a communist society like Cuba. He notes that, by ending alienation, revolutions often destroy the culture of poverty without ending physical need. Harrington clarified his position 20 years later in *The New American Poverty*. In discussing the legacy of the culture of poverty debate, he writes,

> On the other hand, it is terribly wrong to claim, as the conservatives do, that poverty is the expression of a kind of lower-class human nature that cannot be affected by any public policy. . . . The question today is whether the people of the underclass—white, black, brown, and Asian—will be allowed the same opportunities as were given the Irish (and the Jews and the Italians and the other groups), or whether economic and social policies will lock them up in world that has certain tendencies toward crime and disintegrating families. That is a political and economic—not a spiritual—issue [1984, 206].

The works of Lewis, Leibow, and the other, however, share the understanding not only that the culture of poverty was structural in origins but also that—once the culture of poverty exists—changing constraints may leave poverty unaffected.[8] This persistence of preferences is particularly striking; in fact, this literature consistently portrays attitudes as passed across generation. The culture of poverty thesis assumes that (some) poor children are economically disfigured early in life. Oscar Lewis (1969), for example, wrote,

> By the time slum children are of age six or seven they usually have absorbed the basic values and attitudes of their subculture and are not psychologically geared to take full advantage of changing conditions or increased opportunities [i.e., changes in their constraints] which may occur in their lifetime [p. xlv][9]

One finds many of these themes in the current discussion of the underclass. The next section examines this concept and elaborates on the attitudes associates with culture of poverty and the underclass.

The Underclass

The idea that the poor have different attitudes and that these attitudes are transmitted across generations can be found in the current discussion of the "underclass" and of welfare reform.[10] This includes both academic discussions as well as those of the mass media. The latter are of interest because they reflect—and shape—the tenor of public policy debate. This section also considers academic attempts to define and measure the underclass. Many of these definitions include attitudes or preferences. In some cases, analysts try to avoid the controversy that surrounded the culture of poverty by focusing their attention on the poverty of areas or on the behaviors of the poor. The problems with such definitions are discussed below.

The underclass has been the subject of a lively discussion in the popular press. Consider articles from two rather disparate sources.[11] William Tucker's "Our Homestead Plan for the Poor" appeared in the July 1988 issue of the *American Spectator* (pp. 25–28). This discussion evokes the culture of poverty literature:

> The reasons for the collapse of black culture, then are fairly clear .... It is a well-established principle in biology that when monogamy breaks down, the sexual competition between males becomes far more violent. Because every male is no longer asssured a reasonable chance of finding a mate (the implicit social contract of monogamy), the battle for access to women becomes much more intense. Thus, black communities have essentially become a free-for-all where men compete murderously among themselves for the symbols of power (drugs, money, whatever), while women and children remain ensconced in single-parent homes, living off the government. Men become increasingly more attuned to violence, women increasingly more comfortable with welfare; and the chances that [were constraints changed] ordinary human institutions like marriage and the family can be reestablished become increasingly remote ... [Tucker cites the work of Leon Dash, a journalist who spent a year living in a housing project.] Instead, he [Dash] found a world where, for boys and girls alike, having a child became a "rite of passage." Young people simply cannot imagine a life beyond age 19 or so. They are grownups at 12, want children as quickly as possible (in order to prove their man- or womanhood), and place enormous peer pressure on any "good two shoes" who is not sexually active or pregnant by age 15. ... Black teenagers in these circumstances have absolutely no sense of the future. The boys expect to be strung out or dead by 25, the girls to be grandmothers by 35. The whole concept of adolescence as a *preparation* for life, rather than life itself, has been lost. If a 15-year-old does not have a baby with her current boyfriend *right now*, there will never be another chance for her. The idea of postponing any kind of gratification in order to facilitate some great future has become completely lost [pp. 27–28].

The underlying theme is that the accepted means of pursuing one's goals has changed for one group in society. This "culture" encourages self-destructive behavior and reinforces the disadvantaged position of its members in society. Prominent is a chronic disregard for the future.

The implications for poverty policy are clear. The socioeconomic system generally works well; minorities may have suffered historically, but changing poverty now requires the poor to change first. This is at the heart of the culturalist perspective.

A second example comprises a series of articles that appeared in *The New Republic* in 1986 and 1987. Mickey Kaus (July 1986) considers the underclass and its origins. He focuses on the social context of work and on the economic motivaitons of different groups in society. Kaus contends that for the chronically poor, work has become merely a source of money and that this attitude creates welfare dependency. He argues that welfare programs must not only give the poor money but also restore their perceptions of work. Because of their disregard for the future, the poor do not recognize the effect on human capital of holding even a low-paying job. Implicit is the belief that were the nonpoor to face the same opportunities they would work.

Kaus later (October 1986) elaborates that "I don't mean poor blacks are 'ultimately' to blame for their problems. I am talking not about cause or culpability but about *solutions*. Whatever the cause, whoever is to blame, the culture of poverty has taken on a life of its own so that today opening up job opportunities is not enough" (p. 22). This subtle (or dubious) distinction reflects the controversial past of the "culture of poverty" and Kaus's desire to distance himself from its legacy. Kaus does not want to talk about cause or culpability because the perception of "blaming the victim" is what originally banished the term from the realm of "acceptable" ideas.[12] As with the culture of poverty literature, the origins of "bad" attitudes may have structural origins, but their effect would persist even if these constraints were to change. Another familiar chord in Kaus's article is isolation: "Even if whites were a majority of the long-term poor, it would be hard for them to create a poverty 'culture' because poor whites have never been confined to segregated communities" (1986, 23).[13] Murray (in Ehrenreich et al., 1986) adds:

> What Kaus wants to do is bring members of that underclass back into participation in American Society. His diagnosis of what is required is acute and brave. But he is asking the government to behave like a concerned friend or relative or neighbor or church congregation, helping while at the same time holding people responsible for their behavior. Governments cannot do that. They try, and the harder they try the more totalitarian they become, but they never succeed [p. 22].

Again the author suggests that certain members of society are unlike the rest of us: they do not take responsibility for their actions.[14] Opportunities for economic success are available; the problem is that some members of society are ill prepared to take advantage of them.[15]

The notion that the poor are different can be found in recent academic analyses of the underclass as well. Recounting the origin of the term, Jencks (1989) states,

> It soon became clear, however, that those who talked about the underclass had something in mind other than just persistent poverty. The term underclass, with its echoes of the underworld, conjures up sin, or at least unorthodox behavior. Low income may be a necessary condition for membership in such a class, but it is not sufficient [p. 14].

This, however, means more than that the poor are discouraged. Rather, these attitudes are seen as persistent: even if constraints were to change, they would keep the poor in poverty:

> The term "underclass" has been increasingly used in the 1980's to describe a subset of the official poor whose situation seems mostly immune to aggregate economic conditions and compensatory social programs [Danziger 1989, 1].

In the more specific applications of this notion, these "bad" attitudes are also passed across generations.

Consider recent attempts to define the underclass. Most combine spatial, behavioral, and attitudinal dimensions (Ricketts and Sawhill 1988, 317). According to Nathan (1987),

> Underclass conditions are multifaceted. They are economic, behavioral and geographically focused. This is not to say that we can easily put our social science calipers to the task of measuring the underclass. The underclass involves more things that we can measure with conventional economic and demographic indicators—such as low income, long-term unemployment, limited education, and the incidence of welfare dependency. The underclass condition is also attitudinal and behavioral. It involves alienation, and for the long-term welfare subgroup . . . a feeling of "learned helplessness [p. 58].

The National Supported Work Demonstration, for example, based underclass status on three criteria: in particular, members of the underclass (1) have low income; (2) have engaged in some illegal behavior in the past year; and (3) exhibit "some type of asocial attitude toward work.[16]

This discussion has emphasized the prominent place of the attitudes of the poor in analyses of the culture of poverty and in American culture. The notion that the poor are different is also prominent in discussions of the underclass that one finds in the popular press and in some academic analyses. But can one discuss the underclass without addressing the attitudes of the poor? Some analysts have tried, but the results have been somewhat dissatisfying.[17]

Areal definitions, for example, have been employed in numerous analyses: for example, Ricketts and Sawhill (1988) and Jargowsky (1988). Danziger and Gottschalk (1987), for instance, define the underclass as residents of census tracts with poverty rates greater than 40 percent in the 100 largest SMSAs. Such definitions are an important part of social accounting but fail to recognize that proverty status reflects the effects of past and present choices—choices that are the product of constraints and preferences. Such definitions leave key questions unanswered: if, for example, one can detect areal patterns in education, fertility, and welfare reciept, do these patterns involve constraints or preferences; Is underclass a "contagion" of bad preferences, or is the similarity of choices of individuals in these areas the product of having equally poor alternatives?

Ricketts and Sawhill (1988) recognize that poverty status reflects key constrained choices and orient their definition to certain behaviors. They argue that

> . . . most observers agree that the underclass is characterized by behaviors which are at variance with those of mainstream America (such as joblessness, welfare dependency, unwed parenting, criminal or uncivil behavior, and dropping out of high school), . . . actions most likely to inhibit social mobility, to impose costs on the rest of society, or to influence children growing up in an environment where such behaviors are commonplace [p. 317–318].

They define an underclass area as a census tract that has a high proportion of high school dropouts, prime-age males not regularly attached to the labor force, welfare recipients, and households with children headed by women.[18] Once again, however, the reader is left to wonder about constraints and preferences. The authors, in fact, recognize this:

> [I]t is unclear whether these behaviors are an adaptation to external factors (such as a history of discriminatory treatment or a lack of job opportunities) or whether they reflect the development of self-defeating attitudes and lifestyles (which persist even when objective circumstances improve). Mostly likely, the behaviors of the underclass result from a complex interaction between the two. . . . In any case, the testing of hypotheses about the reasons for these dysfunctional behaviors must await better definition and measurement of the underclass phenomena itself. Thus, we can remain agnostic about the fundamental causes of these behaviors and still direct our efforts to the definitional and measurement issues [p. 318].

Unfortunately, their analysis is not only limited in scope but also—in light of American culture and the development of the poverty literature—has unfortunate consequences. In particular, their self-professed agnosticism fosters the notion that the poor are different by emphasizing behaviors (like crime and family structure) historically associated with deviance apart from its social and economic context.

In summary, attitudes are as important in the underclass literature as they were in the culture of poverty debate before it. It is difficult to discuss the poverty of poor families in poor areas without discussing the decisions they make, and it is equally difficult to do so without leaving the impression that the poor are different. This makes the ways in which social scientists treat attitudes especially important. The next section considers the way in which economists treat preferences—revealed preference methodology—particularly with regard to racial differences in wages and employment.

Revealed Preferences and Perfect Markets: The Economic Approach

How might one investigate the importance of preferences in shaping an individual's poverty status? One could study important decisions in the life course and incorporate both individual-level characteristics and a fuller sense of opportunities (e.g., how firms make hiring decisions). This would require comprehensive data with information both on economic and psychological characteristics of the individual as well as on relevant contextual factors. Difficult conceptual work is also necessary: what, for example, are the relevant aspects of an individual's personality that influence economic behavior? How can one characterize a neighborhood empirically and how do these measures enter a utility function? If data are collected along geographic boundaries, what is the areal equivalent to a market? These are difficult questions. Nonetheless, with adequate data (and with an adequate framework to shape their collection), one could weigh the relative importance of constraints and preferences in determining poverty.

In studying individual choice, however, neoclassical economics simplifies matters by making strong assumptions about how individuals make choices, about the setting in which these decisions are made, and about the preferences that shape them: the microeconomic model rests on "the combined assumptions of maximizing behavior, market equilibrium, and stable preferences, used relentless and unflinchingly, [assumptions which] form the heart of the economic approach" (Becker 1976, 5). What is the significance of these assumptions? The first avoids the problem of studying how people actually reach decisions. Economists generally assume that the outcome of interest is not influenced by the process of making decisions (outcome rationality). The second simplifies the task of representing the relevant constraint set. In particular, in a perfectly competitive environment, economic actors are price-takers, and specifying relevant opportunities merely involves knowing the relevant price. For the individual firm, worker, or consumer, quantity supplied, demanded, or consumed is presumed unconstrained at the going price. In the case of labor markets, the relevant price is the wage rate; individuals are assumed able to work any amount at this wage.

The third assumption allows economists to avoid collecting information on preferences directly. In particular, a revealed preference methodology is employed; controlling for constraints (a task made easier by the second assumption) repeated behavior is assumed to reveal *stable* preferences. As Varian (1987) explains:

> Observing the choices of consumers can allow us to "recover" or estimate the preferences that lie behind those choices. The more choices we observe, the more precisely we can estimate the underlying preferences that generated those choices [p. 130].

In empirical work, demographic variables are frequently incorporated to capture differences in preferences.[19]

Note that revealed preference theory fuses one's understanding of preferences with that of markets. Consider a simple example. A family that purchases a green refrigerator when a tan one is available (at the same price) can be seen as preferring green to tan. One need not ask them about their preferences directly. However, if one cannot determine the relevant constraints or misspecifies them, actual preferences remain hidden. If tan refrigerators are backlogged, one cannot say what the family's preferences for color are. The most we know is that they prefer a green refrigerator now to a tan one tomorrow.[20] It becomes very difficult to ascertain what the family would do constraints if were to change.[21] Inferring preferences from behavior is tricky business and is always dependent on the assumed constraints.

One's understanding of preferences, therefore, depends on how one understands and models the relevant constraints. This problem is striking in light of the emphasis one finds in discussions of poverty in both the policy arena and academe. The next section considers this problem in the context of empirical labor economics and its treatment of racial differences in employment and wages.

Labor Economics and the Black-White Wage Gap

Much attention has been focused on black-white gaps in education, employment, and wages (e.g., Smith and Welch 1989; Darity 1982; Freeman 1981; Malveaux 1984). Empirical research has documented that "there were (and continue to be) more low-income individuals than would be predicted from the number of persons with low levels of education" (Williams 1984, 33). Even controlling for education, minorities make up a disproportionate share of low-income families (Farley 1990). Numerous economists have focused on differences in the wage structure underlying these differences in income. [Cain (1986, 760) offers a summary.] In general, these studies suggest that blacks earn between 10 and 20 percent less than comparable white workers. Other studies reveal that blacks are more likely than similar whites to have employment difficulties (e.g., Foster 1990).

What might explain these differences? Basic models of labor supply assume that individuals are largely masters of their own fate. Here, poverty (or at least low wages and frequent unemployment) is dysfunctional, a product of bad choices. Labor markets are modelled as perfectly competitive: individuals allocate their time given the wage that firms are willing to pay them. The latter is a product of worker productivity alone. Firms inclined to pay black workers less are driven from the market by fair-minded, far-sighted, and ultimately more profitable entrepenuers. (Free entry is a condition of perfect competition). The wage rate an individual faces, therefore, is a product of past choices about education and labor supply. (The latter influences wages because experience builds human capital. One might also incorporate on-the-job training which (assuming complementarity of inputs) would be allocated on the basis of worker productivity.)

These assumptions imply that cross-racial differences in wages and employment capture unobserved differences between workers. As Beck, Horan, and Tolbert (1978) note,

> Like Adam Smith's 'invisible hand', the competitive structure presumed by neoclassical theory guarantees that differential placement in the socioeconomic order is accomplished in a manner such that this placement is a reflection of the worker's basic value to the system. From this perspective, inequality of earnings must be a reflection of the dispersion of individual resources; low prestige and poverty wages must be the result of resource insufficiency; sporadic employment and job instability must be the products of inadequate commitment to work or a weak achievement motivation. In short, socioeconomic success or failure is tied directly to the characteristics brought to the marketplace by the individual worker. [p. 704].

Minorities earn less because they produce less: they do not work as hard as whites, or have fewer skills than their education suggests. Differences in employment also reflect preferences. Black workers are unemployment more frequently because they "spend" more of their resources on leisure. Macroeconomists refer to this as "wait" unemployment. Recently economists have shifted their attention to "search" employment: "A worker who enters a state of search unemployment chooses in some sense self-employment in collecting information about job opportunities and wage differentials" (Frisch 1983, 60). In this light, the chronically unemployed are best characterized as deluded as to their true economic worth (i.e., their reservation wage is too high) rather than as simply lazy. The message, however, is the same. As Killingsworth (1983) writes in his survey of labor supply,

> All unemployment is, in effect, a form of leisure time. ... [T]he question of whether or not "unemployment" is "voluntary" is largely semantic; with rather little relevance for normative judgements or policy-making [p. 136, 63].

Note that labor economics creates images similar to those one finds in the poverty literature. They share a similar tone. In particular, both conjure a sense of illness and decay. In discussing the underclass, Crane (1989), for example, poses "an epidemic theory of ghettos," while James Montgomery (1990a) considers whether underclass behavior is "contagious." Characterizing economists' view of unemployment, Summers (1990) writes that "'Problem' unemployment" is largely confined to a few demographic groups that display *pathological* employment instability" (p. 3).

The similarity between labor economics and the underclass/culture of poverty literature is more than a matter of tone. The two focus on similar aspects of preferences. Controlling for education, workers who have a strong preference for leisure (i.e., a high reservation wage) will be more likely to find the wage for available jobs inadequate. As discussed above, this "asocial" attitude toward work is a prominent part of the underclass and workfare discussions:

> *Underclass* has become popular because it seems to grab people's attention. What grabs is the image of a growing horde of ... lazy people who do not carry their part of the economic load, all of them threatening nonpoor Americans and the stability of American society [Gans 1990, 19a].

A high reservation wage may also reflect a high rate of time preference: workers with little regard for the future will undervalue the human-capital-building aspects (i.e., experience) of even menial work.[22] As discussed above, the underclass and culture of poverty literatures repeatedly highlight the inability of the poor to defer gratification. Controlling for education, wage differentials between races will reflect unobserved differences in productivity. This also is a prominent theme in the underclass literature: in *The Underclass*, for example, Auletta (1986) emphasizes the poor work habits (e.g., tardiness) of the chronically poor.[23] Economists have begun to explore unobserved differences in productivity as an explanation for racial differences in wages, and in fact, Thomas Sowell (1978; 1984) and Barry Chiswick (1983a; 1983b) describe them as cultural.

The explanations labor economics offers as to why some individuals would be paid less or unemployed more frequently, therefore, strike a familiar chord. *What is most striking, however, is the presumed exogeneity of preferences*. As discussed above, most of the culturalist and underclass arguments recognize the endogeneity of preferences to some extent. Labor economics, however, stands as an extreme version of these argument.

The theoretical basis of models of labor supply, therefore, forces one to attribute racial differences in wages and employment to differences between individuals or to reject the framework itself. It establishes preferences and constraints as *competing* explanations. The first rest on the notion that the market is more accurate than social scientists in ascertaining the true economic worth of individuals: in wage equations and models of employment status, race is significant because other, productivity-related variables are omitted. The competing hypothesis rests on a different understanding of markets: minorities are discriminated against. Firms *are* able to treat blacks and whites differently. One common explanation for this is the absence of competition (see Cain 1986, 717*ff*). This is certainly a plausible explanation, but it strikes at the core of labor economics. If labor markets are not perfectly competitive, the standard emprical analyses of wages and labor supply need overhauling.

But is there a third way? Is there some way to avoid arguing that blacks and whites are separated by unobserved, exogenous differences in attitudes and productivity or that labor markets are imperfect? Efforts to explain racial differences in wages and employment while retaining the basic framework of labor economics have involved alterations in the environment in which firms compete. This involves consumer tastes and, more recently, uncertainty about worker productivity.

Becker (1957) explored the notion that consumer tastes might produce differences in wages. Primarily, he argued that consumers might be willing to pay a higher price for a product to avoid contact with minorities. This may seem like a simple extension, but in fact is much more significant. In particular, it call into question the basic assumptions economists make about economic—as opposed to social—exchange:

> Classical and neoclassical economics operates, in contrast of with an atomized, *undersocialized* conception of human action, continuing in the utilitarian tradition. The theoretical arguments disallow by hypothesis any impact of social structure and social relations on production, distribution, or consumption [Granovetter 1985, 483–484].

As Granovetter (1985) writes, this assumption is essential because "the elimination of social relations from economic analysis removes the problem of order from the intellectual agenda": in particular, competitive market structure

> . . . makes force or fraud unavailing. Competition determines the terms of trade in a way that individual traders cannot manipulate. If traders encounter complex or difficult relationships, characterized by mistrust or malfeasance,[24] they can simply move on to the legion of other traders willing to do business on market terms; social relations and their details thus become frictional matters [p. 484].

This assumption, in other words, assures us that the competitive market produces the efficient outcome and not merely the triumph of the powerful. Once one recognizes that consumers have preferences not only for a product but also as to whom they buy the product from, the entire structure is called into question. *In particular, if one incorporates this relationship, then why not others, namely firm-worker interaction?* Presumably, the difference is that consumer tastes are fixed in some sense. One, however, wonders why consumers would not recognize that the product they receive is essentially unchanged by the race of who provides it just as some entrepenuers recognize that productivity is not influenced by race.

Ultimately, however, market functioning again returns social interaction to a frictional (i.e., short run) role. Cain (1986, 710), among others, demonstrates that consumer taste for discrimination produce segregation, not discrimination.[25] Minorities experience neither reduced wages nor increased unemployment.

A second attempt to explain racial differences in wages by altering the environment in which firms compete—and not their nature as price takers—involves models of statistical discrimination.[26] These arguments rest on the basic assumption that productivity is unknown, and that available measures of productivity are less reliable for minorities. If firms are risk averse (or there is a cost to matching a worker with a job), groups for whom measures of productivity are less reliable will be penalized with a wage lower than their average productivity.[27]

This argument reconciles perfectly competitive firms, equal productivity across races (controlling for other factors), *and* lower wages for minorities. In a sense, however, this is more of the same. Minorities are still different: one is left wondering why their true abilities are harder to detect. One, however, is also left wondering why firms do not develop better tests.[28] Cain (1986) emphasizes trial work periods as a way for workers to "signal" their productivity to employers.[29]

In conclusion, empirically documented racial differences in wages and employment status suggest that either minorities are discriminated against or that they are less productive or less motivated: either one admits the latter or discards standard analyses of labor supply. If markets are not perfectly competitive, hours worked no longer reveal information about the desire to work in a straightforward fashion. Individuals are no longer price-takers in the conventional sense[30]; the labor supply equation is now a demand-supply hybrid. The measured relationship between hours worked and wages is now biased.

There are two solutions to this problem. One is to model noncompetitive labor markets directly[31]; the other is to incorporate preferences into models of labor supply and wage determination. The latter seems particularly relevant in light of the poverty literature. At first glance, it seems easier as well. Incorporating preferences may mean only adding variables to otherwise standard analyses of wages and employment. If such additions eliminated the effect of race, then our faith in perfectly competitive labor markets would be restored.

Incorporating Preferences

Incorporating preferences, however, creates both empirical and theoretical problems. First, one must determine the relevant dimensions of attitudes and measure them correctly. When economists have included attitudes in their analysis, they have often handled the task poorly. Myers (1989), for example, discusses problems with attempts to measure reservation wages:

> One advantage of the [data examined] is that reservation wages are observed, at least to the extent that workers are asked what wage they would accept for a given job. The question is "If you were offered a job as a ______ would you accept it at $______/hr?" But this wording provokes the fundamental query, "What does the reservation wage measure?" Does it measure the lowest wage that an individual is willing to accept for a given job, as the theory would require, or does it measure something else? Perhaps it measures wage expectations and is, in reality, a response to the question, "What is the job worth?" [Myers 1989, 88].

Myers recognizes that one's understanding of preferences is tied to one's understanding of constraints. The survey question under scrutiny reflects an understanding that wages alone do not capture all relevant characteristics of a job. Tying a potential wage to a particular job is designed to hold nonwage benefits constant. Accepting a job, however, really means accepting a wage profile, and a given job may imply different profiles for different races. In particular, if minorities have limited opportunities for advancement, they may require a higher wage for a job than a white worker. If a white bank teller is more likely to join management than a black one, then the former will probably work for less than the latter. One's understanding of preferences is only as clear as one's understanding of the relevant constraints.

Other examples of the problems associates with measuring preferences are easy to find. Datcher-Loury and Loury (1986) emphasize the importance of whether the majority of a young man's friends are unemployed. Oddly enough, even in attempting to collect information on preferences, these authors are employing revealed preference methodology. They are presuming that a given outcome or behavior (the type of friends one has) reveals preferences accurately. Obviously, this reflects the relevant constraints (the "supply" of employed friends) as well. These authors also find that occupational aspirations are an important determinant of economic success. It, however, remains unclear whether this reflects predictions or desires.[32]

This touches on a second problem with incorporating preferences: standard utility maximization implies that preferences and constraints are independent. The two, however, may develop together over time. Understanding the true significance of preferences requires a broader theoretical perspective, one that specifies the way in which preferences are formed. This necessitates a broader understanding of economic choices and of the impact of making choices.

This requires some elaboration. As discussed above, economists' understanding of markets implies a narrow view of human relationship: in the world of neoclassical economics, individuals trade but do not interact. They are left unchanged by the process of exchange. As James Buchanan (1987) has argued,

> By imposing the condition that no participation in the economic process can independently influence the outcome of the process, all "social" content is squeezed out of individual behavior in market organization. The individual responds to a set of externally determined, exogenous variables, and his choice problem again becomes purely mechanical [p. 27].

The problem, according to Robert Heilbroner (1976), is that

> . . . economics, by its very insistence on dealing with the quantifiable elements of social activity, thereby distorts and misrepresents the activities which it seeks to explain. Economics deals with the economic order as if it were only a mechanism for the generation and allocation of goods and services. *But the fact is that the economic order is also and inextricably a mechanism for the generation of power and privilege, life-style and motive* [p. 62].

Obviously, incorporating this "mechanism" realistically into microeconomic models is challenging. Explaining the origin of preferences—and their ultimate significance—is quite difficult. If one measured the reservation wage correctly and found it to be a significant determinant of labor force behavior, one would not know the extent to which it really *caused* differences in behavior across individuals. In particular, one is left wondering whether better job opportunities engender a regard for the future which would make even a low-paying job—and the training it offers—more attractive.

Conclusion

This analysis has argued that understanding the relationship between employment and preferences is important because of the way Americans have traditionally viewed the poor and because of the effect of these perceptions on public policy. The notion that the poor are deviant in some way was prominent in the culture of poverty debate of the '60s and continues to influence poverty research today. This chapter reviewed efforts to define the underclass and recognized the recurring place of attitudes in this debate. This chapter also reviewed the theories of unemployment and wages on which standard analyses of labor supply are based. It contends that the way in which economists treat preferences reinforces the impression that chronic unemployment (and poverty) is voluntary and that the the chronically unemployed are either lazy, short-sighted, or deluded (or all three). In this light, one must reject perfect competition as a reasonable way of viewing labor markets or accept the premise that minorities are less productive than their education suggests or are unwilling to work.

Models of statistical discrimination were examined as a way to reconcile the two positions but were deemed inadequate. The underlying dilemma is why the fair-minded, far-sighted entrepreneurs that eliminate taste-based discrimination through their willingness to hire blacks on the basis of productivity alone do not develop better tests. Ultimately, statistical discrimination comes to rest on the same foundation as other models of labor supply based on perfect competition: blacks are different in ways that make them unsatisfactory employees.

This analysis considered the addition of preferences to standard empirical analyses as an empirical solution to this problem. Unfortunately, this tactic raises other, underlying theoretical problem. Measuring preferences (i.e., what an individual would do if he or she were unconstrained) is intimately related to how one perceives the underlying constraints. Incorporating preferences also raises disturbing questions about another building block of the economic framework, the stability of preferences. This prompts other questions about economists' understanding of economic exchange and its place in society.

In summary, this chapter offers few solutions to the questions it raises. It is easy to understand why labor economists cling to their framework—it simplifies their task both conceptually and empirically. Tugging at one portion of this edifice seems to destabilize the whole structure.

Notes

1. This takes utility maximization as given—at least in the sense of a taxonomy for grouping different factors influencing the choices of the poor (and nonpoor).

2. Work that integrates the two is rare. To state the obvious, effectively combining model of individual choice with an effective understanding of the constraints created by markets and social relations—that is, integrating mirco with macro—is an ongoing problem in the social sciences.

3. Patterson (1981, 109) summarizes Gallup polls from the 1960s. Heclo (1986) has a relevant discussion.

4. It is frequently argued that "during his campaign for the presidency, [John F. Kennedy] had been shaken by the misery he witnessed first hand in West Virginia" (Patterson 1981, 126). Lemann (1988) provides an interesting history of the development of antipoverty effort during the Kennedy and Johnson administrations. Most programs (particularly the Community Action Programs) treated the poor as "normal": poverty programs during this period placed great emphasis on giving the poor sufficient autonomy to shape their own lives.

To say that a shift in attitudes occurred during the 1960s is something of an oversimplification. Then, as now, some saw the poor as deviant, and the motives of policymakers were mixed. To some extent, the Great Society reflected a concern among elites that some of the poor were trapped in poverty. There was also a general feeling (on the part of activists) that poverty could—and should—be eliminated. Also relevant was the Civil Rights movement and the Cold-War desire to prove our system superior to communism (see Heclo 1986, 336). Heclo emphasizes that the public continued to view poverty largely as a function of preferences and not constraints: "As we look forward, it would be wise to recall that the wide swings between liberal and conservative epochs that historians sometimes identify in domestic policy more generally are largely absent in this area. One of the most striking aspects of public attitudes with regard to the poor and government programs is their immense stability. Delete the dates from relevant public opinion survey questions and it is often difficult to determine whether one is reading results from the present time or from the last half of the 1930's'' (p. 336).

5. It is surprising that a book by Harrington, a socialist, came to be associated with the notion that the poor are to blame for their poverty. To some extent, Harrington was given to rhetorical excess: he wrote that ''the other Americans feel differently than the rest of the nation. They tend to be hopeless and passive, yet prone to burst of violence; they are lonely and isolated, yet often rigid and hostile. To be poor is not simply to be deprived of the material things of this world. It is to enter a fatal, futile universe, an America within an America, a twisted spirit'' (1962, 126). This dramatic emphasis reflected the purpose of the book: as Harrington (1984) noted two decades later, ''The virtue of *The Other America* was not its complex analysis of the economics of poverty but the fact that it demanded that people look around themselves in a time'' of tremendous social change (p. 5). Nonetheless, Harrington's rhetoric—taken out of context—left him with an odd legacy. Patterson (1981) discusses this and other interesting aspects of the culture of poverty episode in poverty research (see ch. 7).

6. See Lewis (1966b, 19, 23). Juvenile delinquency was another behavioral focal point of this debate. See *Delinquency and Opportunity: A Theory of Delinquent Gangs* by Richard Cloward and Lloyd Ohlin (1960). This work exemplifies a structural perspective but illustrates key issues of the day.

7. Quoted in Patterson (1981, 123).

8. Edward Banfield appears to assign the strongest independent role to culture in *The Unheavenly City* (1968).

9. Indeed, some took the argument even further: ''The basic psychological potential of the children of the poor may even be damaged before they are born. The dietary deficiencies and the emotional stress of mothers in poverty before conception and during pregnancy may hamper the development of their offspring during the embryonic and fetal stages . . . '' (Hunt 1970, 54). This need not involve preferences, but this quote is striking given the recent attention paid to so-called ''crack babies.''

10. Corcoran and associates (1985) and Wilson (1988) also discuss the close link between the underclass and the culture of poverty literature.

11. This is not to slight the role of television. As in all matters, it strongly influences the public's perception of the poor and poverty. Bill Moyer's ''CBS Report'' is a prominent example. Moyer's special illustrates a point that will be emphasized throughout this work: the continual emphasis on hopelessness of the ghetto poor—while well intentioned—creates an individual-level focus of blame. It fosters an aura of hopelessness around the whole problem. Wilson (1988) offers a related discussion.

12. See Valentine (1968) or Ryan (1976). Furnham and Lewis (1976) summarize criticisms of the culture of poverty.

13. More to the point, he adds that ''it is simply stupid to pretend that the culture of poverty is not a black culture'' (p. 22).

14. Piven and Cloward (1985) cite this as a key tenet of Reagan social policy: ''Indeed, when the several major policy initiatives of the Reagan initiative are laid side by side, something of a coherent theory can be detected. But it is not a coherent theory of the workings of the economy. . . . It is the archaic idea that people in different social classes have different human natures and thus different basic motivation. The affluent are one sort of creature and working people another. It follows that these different sorts of creatures require different systems of incentives and disincentives if they are to be prodded to greater economic effort. The affluent exert themselves in response to reward—to the incentive of increased profitability yielded by lower taxes. Working people respond only to punishment—to the economic insecurity that will result from reductions in the income support programs. . . . The basic assumption of

classical *laissez-faire* economic theory—that all people are rational and self-interested—was thus twisted to mean that the rationality and the self-interest of the great majorities who were poor could be activated only by economic insecurity'' (p. 38).

15. This section has focused on two articles, but other examples are easy to find. See, for example, Vinovkis (1988): She writes that ''to understand the rise in out-of-wedlock births, one must also consider changes in values and culture. While values and culture are shaped to a large degree by the social and material environment in which we live, our values and cultural heritage—once in place—can play an independent, though constrained, role in our perceptions of the world and our actions in it. They have played an important part in the increasing proportion of out-of-wedlock births for both blacks and whites, and have contributed to the differences between black and white marital behavior'' (p. 92).

16. Discussed in Carson (1986, 348).

17 The vitriol that characterized the culture of poverty debate provided ample incentive (until recently) to avoid discussing the attitudes of the poor. Wilson (1988) discussed this period in social science.

18. A ''high'' proportion is defined as a proportion one standard deviation above the rate for the country as a whole.

19. Note that preferences are revealed by repeated choices. By adding demographic variables to the analysis of cross-sectional data, the analyst is implicitly assuming that the choices of similar individuals is the same as repeated choices by the same individual.

20. The problem is that we have one outcome and two unknowns—the rate of time preference and color preference.

21. The underlying problem is that prices alone (or at least a single price) do not tell us enough about the economic environment. Presumably, over the long run, if individuals tended to have a high rate of time preference and tan refrigerators were consistently backlogged, their price would fall. The long run, however, may not be relevant. (The milk will have spoiled.) Advertising, for example, may maintain the price of tan refrigerators.

This is a bit simplistic. Economists have developed econometric methods to deal with piecewise-linear budget constraints: here individuals chose from an opportunity set represented by a vector of prices. One encounters these methods in attempts to model, for example, the effect of social security on the work effort of older workers; see Hurd (1990) for a general survey. The underlying problem is theoretical, not econometric.

22. Experience (as human capital) is one of the fundamental building blocks of wage equations.

23. Preferences and productivity are closely related: ''The productivity of a given worker is also influenced by the tastes of that worker, . . . [i.e.,] a willingness to produce'' (Cain 1986, 698).

24. Surely discrimination would fall into this category.

25. This assumes costless mobility and some variance in the nature of the consumer-worker relationship.

26. Since this argument retains perfect competition, it portrays unemployment as a form of leisure.

27. Even if neither of these conditions is met, the wage-education (or productivity) profile will be flatter.

28. This is particularly striking in light of the societal preoccupation with tests characteristic of the managerial age (c.f. Darity 1990). The reluctance of firms to develop better tests may reflect the controversy over what they mean and how they are applied. (Consider the trouble firms would have were they to use the Scholastic Aptitude Test in hiring decisions.)

29. Also note that much of this discussion has treated a worker's productivity and education

as given. The differential returns to education may generate inequality by reducing the education of the minority group.

30. In that they can work as much as they like at the going wage.

31. One might base such a model on dual labor market theory. Taubman and Wachter (1986) summarize this literature.

32. This is particularly striking given the author's emphasis on an individual's propensity to adjust wage expectations in line with actual job possibilities.

References

Auletta, K. 1982 *The Underclass*. New York: Random House.

Banfield, E.C. 1968. *The Unheavenly City: The Nature and Future of Our Urban Crisis*. Boston: Little, Brown.

Beck, E.M., Horan, P.M., and Tolbert, C.M., II. 1978. "Stratification in a Dual Economy." *American Sociological Review* 43: 704–620.

Becker, G.S., 1971. *The Economics of Discrimination*. Second Edition. Chicago: University of Chicago Press, 1971.

———. 1976. *The Economic Approach to Human Behavior*. Chicago: University of Chicago Press.

Buchanan, J.M. 1987. *Economics: Between Predictive Science and Moral Philosophy*. College Station: Texas A&M Press.

Cain, G.G. 1986. "The Economic Analysis of Labor Market Discrimination: A Survey." In *Handbook of Labor Economics*, Vol. 1, O. Ashenfelter and R. Layard, eds., 693–785.

Carson, E.D., 1986. "The Black Underclass Concept: Self Help vs. Government Intervention." *American Economic Review* 76: 347–350.

Chiswick, Barry R. 1983a. "An Analysis of the Earnings and Employment of Asian-American Men." *Journal of Labor Economics* 2: 197–214.

———. 1983b. "The Earnings and Human Capital of American Jews." *Journal of Human Resources* 18: 313–336.

Cloward, R.B., and Ohlin, L. 1960. "Delinquency and Opportunity: A Theory of Delinquent Gangs." New York: ??.

Clark, K. 1965. *Dark Ghetto: Dilemmas of Social Power*. New York: Harper and Row.

Corcoran, M., et al. 1985. "Myth and Reality: The Causes and Persistence of Poverty." *Journal of Policy Analysis and Management* 4: 516–536.

Crane, J. 1989. "The Epidemic Theory of Ghettos." Cambridge, MA: Center for Health and Human Resources Policy Discussion Paper Series.

Danziger, S. 1989. "Overview." *Focus* 12 (Spring/Summer): 1–5.

Danziger, S. and Gottschalk, P. 1987. "Earnings Inequality, the Spatial Concentration of Poverty, and the Underclass." *American Economic Review* 77: 211–215.

Darity, W.A., Jr. 1982. "The Human Capital Approach to Black White Earnings

Inequality: Some Unsettled Questions.'' *Journal of Human Resources* 17: 72–93.
————. 1990. ''Racial Inequality in the Managerial Age: An Alternative to the NRC Report.'' *American Economic Review* 80(May): 247–251.
Darity, W.A., Jr., and Myers, S.A. Jr. 1983. ''Changes in Black Family Structure: Implications for Welfare Dependency.'' *American Economic Review* 73: 59–64.
Darity, W.A., Jr., and Williams, R. 1985. ''Peddlers Forever? Culture, Competition and Discrimination.'' *American Economic Review* 75: 256–261.
Datcher-Loury, L., and Loury, G. 1986. ''The Effects of Attitudes and Aspirations on the Labor Supply of Young Men.'' In *The Black Youth Employment Crisis*, R.B. Freeman and H.J. Holzer, eds., 377–399. Chicago: University of Chicago Press.
Duncan, G.J., ed. 1984. *Years of Poverty, Years of Plenty*. Ann Arbor, MI: Institute for Survey Research, University of Michigan.
Ehrenreich, B., et al. 1986. ''Welfare and Work: A Symposium.'' *The New Republic* 6 October: 18–23.
Ellwood, D. 1989. ''The Origins of 'Dependency': Choices, Confidence or Culture?'' *Focus* 12 (Spring/Summer): 6–13.
Farley, R. 1990. ''Blacks, Hispancis, and White Ethnic Groups: Are Blacks Uniquely Disadvantaged?'' *American Economic Review* 80: (May): 237–241.
Foster, E. Mi. 1990. ''Racial Differences in the Likelihood of Chronic Unemployment.'' Mimeo.
Freeman, R. 1981. ''Black Economic Progress Since 1964: Who Has Gained and Why?'' In *Studies in the Labor Market*, S. Rosen, ed. Chicago: University of Chicago Press.
Frisch, H. 1983. *Theories of Inflation*. Cambridge: Cambridge University Press.
Furnham, A., and Lewis, A. 1986. *The Economic Mind*. New York: St Martin's Press.
Gans, H.J. 1990. '''Underclass' is a Dirty Word.'' *The Philadelphia Inquirer* 20 (September): 19a.
Granovetter, M. 1985. ''Economic Action and Social Structure: The Problem of Embeddedness.'' *American Journal of Sociology* 91: 481–510.
Hannerz, U. 1970. *Soulside: inquiries into Ghetto Culture and Community*. New York: Columbia University Press.
Harrington, M., 1962. *The Other America: Poverty in the United States*. New York: Macmillan.
————. 1984. *The New American Poverty*. New York: Holt, Rinehard, and Winston.
Heclo, H. 1986. ''The Political Foundations of Antipoverty Policy.'' In *Fighting Poverty: What Works and Doesn't Work*, S. Danziger and D.H. Weinberg, eds., 312–340. Cambridge: Harvard University Press.
Heilbroner, R. (1976) ''On the Limited 'Relevance' of Economics.'' In *The Economic Approach to Public Policy*, R.C. Amacher, R.D. Tollison, and T. Willett, eds., 54–66. Ithaca, NY: Cornell University Press.

Hunt, J. McV. 1970. "Poverty Versus Equality of Opportunity." In *Psychological Factors in Poverty*, V.L. Allen, ed., 47–63. Chicago: Markham Publishing.

Hurd, M. 1990. "Research on the Elderly: Economic Status, Retirement, and Consumption and Saving." *Journal of Economic Literature* 28: 565–637.

Jargowsky, P. 1988. "Ghetto Poverty: Who and How Many?" *Research Bulletin: Center for Health and Human Resources Policy* 7: 1–3.

Jencks, C. 1989 "What is the Underclass–and Is It Growing?" *Focus* 12 (Spring/Summer): 14–26.

Kaus, M. 1986a. "The Work Ethic State: The Only Cure for the Culture of Poverty." *The New Republic* 7 (July): 22–33.

———. 1986b. "Up from Altruism." *The New Republic* 15 (December): 17–18.

Killingsworth, M. 1983. *Labor Supply*. Cambridge: Cambridge University Press.

Kluegel, J.R., and Smith, E.R. 1986. *Beliefs About Inequality: Americans' Views of What Is and What Ought to Be*. New York: Aldine de Gruyter.

Leibow, E. 1967. *Talley's Corner: A Study of Negro Streetcorner Men*. Boston: Little, Brown.

Lemann, N. 1988. "The Unfinished War." *The Atlantic* (December): 37–56.

Lewis, Oscar. 1959. *Five Families: Mexican Case Studies of Poverty*. New York: Basic Book.

———. 1966a. *La Vida: A Puerto Rican Family*. New York: Random House.

———. 1966b. "The Culture of Poverty." *Scientific American* 215: 19–25.

———. 1969. "The Culture of Poverty." In *On Understanding Poverty*, D. Moynihan, ed. New York: Basic Books.

Malveaux, J. 1984. "Theoretical Explanations for the Persistence of Racial Unemployment Differentials." In *Labor Economics: Modern Views*, W. Darity, Jr., ed., 91–118. Boston: Kluwer-Nijhoff Publishing.

Melville, K., and Doble, J. 1988. *The Public's Perspective on Social Welfare Reform*. New York: The Public Agenda Foundation.

Montgomery, J.D. 1990a. "Is Underclass Behavior Contagious? A Rational-Choice Analysis." Manuscript, March 8.

———. 1990b. "Revisiting Talley's Corner: Mainstream Norms, Cognitive Dissonance, and Underclass Behavior." Manuscript, July 15.

Myers, S.L., Jr. 1984. "Labor Economics, Preferences, and the Rationality Assumption: A Comment on Blau, Dickens, and Malveaux." In *Labor Economics: Modern Views*, W. Darity, Jr., ed., 257–268. Boston: Kluwer-Nijhoff Publishing.

Nathan, R. 1987. "Will the Underclass Always Be With Us?" *Society* 57–62.

Patterson, J.T. 1981. *America's Struggle Against Poverty, 1900–1980*. Cambridge, MA: Harvard University Press.

Piven, F.F., and Cloward, R.A. 1985. *The New Class War: Reagan's Attack on the Welfare State and Its Consequences*, 2nd ed. New York: Pantheon Books.

Rainwater, Lee. 1966. "Crucible of Identity: The Negro Lower-Class Family." *Daedalus* 95 (Winter): 176–216.

———. 1967. "The Lessons of Pruitt-Igoe." *The Public Interest* 116–126.

————. 1970a. *Behind Ghetto Walls: Black Families in a Federal Slum.* Chicago: Aldine.

————. 1970b. "Neutralizing the Disinherited: Some Psychological Aspects of Understanding the Poor." In *Psychological Factors in Poverty*, V.L. Allen, ed., 9–28. Chicago: Markham Publishing.

Rickets, E.R., and Sawhill I.V. 1988. "Defining and Measuring the Underclass." *Journal of Policy Analysis and Measurement* 7: 316–325.

Ryan, W. 1976. *Blaming the Victim.* Lexington, MA: Vintage Books.

Sarbin, T.R. 1970. "The Culture of Poverty, Social Identity, and Cognitive Outcomes." In *Psychological Factors in Poverty*, V.L. Allen, ed., 29–46. Chicago: Markham Publishing.

Smith, J.P., and Welch, F.R. 1989. "Black Economic Progress After Myrdal." *Journal of Economic Literature* 27: 519–564.

Sowell, T. 1978. *American Ethnic Groups.* Washington, DC: The Urban Institute.

————. 1984. *Civil Rights: Rhetoric or Reality*? New York: Morrow.

Summers, L. (with K.B. Clark). 1990a. "Why is the Unemployment Rate So Very High Near Full Employment?" In *Understanding Unemployment*, L. Summers, ed., 286–328. Boston: Massachusetts Institute of Technology.

————. 1990b. "Labor Market Dynamics and Unemployment: A Reconsideration." In *Understanding Unemployment*, L. Summers, ed., 3–47. Boston: Massachusetts Institute of Technology.

Taubman, P. and Wachter, M.L. 1986. "Segmented Labor Markets." In *Handbook of Labor Economics*, Vol 2, O.C. Ashenfelter and R. Layard, eds. New York: North Holland.

Tucker, W. 1988. "Our Homestead Plan for the Poor." *The American Spectator* (July): 25–28.

Valentine, C. 1968. *Culture and Poverty: A Critique and Counter-Proposals.* Chicago: University of Chicago Press.

Van Haitsma, 1989. "A Contextual Definition of the Underclass." *Focus* 12 (Spring/Summer): 27–31.

Varian, H.R. 1987. *Intermediate Microeconomic.* New York: W.W. Norton and Co.

Vinovkis, M.A. 1988. "Teenage Pregnancy and the Underclass." *The Public Interest* (Fall): 87–96.

Wacquant, L.J.D., and Wilson W.J. 1988. "Living in the Ghetto: The Cost of Racial and Class Exclusion in the Inner City." Mimeo. (Forthcoming in *The Annals of the American Academy of Political and Social Science*, special issue on "The Ghetto Underclass: Perspectives from the Social Sciences.")

Williams, R.M. 1984. "The Methodology and Practice of Modern Labcr Economics: A Critique." In *Labor Economics: Modern Views*, W. Darity, Jr., ed., 23–25. Boston: Kluwer-Nijhoff Publishing.

Wilson, W.J. 1978. *The Declining Significance of Race: Blacks and Changing American Institutions.* Chicago: University of Chicago Press.

————. 1987. *The Truly Disadvantaged: The Inner City, the Underclass, and Public Policy.* Chicago: University of Chicago Press.

————. 1988. "The American Underclass: Inner-City Ghettos and the Norms of Citizenship." The Godkin Lecture delivered on April 26, 1988, at the John F. Kennedy School of Government at Harvard University.

Wright, E.O. 1979. *Class Structure and Income Determination*. New York: Academic Press.

CONTRIBUTING AUTHORS

Jeremiah Cotton is Associate Professor of Economics at the University of Massachusetts at Boston. He is currently conducting a study of poverty in the black and Hispanic communities of Boston funded by a grant from the Boston Foundation's Persistent Poverty Project. His most recent publications are "The Economic Performance of Black Hispanics and White Hispanics: An Intracultural Analysis," *Social Science Quarterly*, forthcoming 1992; "Regional Differences in Black and White Earnings, 1974–1988," *The Review of Black Political Economy*, forthcoming 1992; and "The Gap at the Top: Relative Occupational Earnings Disadvantages of the Black Middle Class," *The Review of Black Political Economy* Vol. 18:3 Winter 1990 pp. 21–38.

William Darity, Jr., is the Cary C. Boshamer Professor of Economics at the University of North Carolina at Chapel Hill. His current research interests include determinants of racial and ethnic economic inequality in the United States, North-South models of trade and growth, the role of the slave trade and slavery in European industrialization, the hysteresis effects of unemployment exposure, and interpretations of Keynes's economics.

William T. Dickens is Associate Professor of Economics at the University of California at Berkeley. A prolific scholar, his collaborative research with

Kevin Lang has led to the development of porcedures for testing for the existence of labor market segmentation. He also has contributed to the development of empirical work on various aspects of the New Keynesian view of labor market dynamics, in particular the efficiency wage hypothesis.

Alfred Field, Jr., is Professor of Economics at the University of North Carolina at Chapel Hill. He is a trade/development economist who is particularly interested in structural adjustment issues. Recent publications include *International Economics* [Richard D. Irwin Inc., 1992, with Dennis R. Appleyard], "The Impact of Gender and Working Life Cycle Position on the Likelihood and Accumulation of Formal On-the-Job Training," *Population Research and Policy Review* Vol. 10:1 1991 pp. 47–66 (with Arthur Goldsmith), and "The Effects of Customs Unions on the Pattern and Terms of trade in a Richardian Model with a Continuum of Goods," *Journal of International Economics* Vol. 27 1989 (with Dennis R. Appleyard and Patrick J. Conway). Current research interests include contemporary issues of economic integration; employment, trade, and production in the North Carolina and U.S. textile and apparel industry; and issues relating to trade and structural change.

E. Michael Foster is currently on the faculty at Vanderbilt University in the School of Education and with the Vanderbilt Institute for Public Policy Studies. He was recently a postdoctoral fellow in aging at the Population Studies Center at the University of Pennsylvania. His research focuses on economic demography, particularly on matters of policy significance. Recent work examines the consequences of early childbearing using sister pairs and considers the intergenerational determinants of idleness among young men. Ongoing work involves the link between neighborhood quality and status attainment as well as residential mobility among the poor.

Arthur Goldsmith is Associate Professor of Economics at Washington and Lee University. His current research interests include social psychology and the unemployed, the meaning of full employment, executive perceptions and investment, expectations and labor demand, and alternative means of testing rational expectations. Recent articles include "Social Psychology, Unemployment Exposure and Equilibrium Unemployment," *Journal of Economics and Psychology* forthcoming 1992 (with William Darity, Jr.) and "The Impact of Gender and Working Life Cycle Position on the Likelihood and Accumulation of Formal On-the-Job Training," *Population Research and Policy Review* Vol. 10:1 1991 pp. 47–66.

James J. Heckman is the Henry Schultz Professor of Economics at the University of Chicago. The recipient of the prestigious John Bates Clark Award in 1983, he has made signal contributions in the areas of labor economics, econometrics, and economic demography. His theoretical and applied work on sample selection bias is the source of widely used procedures to correct for the problem of nonrandom samples.

Alexander Keyssar is Professor of History at Duke University. He is the author of *Out of Work* [Cambridge University Press, 1986] which was awarded the Frederick Jackson Turner Award of the Organization of American Historians, as well as the Philip Taft Labor History Award. He also has published articles about more recent trends in unemployment in *Social Research*, in Julian Simon (ed.), *The Resourceful Species*, and in popular outlets such as the *Nation* and *The New York Times*. His current research deals with the history of class and political participation in the United States.

Kevin Lang is Professor of Economics at Boston University and Faculty Research Fellow of the National Bureau of Economic Researach. He edits a monograph series on sociology and economics for Aldine de Gruyter and conducts research on topics of interest to researchers in both disciplines, including labor market segmentation, discrimination, and education. Among his recent publications are "The Effects of Hours Constraints on Labor Supply Estimates, "*Review of Economics and Statistics* November 1991 (with Shulamit Kahn), "The Contractor's Game," *Rand Journal of Economics* Autumn 1991 (with Robert Rosenthal), "Persistent Wage Dispersion and Involuntary Unemployment," *Quarterly Journal of Economics* February 1991, and "Efficiency Wage Models of Unemployment: A Second View," *Economic Inquiry* April 1990 (with Shulamit Kahn).

Michael Syron Lawlor is Associate Professor of Economics at Wake Forest University. His research areas include monetary theory, doctrinal history, and macroeconomic policy. His current research involves provocative work on interest rate theory and the implications for contemporary theory of the Keynes-Hayek-Sraffa debate of the 1930s.

Thomas MaCurdy is Professor of Economics at Stanford University. A prominent scholar in the labor economics arena, he is most noted for his careful research using aggregative data to uncover the actual dynamics of labor markets. Collaborative work with James Heckman dates from the early 1980s when the two of them produced a major paper on female labor supply. His research includes both theoretical and applied aspects of econometrics and labor economics.

Rhonda M. Williams is an Assistant Professor of Economics and African-American Studies at the University of Maryland at College Park. Her research interests include capitalist development, culture and competition, and the evolution of gender and ethnic divisions of labor in the United States.

Stephen Woodbury is Professor of Economics at Michigan State

University and a Senior Economist at the W.E. Upjohn Institute for Employment Research. Aside from the interesting body of research he has now undertaken on economic outcomes for black immigrant populations to the United States, his general research interests include wage and nonwage compensation and social insurance policy.

SUBJECT INDEX